NATIONAL GEOGRAPHIC

TRAVELER
Panama

NATIONAL GEOGRAPHIC

TRAVELER
Panama

Christopher P. Baker
Photography by Gilles Mingasson

National Geographic
Washington, D.C.

Contents

How to use this guide 6–7 About the author & photographer 8
The regions 57–238 Travelwise 229–265
Index 266–270 Credits 270–271

Page 1: A monkey in Azuero Province
Pages 2–3: A young Kuna Indian, El Porvenir, San Blas
Left: Fireworks over Iglesia San Pedro honor Santa Carmen, patron saint of fishermen, in Isla Taboga.

How to use this guide

See back flap for keys to text and map symbols

The *National Geographic Traveler* brings you the best of Panama in text, pictures, and maps. Divided into three main sections, the guide begins with an overview of history and culture. Following are eight regional chapters with featured sites selected by the author for their particular interest and treated in depth. Each chapter opens with its own contents list for easy reference.

The regions, and sites within them, are arranged geographically. A map introduces each region, highlighting the featured sites. Walks, plotted on their own maps, suggest routes for discovering an area. Features and sidebars offer detail on history, culture, or contemporary life. A More Places to Visit page generally rounds off the regional chapters.

The final section, Travelwise, lists essential information for the traveler—pre-trip planning, getting around, communications, money matters, and emergencies—plus a selection of hotels, restaurants, shops, and entertainment.

To the best of our knowledge, site information is accurate as of the press date. However, it's always advisable to call ahead.

Color coding

Each region is color coded for easy reference. Find the region you want on the map on the front flap, and look for the color flash at the top of the pages of the relevant chapter. Information in **Travelwise** is also color coded to each region.

Museo del Canal Interoceánico
www.museodelcanal.com
✉ Plaza de la Independencia
☎ 211-1649
🕐 Closed Mon.
$ $

Visitor information

for major sites is listed in the side columns (see key to symbols on back flap). The map reference gives the page where the site is mapped. Other details are the address, telephone number, days closed, entrance fee ranging from $ (under $5) to $$$$$ (over $20), and the nearest metro stop or transportation options. Visitor information for smaller sites is provided within the text. Admission fees are based on the prices foreigners pay.

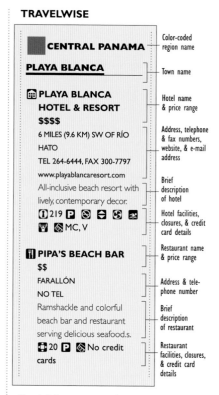

TRAVELWISE

CENTRAL PANAMA — Color-coded region name

PLAYA BLANCA — Town name

🏨 **PLAYA BLANCA HOTEL & RESORT** — Hotel name & price range
$$$$
6 MILES (9.6 KM) SW OF RÍO HATO — Address, telephone & fax numbers, website, & e-mail address
TEL 264-6444, FAX 300-7797
www.playablancaresort.com
All-inclusive beach resort with lively, contemporary decor. — Brief description of hotel
ⓘ 219 🅿 🅂 🖥 🆂 🌊 🆃 MC, V — Hotel facilities, closures, & credit card details

🍴 **PIPA'S BEACH BAR** — Restaurant name & price range
$$
FARALLÓN — Address & telephone number
NO TEL
Ramshackle and colorful beach bar and restaurant serving delicious seafood.s. — Brief description of restaurant
⛱ 20 🅿 🆂 No credit cards — Restaurant facilities, closures, & credit card details

Hotel & Restaurant prices

An explanation of the price bands used in entries is given in the Hotels & restaurants section beginning on p. 236.

REGIONAL MAPS

Mountain peak
Drive start point
Point of interest
Airport
Highway number
Important featured town
Map reference

- A locator map accompanies each regional map and shows the location of that region in the country.
- Adjacent regions are shown, each with a page reference.

WALKING TOURS

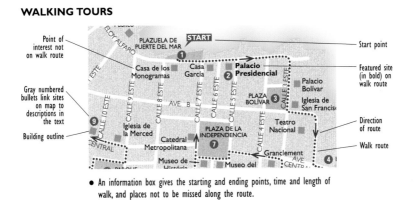

Point of interest not on walk route
Start point
Featured site (in bold) on walk route
Gray numbered bullets link sites on map to descriptions in the text
Building outline
Direction of route
Walk route

- An information box gives the starting and ending points, time and length of walk, and places not to be missed along the route.

DRIVING TOURS

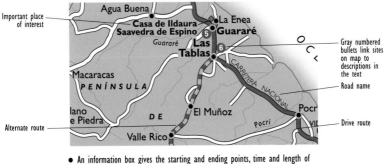

Important place of interest
Gray numbered bullets link sites on map to descriptions in the text
Road name
Alternate route
Drive route

- An information box gives the starting and ending points, time and length of drive, and places not to be missed along the route.

NATIONAL GEOGRAPHIC

TRAVELER

Panama

About the author & photographer

After studying geography at the University of London and Latin American studies at the University of Liverpool, author Christopher P. Baker settled in California and established a career as a travel writer, photographer, and lecturer. He has written several guidebooks about Cuba and Havana, as well as ones to Jamaica, The Bahamas, Turks & Caicos, and California. For National Geographic he has written the *National Geographic Traveler: Costa Rica* (2000) and *National Geographic Traveler: Cuba,* as well as *Mi Moto Fidel: Motorcycling through Castro's Cuba* (2000).

Photographer Gilles Mingasson grew up in Grenoble, France, before moving to Paris to pursue photojournalism. After being sent to the United States on assignment, he made Los Angeles his base. In 1990 Mingasson spent six months bicycling 7,500 miles across the Soviet Union with two cameras (and a serious saddle rash). On the eve of profound changes that few had yet to grasp, he photographed ordinary people who had lived their entire lives under the Soviet state. Today, Mingasson works on feature and travel stories for clients including *Newsweek, Fortune, Reader's Digest, Scholastic, Sky, Le Nouvel Observateur, L'Equipe* magazine, *Reppublica Delle Donne, Espresso, Elle, and Le Figaro.* Some of his projects have included the NASCAR Dads, global warming in an Eskimo village, and a documentary on Latinos in the United States. Assignments have taken him to Asia, Australia, Latin America, Europe, India, and North Africa.

History & culture

Monumento Homenaje a la Democracía, Panama City

Panama today

GRANDIOSE, DRAMATIC, SPANNING AN ENTIRE CONTINENT: THE PANAMA Canal is synonymous with the country it bisects. The world's most concentrated highway of commerce, in fact, birthed the nation of Panama, and cosmopolitan Panama City basks in wealth brought by the canal's liquid power. But the canal's importance has, until recently, overshadowed the country's diverse and remarkable treasures. In Panama, a slim-waisted tropical nation about the same size as South Carolina, you can find sweeping rain forests teeming with exotic animals and birds, cloud forests cloaking the summits of rugged mountains, and vibrant indigenous cultures that predate the *conquistadores*. A cornucopia of wildlife wonders side by side with fortresses and sleepy colonial villages, Panama is a country just awakening to its vast potential.

Tourism has come late to Panama, partly because of a recent history tarred by the excesses of a notorious dictator. The lingering perception of the country as a banana republic is now outdated. Gen. Manuel Antonio Noriega (1938–) is long gone, following a U.S.

military invasion in 1989, and democracy is soundly established. True, Panama still has political and economic problems, including areas marked by poverty and drug trafficking, and it may have more than its fair share of rogues and latter-day pirates. Their presence, however, is usually nothing more than a footnote for tourists, many of whom thrill to a fascinating history associated with a more distant pirate past.

The ancient fortresses of Portobelo and San Lorenzo still echo with the clash of cutlasses and the roar of cannon. The ruins of Panama Viejo provide mute testimony to the ferocity of pirate Henry Morgan's (1635–1688) ruthless attack. And cobbled remnants of the Camino Real and Camino de Cruces treasure trails, which once linked

Panama Viejo and Portobelo, still peek forth from the jungled terrain. Walking the mossy pathways, it is easy to imagine you hear the braying of mules laden with bullion destined for Spanish galleons.

Panama City—a modern metropolis pinned by glittering skyscrapers—equally prizes its past, especially as seen in the colonial jewel of Casco Viejo. This old neighborhood is full of museums, cathedrals, trendy restaurants and jazz clubs, and quaint mansions painted in soft impressionist colors: lemon yellow, tangerine, guava green. Old and new, kitschy and glitzy—vibrant Panama City is all this and more.

Contrasts abound in this sultry nation. The Canal Zone—the green beltway that surrounds the canal—is a seamless blend of moisture-laden forests merging southward into Darién, a vast rain forest that is home to jaguars, monkeys, poison dart frogs, and other wildlife species of every stripe, spot, and hue. In the Península de Azuero, the tapestry changes to dusty tan; cowboys trotting through rustic colonial-era hamlets add quaint notes to the lyrical landscape. The Chiriquí highlands comprise rugged mountains flanked by rows of glossy green coffee bushes. Shading them are mist-shrouded forests that shelter the resplendent quetzal, a bird known for its astounding beauty. The Caribbean Sea—embroidered with offshore coral reefs and cays licked by calm waters the color of jade—offers the appeal of distinctive cultures: one rooted in an Afro-Caribbean heritage, the other deriving from the indigenous Kuna peoples, whose women are garbed as flamboyantly as the most exotic of scarlet macaws.

Ah, yes... the birds! Visitors speak rapturously of phenomenal birding. Panama—a crossroads between two continents and two oceans—has many more species than Costa Rica, the neighbor whose spot in the ecotourism limelight has forced Panama to wait unrecognized in the wings. But birders are finally flocking to the country—as are surfers rushing to catch

Sparkling by night, Panama City's modern Bella Vista district is a center for banking, deluxe hotels, and fine restaurants.

Panama's rising wave. Sportfishers are also being lured by seas filled with trophy contenders—dorado, blue marlin, yellowfin, even peacock bass—lining up for the hook. Hikers take in the mountain highs in Parque Nacional Volcán Barú and Parque Internacional La Amistad. The scuba diving is simply astounding. You can take your pick of two dozen beaches where you can see marine turtles nesting and even top off your adventure tour by whale watching off the Archipiélago de las Perlas. And no visit to Panama is complete, of course, without a boat trip through the gargantuan locks of the almighty canal.

THE PANAMANIANS

If ever a country were a melting pot, Panama—whose population tops three million—is it, with every conceivable ethnicity thrown into the *sancocho* stew. Elaborately costumed Kuna Indians. Barely costumed Emberá-Wounaan Indians. Afro-Caribbeans.

Hindu merchants. Chinese supermarket owners. "Pure blood" Spanish elites sipping cocktails at Panama City's exclusive Club Unión. Beyond Panama City, the country is predominantly mixed-blood mestizo.

The early Spanish colonists who came in search of gold encountered thriving indigenous cultures. Many of these tribes quickly succumbed to European disease and the ruthlessness of 16th-century Spanish conquistadors, though eight pure-blood

A boat is ready for loading in the small town of Sambú on the Río Sambú. Motorized launches are the main means of transport in the watery interior of Darién.

indigenous groups survive today. The mixing of native Indian and Spanish blood produced an exotic mestizo population (today comprising 70 percent of the nation), while French, Dutch, and English merchants and pirates added their singular contributions.

These foreign groups were quickly assimilated into the mainstream Spanish-speaking culture, as were large numbers of African slaves imported to Panama throughout the 16th and 17th centuries. Many slaves, however, escaped to remote jungle hideouts and established communities whose occupants today proudly wear their badge as descendants of *cimarrones* ("runaways"). Their unions with indigenous peoples resulting in mixed-blood *mulatos* added further spice to the pot.

Thousands of North Americans moved through Panama during the 1840s en route to or from the California gold rush. To ease their passage, Chinese and Indian indentured laborers were brought in to lay the Panama Railroad—a daunting endeavor for which thousands paid with their lives (many Chinese laborers committed suicide en masse). The ultimately ill-fated French effort to build a canal, initiated in 1881, elevated the cosmopolitan nature of Panamanian society to

a new level. A large influx of French immigrants, of course, introduced Gallic ways. But Ferdinand de Lesseps's *grande enterprise* employed laborers and technicians from around the globe, while prostitutes of every desirable kind were in such demand that "*langoustes arrivées*" ("lobsters coming") was telegraphed down the line whenever a new shipload docked. Meanwhile, other European immigrants—mostly Swiss and central European farmers—settled the Chiriquí

The Río Caldera carves a gorge into the slopes of Boquete. This area of northwest Panama is farmed for coffee.

highlands, where they established coffee fields and market gardens.

Came the 20th century and with it the United States' epic, century-long involvement in Panama. During the ten years of canal construction, from 1904 to 1914, U.S. engineers commanded nearly 60,000 workers

from around the world, most from the
Caribbean islands. Many stayed, alongside the
families of almost 10,000 U.S. workers
("Zonians," who ran the canal) and an even
greater number of U.S. military personnel
who arrived to stitch North American
customs into the cultural quilt of the nation.
Recent decades have witnessed a new
influx of North Americans and Europeans
seeking to retire in the sun, principally
around Boquete and Bocas del Toro.

NATIONAL IDENTITY

Panamanians are schizophrenic about their
relationship with the United States. Panama
was wrested from Colombia by the first-ever
display of U.S. gunboat diplomacy, and the
U.S. wrote the 1903 constitution to guarantee
Panamanian independence only on a short
leash. The 10-mile-wide (16 km) Panama
Canal Zone spanning the waterway's entire
50-mile (80 km) length became U.S. territory,
and more than a dozen military bases were

maintained there (Zonians were a privileged class, living rent free), rankling Panamanian sensibilities. In 1964, simmering resentments boiled over in deadly riots. The subsequent success of President Omar Torrijos Herrera (1929–1981) in negotiating the Panama Canal Treaty—which gave the canal back to Panama—resulted in a rush of *soberanía*, sovereignty fever (a national park and even a beer were named after that sentiment). Since 1999, Panamanians have been on their own.

Diablos (devils) dance in front of the Santo Domingo church in Los Santos during the Corpus Christi festival.

Feelings are mixed. Many Panamanians look back with nostalgia to the days when the U.S. military directly employed thousands of local civilians (at preferential wages) and pumped 350 million dollars into Panama's economy every year.

About 57 percent of the population is

urban: One in every four citizens lives in Panama City. Except for Colón and David, most other towns are relatively small agricultural and commercial centers. The majority of rural folk live a simple life, tending coffee and arable farms in the highlands and cattle on the lowlands, where everyday life evokes the cowboy spirit—notably in the Azuero peninsula, heartland of Panama's unifying folkloric traditions.

STANDARDS OF LIVING

Panamanians' life expectancy is on a par with that of developed nations, although infant mortality is triple that of the United States.

The population enjoys free public education and decent public health care, although some regional disparities exist. The telecommunications system is advanced; so, too, the financial and service sectors. Panama City is a leading international banking center with a large and forward-focused middle class.

While Panama's per-capita income of $4,600 is high for Central America, its society is far from egalitarian. Panama's prosperity is evident. Yet there is no avoiding the impoverishment found nationwide: Almost 40 percent of the population lives in poverty (17 percent in extreme poverty), many

Lightning dances over the small fishing village of San Pedro, Isla Taboga.

continue to face discrimination. Family trumps most other considerations in business and politics. Dynasties are evident in the government, where blood connections open doors. And many trades are monopolized by single groups: Throughout Panama, for example, Chinese merchants own a majority of supermarkets and corner stores—known colloquially as *chinitos*.

INDIGENOUS PEOPLES TODAY

Panama has about 285,000 indigenous people, about ten percent of the total population. Most live within five autonomous districts *(comarcas)* where indigenous groups are guaranteed rights to self-government. Suffering high rates of malnutrition and politically disempowered on a national level, these groups remain suspicious of outsiders. Despite the passage of well-intentioned laws intended to safeguard their heritage, the government continues to issue rights to powerful mining and logging entities that whittle away at the Native Americans' lands.

Panama's most numerous indigenous people are the Ngöbe-Buglé (population 130,000), who live a reclusive existence in the western highlands. The arrival in the 1930s of transnational banana corporations and non-indigenous cattle ranchers forced the Ngöbe from many of their traditional coastal habitats; caught in a cycle of poverty, they practice slash-and-burn agriculture while others migrate to work seasonally as coffee-pickers or plantation workers. In October 1996, several hundred Ngöbe-Buglé men, women, and children marched to Panama City to demand their own comarca, which was established the following year. Covering almost one-tenth of Panama's surface area, it spans Bocas del Toro, Chiriquí, and Veraguas Provinces.

The Kuna (pop. 62,000) inhabit the southern Caribbean zone and San Blas archipelago, which they have occupied for only a few hundred years. During the early 20th century, the newly formed Panamanian government tried to suppress Kuna traditions

in urban slums marked by unemployment and crime. Thousands of impoverished *colonos* (non-Indian migrant farmers) continue to practice subsistence slash-and-burn agriculture, felling precious forests for cattle. And some critics believe that Panama City's wealthy elite, secluded in the deluxe high-rise condos of Punta Paitilla, is out of touch with the plight of impoverished Ngöbe-Buglé Indians or Dariénitas (inhabitants of Darién Province, many of them descendants of African slaves).

An unofficial racial pecking order exists, closely related to socioeconomic status; the country's indigenous people and blacks

and forcibly Westernize the culture. Following a violent revolt in 1925, the Kuna were granted cultural and political autonomy. These people, who have traditionally lived from fishing and harvesting coconuts for sale, passionately protect their land. Nevertheless, declining fish stocks have forced the Kuna to look to tourism to bolster their fortunes, while increasing numbers have migrated to Panama City and other towns to earn a living.

The rain forest–dwelling Emberá-Wounaan (pop. 9,000) of Darién are a gentle and friendly people culturally related to Amazonian tribes. Though referred to jointly, the two groups are ethnically and linguistically separate. They live off fishing, subsistence farming, and hunting using blow darts tipped with the deadly skin secretions of certain frogs. Though traditionally nomadic and lacking tribal organization, in recent years they have coalesced to form permanent villages, encouraged by the Panamanian government. They lack the political clout of the more numerous and organized Kuna; the influence of missionaries and other Westerners continues to dilute traditional practice.

GOVERNMENT & POLITICS

Panama is defined by the constitution of 1972 as a democratic republic run by an elected president (assisted by two vice presidents) and a 12-member cabinet. Presidents serve a single five-year term and may not serve consecutive terms. Power resides in the unicameral Asamblea Nacional (National Assembly), which makes legislation and is composed of 78 elected members representing the nation's provinces plus the Kuna comarca. Members serve five-year terms and sit in the high-rise Palacio Legislativo overlooking the Parque Legislativo in Panama City. The Supreme Court comprises nine appointed judges who serve ten-year terms. Voting is compulsory for citizens 18 and over (though there are no penalties for anyone choosing not to vote). Elections are overseen by an electoral tribunal.

Panama is divided into nine provinces— Bocas del Toro, Chiriquí, Coclé, Colón, Darién, Herrera, Los Santos, Panamá, and Veraguas—each overseen by an appointed governor. In addition, the five autonomous indigenous regions have representation in the central government.

POLITICAL PARTIES & PERSONALITIES

Between 1968 and 1989, when the U.S. overthrew Manuel Noriega, the president and legislative assembly were under the sway of military dictators. Political parties were relatively weak. Even now, Panamanian parties still revolve around the personalities of their leaders, rather than emphasizing a clear philosophy.

President Martín Torrijos Espino (1963–), son of Maj. Gen. Omar Torrijos, was elected to office in May 2004. He represents the Partido Revolucionario Democrático (PRD), founded in 1978 by supporters of Omar Torrijos to give

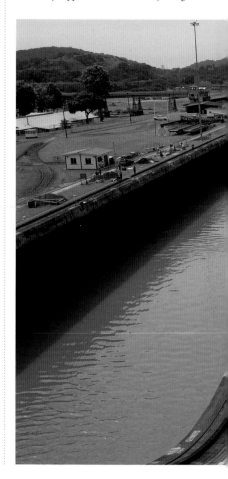

his military rule legitimacy. It draws its strongest support from labor unions and the urban middle class. The main rival party is the Panamenista Party (formerly the Arnulfista Party), founded in 1936 by Arnulfo Arias Madrid (1901–1988). This centrist party draws its main support from the provinces and is strongly nationalistic. Arias's ex-wife, Mireya Moscoso de Gruber (1946–), headed the party in the 1990s and in 1999 became Panama's first woman president. The Partido Popular is akin to the U.S. Democratic Party and has a defined ideology espousing concern for social welfare. Though party affiliations are defended fiercely, this has more to do with personal interest than philosophy.

The government is known for corruption, and public cynicism is rife. President Martín Torrijos has espoused "zero tolerance" for corruption and has enacted laws to make government more transparent, including formation of a National Anti-Corruption Council.

Following the U.S. invasion to topple Noriega in December 1989, his notorious Panama Defence Force was disbanded and the country today has no armed forces. A heavily armed police force looks after the nation's security, while the U.S. military reserves the right to intervene to protect the canal. ■

A locomotive known as a *mula* (mule) guides a ship through Miraflores Locks along the Panama Canal.

Food & drink

PANAMA HAS LONG BEEN A CULTURAL CROSSROADS FOR THE WORLD, AND the fusion of international flavors is reflected in the restaurant scene. Every town has its Chinese restaurant, South American *parrillada* (steakhouse), and pizzeria. Thai and Japanese restaurants, even Indian and Middle Eastern cuisine, abound in Panama City, which competes with international cities around the world for the variety and quality of its cuisines. And gourmands will find no shortage of hip fusion restaurants.

Panama's uniquely flavorful native cuisine melds indigenous, Spanish, and African influences into a mouth-watering mélange of (rarely spicy) dishes. The dish most associated with the country is *sancocho,* a soup that comes in regional variations and may contain corn, yucca, and any number of other vegetables. *Sancocho santeño,* from Los Santos, is made from yams, with cilantro, garlic, and chicken. The folks of Bocas del Toro like to add pig's tails. Panamanians are big on meats. They're fond of roast pork (especially at fiesta time) and *patacón con puerco*, pork with banana-like plantain. *Pollo asado* (roast chicken) is a staple of *comida criolla. Bistec* (steak) is also popular. *Arroz con pollo* (rice and chicken) is another favorite, often seasoned with onions and garlic or served topped with peas or even crumbled hard-boiled egg yolk at breakfast.

More often, Panama's *desayuno típica* (typical breakfast) includes thick corn tortillas with fresh cheese, roast meats, and eggs. Among the urban middle class, American dining habits have ousted the Panamanian tradition of rice and beans, and internationally known fast-food joints have made inroads everywhere.

The name Panama is an indigenous word for "abundance of fishes." No wonder, then, that seafood also abounds on local menus. Almost every seafood restaurant worth its salt features *ceviche,* raw fish marinated with chopped onions and peppers. The fish of choice are tilapia and *corvina* (sea bass), often served with *ajo* (garlic), while dorado (mahi mahi) and *pargo* (snapper) are also favored. Peruvian seafood restaurants add their own distinct flavors. The Caribbean coast simmers its lobster, shrimp, and other seafoods in unique spices and coconut milk. And trout is a local delicacy in Boquete.

Panamanians' use of corn reflects indigenous traditions, as in a *tamal*—cornmeal pastry stuffed with stewed chicken or pork, peppers, garlic, and onions, then wrapped in a banana leaf and boiled. *Chiricanos,* typical of the Azuero peninsula, are baked pastries made of ground corn and shredded coconut sweetened with sugarcane juice and honey. Panamanians have a weakness for *dulces* (sweets) made of coconut and sugar, as in *cocadas,* sold by the roadside. Milk is used in *arroz con leche* (sweetened rice with milk, sugar, and cinnamon) and *flan* (custard).

Other dishes to try include:
Plátano en tentación: a popular side dish consisting of baked plantain sweetened with molasses and cinnamon.

Carimañolas: mashed boiled yuccas stuffed with beef and then deep fried.

Chicheme: a drink of ground corn and milk flavored with cinnamon and vanilla.

Ensalada rosada: potato and mayonnaise salad with beets; popular at Carnival time.

Tamal de olla: oven-baked corn tamales stuffed with meat and vegetables, plus raisins.

At lunchtime, look for inexpensive *comida corriente*—set meals containing a combination of local dishes.

Regional markets are cornucopias of tropical fruits, such as mangoes, melons, papayas, pineapples, and strawberries fresh from the Chiriquí highlands. These and local favorites such as *marañón* (cashew fruit) and guanábana find their way into *batidos,* delicious iced shakes made with water or milk. *Agua de pipa*—water from a green coconut—is drunk as the perfect pick-me-up on hot days. Panama's local lager-style brews (e.g., Soberana and Balboa) are also perfectly suited to the tropical climate when served chilled, *bien fría.*

The urban workingman's drink is *seco,* a harsh sugarcane liquor often drunk with milk; his country cousins favor *vino de palma,* a rough alcohol made from palm sap. The country's prized Carta Vieja rum is light-bodied and smooth in flavor. Wine is popular with the middle classes, and most upscale restaurants have a wide selection of quality imported wines.

Panama's light-roast *arabica* coffee is also world class, and individual labels regularly make the top-ten list of international-al coffee critics, but most of the good stuff is exported. Coffee in Panama is typically drunk American-style or thick and heavily sugared, *espresso* style. ■

Puerco frito con patacones—fried pork and plantains—is a Panamanian culinary staple (top). Made of chicken, garlic, onions, yams, and spices, *sancocho panameño* is a delicious local soup (above). A worker fills bags of coffee at El Tute Café factory in Santa Fé, reputed to produce one of the best coffees in Panama (below).

Panamanian history

WHEN ON AUGUST 15, 1914, THE PANAMA CANAL WAS OFFICIALLY OPENED with the passage of the SS *Ancón,* it marked the culmination of a dream dating back five centuries. Panama has always been a path between seas. For centuries, pre-Columbian Indians who lived at this crossroads between two oceans and two continents followed a trail across the country. As early as 1529, Spanish conquistadors drew up the first working plan for a canal on the orders of King Charles V. And during the height of the California gold rush, fortune hunters crossed the narrowest point of the isthmus along the same trail used by Spanish mule trains laden with Indian treasure.

Pre-Columbian carvings cover the Piedra Pintada (Painted Stone), near El Valle.

FIRST PEOPLES

People migrating south may have occupied the region we know today as Panama as early as 12,000 years ago. Nearly a million indigenous people are thought to have inhabited the region by the time of the Spanish conquest in the 1500s. Several dozen diverse tribes, distinguished by their distinct ceramics and artifacts, were divided into three cultural zones in west, east, and central Panama. Most succumbed to the brutality of Spanish occupation and to European diseases, and only eight indigenous tribes exist today.

The country is speckled with rocks bearing mysterious petroglyphs. Dozens of archaeological sites have also been uncovered throughout the region, though no massive pyramids or even towns have been unearthed, and most sites date back no more than two thousand years. Although trade links existed between the cultural groups and with more advanced cultures to the north and south, the Panamanian peoples seem not to have evolved the complex sociopolitical structures of societies elsewhere in the Americas, such as the Maya, Aztec, and Inca. Panama's peoples never unified to form a kingdom but remained under chieftains *(caciques)* who ruled over competing areas and whose names were adopted by the Spanish for each tribe and the regions they inhabited.

Western cultures

The Barriles culture is considered Panama's earliest major civilization. It originated in today's Costa Rica and moved into Panama about 500 B.C., when the group settled the Chiriquí highlands around a ceremonial site on the slopes of Volcán Barú. Eventually the culture extended to the Caribbean and Pacific coasts. It evolved from simple agricultural communities based on cultivation of corn and beans to ranked societies, reaching a zenith about A.D. 500 before being abruptly destroyed when Volcán Barú erupted.

An ancient mortar and pestle at Sitio Barriles date from the ancient culture of the Barriles.

The Barriles left behind monochrome pottery, *metates* (three-legged stone corn-grinding tables), and life-size stone statues showing men (often clutching severed heads in their hands) being borne on the shoulders of slaves. In time, the Barriles were replaced by the Cultura Coclé and the classic Chiriquí and Veraguas cultures who left behind elaborate earthenware, including ceramics painted with "lost-wax" designs.

Central cultures

The most important (and oldest) archaeo-logical sites thus far discovered are in the Pacific lowlands, centered on the current provinces of Coclé, Herrera, and Veraguas. Groups that settled along the Pacific coast introduced agriculture about 3000 B.C. By A.D. 500, complex societies had evolved based on intensive slash-and-burn agriculture, although they also relied upon fishing and commercial trade with other groups throughout Mesoamerica. Headed by power-ful caciques, they also warred with other tribes for control of the most productive land.

The largest site, Sitio Conte, near the current town of Penonomé, served as an important pre-Columbian burial site for at least 200 years. It was discovered in the 1930s when the Río Grande changed course and exposed fabulous burial treasures, most of which now reside in museums around the world. More than 1,000 gold *huacas* (small ornaments) were unearthed from 60 graves.

Gold objects—and the lost-wax metallurgical technique employed to make them—were introduced from Peru around 2,000 years ago. Metallurgy was quickly adopted by local tribes, who shaped animal figurines and decorative body items, such as bracelets, pendants, and chest plates, reserved for caciques. When they died, caciques were buried with their wives, servants, and possessions, including ceramics such as vases and pedestals painted with elaborate zoomorphic designs.

Parque Arqueológico El Caño, near the town of Natá, dates from around A.D. 1100 and, like Sitio Conte, features geometrically aligned stone columns, some carved into the shape of animals and humans. Most of the stones were removed at the time of discovery.

Eastern cultures

The eastern cultures were the first to experience the brutality of early Spanish conquistadors, who enacted a policy of extermination. Little is known about these

Spanish explorer Vasco Núñez de Balboa sees the Pacific Ocean in 1513.

peoples, not least due to the rugged inaccessibility of much of the terrain and their near-total destruction at the hands of the Spanish. These hunter-gatherers spoke a *chibcha* language and were related to Amazonian tribes. (The Choco tribe—known as the Emberá-Wounaan Indians—who inhabit the area today migrated from Amazonian regions around the 18th century.)

The eastern peoples lived in circular huts

constructed on pole frames with walls of cane and roofs of thatched palm, similar to those in which many of their descendants live today. Spanish conquistadors reported that caciques lived in the largest huts, which contained the smoked bodies of ancestors wearing gold masks. The ceramics of these groups were comparatively crude, although they were skilled at using stone tools to fashion sleek canoes from logs hollowed by fire. Women wore an apron-like bark skirt; men wore penis coverings and necklaces of shells and stone beads, while nobles were adorned with gold ear plugs, nose plates, and arm and leg bands.

FIRST EUROPEANS

The first European to sight Panama was Spanish explorer Rodrigo de Bastidas (1460–1527), who sailed along the Caribbean shore of Darién in 1501. The region's indigenous peoples greeted the newcomers while adorned in their finest gold bracelets, earrings, and chest plates. The following year, Christopher Columbus (1451–1506) arrived during his fourth and final voyage to the New World; he explored the shoreline between Bocas del Toro and Darién and established an ill-fated settlement near the mouth of the Río Belén. He named the region Veraguas after a local tribe.

In 1510, Vasco Núñez de Balboa (1475–1519)—a former member of Bastidas's crew—stowed away aboard a merchant vessel to escape his creditors. He ended up in Darién as an early settler of Santa María la Antigua del Darién, the first successful town constituted in the isthmus by the Spanish crown. Balboa quickly rose to become governor of the region. Three years later, he crossed the isthmus and, on September 25, 1513, became the first European in the Americas to see the Pacific Ocean. Clad in armor, Balboa famously waded into the ocean (which he named Mar del Sur, Southern Sea) to claim it for Spain. The momentous discovery positioned Panama as a staging point for the conquest of the Pacific coast of the Americas.

Balboa's discovery of the Pacific and the pearl-rich Archipiélago de las Perlas fueled the jealousy of rival conquistador Pedro Arias de Ávila (1440–1531), alias Pedrarias Dávila, who connived to have himself named as Balboa's successor. In 1519, the new governor had Balboa tried for treason on trumped-up charges and put to death. Ávila then founded Nuestra Señora de la Asunción de Panama (Panama City) as the first Spanish settlement on the Pacific and relocated the capital there. Balboa's even-handed treatment of the indigenous peoples was replaced by brutal tyranny and exploitation. Entire communities were put to the sword, while others were enslaved to extract gold from the Darién jungles. By the mid-16th century the indigenous peoples had christened the Spaniards *guacci-guacci* after a kind of predatory mammal. Whole tribes withered and died under the intolerable hardships of forced labor. European diseases such as smallpox, measles, and tuberculosis, against which they had no resistance, hastened their demise. Groups such as the Buglé fought long bitter struggles against the Spanish but gradually retreated into the thickly forested mountains of the Cordillera Central and the Caribbean coastal plains of Veraguas.

TREASURE ROUTES

After the conquest of Virú (today's Peru) by Francisco Pizarro (1478–1541) in 1532, the plundered wealth of the Incas began filling the vaults of Panama City—capital of the province then known as Castillo de Oro, an ever changing district that also included much of today's Nicaragua and Costa Rica—as down payment on a glittering future. The settlement grew swiftly as the chief entrepôt for the wealth of the New World being transferred to Spain. Unimaginable quantities of silver, gold, emeralds, pearls, and other treasures were transported by mule across the isthmus in a one-week journey for shipment to Spain.

In 1517, conquistador Gaspar de Espinosa (1484–1537) had begun construction of the Camino de Cruces connecting Panama to the Caribbean port of Nombre de Dios (founded in 1510). The harbor at Nombre de Dios was ill-chosen, however, due to its exposure to hurricanes. Thus, in 1585, work began on a more suitable site named San Felipe de Portobelo in honor of the king. A royal decree ordered construction of a second mule trail, the Camino Real (Royal Road), branching off

A captured Spaniard bows before Sir Henry Morgan during the Welsh privateer's sacking of the city of Panama in the 1670s.

the Las Cruces trail, to connect to the new city; a tax on precious metals was levied to pay for building and maintaining the route.

The treasure-laden mule trains that followed the trails were timed to coincide with the annual arrival of the Spanish *flota* (fleet) bearing the products of the Old World. The fleet reached Cartagena following a ten-week journey from Spain and split into two fleets, bound separately for Mexico and Panama, while couriers were sent ahead to inform the king's agents and merchants of the ships' impending arrival. Hundreds of vessels converged on Nombre de Dios and, later, Portobelo. The annual fairs (in which silver and raw materials were traded for manufactured goods) drew thousands of Spanish merchants, soldiers, clerics, merchants, and scribes. Nombre de Dios and Portobelo grew from sleepy *pueblos* to bustling treasure ports. By law one-fifth (the *quinto*) of New World treasure had to go to the King of Spain, whose own galleons got priority in the treasure ports of the Spanish Main. More than 200,000 tons (181,400 metric tons) of silver were shipped to Spain through Portobelo from 1550 to 1650. (Spain's debts were so great, however, that much of it was shipped directly to European bankers in Venice.) So much silver was shipped aboard bulging merchantmen that mountains of bullion were left behind in the street.

The vast wealth drew the larcenous attention of pirates: cold-hearted cutthroats capable of astoundingly inhumane deeds. English slave-trader-turned-pirate Sir Francis Drake (1540–1596) attacked Nombre de Dios in 1572; the following year he successfully waylaid a mule train laden with treasure. The Spanish developed a flotilla system to guard the creaking treasure ships, with one galleon for every ten merchant vessels. They also built fortifications to guard Portobelo and the mouth of the Río Chagres. In 1595, Drake and John Hawkins (1532–1595) set out with 26 ships and an audacious plan to sack Nombre de Dios and Panama City. Hawkins died en route, while Drake fell ill and on January 27,

1596, died and was buried at sea near the mouth of Portobelo. Pirate William Parker (1587–1617) successfully sacked Portobelo in 1602, and in 1668 Welsh pirate Henry Morgan sacked the town and held the occupants for ransom. In 1671, Morgan even used the mule trails to attack Panama City, which he burned to the ground. After the sacking, the residents reestablished their city a few miles west at a more defensible position—today's Casco Viejo. Panama and Portobelo suffered so many depredations that Spain finally permitted passage of ships around Cape Horn, ending the golden age of Portobelo as the "richest little city in the Indies."

COLONIAL ERA

Spain's monopoly on the isthmus was challenged in 1698 when the Company of Scotland was founded to establish a colony of Scots on the Caribbean coast of Darién. The

colony of New Edinburgh was a fiasco (most of the 1,200 settlers soon perished from starvation or disease) and the financial fallout forced Scotland to give up all notion of independence from England.

During the early 18th century, arch-enemies England and Spain settled into a period of more or less peaceful coexistence. In 1731, however, English sea-trader Robert Jenkins, sailing in the West Indies, was arrested by Spanish coast guards, who cut off his ear. Seven years passed before Jenkins told his story—and showed his shriveled ear—to the House of Commons. The aroused parliamentarians voted for war (now sometimes known as the "War of Jenkins' Ear") and reserve naval officer Sir Edward Vernon (1684–1757) set off for the Caribbean in command of six warships. On November 20, 1739, he arrived off Portobelo which, notwithstanding its formidable fortifications, surrendered after a short resistance. The

fortresses were promptly blown up. The Spanish lost no time in building larger, more modern defenses.

The Spanish imperial age was waning, however, ushering in a period of stagnation for Central America. Panama's fortunes diminished and the region was relegated to backwater status. Occasionally, civil wars inspired by growing nationalist sentiments spilled into the province as independence sentiments swept through Spain's weakened Latin American empire. On November 10, 1821, the residents of La Villa de los Santos township petitioned Latin American liberator Simón Bolívar (1783–1830) for independence in a letter, the *Primer grito de independencia* (first call for independence). Eighteen days later, Panama broke from Spain and joined Gran Colombia, a union that initially included Colombia, Ecuador, Peru, and Venezuela. In 1826, Bolívar initiated an ultimately unsuccessful congress (hosted in Panama City's Casco Viejo) to create a pan-American union of all the republics. In 1830, Gran Colombia fractured. Panama proclaimed independence, but neighboring Colombia forced it to reunite, with Panama becoming one among Colombia's many provinces. Panama's union with Colombia was uneasy, however, and more than 50 rebellious incidents and three major attempts to sever the union were violently suppressed.

CANAL FEVER

In 1848 the outpost province of Colombia was thrust back onto the world stage by the discovery of gold in California. No railroad yet spanned the United States, and adventurers from around the world landed in Panama to cross the isthmus via the old Camino de Cruces. Bandits preyed upon the gold-seekers as they stumbled along the grueling weeklong trail. Thousands succumbed to yellow fever, malaria, and other diseases. Demand for mule transport fostered exorbitant prices. Future Civil War hero and U.S. president Capt. Ulysses S. Grant (1822–1885) was forced to use his own money to meet the extortionate fee charged for mules to transport the cholera-stricken U.S. Fourth Infantry across the peninsula en route to San Francisco. Then came William Henry Aspinwall (1807–1875), an entrepreneur who founded the Pacific Mail Steamship Company and the Panama Railroad, completed in 1855 at a cost of some 6,000 lives. Between 1848 and 1869, about 375,000 argonauts crossed the isthmus via mule and, eventually, rail from the Atlantic to the Pacific. Some 225,000 crossed in the opposite direction.

The success of the Panama Railroad sparked notions of something grander. Step in French engineer Count Ferdinand de Lesseps (1805–1894), who had just succeeded in building the Suez Canal and now set his eyes on building a sea-level canal through the Isthmus of Panama. His Compagnie Universelle du Canal Interocéanique de Panamá was launched in 1880; de Lesseps purchased (from Colombia) the exclusive right to build a canal, and stock was issued to finance the effort. The stubborn Frenchman resisted all entreaties to abandon the ill-

French engineer Ferdinand de Lesseps failed in his attempt to build a canal across Panama in the late 1800s.

conceived sea-level idea and adopt a dam-and-lock system until it was too late. The cost and difficulties of digging *La Grande Tranché* (great trench) through mountains and taming the Río Chagres and devastating tropical diseases were simply too great. About 22,000 laborers died (most were Caribbean islanders felled by malaria and yellow fever) before the company foundered in 1889, bringing financial ruin to investors. The French government also collapsed in the fallout as financial frauds, political bribes, and influence peddling were revealed; eventually, de Lesseps and his son Charles were each sentenced to five years in prison.

A brief and bloody interlude—the Prestan Uprising—occurred in 1885 after Rafael Aizpuru (1843–1919), former president of the department of Panama, seized power. Colombian troops were dispatched from the Caribbean port of Colón. Pedro Prestan, a rabble-rousing Haitian mulatto, took advantage of the troops' absence to seize control of Colón. Prestan demanded that the captain of a boatload of armaments hand over the goods. When the captain refused, Prestan took five Americans hostage and threatened to kill them if the captain of the U.S. gunboat *Galena* (which was anchored offshore) landed troops. The U.S. captain had instructions not to intervene unless the Panama Railroad was threatened. Having been promised the arms, Prestan released the hostages, but the *Galena* swiftly towed the arms-bearing ship beyond reach. Colombian troops returned to Colón and routed Prestan and his mob, but not before the rebel put the town to the torch. The wooden town was almost entirely destroyed. Prestan was captured and hanged while Aizpuru was deposed by U.S. marines and handed over to Colombian troops.

THE CANAL & INDEPENDENCE

Meanwhile, the United States had decided that a shortcut between the seas was crucial to its evolving naval power and had grown determined to build a canal, with Nicaragua the most likely route. That Panama was eventually chosen is due largely to the indefatigable efforts of one man: Philippe Bunau-Varilla (1859–1940), former chief engineer of the Compagnie Universelle du Canal Interocéanique de Panamá. In 1894, Bunau-Varilla had organized the Compagnie Nouvelle, which acquired the French rights to build a canal; in 1904, he sold the rights to the United States for 40 million dollars. This one-man whirlwind pursued a relentless, brilliant, and ultimately successful campaign to influence the U.S. Congress and President Theodore Roosevelt (1858–1919) on behalf of the Panama route. Once the decision was made, the United States was determined to bully the Colombian government into negotiating a canal treaty on dictated terms.

When Colombia refused to agree to the U.S. terms, a plot was hatched to sever the province of Panamá. Prompted by Bunau-Varilla, prominent and ambitious Panamanian citizens conspired with Panama Railroad officials. On November 3, 1903, they declared independence from Colombia (Bunau-Varilla's wife had even stitched together the first flag of Panama). By prearrangement, Roosevelt had sent the gunboat *Nashville* to Panama to prevent Colombian troops from landing to suppress the insurrection. When the Colombian troops already ashore were rushed from Colón to Panama City, swift-thinking Panama Railroad

officials insisted that the Colombian officers ride in the front of the train as a matter of protocol; they then uncoupled the rear carriages, leaving the troops behind. Upon arrival in Panama City, the Colombian officers were arrested by their own soldiers, who had been bought off by the conspirators.

The United States instantly recognized the breakaway republic. Meanwhile, the ever wily and prescient Bunau-Varilla had gotten himself named Panama's ambassador to the U.S. Preempting the arrival in Washington of an official Panamanian delegation to negotiate the terms of a new canal treaty, the Frenchman negotiated the Hay-Bunau-Varilla Treaty committing the United States to build a canal across the isthmus of Panama on terms highly preferential to the U.S. The treaty granted the United States sovereignty of the canal and a 10-mile-wide (16 km) Canal Zone that would be governed exclusively by the United States in perpetuity; the U.S. government paid the new Panamanian government 10 million dollars, plus an annual payment of $250,000. Panama's constitution was even written by Bunau-Varilla in a New York hotel room and rigged to let the United States meddle whenever it pleased. The Hay-Bunau-Varilla Treaty—a fait accompli delivered to a stupefied and livid official Panamanian delegation—became a bone of contention between the two nations for decades.

On May 4, 1904, the French-owned assets in Panama were handed over to the United States, and the Stars and Stripes were raised.

THE GREATEST ENGINEERING FEAT OF ALL TIME

U.S. engineers understood, where the French had not, that a sea-level canal was out of the question. The U.S. plan called for damming the Chagres, the principal river in the canal's path, to create a massive lake 85 feet above sea level, with three lock chambers at each end of the lake to raise and lower ships to sea level: The isthmus would be bridged, not severed. Cuban doctor Carlos Finlay's (1833–1915) irrefutable proof that yellow fever was transmitted by mosquitoes was another key element in the canal's success. An all-out and ultimately successful effort was made to eradicate the *Aëdes aegypti* and *Anopheles* mosquitoes (transmitters of yellow fever and

Massive metal gates at Gatún Locks dwarf workers in 1910, during construction of the canal.

malaria, respectively) under far-sighted medical officer Col. William C. Gorgas (1854–1920). Meanwhile, Chief Engineer John F. Stevens (1853–1943) set up a flatbed train system that would be essential for hauling out rock as the canal was blasted through the Culebra Cut, 9 miles (14 km) of mountains forming the continental divide. In 1907, Stevens resigned and was replaced by Col. George W. Goethals (1858–1928), an efficient military engineer who saw the effort by the U.S. Army Corps of Engineers to fruition.

When completed after ten years of grueling effort, the canal extended some 50 miles (80 km) from Limon Bay on the Atlantic to Panama Bay on the Pacific. On January 7, 1914, an old French crane boat, the *Alexandre La Valle*, made the first complete passage, although the canal wasn't officially opened until August 15, 1914, when the SS *Ancón* transited. On August 3, 1914, the same day that the dark clouds of World War I broke over Europe, the first oceangoing vessel—the *Cristobal*—passed through the canal.

Theodore Roosevelt's Big Ditch had chopped 9,000 miles (14,484 km) off the journey for ships sailing from New York to San Francisco.

SHAPING PANAMA

The years following completion of the canal witnessed marked economic progress in Panama as roads, telephones, and other elements of modern infrastructure were installed throughout the nation. Democracy, however, was slow to take hold. Turbulent politics caused the United States to intervene militarily in Panama's domestic affairs in 1908, 1912, and 1918, and again in 1925 when the Panamanian government's forced suppression of Kuna culture provoked a violent revolt in San Blas. Led by Nele Kantule and Simral Colman, the Kuna declared independence and established their own nation, the Republic of Tule. The United States intervened, but not before 22 policemen and 20 tribesmen had been killed. Self-rule was granted to the Kuna in 1938.

In 1936, the right of U.S. intervention was revoked when the Hull-Alfaro Treaty replaced the Hays-Bunau-Varilla Treaty. The treaty was named for Arnulfo Arias Madrid (1901–1988), leader of Acción Comunal, a radical group that in 1931 violently overthrew the government of Florencio Harmodio

virulent enmity for *arnulfistas.* Nonetheless, Arias is credited with having established Panama's social security system.

Arias's chief nemesis was José Antonio Remón Cantera (1908–1955), commander of the National Police. Elected to the presidency in 1952, he initiated progressive reforms before being assassinated in a machine-gun attack at the horse-racing track that now bears his name.

FLAG RIOTS

Arias's anti-U.S. rhetoric was shared by much of the populace, who resented the overbearing presence of the United States and its repeated interference in Panama's domestic affairs. The first serious riots occurred in 1947, when Panama's national legislature met to consider

U.S. Secretary of State Henry Kissinger and Panamanian President Omar Torrijos Herrera after the signing of the Panama Canal Treaties in 1977. The two new treaties would ultimately give the canal back to Panama in 1999.

Arosemena (1872–1945). After a short interlude, Arias's brother was installed as president. A charismatic populist, Arias espoused *panameñismo,* a vehemently racist, fascistic, and anti-U.S. nationalism. His popularity among the poor was such, however, that he was elected president three times between 1940 and 1984; each time he was deposed by the police, who evolved a

extending rights for the U.S. military to use bases outside the Canal Zone. The simmering resentment boiled over in the so-called Flag Riots that erupted on January 9, 1964. The Kennedy administration had agreed to fly the Panamanian flag next to the Stars and Stripes in the Canal Zone. When his successor Lyndon Johnson announced plans to reduce the number of flags flown in the Zone, many

Zonians (U.S. residents of the Zone) took slight. A flag-raising initiative was organized. When students at Balboa High School raised an American flag in defiance of the governor's orders, Panamanian students from the Instituto Nacional set out to raise their national flag alongside. Their flag was torn down. Tempers flared and before long full-scale riots broke out. Panamanians from all walks of life were drawn into the maelstrom, which left 27 dead, the majority Panamanians shot by U.S. troops. The Flag Riots were a seminal moment in Panama's history and marked a turning point in U.S.–Latin American relations. President Johnson thereafter announced that the United States would negotiate a new canal treaty.

In 1968, Arnulfo Arias was elected for a third time. Immediately he called for the canal to be turned over to Panama. However, he was toppled by the military only 11 days into his term. In the resulting chaos, a handsome, charismatic National Guard colonel, Omar Torrijos Herrera, seized power, initiating a 21-year spell of military rule. After swiftly overcoming a countercoup, Torrijos established himself as a popular leader who engaged the state more actively in the economy and instituted sweeping and progressive reforms. Panama's socialized health service was expanded. An agrarian reform distributed land to impoverished peasants. And a modernization program invested millions of dollars in Panama City. However, the constitution was suspended, the press was censored, and many political opponents were murdered.

Torrijos (who is remembered fondly by Panamanians to this day) consolidated his popularity with the Torrijos-Carter Treaty. Signed by Torrijos and President Jimmy Carter in Washington on September 7, 1977, the treaty called for the increasing involvement of Panamanians in canal operations, the eventual transfer of the canal to the Republic of Panama, and the closure after a 20-year term of all U.S. military bases. Torrijos's triumph was greeted with a rush of *soberanía*—sovereignty fever. A digital clock was even set up outside the canal administration building, where it ticked down the seconds until the canal finally passed fully into Panama's hands.

THE NORIEGA YEARS

On July 31, 1981, Torrijos was killed when his small plane mysteriously crashed into a mountain. His untimely death left a vacuum in which a series of military figures jostled for power. Torrijos had named one of his supporters, Lt. Col. Manuel Antonio Noriega (1938–), as head of military intelligence. Noriega soon gained control of the National Guard (which he renamed the Fuerza de Defensa de Panama—Panama Defense Force) and the country, which he proceeded to rule through fear and intimidation, while a constitutional president and fraudulent elections maintained the sham of democratic proceedings.

In September 1985, Torrijos's protégé and vocal Noriega opponent Dr. Hugo Spadafora (1940–1985) was seized while returning to Panama from exile in Costa Rica. Discovery of his decapitated and brutally tortured corpse catalyzed growing disgust with Noriega's corrupt, thuggish rule, which used paramilitary "Dignity Battalions" to terrorize and murder opponents. Nonetheless, Noriega, who had been on the CIA payroll since the early 1970s (then-CIA director George H. W. Bush had authorized an annual payment of $110,000 to Noriega), continued to receive tacit U.S. support. The U.S. government turned a blind eye to Noriega's involvement in drug trafficking and money laundering hand-in-hand with Colombia's Medellín cartel. In 1987, former Noriega supporter Col. Roberto Díaz Herrera went public with claims that Noriega was behind the deaths of Torrijos and Spadafora. The public outcry resulted in a "Civic Crusade" in which Panama's middle class took to the streets calling for Noriega to step down. Noriega responded by organizing his own demonstrations from among his base, the urban (mostly nonwhite) underclass.

Noriega's political opponents rallied to support Guillermo Endara Galimany (1936–) in the May 1989 elections against Noriega's handpicked candidate, Carlos Duque. When it was clear that Duque had lost by a wide margin, Noriega canceled the election he had shamelessly attempted to rig. Former president Jimmy Carter, in Panama as an observer, denounced Noriega, who unleashed his paramilitaries to suppress demonstrations.

Anti-government demonstrations erupted in Panama City on March 14, 1988, following a failed coup against Gen. Manuel Noriega (above). U.S. troops landed near Santiago, Panama, during Operation Just Cause, a military invasion in 1989 that toppled Noriega (below).

Panamanian President Martín Torrijos in 2006 announced plans to expand the canal.

Endara and his two vice-presidential running mates were seen on television being beaten by Noriega goons wielding steel pipes.

Washington's mood had now shifted. The U.S. imposed economic sanctions, halted all canal payments, and encouraged a coup (which it declined to support at the vital moment). The coup occurred on October 3, 1989. Noriega, however, managed to rally his most loyal troops and the coup failed. Bloody reprisals were enacted as the increasingly paranoid Panamanian leader began to rely on his vicious paramilitary units. On December 15, the Panamanian legislature declared Noriega president. Meanwhile, clashes between Noriega's forces and U.S. troops stationed in Panama escalated and came to a head on December 17, when a U.S. Marine in civilian clothes was shot dead.

On December 20, 1989, President George H. W. Bush ordered a military invasion—Operation Just Cause—to capture Noriega, who took refuge in the Vatican embassy. After ten days of psychological warfare (rock music was blasted day and night), Noriega surrendered and was extradited to the United States, where in 1992 he was sentenced to a 30-year prison term for racketeering, drug trafficking, and money laundering (though since has received deductions in his punishment for good behavior). Although only 23 U.S. soldiers were killed during the invasion, as many as 4,000 Panamanian civilians may have died, and thousands more were rendered homeless after U.S. forces attacked El Chorrillo, a poor, densely packed district of Panama City and the setting for Noriega's command center. Upon his release from prison, Noriega faces extradition to Panama, where in 1995 he was sentenced in absentia for murder.

NEW DEMOCRACY

Following Noriega's ouster, the Panama Defense Force was disbanded and Guillermo Endara Galimany was sworn in as president. Despite the difficulties of trying to reestablish democracy in the wake of a military invasion,

Endara's term is considered a success.

The mid-1990s saw Torrijos's Partido Revolucionario Democrático return to power in the form of Ernesto Pérez Balladares (1946–), a PRD cofounder who followed pro-market policies, including privatization of key industries. In 1999, Panamanians elected their first female president, Mireya Moscoso, ex-wife of former president Arnulfo Arias. Her administration became mired by corruption charges. That same year, a Kuna legislator, Enrique Garrido, became the first-ever indigenous person to head the nation's Legislative Assembly.

At noon on December 31, 1999, the Republic of Panama assumed full

responsibility for the canal under the control of the Autoridad del Canal de Panama (ACP). All 11,000 U.S. troops departed and 14 major military bases and dozens of "Small Town, U.S.A." townships were turned over to the Panamanian government. America's century in Panama was finally over, although a bilateral treaty gives Uncle Sam the right to come back if the canal's security is threatened. The ACP has since operated the canal as a profitable business (the U.S.-run Panama Canal Commission was a break-even entity). In 2006 the ACP published plans to expand the canal and build a new megaport at the Pacific entrance. International commerce is increasing and ships now come in sizes never

dreamed of when the canal was built.

In May 2004, Martín Torrijos (1963–), son of Omar Torrijos, was elected president. He named former presidential contender and Grammy-winning salsa singer/actor Rubén Blades (1948–) as minister of tourism. The past few years have witnessed a boom in tourism. The country faces major problems, including poverty, a reputation as a drug transshipment center, and the spillover effects of Colombia's four-decades-old civil war. Still, Panama's future looks bright. The canal expansion promises a mammoth boost to the national economy. And the country's vast tourist potential has barely been tapped. ■

Land & landscape

DESPITE ITS DIMINUTIVE SIZE—AT 30,134 SQUARE MILES (78,046 SQ KM) slightly smaller than South Carolina—Panama is a kind of microcontinent unto itself. Elongated and shaped in a gentle S-curve aligned roughly east–west, the isthmus is between 30 and 120 miles (48 and 193 km) wide and narrowest at its tendril-thin waist-line, where the Panama Canal cuts through. A tenuous land bridge barely separating two great oceans and two American continents vastly different in character, Panama is sculpt-ed to show off the full potential of the tropics. Its landscapes are kaleidoscopic, and scenery changes around every corner. The terrain varies from rain forest as lush as the bib-lical Garden of Eden to cloud forest steeped in swirling mists atop Volcán Barú. To either side, forested hills rise to a backbone of mountains that gradually broadens and forms a rugged buffer zone with Colombia and Costa Rica.

The isthmus is relatively youthful. The land we see today began to rise from the sea barely three million years ago, the product of geological upheavals caused by the jostling of three tectonic plates. Panama sits above the juncture of the Cocos, Nascos, and Caribbean plates, which move against each other, the Cocos overriding the Caribbean plate, causing occasional earthquakes and the infrequent eruptions of Volcán Barú, Panama's only volcano.

Despite Panama's location entirely within the tropics, vast extremes of elevation and relief spawn a profusion of microclimates. The arid flatlands of Azuero and the sodden coastal plains of Colón could belong to different worlds, notwithstanding their similar elevation and close proximity. Though temperatures in any one place scarcely vary year-round, the smothering heat of the lowlands contrasts markedly with the crisp cool of the highlands. And despite the narrowness of the isthmus, the climate differs markedly between Pacific and Caribbean sides: The latter receives the moisture-laden trade winds and considerably more rainfall.

There are only two seasons: wet (May to November) and dry (December to April), though the nation is a quilt of regional variations and in many parts of the country the seasons might more correctly be termed "wet" and "less wet." The humidity is less oppressive on the Pacific side, although heavy enough to cling like a damp shawl in wet season, when the cooling breezes die, gray cascades of rain pour down in torrents, and the forests of trees and skyscrapers vanish behind a thick silver veil. Panama lies outside the hurricane belt.

Up to 35 percent of the nation is sheltered in 15 national parks and 48 other protected areas, some 1,300 square miles (3,367 sq km) of it in seven national parks bordering the Panama Canal in a 10-mile-wide (16 km) forested watershed. Marine parks protect some of the more than 1,500 islands that stud the oceans close to shore. Many of these isles are ringed by coral reefs, while the country hosts America's largest mangrove estuaries.

The Panamanian government has long been a keen advocate of ecological preservation, at least on paper. Nonetheless, the nation is severely threatened. During the past century, as much as 65 percent of Panama was denuded by cattle ranching and slash-and-burn agriculture. Much of the Azuero peninsula and the foothills of the Cordillera Central have been virtually deforested. More recently, the extension of the Interamerican Highway into western Darién has been calamitous for the forests, which have been felled by loggers and land-hungry farmers. And in 2002, President Mireya Moscoso introduced plans to carve a road between Volcán Barú and La Amistad National Parks, with potentially devastating consequences.

From semi-desert to rain forest paradise, Panama's range of terrains reflects the full diversity of the tropics, and each region is as distinct as a thumbprint.

WESTERN HIGHLANDS
Dominating the landscape of far western Panama, dauntingly rugged mountains rise dramatically from the coastal plains, sepa-rating the Caribbean and the Pacific like a

An untouched jungle-like mountain forest in Parque La Amistad, a favorite destination for birders and hikers alike

great wall. Rising to 10,945 feet (3,336 m) atop Cerro Fábrega, on the border with Costa Rica, these great cerros, or peaks, are folded in serrated pleats—the Cerro Trinidad, Cordillera de Tabasará, and Cordillera Central—cut by deep valleys. Towering and sodden, they have been little explored, although they are cross-hatched by pathways known only to Indians who live on the mid- and low-level slopes.

Moisture-bearing winds from the Caribbean dump their liquid cargo on the soggy eastern slopes, feeding lush rain forests profusely smothered in bromeliads and delicate orchids that merge into a seamless wall of aqueous greenery. Clouds swirl about windswept summits, where mosses and ferns thrive in the mists haunted by the whistles of resplendent quetzals. Much of this velveteen jungle is protected within Parque Internacional La Amistad, a refuge for endangered wildlife. Volcán Barú, 11,411 feet high (3,478 m), rises amid these mountains and last erupted in the 16th century. Bubbling hot springs and steaming fumaroles attest to the latent power of the sleeping giant. Its slopes are clad in coffee plants; fertile high valleys support market gardens around Cerro Punta, and the delightful alpine town of Boquete combines lovely hotels, intriguing coffee farms and gardens, and splendid hiking.

CENTRAL PANAMA

About two-thirds of Panama's population lives in a belt spanning the isthmus at its narrowest and lowest point. More than one-quarter lives in Panama City, a sprawling coastal metropolis at the southern entrance to the Panama Canal (because the isthmus runs east–west between the oceans, the canal runs more or less north–south). The rest of the populace is concentrated west of the city in provincial towns and dusty agricultural villages in a belt stretching along the foothills of the Cordillera Central and linked by the Interamerican Highway. The expansion of population eastward is a recent phenomenon, and most settlements are small and inconsequential. The country is effectively divided in two, metaphorically and literally, by the canal.

The Panama Canal, a sightseeing attraction in its own right, forms a great trench through the low-lying center, flanked to each side by mountains cloaked in a dozen shades of tropical green. Broken into peaks and troughs like a tormented sea, these lushly forested heights span a half dozen or so national parks protecting the water

sources—not least the mighty Río Chagres—that feed the canal, and thereby the country's economy. The Chagres drains a basin the size of Rhode Island. Home to Emberá Indians, and a source for exhilarating white-water river trips, the Chagres region harbors a mind-boggling array of bird and wildlife species, including large populations of monkeys, jaguars, and harpy eagles. The tempestuous Chagres feeds west into Gatún Lake, which flooded 164 square miles (425 sq km) of forest when the river was dammed in 1906. The lake is still littered with half-drowned trees and studded with islands where wildlife thrives.

At the canal's southern end, the nation's cosmopolitan capital, Panama City, faces the

Golfo de Panama. Nearby Isla Taboga draws day-trippers by ferry, while farther out, the Archipiélago de las Perlas offers tantalizing beaches and superlative snorkeling and diving. The capital city seeps eastward along the Interamerican Highway, unspooling through spongy, half-drowned coastal lowlands filled with brackish swamps. Westward the highway grants access to a string of beaches popular with city-dwellers on weekends. The Altos de Campana rise inland, a partially deforested mountain range composed of isolated, sheer-sided craggy mounds and rugged vales traversed by marked trails. One broad vale, El Valle de Ancón, stands out for its exquisite beauty and springlike climate. Colón, a down-at-the-heels Caribbean port city, commands the canal's northern gateway. Spanish fortresses still guard the mouth of the Chagres and the entrance to the ancient treasure port of Portobelo.

EASTERN CARIBBEAN

Arcing southeast for 142 miles (230 km), this enticingly beautiful coastline is decorated with the San Blas Islands, more than 350 coral-based isles in jade-colored waters a short distance offshore. Hemming in the

Aging structures in Bocas del Toro once served the United Fruit Company— a reminder of the lush, fertile land for which the region is renowned.

coast, a backdrop of lush green mountains forms a spine separating the Caribbean from Darién Province. Comprising the autonomous Kuna Yala *comarca* (district), this is purely Kuna Indian terrain. No non-Kuna live here, ensuring that the indigenous culture remains one of the most intact native communities in the world. The Kuna population is concentrated on about one

north by the Serranía de San Blas and Serranía de Darién mountains and to the south by mountain chains that rear above the Pacific coastline. The mountains cup a huge basin some 155 miles long (250 km), drained westward through the broad Golfo de San Miguel. Prodigious rainfall pummels the region. In rainy season, rivers become seething torrents, bounding down the

Adobe houses with fired-clay tile roofs reflect the simplicity of the Azuero peninsula.

dozen densely packed islands. Many isles have humble facilities for tourists. Simple watercraft are the main mode of travel, permitting access to uninhabited islands fringed by soft sand beaches and warm tropical waters perfect for snorkeling. Pale green in the shallows, the water becomes aqua, azure, and then sapphire where a barrier reef stems the waves. The reef peters out to the east, ending its protection. The coastal plain is farmed with coconut groves although mainland settlements are few, and none exist in the thickly forested Serranía de San Blas and Serranía de Darién mountains, accessible only in the Área Silvestre Protegida de Narganá.

THE DARIÉN ISTHMUS

Panama's vast, sparsely populated southeast quarter broadens eastward, framed to the

mountains in angry leaps to spill their coffee-colored waters into the gulf. The rivers form liquid highways for isolated communities of Emberá-Wounaan Indians and Afro-Antillean peoples.

Construction of the Interamerican Highway in the 1970s opened the intermontane valley to loggers and farmers. Much of the rain forest that carpeted the region has since disappeared. The highway ends at Yaviza, beyond which fully half of Darién is still smothered by the Western Hemisphere's second largest rain forest. In the spongy heat of Parque Nacional Darién, the vegetation is as luxuriant as anywhere on Earth. Giant cedar trees tower a hundred feet (30 m) in the air, orchid species are counted in their hundreds, and you can almost sense the vegetation growing around you. Much of the park is mountainous, reaching 6,152 feet (1,875 m) atop Cerro Tacarcuna. East of the Golfo de San Miguel, the lonesome shoreline unfurls ruler-straight, lined with black sand beaches.

WESTERN PACIFIC

The southern foothills of the western highlands ease onto broad, rolling coastal plains that curve around the Golfo de Chiriquí. The

crawl onto lonesome beaches to lay their eggs.

Offshore, Parque Nacional Marino Golfo de Chiriquí protects warm waters thronged by marine life: sharks, manta rays, marlin, and smaller fry gamboling amid the coral reefs. Farther out lies uninhabited Isla Coiba, Panama's largest island and today a nature reserve occupied mostly by monkeys, iguanas, and birds such as scarlet macaws.

Visitors head to a suspended zipline ride through the treetops near El Valle.

llanura (plain) narrows eastward, and westward curls around the Bahía de Charco Azul to the long, slender tip of Punta Burica. The western flatlands are smothered in banana plantations extending all the way to the Costa Rica border.

The deeply indented and irregular Pacific shore stretches in total for 767 miles (1,234 km). The Pacific Ocean tides are tremendous—rising and falling by as much as 20 feet (6.1 m). Beaches like ribbons of silver lamé unspool along the clawlike Burica peninsula and along the gulf's wild eastern shoreline, washed by rugged waves favored by surfers. The waters along the central shore are thick with mangroves forming a braided maze that comprises the Manglares de David, the largest such complex in Panama. The riparian system teems with birds, while marine turtles

Sportfishers and scuba divers rate these waters as world class. The city of David sits square in the center of the region and, occupying a barren plain, can be stiflingly hot, the air often still as a stone.

AZUERO PENINSULA

This oblong region jutting south into the Pacific Ocean is Panama's dry quarter. Cactuses thrust up from the parched earth that culminates in the Saharan landscapes of Parque Nacional Sarigua, shimmering in the searing summer sun like a dream world. A rugged mountain chain to the west files eastward to a featureless plain the color of honey. The lowlands have long been cleared of forests to make room for ranches and, later, sugarcane. Cattle rest in the cool penumbra of broad trees spreading their gnarled branches

The **Río Sambú** mirrors storm clouds that are an almost daily occurrence in the rain-soaked Darién region (left), while sunshine drenches the palm-studded isles of **San Blas** (above).

to the ground. In spring and summer, yellow bark, purple jacaranda, and bright orange flame-of-the-forest speckle Azuero, and the hot, heavy air is redolent with fragrance. A string of time-warp colonial towns—nostalgic communities where Panama's folkloric traditions run deep—color the main highway running inland of the eastern shore. Here women sew lacy *polleras* and men dress in pleated *montunos* (shirts) and *sombreros montunos* (straw hats). Remarkably, few tourists know of Azuero's relaxed charms. Surfers are drawn to the waves rolling ashore onto broad slivers of taupe sand. Shorebirds in their thousands flock to the flats. Offshore, Refugio de Vida Silvestre Isla Iguana, a rookery for frigate birds, dots the warm waters that nourish coral reefs and draw humpback whales to breed. This refuge, as well as the nearby Refugio de Vida Silvestre Isla de Cañas, are also vital nesting sites for marine turtles.

WESTERN CARIBBEAN
The relatively smooth Caribbean shore is 477 miles (768 km) long in total. Its western portion extends southeast from the Río Sixaola and the Costa Rica border, a broad coastal plain forming a vast sea of banana trees separated from the sea by a complex of mangroves and swamps. The dusty service center of Changuinola is choked with truck traffic linking the *fincas* (plantations) of international fruit companies to the port of Almirante, a funky gateway (by water taxi) to the Archipiélago de Bocas del Toro. The islands of Bocas del Toro draw adventure-seeking tourists to the charming, colorful Afro-Caribbean-flavored center of Bocas Town. The reef-combed and mangrove-lined isles enfold the tranquil Laguna de Chiriquí, where dolphins cavort in the bay of Bocatorito. Parque Nacional Marino Isla Bastimentos—famous for its strawberry-colored poison dart frogs—protects a mosaic of mangroves, towering rain forest, and pristine coral reefs. To the east, the Península Valiente hooks around the lagoon, beyond which the Caribbean coast curves along the Golfo de los Mosquitos—a remote, sparsely inhabited world where the air smells of greenhouse fecundity. Hard-pressed Ngöbe-Buglé and Teribe communities speckle the region: Many welcome visitors as they turn to ecotourism as an alternative to destructive slash-and-burn agriculture. ■

The swallowtail butterfly is one of more than 1,000 species of butterflies found in Panama.

Flora & fauna

PANAMA, A PIVOTAL REGION AT THE JUNCTURE OF THE TWO AMERICAS, IS A meeting point for the biota of each. Profuse in wildlife, the lush environment is a veritable tropical Eden, a cornucopia of biodiversity that was reflected in the words President Theodore Roosevelt wrote to his daughter after his canal visit in 1906: "It is a real tropic forest, palms and bananas, breadfruit trees, bamboos, lofty ceibas, and gorgeous butterflies and brilliant colored birds fluttering among the orchids." This diversity of plants and animals exists despite the fact that the country lies wholly within the tropics, between 7 and 9 degrees north of the equator. Nevertheless, Panama boasts ten distinct ecological zones, from coastal mangrove forests and swampy wetlands to cloud forests shrouded in ethereal mists atop the higher peaks. The colorful canvas even has its dun patches, pockets of dry deciduous forest merged into the parched savannas of Azuero.

LUXURIANT GREENHOUSE

Panama is steeped in humidity and near-constant high temperatures, with the sun passing almost directly overhead throughout the year. Combined with profuse rainfall that tops a drenching 200 inches (500 cm) in many places, the heat fuels luxuriant growth. The bountiful country hosts more than 10,000 known plant species, including more than 1,500 varieties of trees and at least 678 fern species, some 13 feet tall (4 m) with fiddlehead fronds that could grace titanic cellos.

Orchids & other flowers

Panama is singularly rich in orchids: About 1,200 orchid species have been identified so far, including the Flor del Espíritu Santo, or Holy Ghost orchid, the beautiful white national flower. Thriving on moisture, these exquisite plants are found at every elevation, from sea level to the misty upper slopes of Volcán Barú. At any time of year, dozens of species are in bloom, ranging from the pinhead-sized *Platystele jungermanniodes* to the sinister beauty of the Dracula species, such as *Dracula vampira,* with black tapering leaves up to 12 inches long (30 cm).

Most orchid species are epiphytes (Greek for "air plants"), arboreal nesters that root on other plants, drawing their moisture through spongelike roots direct from the air. Other epiphytes include bromeliads, whose thick, tightly whorled spiky leaves form cisterns that trap water and falling detritus whose decay sustains the plants. Many tropical forests resemble vast galleries, so dense are the colonies of air plants thriving in the compost atop massive boughs.

The landscapes flare with color: orange and purple angel trumpet vines; anthuriums in whites, reds, and pinks; begonias; heliconias (more than 30 species); carnal red passionflowers; and *labios ardientes* ("hot lips") looking like Marilyn Monroe's kiss-me pout. Even the rare tropical dry broadleaf deciduous forests of Azuero explode in vivid colors in dry winter months, when *corteza amarilla* (yellow bark), purple jacaranda, and flame-red *Spathodea,* or African flame-of-the-forest, brighten the landscape before dropping their petals like colored confetti.

Mangroves & wetlands

Panama's shorelines are home to five species of *manglares* (mangroves). These halophytic plants—terrestrial species able to survive with their roots in salt water—thrive in alluvium washed down to the coast. Vast forests of mangroves grow along the estuarine shoreline, especially along the Golfo de Chiriquí, Bahía de Panama, and Golfo de San Miguel. Standing over the dark waters, their interlocking stilt roots forming a tangle among the braided channels, mangroves rinse silt from the slow-flowing rivers to form new land by the shore. Thus, they fight tidal erosion and trap nutrients that nourish a profligate world. Migratory waterfowl, wading birds, and small mammals abound, thriving on amphipods, crabs, mussels, and other tiny creatures that inhabit the watery sloughs— vital nurseries, too, for dozens of fish species and marine invertebrates.

Water hyacinths crowd Lago Gatún and Lago Bayano in the center of the country. Other grassy wetlands, swamp forests, and freshwater pools concentrate inland of the Bahía de Panama, drawing migratory shorebirds. The marshes of Área Protegida Ciénaga de las Macanas and Refugio de Vida Silvestre Cenegón del Mangle, on the Pacific coast, and those of San San Pond Sak, on the Caribbean coast, flood in rainy season, when they are flush with fulvous whistling ducks and other waterfowl.

Rain forests

Crown jewels of neotropical life, rain forests are among the most complex ecosystems on Earth. Biologists recognize at least 13 types of rain forest, ranging from the lowland jungle to high-mountain cloud forest at elevations around 4,000 feet (1,220 m), where branches drip with mosses and epiphytes thrive in the near-constant mists. Different forests stem from differences in altitude, rainfall, and soil. Thus the same latitude in Panama may be

White flowers of the *carachuca,* or frangipani, brighten Panama's dry zones.

Mist shrouds the forested heights of Volcán Barú, feeding luxuriant growth.

marked by tropical evergreen rain forest on the Caribbean coast and seasonally dry evergreen forest on the Pacific coast. All rain forests receive more than 100 inches (250 cm) of rainfall per year. The true lowland rain forests that smother the *llanuras* (flatlands) of the Caribbean plains and Darién may receive up to 300 inches (750 cm).

The lowland rain forest is a multilayered riot of green so densely shaded that little undergrowth survives on the floor. Trees of Gothic proportion grow to 100 feet (30 m) or more before merging like giant umbrellas, forming a solid canopy. Some species with trunks like great Corinthian columns, such as the mahoganies and ceiba or silk cotton, soar past their neighbors. The hundreds of tree species are festooned with bromeliads, parasitic plants, and tangled creepers.

In the hot, humid tropics, plants grow year-round. Dead leaves decompose quickly and nutrients are recycled into the forest canopy. Thus, tropical soils are thin, and the massive hardwood trees spread their great roots wide, like giant serpents; the huge trees are flanged at their bases, like rockets, to prevent their toppling over.

Only about 10 percent of the sunlight reaches the cool, dank forest floor, where plants such as the "poor man's umbrella" (*sombrilla de pobre*) put out broad leaves to soak up the subaqueous light. The lack of sunlight precludes growth so that the saplings of many high-canopy species stop growing once they reach about 10 feet (3 m) in height, then wait until a tree falls, opening a patch of light, before erupting into explosive growth. Much of the life of the forest takes place in the sunlit upper canopy, which resounds with the calls of birds and unseen creatures.

BOUNTIFUL ARK

Panama is home to almost 1,000 bird, 225 mammal, 214 reptile, and 155 amphibian species, including more than 104 species of frogs and toads. Insect species number in the tens of thousands and countless marine species swim and crawl out at sea. Over the eons, life-forms from the north and south

have migrated through the narrow land bridge and diversified remarkably as an adaptation to the varied local relief and climate.

Birds

Ornithologists' hearts take flight in Panama, which despite its comparatively tiny size boasts an astounding 960 or so species of birds, 12 of them found only here. Some 150 species are migrants—the isthmus is a bottleneck for birds migrating between the Americas. Panama's coastal wetlands are particularly rich in migratory shorebirds, such as sandpipers, willets, and whimbrels, often seen in tens of thousands. White ibis, spoonbills, and herons pick for morsels down by the shore, where coastal mangroves prove ideal nesting sites for pelicans, frigate birds,

and even boobies, which can be seen on Isla de los Pájaros (Swan's Cay) and on islands off the Azuero peninsula.

The forests are alive with the squawks and screeches of parrots barreling overhead in jet-fighter formation. Panama has 18 species, from the diminutive Panama Amazon to the giant blue-and-gold macaw, one of six endangered macaw species found here. Large flocks of scarlet macaws can be seen on Isla Coiba, plunging between the treetops like flying rainbows.

Keel-billed and chestnut-mandibled toucans, with their bananalike beaks, are common throughout the country. So, too, are cattle egrets, easily seen in pastures. And quetzals, the emerald jewels of the cloud forest, are more numerous here than anywhere else in Central America. They're a dime a dozen around Volcán Barú, especially in springtime when the ardent males are given to wooing their prospective mates with daring soar-and-swoop displays. Visitors should listen for the quetzal's mournful two-note whistle.

The country also hosts dozens of species of tanagers and trogons and doves, plus bellbirds, umbrellabirds, and antbirds scavenging on insects and lizards flushed out by columns of army ants. The list goes on and on.

Panama's national bird is the massive harpy eagle, largest by far of the nation's 50 or so raptor species. It nests atop the tallest trees, keeping a sharp eye out for monkeys and other potential snacks that it will snatch up on the wing. Although the bird is endangered throughout its range, the

Fondo Peregrino-Panama has a successful breed-and-release program.

Mammals

Almost half of Panama's mammal species are bats, ranging from fruit eaters and vampires (feeding mainly on the blood of sleeping cattle) to hawk-size fishing bats with large claws adapted for snatching fish on the fly. Most mammal species are shy and not easily seen by visitors, as with Panama's six species of elusive and well-camouflaged tropical cats.

Far more easily viewed are the country's seven species of monkeys, from the tiny endemic Geoffrey's tamarin and the omnivorous white-faced capuchins to herbivorous mantled howlers. Male howlers are heard as often as seen; the forests vibrate to their stentorian roars. Two- and three-toed sloths (*perezosos*) are commonly seen snoozing in treetops. And capybaras, the world's largest rodents, inhabit watery sloughs at the northernmost end of their range.

On the ground, the adorable raccoonlike brown coati (*pizote*) is ubiquitous. Herds of potentially aggressive white-lipped and collared peccaries are sometimes encountered deep in the rain forests. Baird's tapirs—trunknosed distant cousins of elephants—inhabit both lowland montane forests. Agoutis (large rodents), anteaters, and armadillos are other common mammals. And otters swim in the rivers of Parque Nacional Chagres.

Amphibians & reptiles

Amphibians and reptiles thrive in the hot, damp tropics. Snakes, of which Panama has more than 120 species, are ubiquitous, although usually well camouflaged and not easily seen. A swaying vine turns out to be an eyelash pit viper, so green as to be almost iridescent, curled in sensuous coils on a branch. Boas up to 10 feet long (3 m) are often spotted along riverbanks. Most snake species are small, preying on small birds, lizards, and rodents. Fewer than 10 percent are venomous. The viper family includes the much-feared, burnished brown fer-de-lance (locally called *equis*—"X"—for the marks on its back), an aggressive giant that accounts for most of the fatal snake bites in Panama. Brightly banded

coral snakes account for many of the others. Fortunately, there are no known occurrences of humans being bitten by the highly venomous black-and-orange sea snake often seen in swarms in the Bahía de Panama.

Frogs abound, including red-eyed tree frogs and gaily colored poison dart frogs hopping about the forest floors, secure in the Day-Glo liveries meant to warn off predators. In recent decades, a deadly fungus has killed off many frog and toad species and threatens Panama's endangered and earless golden frog (*Atelopus zateki*), a national symbol revered for its ability to communicate by a kind of semaphore.

American crocodiles (*cocodrilos*), which reach lengths of up to 15 feet (4.5 m), infest the river estuaries and lowland waterways, including Lago Gatún. Their diminutive cousins, caimans, rarely grow beyond 6 feet (1.8 m). The tree-dwelling iguana inhabits both wet and dry lowland forests and can grow to 3 feet (0.9 m); its population has been greatly reduced by *campesinos* for its tasty meat. A highlight among the dozens of smaller reptiles is the basilisk lizard, a lowland dweller nicknamed the "Jesus Christ lizard" for its ability to run across water on its hind legs.

Five species of marine turtles come ashore to lay their eggs at beaches on both Caribbean and Pacific shores. The most exhilarating sight is the synchronized mass nestings of olive Ridley turtles that takes place at Refugio de Vida Silvestre Isla de Cañas during full moons in autumn.

Marine life

The warm waters off Panama's coasts are thickly populated by fish and marine mammals. Manatees, endangered marine herbivores, inhabit the watery seclusion of San San Pond Sak. The waters of the Golfo de Chiriquí and Golfo de Panama teem with gamefish, luring anglers seeking dorado, tuna, and marlin. Humpback whales and even sperm whales and orcas gather to mate and give birth in the nutrient-rich gulf waters.

Harmless manta rays, whale sharks, octopuses, crabs, and spiny lobsters the size of house cats: These and other creatures thrill scuba divers in Panama's Pacific waters. On

The keel-billed toucan, with its extravagant, rainbow-hued beak, resides in Panama's forests.

the Caribbean side, a kaleidoscopic array of fish plays tag in the coral-laced waters of the San Blas Islands and Bocas del Toro, where dolphins perform like a circus troupe.

Insects
Incalculably rich in insect fauna, Panama resounds to a cacophonous buzz. The country is thought to have more than 18,600 insect species per acre (about 46,000 per hectare), from microscopic flower mites that hitch rides inside the nostrils of hummingbirds to the 3-inch-long (7.5 cm) rhinoceros beetle. Tiny Isla Barro Colorado alone has more than 200 ant species, from vast swarms of army ants to the less aggressive leaf-cutters scurrying along well-worn pathways with shards of scissored leaves above their heads. Some 1,600 species of butterflies flit about the country, including the electric-blue morpho butterflies. ■

Culture

FROM AFRO-CARIBBEAN RHYTHMS TO CLASSICAL MUSIC AND RACY JAZZ tunes, Panameños are proud of their vibrant cultural scene. Although comparatively undeveloped and lagging in certain genres—namely, literature—the country is incomparably rich in folkloric tradition. The visual arts have shed prescriptive straightjackets to arouse the admiration of the rest of the world. And classical and contemporary music are vibrant avatars of the nation's lively cultural spirit, recalling rich indigenous traditions that predate the Spanish arrival.

The Museo de Arte Contemporáneo (above) and Instituto Nacional de Cultura (opposite) exemplify Panama City's art scene.

VISUAL ARTS

Panama has an artistic tradition dating back 10,000 years, to a time when pre-Columbian peoples adorned their ceremonial bowls and other ceramics with stylized red, black, and ocher motifs. During the colonial period, most artistic expression was relegated to religious art. Post independence Panamanian art is associated above all with Roberto Lewis (1874–1949), whose allegorical, romantic murals, inspired by the belle époque of France, adorn the Palacio Presidencial and Teatro Nacional. Lewis became director of Panama's first art academy, the Escuela Nacional de Pintura, in 1939, and influenced an entire generation of artists. Manuel E. Amador's (1869–1952) modernism led the way for more abstract art, typified by Eudoro Silvera (1917–), Alfredo Sinclair (1915–), and Guillermo Trujillo (1927–), known for his distinctive works that fuse love of country with the mythology of its indigenous people.

Panama's eclectic fine-arts scene—long overshadowed by the U.S. presence—has lacked a recognizable national theme, and identifiably Panamanian issues are rarely addressed on canvas. An exception is the work of acclaimed artist Brooke Alfaro (1949–), who in 2000 moved from working on canvas to video art to create portraits of the life of Panama's marginalized underclass. Meanwhile, inspired by the works of Cuba's Wilfredo Lam (1902–1982), Colón native Arturo Lindsay (1946–) has concentrated on exploring African spiritual and aesthetic traditions from the Taller Portobelo art school, which he co-founded, on the Caribbean.

The nation's largest collection of works by Panamanian artists is found in permanent and revolving exhibitions in Panama City's Museo de Arte Contemporáneo. The museum hosts weekly workshops and every two years hosts the Bienal de Art.

Earning international recognition for their photography are Iraida Icaza (1952–) and Sandra Eleta, known for her book, *Portobelo: Fotografías de Panamá* and her recent photo-documentaries of the Emberá-Wounaan, who decorate their bodies with patterns etched with the juice of the jagua.

Sculpture

The sculptural landscape is undistinguished, notwithstanding a strong heritage of ritualistic sculptures associated with pre-Columbian

cultures. Creation of the Instituto de Artes in 1907 spawned a school of sculptors (mostly Europeans) working in neoclassic style. In the 1940s, José Mora Noli emerged as the first contemporary Panamanian sculptor. Today's preeminent sculptor is Isabel de Obaldía (1957–), who works predominantly with glass.

Crafts

On the crafts front, Panama is famed for its stitched appliqué *molas* exclusive to the Kuna people, for elaborately embroidered white lace pollera dresses, and for grotesque papier-mâché devil masks from the towns of Azuero. The popular masks are collector's items from the hands of such master mask-makers as Darío López and Iván de León.

Market stalls are brimful of straw hats, available in a variety of styles (though the famous "Panama hats" are actually made in Ecuador). Some of the highest-quality weaves and designs are achieved by the Ngöbe-Buglé people, who normally wear straw hats for celebrations, when they adorn their hats with feathers. Most hats derive from the provinces of Coclé and Herrera, where weaving is a true cottage industry in Azuero hamlets such as Ocú and Pedregosa. The very best hats are made in the early morning or late at night. The rest of the day the sweat builds up on the weaver's fingers, and atmospheric conditions are too variable for the absolute continuity necessary in a *fino.* Such hats can last for decades. They are also rare and expensive. Most hats today, however, are relatively coarse, inexpensive weaves.

Tourism has stimulated the production of indigenous crafts whose secrets are passed down through generations. The Emberá-Wounaan are acclaimed for tightly woven flat basketry adorned with animal motifs, and for their skill as carvers who turn *tagua* palm nuts into small animal figurines. The Ngöbe-Buglé are known for their unique *chácaras,* bags intricately hand-knitted from the leaf fibers of the cabuya and pita plant. These range from tiny purses worn to carry charms and talismans to large bags used as cradles for babies. Their designs commemorate ancestral legends, and the styles are considered to have been invented by supernatural beings *(magatda).* Common design elements in all

Ngöbe-Buglé art are the triangle, representing both mountain and valley of the culture's home environment, and snake designs *(culebrakrays)* that reflect the importance of snakes in Ngöbe-Buglé mythology. These peoples excel, too, in the beauty of their *chaquiras*—exquisite glass bead necklaces up to 12 inches wide (30 cm).

LITERATURE

Panama was slow to evolve a literary culture or writers of distinction. The early exceptions were novelist and dramatist Víctor de la Guardia (1772–1823), poet Dario Herrera (1870–1914), and nationalist poet Amelia Denis de Icaza (1836–1911), best known for her patriotic poem, "Al Cerro Ancón," about Ancón Hill. The nation found its most vital expression in the mid-20th century through the pens of such novelists as avant-garde Guillermo Sánchez Borbón (1924–2005), who wrote under the pseudonym Tristán Solarte, and Ricardo Miró (1883–1940), who wrote the poem "Patria," a homeland homage. Acknowledged as Panama's literary luminary, Miró lends his name to the nation's highest literary honor, the Ricardo Miró National Literature Award.

Despite a high literacy rate, Panamanians as a whole are dispassionate about literature. Inward-looking and intensely focused on themes of daily life on the isthmus, local authors still produce mostly poems and short stories that tend toward the prosaic. Latter-day standouts include poet Joaquín Beleño (1922–), known for his novels *Luna Verde* and *Gamboa Road Gang,* nationalistic works about injustices of the Panama Canal, and Carlos Francisco Changmarín (1922–), who writes mostly on countryside themes. Prominent among contemporary authors, Enrique Jaramillo Levi (1944–) also edits Panama's literary review, *Maga.*

THEATER

Panama has a lively theater scene, with everything from the classics to experimental pieces performed in venues large and small. Noted Panamanian-born stage director José Benjamin Quintero (1924–1999) pioneered the off-Broadway movement of the 1950s and was a cofounder of New York's leg-

endary Circle in the Square Theatre. The
Theater Guild of Ancón performs in English
at the art deco Teatro Balboa in Panama
City. The nation's leading theater is the
Teatro Nacional.

MUSIC & DANCE

Panama today swings to a salsa beat.
Nonetheless, Panama's folkloric tradition
runs deep, although *música folclórica* (often
referred to as *típico* or *pindín*) is performed
today only in festivals and stage presentations.
Panama's típico music fuses the sound of the
five-string *mejorana* guitar with *tambores*
(African bongo drums) and pre-Columbian
musical instruments such as tagua seedpods
and *churucas* (gourd rattles). Dances are
typified by the *punto,* the *mejorana,* the
tamborito (Panama's national dance), and
similar stomps for couples dressed in
traditional clothing: the *montuno* hat and
white shirt for men and the ankle-length,
frilled lace pollera for women. Traditional
dancing is based on the stylized Spanish *paseo,*
with men and women alternately circling each
other, accompanied by much "yip-yipping"—
in Panama the shouts are called *saloma*—and
tossing of scarves and straw hats.

**Women dance in the Festival Nacional
de la Pollera in Panama City (above)
while men play traditional music (top).**

Every week a folkloric festival seems to
be taking place somewhere in the Azuero, the
heartland of Panamanian music and dance.
None is more colorful than the Corpus Christi

Grammy-winning musician Rubén Blades also serves as Panama's minister of tourism.

festival, highlighted by devil dancers in masks and elaborate costumes. The Ngöbe-Buglé, Emberá-Wounaan, and Kuna communities also enjoy demonstrating their centuries-old traditional dances, performed to the accompaniment of drums and Pan-style flutes.

Many típico dances, such as *los enanos* (the dwarfs) and *el zaracundé,* are derived from African culture and performed during festivals by dancers dressed in dry banana leaves. Colón Province is known for its *congos,* performances featuring drama, music, and dance that recount the history of Panama's Afro-Antillean people. Contemporary island tunes also infuse the culture: The Bastimentos Beach Boys, from Bocas del Toro, are legendary exponents of Calypso.

On the classical front, the national symphony orchestra was created in 1941 under the baton of celebrated Spanish composer Alberto Galimany (1889–1973). The Ballet Nacional de Panamá was founded in 1970. The popularity of the classical genres among urbanites was boosted when British ballerina Dame Margot Fonteyn (1919–1991) settled in Panama. Panama hosts the Festival Nacional de Ballet each October. Today classical music is sponsored by the private Asociación Nacional de Conciertos, founded by Panamanian pianist Jaime Ingram (1928–).

The capital's cosmopolitan jazz scene finds its major outlet in the annual Panama City Jazz Festival each January. The festival's founder is Panama's well-known jazz composer, pianist, and Grammy-winner Danilo Pérez. He was recently named cultural ambassador for Panama.

The younger generation has forsaken traditional forms of music and dance for hip-hop, rock, and Latin rhythms—salsa, cumbia, and hip-swiveling merengue. Panama City's nightclubs throb on weekends to the *vida loca* vibe. Hot performers include the Latin rock band Los Rabanes and top-selling cumbia artists Sammy and Sandy Sandoval. Panama's undisputed ambassador of contemporary sound is salsa superstar (and politician) Rubén Blades. Born into an artistic family, Blades attained national hero status for his lyrics on social and nationalist themes. ■

W orld-class on many levels, this vibrant financial capital teems with cosmopolitan restaurants, hotels, and nightlife. The historic quarter is chock-full of churches, small museums, and pocket-size plazas, while nature and the Panama Canal are never far away.

Panama City

The seawall at Plaza de Francia

A couple admires the view of Punta Paitilla's modern skyline from Monumento Balboa.

Panama City

COSMOPOLITAN, COMPACT, AND STEAMY, PANAMA'S CAPITAL CITY SPREADS along the shore of a broad Pacific bay at the southern entrance to the canal. Its hot, humid, tropical maritime climate at times feels like a Turkish sauna. Hotter still is the city's cool Latin vibe. At once both colonial and contemporary in mood and setting, this burgeoning city of around 750,000 people (Panamanians know it simply as "Panama") is the most sophisticated metropolis between Miami and Maracaibo.

A crossroads between two continents and two oceans, the city has been motivated by commerce for 500 years. Founded in 1519 at the mouth of the Río Abajo, the ancient city prospered as the Pacific marshaling point for treasures bound for Spain via the *camino real*. In 1671, cutthroat pirate Henry Morgan ravaged the city, leaving charred ruins in his wake. A fresh start was

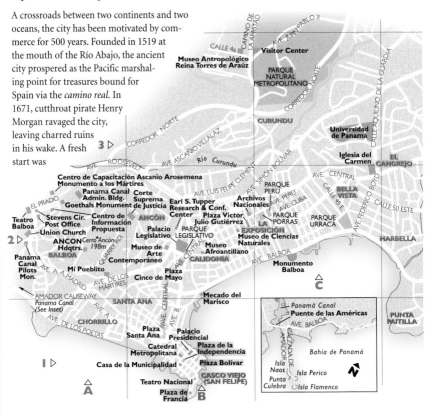

made on a promontory known as San Felipe. Safe behind thick for-tress walls, the new city evolved fine mansions in Spanish colonial style. The city's fortunes were also boosted by the mid-19th-century California gold rush and construction of the Panama Railroad, with its terminus in Panama City, while the arrival of the Compagnie Universelle du Canal Interocéanique in the 1880s added Parisian flavors to the quarter now known as Casco Viejo.

Independence in 1903 and canal construction thrust the city headfirst into the 20th century. Entire new districts—Ancón, Balboa, Quarry Heights—went up overnight alongside U.S. military bases. For eight decades, Zonians (U.S. residents of the Canal Zone) lived a pampered colonial lifestyle with their own schools, hospitals, commissaries, and social clubs. Though the U.S. bases have closed, the tidy neighborhoods of white bungalows and town houses surrounded by shade trees retain their charm.

Positioned by the canal as a center of international commerce, the city has since evolved into a sprawling metropolis. Today, Panama City is a major international banking center humming with modernity. The glass-and-marble towers

of the banking district, the high-rise condo-miniums of Punta Paitilla, the commercial district of El Cangrejo teeming with shoppers—all are a far cry from the ancient ruins of Panama Viejo (the original city) and the cobbled streets of Casco Viejo.

A quilt of loosely defined neighborhoods and multiple ethnicities, the city offers star-tling contrasts. The middle- and upper-class districts of Bella Vista, El Cangrejo, and Marbella, boasting boutique hotels and sophisticated restaurants, are in the midst of a high-rise building boom. The expansion has failed to engulf the ancient quarter, still rich in colonial-era allure. Brimming with scenic plazas, museums, and ecclesiastical treasures, Casco Viejo is on the upswing as savvy investors turn ugly ducklings into gracefully remodeled mansions, hip restaurants, and trendy cafés.

Much of Panama City, however, is more Mean Street than Main Street. English-speaking guides are available on the crowded sidewalks of Casco Viejo, where a strong police presence helps keep crime at bay. However, parts of Casco Viejo are best avoided. So, too, are the neighboring streets of Salsipuedes, Santa Ana, and El Chorrillo, where labyrinthine streets are lined with crime-ridden tenements. ■

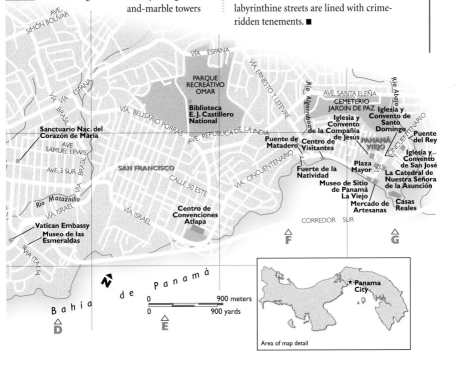

Casco Viejo

Founded in 1673 following the sacking of Panama Viejo, the "Old Quarter" is the most colorful and intriguing part of the city. Though now lacking its fortified walls and decrepit in parts, this timeworn and earthy living museum is full of historic buildings, quaint plazas, charming sidewalk cafés, and eclectic museums. Declared a UNESCO World Heritage site in 1997, this delightful quarter known colloquially as San Felipe is a world apart and centuries away from the 21st-century high-rise metropolis of modern Panama City.

Weathered homes dating back to the 18th century lend unique charm to Casco Viejo.

In 1878, a devastating fire—the worst in a series of destructive blazes—razed one-third of the ancient city. Many of the buildings that remained declined quickly in the tropical climate. An ambitious restoration project was begun in 1997 to restore Casco Viejo to its former grandeur. A decade on, the area—resembling in many ways New Orleans's French Quarter—has regained its vitality as well as a new luster. Even the poorest streets have a lingering dignity beneath the grime baked in by centuries of tropical heat.

The neighborhoods seem to spring from the pages of history books as you roam the narrow brick-paved streets, lined with gaily painted colonial confections in stone.

Wrought-iron balconies drip with giddily colorful flowers, while walls of variegated tropical pastels smolder gold in the late afternoon sunlight. In the evening, it is a pleasure to sit beneath the street lamps illuminating the patios of a fashionable new generation of restaurants and bars.

Here you'll find some of the city's most alluring sites: Iglesia de San José, Plaza de la Independencia, Plaza Bolívar, Palacio de las Garzas, and—a good place to begin your visit—Plaza de Francia, French Plaza.

Note that although gentrification is on-going, pockets of depression remain, and caution is required while walking at night. Even by day avoid the Chorrillo area immediately west of Casco Viejo. ∎

Plaza de Francia

THIS PLAZA OPENS TO THE SEA AIR AT THE TIP OF THE peninsula, where Casco Viejo meets the bottle-green bay. Originally it supported a fort that was torn down at the turn of the 20th century. At that time, it was renamed in honor of the French and their pioneering attempt to construct the canal.

Shaded by jacaranda and palms, the plaza is dominated by a pencil-thin obelisk crowned by a Gallic cockerel and guarded at its base by bronze busts of Ferdinand de Lesseps and four other figures prominent in the French effort to build a canal. The story of the canal's construction and of the 22,000 workers who gave their lives is visible on stone tableaus engraved in the walls of a half-moon gallery beneath the **Paseo Estebán Huertas** esplanade. Also honored by a plaque is Carlos J. Finlay, the Cuban physician who discovered the link between the *Aëdes aegypti* mosquito and yellow fever.

In rough weather, waves crash against the eastern seawall; in Spanish colonial days, condemned convicts were chained to this wall and drowned. Today nine vaults built into the wall—**Las Bóvedas**—house an art gallery plus the Restaurant Las Bóvedas, hosting jazz on Friday nights. Immediately north is the gleaming white, triple-tiered **Instituto Nacional de Cultura** (National Institute of Culture), the government agency responsible for the nation's museums and other cultural institutions. The building also holds the tiny **Teatro Anita Villalaz** *(tel 501-4017 ext. 4020).*

Facing onto the plaza on the north side is the robin's-egg blue **French embassy** *(tel 211-6200, Calle 1 at Plaza de Francia),* admired from its east side by a life-size bronze effigy of Pablo Arosemena (1836–1920), principal negotiator with the U.S. government of the canal treaty and later president of the Republic of Panama (1910–1912 and 1920). Each July 14, the embassy hosts an outdoor party complete with fireworks.

NEAR THE PLAZA

The ruins two blocks northwest of the plaza are those of the **Iglesia y Convento de Santo Domingo** *(Ave. A at Calle 3),* built by Dominicans in 1756 on the site of earlier churches destroyed by fire. The adjacent **Museo de Arte Religioso Colonial** is a trove of religious artworks dating back to the 16th century, including the convent's original baroque altar. ∎

Plaza de Francia
⚏ 58 B1

Instituto Nacional de Cultura
www.inac.gob.pa
✉ Plaza de Francia
☎ 211-4000
🕐 Closed Sat. & Sun.

Museo de Arte Religioso Colonial
✉ Ave. A at Calle 3
☎ 501-4127
🕐 Closed Mon.
💲 $

Plaza de la Independencia

FORMERLY CALLED PLAZA DE LA CATEDRAL, THE LARGEST
and the most important of the Old Quarter's squares is ringed by
colonial-era buildings and has an octagonal pergola at its heart. The
Spanish classicism of aristocratic homes blends with 19th-century
French rococo, with the humble and haughty side by side. In dry
season, the park explodes in a bouquet of colors: canary-bright
yellow bark, delicate pink poui, and flame-red royal poinciana ignite
the square.

Dominating the square on the west
side is the **Catedral Metropolitana** *(Calle 7 Este at Ave. Central;
see pp. 64–65)*, begun in 1688 and
completed in 1796. The city's colonial ecclesiastical masterpiece pre-
sents a striking facade, with a centerpiece—part Moorish, part rippling baroque—built with stones
from the ruins of the Convento de
la Merced in Panama Viejo. It is
flanked to each side by triple-tiered
bell towers, inlaid with mother-of-
pearl and dazzlingly white in the
phosphorescent light of midday.
The cathedral played host to the
signing of the declaration of independence from Colombia on November 3, 1903. A reliquary toward
the front of the church contains the
skeleton of Santo Aurelio; it is hidden behind a painting of Jesus.

Diagonally across from the
cathedral, on the square's southwest
corner, is the **Casa de la Municipalidad** *(tel 506-5705)*, dating from
1910 and designed in beaux arts
style by Italian architect Gennaro
Nicola Ruggieri. On the second
floor, the tiny, two-room **Museo
de História de Panamá** traces the
nation's history from the arrival of
Balboa until 1977. Exhibits include
armaments, scale models of ancient
fortresses, old maps, and documents.
Signs are in Spanish only.

Built in quintessential French
colonial fashion, the grand three-
story edifice with mansard roof on
the square's southeast side is the

splendid **Museo del Canal Interoceánico,** which opened in 1997 in the former headquarters of the Compagnie Universelle du Canal Interocéanique. The building began life as the Grand Hotel (where Ferdinand de Lesseps was fêted with a banquet in 1879) and later housed the U.S. Canal Commission from 1904 to 1912. The eclectic exhibits recalling the Herculean canal-building efforts are laid out chronologically and include mementos of the California forty-niners, an informative section on the building of the Panama Railroad, and model ships that include the S.S. *Ancón,* the steamer that made the first official Panama Canal transit. The upstairs *sala* exhibits coins and stamps, including Canal Zone stamps, plus a copy of the Torrijos-

Hemmed by twin campaniles, the baroque Catedral Metropolitana offers an imposing facade to Plaza de la Independencia.

CATEDRAL METROPOLITANA

Inside Catedral Metropolitana

Panama's municipal cathedral, built between 1688 and 1796 and featuring a multi-toned sandstone facade, is a supreme example of religious colonial architecture. The two imposing belfries are inlaid with mother-of-pearl from the Islas Perlas, and the bells were made in Toledo, Spain. According to legend, a dash of gold accounts for the bells' musical tone. The country's Declaration of Independence was signed in the park in front of the cathedral.

Belfry

Nave

Altar

Facade

Front doors

The glistening lobby of the Museo del Canal Interoceánico reflects its origins as a 19th-century hotel that once welcomed Ferdinand de Lesseps.

Palacio Presidencial

🅜 58 B1

✉ Ave. Eloy Alfaro, between Calles 6 Este & 7 Este

☎ 227-9740.
Fax: 527-9073

🕐 Tours 3 times daily, Tues., Thurs., & Fri. 24-hour written notice required. No shorts, jeans, T-shirts, or sandals.

Carter Treaty of 1977 that committed the United States to handing the canal to Panama. Other »exhibits include pre-Columbian gold, Spanish armor and weaponry, and the desk at which Panama's declaration of independence was signed. The labels are solely in Spanish, although English-speaking guides are available with advance notice. Audio tours are offered for a fee.

IN THE VICINITY
The former **Iglesia y Convento de la Compañia de Jesús** (*Calle 7 Oeste*), just south of the plaza, is now but a shell with a baroque facade and columns; its innards are in ruins. It was founded by Jesuit bishop Francisco Javier de Luna in 1749 and enjoyed a brief life as a university—the Universidad Javeriana—before being destroyed by fire in 1781 (the Jesuit order had been expelled from Panama in 1767).

Reputedly the oldest house in Casco Viejo, the simple two-story **Casa Góngora** (*Ave. Central at Calle 4 Oeste, tel 506-5836, closed*

Mon.), one block east of the plaza, was built for a Spanish pearl merchant in 1756. It survived the ravages of three fires and today functions as an art space and concert hall. Tours are given in Spanish only.

The official residence of the Panamanian president, the **Palacio Presidencial** occupies an entire block one block north of the plaza. Visits are by prior request only. Erected in 1673 and rebuilt in 1921 in Moorish style, the palace is colloquially called the Palacio de las Garzas (Palace of the Herons) for the herons that strut around the Patio Andaluz, the marble-floored lobby centered on a fountain inlaid with mother-of-pearl. Highlights include a gallery of life-size bronze statues representing the virtues and the elaborate Salón Amarillo and Salón Los Tamarindos, adorned with beautiful murals by Roberto Lewis. Visitors are also shown the Salón de Gabinete, where the president's weekly cabinet meetings are held (the president doesn't actually live here). ■

Plaza Bolívar

WITH ITS NEATLY CLIPPED TREES AND COLORFUL BUILDINGS, this delightful plaza is the most intimate of Casco Viejo's squares. The plaza is enlivened by chic bars and cafés and vibrates with guitar music in the voluptuous heat of the night. It is named for Simón Bolívar (1783–1830), the Latin American "Great Liberator" who led the fight for independence from Spain.

Royal palms shade a dramatic **monument of Bolívar,** who in 1826 organized a congress (the Congreso Anfictiónico) here for the cause of Latin American union. Though Bolívar never attended, the meeting convened in a convent schoolhouse on the park's northeast corner. Today the **Palacio Bolívar** (alias the Antiguo Instituto Bolívar) houses the Ministerio de Relaciones Exteriores, or Foreign Ministry. Beyond the carved wooden portal, the inner courtyard—the Plaza de Los Libertadores—is adorned with the coats of arms of the republics that participated in the congress; on its east side a bronze bust of Bolívar gazes down on an excavated portion of the original convent. The mosaic floor inset with a huge compass is protected by a vast skylight. The courtyard can be explored during business hours, as can the twin-room **Sala Bolívar.** The Sala Capitular (Meeting Room) where the congress was held contains a copy of Bolívar's gold ceremonial sword encrusted with 1,374 diamonds; an upstairs room displays the original congress documents.

The adjoining Romanesque **Iglesia y Convento de San Francisco de Asís** (Calle 3 Este at Ave. B, tel 262-1410) dates from 1761 and has a see-through belfry and a fairly austere interior. Permission to climb the campanile can be obtained at the office to the rear of the church. Feeling like Quasimodo staring from between the bells, you gain a fine vantage over Casco Viejo, including the recently renovated **Iglesia San Felipe de Neri** (Ave. B at Calle 4), built in 1688 and thereby one of the oldest structures in Panama. Its bell tower is adorned with mother-of-pearl.

Spectacular after a recent renovation, the **Teatro Nacional,** on the plaza's southeast corner, was inaugurated in 1908 with a performance of Aida. A mini La Scala in the tropics, it was designed by Gennaro Nicola Ruggieri in Italianate style and is decadently adorned in rococo fashion. Its three-tier, horseshoe-shaped auditorium still has the original gilt-and-red-velvet seats and is capped by a dome with masterful, patriotically themed murals by Panamanian artist Roberto Lewis. Lewis's bust occupies the lobby alongside that of Dame Margot Fonteyn, the British ballerina and long-term Panama resident, who performed here. ■

Plaza Bolívar
⬛ 58 B1

Palacio Bolívar
✉ Antiguo Instituto Bolívar, Plaza Bolívar, Calle 3
🕐 Closed Sat. & Sun.

Teatro Nacional
www.teatrodepanama.com
✉ Ave. B at Calle 3 Este
☎ 262-3525
💲 $

Simón Bolívar looks over Casco Viejo from his pedestal in Parque Bolívar.

A walk around Casco Viejo

This walk explores the nation's most complete colonial region: a veritable trove of exquisite historic buildings, from early 17th-century fortress ruins to French-style 19th-century mansions and even early 20th-century art deco treasures. Concentrated around four main plazas, the region includes much of the city's finest domestic and ecclesiastical architecture. An ongoing renaissance by conscientious investors has saved much of the area from demolition while turning near-ruins into chic restaurants, boutiques, and bars.

Blossoms of a "flame of the forest" emblazon Plaza de Francia.

Walking the main streets, tiled with red bricks, is quite safe due to a heavy police presence and the availability of *asistentes de turismo* (licensed guides). Nonetheless, much of Casco Viejo remains down-at-the-heels and poses risks for anyone venturing even one or two blocks off this beaten track.

Begin the walk at **Plazuela de Puerta del Mar ❶**, a tiny triangular plaza giddy with bougainvillea. Pause here to admire the handsome sepia facade of the **Casa de los Monogramas,** which began life as a convent in 1743 and is graced by wooden balustrades with lathe-turned bars. Walk 50 yards (46 m) east to the police guard post *(at Calle 7 Este).* After being searched, you pass into the secure zone of the presidential palace. Immediately on your right, note the **Casa García** and beyond, the ornate gleaming white Moorish-influenced **Palacio Presidencial ❷** (see p. 66); herons can be seen strutting around in the courtyard beyond the well-guarded gates.

Follow Avenida Eloy Alfaro east to Calle 3 Oeste. Turn right and walk 50 yards (46 m) to the entrance of the **Palacio Bolívar** (see p. 67). After visiting the **Sala Bolívar,** exit the former convent. If your timing is good, the bell tower of the **Iglesia de San Francisco** (see p. 67) will be open for you to ascend to take in the fine view over **Plaza Bolívar ❸** (see p. 67), where steps lead up to the **Monumento Bolívar.** The exquisite Moorish-in-

0   300 meters
0   300 yards

B a h í a   d e   P a n a m á

spired three-story building on the north side is an apartment complex with restaurants on the ground floor.

Cross to the southeast corner to enter and explore the **Teatro Nacional** (see p. 67), then follow Ave. B around to **Plazuela de las Mojas ④.** The beautifully restored three-story colonial building on the south side is the private **home of Rubén Blades,** famous salsa-singer-turned-minister-of-tourism. Fifty yards (46 m) beyond, ascend the steps to follow **Paseo General Esteban Huertas,** a waterfront ramp that leads to **Plaza de Francia ⑤** (see p. 61), with its busts and plaques honoring the French effort at building the canal. Passing **Las Bóvedas** and **Instituto Nacional de Cultura** on the east side of the plazas, and the **French embassy** on the north side (see p. 61), follow Calle 2 Oeste its 50-yard (46 m) length to tiny **Plaza Charles V ⑥,** with a bust of the namesake Holy Roman Emperor (1500–1558) framed by bougainvillea.

Turn left onto Avenida A, passing the ruins

🔲 See area map pp. 58–59
▶ Plazuela de Puerta del Mar
🔄 1.5 miles (2.4 km)
🕓 4 hours
▶ Casa de la Municipalidad

NOT TO BE MISSED
- Palacio Presidencial
- Teatro Nacional
- Plaza de Francia
- Museo del Canal Interoceánico
- Catedral Metropolitana

---

of **Iglesia de Santo Domingo** (see p. 61) on your right. Call in at the adjoining **Museo de Arte Religioso Colonial** (*Ave. A at Calle 3 Este, tel 2280 2897, closed Sat.–Sun.*), containing antique religious icons. Then follow Calle 2 Oeste north one block to Avenida Central. Turn left for a well-earned break at **Granclement** (*tel 228-0737*), serving delicious gelato ice creams. One block farther

A WALK AROUND CASCO VIEJO

The **Baluarte Mano del Tigre** (above) is the sole remaining section of the city wall. A baroque altar draws visitors to the Iglesia de San José (below).

brings you to **Plaza de la Independencia** ⑦ (see pp. 62–66). Stroll about the square counterclockwise, calling in at the fascinating **Museo del Canal Interoceánico** (see pp. 62–63) and, next door, the motley **Museo de História de Panamá** (see p. 62). After ex-

ploring the **Catedral Metropolitana** (see p. 62) on the west side of the plaza, follow Calle 7 Oeste south one block and turn right onto Avenida A. You are now entering a rough area; ask an *asistente de turismo* to accompany you.

After one block you reach **Iglesia de San José** *(Avenida A bet. Calle 8 & Calle 9),* a diminutive church whose simple exterior belies the gorgeous baroque altar within. According to legend, the gold altar originally graced the Iglesia de San José in Panamá Viejo. Painted black on the eve of Henry Morgan's sack of that city, it survived the pirate's predation and was later moved to its current location. Stepping from the church, head one block west to **Parque Herrera** ⑧, a rundown plaza with a life-size bronze statue of Gen. Tomás Herrera on horseback. Continue west 50 yards (46 m) to the **Baluarte Mano de Tigre,** a watchtower and sole remnant of the colonial city wall. Retrace your steps to the park and follow Calle 9 Oeste one block north to the **Iglesia de la Merced,** boasting an exquisite baroque west facade. The handsome neoclassic building diagonally across, on the west side of Calle 10 Este, is the **Casa de la Municipalidad** ⑨, headquarters of city government and the end of your tour. ∎

Parque Natural Metropolitano

Parque Natural Metropolitano
www.parquemetropolitano.org

58 C3

Ave. Juan Pablo II

232-5552

Visitor center closed Sun. Guided hikes by appt.

$

TROPICAL AMERICA'S ONLY FULLY FLEDGED WILDLIFE refuge and forest environment within city limits, this park teems with animals and birds and protects one of the last vestiges of Pacific seasonally dry forest in Central America. City-dwellers flock here for outdoor recreation, including mountain biking.

Established in 1985, the 655-acre (265 ha) Metropolitan Nature Park is only a ten-minute drive north of the city center and is reached via Corredor Norte, which runs along the park's eastern edge. Covering the hills on the city's north side, this rare remnant of lowland semideciduous Pacific dry forest forms a biological corridor linked to Camino de Cruces and Soberanía National Parks. The forests explode in riotous color during the dry season, when many of the trees drop their leaves and the wildlife is more easily seen.

More than 250 bird species flit about the forest, including bluecrowned motmots, keel-billed toucan, oropendolas, lance-tailed manakins, Baltimore orioles, and yellow warblers. Iguanas and boa constrictors are among the 36 reptile species. Turtles scuttle about in the Río Curundu, where caiman keep a hungry eye out for fish. Sloths creep along the branches, Geoffrey's tamarins cavort in the treetops, and coatis and white-tailed deer are sometimes seen at ground level. An early morning visit is best for wildlife viewing.

Begin at the **visitor center** (tel 232-5516) at the park entrance near the junction of Camino de la Amistad and Avenida Juan Pablo II. It has maps and displays on local flora and fauna. Orchids blossom profusely in the orquideario outside. Well-signed paths begin here and weave through the park, although hiking alone isn't advised for safety reasons. The 0.4-mile (0.6 km) **Sendero La Momótides,** being flat, provides a short introductory walk; blue-crowned motmots are often seen here. The interpretative **Sendero La Cienaguita** nature trail is best for wildlife viewing (buy a self-guided booklet at the visitor center before setting out) and forms a loop with the **Camino del Mono Tití,** which claws its way up through the forest to the **Cerro Cedro** mirador (observation platform). At 492 feet (150 m), it grants sweeping vistas over the city and Miraflores Locks.

The Smithsonian Tropical Research Institute (tel 212-8000, www.stri.org) has a crane soaring 138 feet (42 m) into the forest canopy. Used for research into life in the upper branches, it may be open by request. ∎

Offering distant views over Panama City, Parque Natural Metropolitano is a tropical forest in a concrete jungle.

Calidonia & La Exposición

FLANKED BY THE CITY'S TWO MAIN ARTERIES—AVENIDA Balboa and Vía España—these twin districts clasped between Casco Viejo and Parque Natural Metropolitano play host to most of the city's museums, as well as to many of the city's budget-oriented and mid-range hotels.

AVENIDA CENTRAL

Connecting Casco Viejo to Calidonia, this broad street is worth the stroll to gain an intimate impression of life in Panama City. A suitable starting point is **Plaza Santa Ana,** where **Café Coca Cola** *(tel 228-7687)*—supposedly the oldest coffeehouse in the country and a local institution—is good for a fortifying espresso and a sampling of the local atmosphere.

Avenida Central north of the plaza is brick-paved and pedestrian-only. Lined with budget hotels and discount shops, the boulevard is a whirligig of color and motion. Here you will see Kuna women gorgeously costumed in flashes of tropical hues; street vendors selling *guarapa* (sugarcane juice) freshly squeezed in traditional presses; and local youth dolled up in the latest fashions, jiving to brassy salsa tunes meant to beckon custom into predominantly Hindu-owned stores.

Stick to the pedestrian boulevard. The hardscrabble Santa Ana area and the Salsipuedes district east of Plaza Santa Ana are run-down and require caution, especially by night. The Salsipuedes area includes **Barrio Chino,** a tiny "Chinatown" centered on Calle 15 Este. Its gaudily painted **Chinese arch** with red dragons and yellow lanterns was a gift following the visit to Panama in 2003 by Taiwanese President Lee Teng-hui.

PLAZA CINCO DE MAYO

The pedestrian precinct leads north to the maelstrom of triangular Plaza

Cinco de Mayo, centered on a small fountain that doubles as the **Monumento a los Caídos** (Monument to the Fallen), or firefighters' monument. The memorial honors six *bomberos* killed on May 5, 1914, when the blaze they were fighting ignited an adjacent fireworks factory. Every November 27 the plaza is the setting for a torch-lit parade by the nation's Cuerpo de

Bomberos, who don their spiffy dress uniforms—blue for the officers, fire-engine red for the rank and file—and march through town to mark the 1885 creation of the fire brigade.

On the plaza's east side is the erstwhile Pacific Railroad station, Plásticas (School of Plastic Arts) and schools of dance and theater (Escuela Nacional de Danza and Escuela Nacional de Teatro). To the rear of the building and worth a browse is the open-air **crafts market** *(Ave. 4 Sur at Calle 23 Este).* One block north, a triangular

an imposing neoclassic edifice erected in 1912 with a facade graced by great Doric columns. It reopened in 2000 as the nation's anthropological museum, but the structure's deteriorated physical condition forced a closure in 2005. Slated to be renovated, it is scheduled to reopen in 2008 as the home of the **Instituto Nacional de las Artes'** Escuela Nacional de Artes

plazuela—a twin to Plaza Cinco de Mayo—contains a **statue of Mahatma Gandhi,** usually garlanded in flowers placed by members of the city's large Hindu population.

The **Museo Afroantillano de Panamá** (West Indian Museum of Panama) recalls the contribution made by West Indian laborers in the construction of the Panama Railroad and Canal. Housed in a

A colorful *diablo rojo* (red devil) bus threads its way through the congested streets of Calidonia.

Museo de Ciencias Naturales

- 58 B2
- Ave. Cuba, 29 E & 30 E
- 501-4125
- Closed Sat. & Sun.
- $

two-story wooden structure that was once a Christian mission church, this humble gem displays photographs and paintings, plus quilts and other exhibits of fine needlework alongside period furnishings and personal belongings. The displays intimately recall the hardships faced, and the skills and fortitude possessed, by the 20,000-plus ill-treated Caribbean islanders (principally Barbadians) who toiled in the jungles of Panama.

VICINITY OF PARQUE LEGISLATIVO

The nation's Asamblea Legislativa (Legislative Assembly) performs its duties in the **Palacio Legislativo** *(tel 512-8300),* to the northwest of Plaza Cinco de Mayo. The building stands in **Parque Legislativo,** freshly invigorated after a recent cleanup. Soaring over this raised plaza is a black granite monument, **Friso Alegórico a la Justicia** (Allegorical Frieze to Justice), by Peruvian sculptor Joaquín Roca Rey (1923–). It was erected in memory of assassinated president José Antonio Remón Cantera (1908–1955) and the plinth bears his words: "Neither alms, nor millions, we want justice."

On the north side of Avenida de los Mártires, the **Monumento a los Patriotas** (Monument to the Patriots) features three human figures clambering up a flagpole, an homage to the nationalists who died during the "Flag Riots" of January 1964. Only 100 yards (91 m) north is the Smithsonian Tropical Research Institute's **Earl S. Tupper Research & Conference Center** *(Tupper Building, 401 Roosevelt Ave., tel 212-8076).* Its splendid bookstore and research library are open to the public, and a 176-seat auditorium and exhibit hall host free science-related seminars every Tuesday from 12 noon to 1 p.m.

PLAZA VICTOR JULIO GUTIÉRREZ

Laid out in a grid, La Exposición extends northeast of Calidonia and has three small parks at its heart. The roofed **Plaza Víctor Julio Gutiérrez** *(Aves. Perú/Cuba at Calles 31 Este/32 Este)* is the setting for the twice-weekly drawing of the national lottery at the **Edificio de la Lotería** *(Ave. Cuba & Calles 31/32),* the Lottery Building, on the east side of the concrete plaza. Each drawing is a fiesta, with folkloric performances and celebrations (see sidebar p. 76).

The main draw nearby is the **Museo de Ciencias Naturales** (Museum of Natural Sciences), one block west of the plaza. It has four rooms dedicated to entomology and marine biology, geology and paleontology, vertebrates, and foreign fauna. Albeit modest in scale and scope, it provides a summary of animals you might hope to see in the wild: jaguars, howler and spider monkeys, harpy eagles, quetzals, and more, mounted for posterity. Animals from beyond the Americas are also represented, including antelopes, lions, tigers, and even a rhino unfortunate to have been sighted within a hunter's scope.

Note the magnificent building in neoclassic style with four Corinthian columns, circa 1924, on the square's north side. It houses the **Archivos Nacionales** *(Ave. Perú at Calles 31/32, tel 501-6151),* the national archives.

PARQUE BELISARIO PORRAS

This rather formal park *(Calles 33 Este/34 Este at Aves. Peru/Cuba)* surrounded by Spanish-colonial centenary buildings is the unlikely setting for the city's premier annual event: Carnival! Down its center median come the *comparsas* (processions) graced by girls in *polleras*

and, on the final day, others in sequined G-strings and gaudy feathers, gyrating like the most exotic and excited of tropical birds. Pinning the park is **Monumento Belisario Porras** by Spanish sculptor Víctor Macho (1887–1966) commemorating Belisario Porras (1856–1942), the three-time president and a founding father of the nation. Cuban nationalist heroes José Martí and Antonio Maceo are also honored. The Romanesque **Iglesia de Don Bosco** *(Ave. Central at Calle 34),* one block to the northwest, was built in the 1950s with a minaret-like tower.

One block east of the park is leafy **Parque Perú,** marked by a bust of Francisco Arias Paredes (1886–1946), a radical politician who led the 1931 coup that toppled corrupt U.S.-backed president Florencio Arosemena. Numismatists and philatelists on a busman's holiday should head to the nearby **Casa Museo Banco Nacional** in a charming little upper-class home dating from 1925. Adorned within by a marble staircase, ornate wrought-iron fixtures, and gleam-

ing tile floors, the museum boasts a collection of coins and stamps dating back to the conquistadors.

AVENIDA BALBOA

Curving along Panama Bay like a shepherd's crook, the broad seafront boulevard links Casco Viejo to the ritzy district of Punta Paitilla. A well-maintained promenade, or *malecón,* provides a pleasant amble despite the roar of buses and the whiff of sewage. Use caution crossing the boulevard, as traffic flies along at warp speed. The seawall is adorned with mosaics of fishes and other thalassic designs.

Midway along the avenue is a small park with the marble **Monumento Balboa** *(between Calles 35/36).* Holding his sword in one hand and the flag of Spain in the other, larger-than-life conquistador Vasco Núñez de Balboa gazes proudly out over the ocean he "discovered" in 1513.

Gaily painted fishing boats unload their catch at the wharves at the southern end of Balboa, where fresh seafood is sold at **Mercado del Marisco** *(Calle 23 Este).* ■

Surveying the ocean he discovered for Spain, Vasco Núñez de Balboa takes pride of place from atop a marble plinth at Monumento Balboa.

Casa Museo Banco Nacional

✉ Ave. Cuba at Calle 34 Este

☎ 507-1276

🕐 Closed Sat. & Sun.

La Lotería

Virtually every street corner in Panama has one or more vendors selling lottery tickets; about 10,000 such vendors are licensed nationwide. Panamanians love a good bet, from wagering on horses at President Remón racetrack to personal bets on which presidential candidate will win an election. It's the national lottery, however, that commands the entire country's attention, with all eyes on the twice-weekly drawing.

Every Wednesday and Sunday afternoon, crowds pack into the Parque Víctor Julio Gutiérrez—headquarters of La Lotería Nacional de Beneficia *(tel 507-6800, www .loterianacional.com.pa)*—for the fiesta-like drawings, which are broadcast live on radio and TV. Lasting several hours, each drawing is preceded by musical performances and folkloric dances with beauty queens adorned in polleras. Dignitaries arrive, including three children dressed in their Sunday best and chosen for the honor of selecting the four winning numbers. In a tradition dating back to the lottery's founding in 1919, a globular metal cage is used as a receptacle (when officials replaced the antiquated cage with an electronic system, the public angrily protested and the old system was reinstated). Lottery balls, each containing a single number, are placed in the cage, which is spun…and spun…and spun by a spindled handle. After an interminable number of revolutions, the globe is stopped and the chosen child nervously steps forward

to choose a ball. The ball is opened with tense solemnity to reveal the hidden number.

The process is repeated four times to generate the winning combination, good for a $2,000 first prize in the regular lottery. Two sets of four numbers are also chosen to produce the second ($600) and third ($300) prizes. Tickets cost as little as 25 cents for two-number tickets that pay out smaller winnings if the numbers correspond to the last two digits of the winning combination. On the last Friday of every month, Panamanians wait breathlessly for the results of a special drawing called *Gordito del Zodiaco* (little fattie of the Zodiac), named, one supposes, for the stars that align for the winner of the $600,000 grand prize. ∎

Twice-weekly drawings for the national lottery cast a hypnotic spell across the nation (above left). Lottery ticket vendors do a thriving business in front of a supermarket on Vía España (below).

El Cangrejo & Bella Vista

Santuario Nacional del Corazón de María

www.santuarionacional.net

🅰 59 D2

✉ Calle 53 Este & Aves. 2a Sur/3a Sur

☎ 263-9833

A FOREST OF MIRRORED SKYSCRAPERS TOWERS OVER THE ritzy neighborhoods at the pulsing, trend-setting, commercial heart of the modern city. El Cangrejo is known for its casinos, Bella Vista for fine restaurants and a sizzling night scene hot enough to cook the pork. The banks of Marbella glitter gold in the evening sunlight alongside the gleaming condominiums of the residential Punta Pacifica and Punta Paitilla peninsula.

Sites of touristic interest are few here. An exception is **Parque Urracá** *(Ave. Balboa at Calle 45 Este)* in Bella Vista, shaded by trees that bloom impressionistically each spring. The park is the starting point for the annual Christmas Parade and the Parade of Torches, held each November 2, when firefighters march the first flag of the Republic to Plaza de la Independencia. Avenida Federico Boyd leads north from the park to busy Vía España. Rising over the junction is the white-and-gray neo-Gothic facade of **Iglesia del Carmen** *(Vía España at Ave. Manuel E. Bautista)*. A twin-spired medieval inspiration built in 1947, the church features a Byzantine altar and pleasing murals.

The sprawling **Universidad de Panamá** *(Ave. Manuel E. Bautista, tel 523-5000)*, the national university, is one block north, in El Cangrejo. The campus hosts the **Instituto Geográfico Nacional Tommy Guardia** *(Calle 57 Oeste at Ave. 6a Norte, tel 507-9684)*, the best source in town for maps of Panama.

Despite its seeming antiquity, the **Santuario Nacional del Corazón de María,** also in El Cangrejo, was dedicated on August 22, 1949. Its facade—part Romanesque, part Spanish colonial style—is at odds with the sea of modernity. The interior has fine stained glass, and a side entrance opens to a courtyard

with a fountain and peacocks.

The city's most exclusive area, **Punta Paitilla,** at the eastern end of Avenida Balboa in Marbella, is a veritable Manhattan in the tropics, its glass-and-marble condominium towers reflecting the wealth of their occupants. Nestled in their shadow is the **Vatican embassy** *(Ave. Balboa at Ave. de Italia)*, where Gen. Manuel Noriega famously sought asylum. ∎

An angel greets visitors at the Sanctuario Nacional del Corazón de María in Bella Vista.

The real tailor of Panama

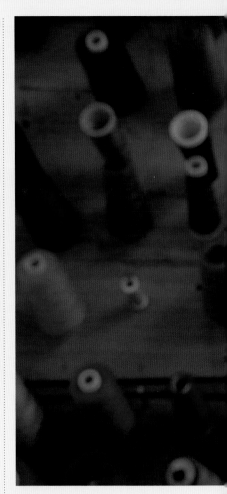

A fine suit speaks volumes in Panama, and when it comes to sophisticated duds for the country's elite, the universal choice is a Savile Row–style boutique straight from the pages of novelist John le Carré's thriller *The Tailor of Panama.*

"La Fortuna, since 1925" it reads in elegant letters on the *rótulo* (sign) outside the Orión commercial building on Vía España, 100 yards (9 m) east of Vía Argentina. Loosely portrayed as Pendel & Braithwaite Limitada in le Carré's thoughtfully textured spy thriller, this establishment *(tel 263-6434, closed Sun.)* is known to Panameños of discernment as the real "tailor of Panama."

In le Carré's satire, anybody of importance in Central America passes through Harry Pendel's doors. He dresses everyone from crooks and spies to the Panamanian president. His fitting room hears more confidences than a priest's confessional. While le Carré's tale of a tailor reluctantly engaged as a tattletale for a British agent was fictional, there is more than a kernel of truth to the notion of a Panamanian tailor being privy to everyone's secrets. La Fortuna has long

been the *sastre* (tailor) of choice for presidents, ambassadors, generals, and members of Panama's Asamblea. Omar Torrijos, the late dictator-president, once joked that La Fortuna's owner, José Abadi, was the only man for whom he would drop his trousers. José even made suits for actors Pierce Brosnan and Geoffrey Rush when they came to Panama in 2000 to film the screen version of le Carré's novel.

José Abadi has since semiretired from the company his father founded in 1925 to cater to a select clientele (La Fortuna was named after José's mother, Fortuna). Today his son Adán Abadi oversees a cadre of 17 highly skilled tailors. Nonetheless, the senior Abadi

can still often be found on the premises, fussing over the cut of a suit and happy to regale you with tales of the visits by current Panamanian president, Martín Torrijos Espino (whom José first measured for a suit when Torrijos was still a child) and by actors Rush, Brosnan, and Jamie Lee Curtis. You'll leave the store wondering just what *real* secrets José might have gleaned in his years in the business.

The shop walls are lined with racks of precisely cut chiffon shirts and inky blue suits of thin silk cashmere. A fitted hand-stitched shirt can be made in as little as two days. A bespoke tailored suit takes at least ten days and requires two fittings.

Fabric waits to be transformed into custom suits at La Fortuna (top left), where skilled tailors work under the watchful instruction of José Abadi and his son Adán (above).

The Abadis can craft a suit to match any photograph you bring in, whether you want to evoke scholar, urban warrior, or business bigwig. A double-breasted herringbone or a trimly fit monochrome suit of Armani, Ferré, or Versace cloth can be had for around $500, complete with a personalized panel sewn inside the jacket denoting that the suit was made exclusively for you. ■

A tugboat kicks up a wake in the entrance to the Panama Canal, framed by the Calzada de Amador and the sharp high-rises of Punta Paitilla beyond.

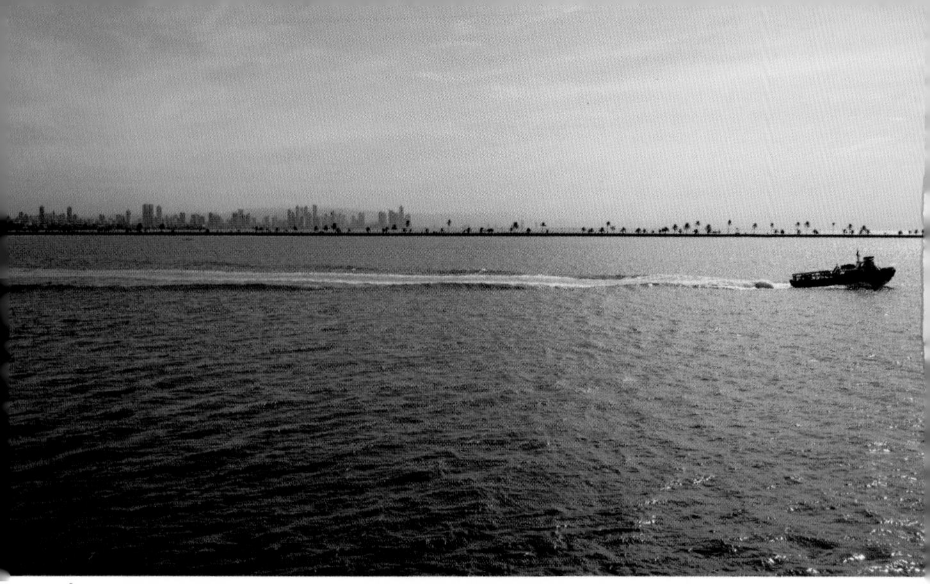

Amador Causeway

WITH GORGEOUS VIEWS TOWARD PANAMA CITY ON ONE side and the Bridge of the Americas and busy canal channel on the other, the breakwater known as Calzada de Amador is one of the city's most appealing recreational areas. In recent years, the causeway has become a trendy venue for hip youth and, following major investment, a hub for international visitors.

Amador Causeway
58 A1

The palm-lined *calzada* (causeway) is fringed by a recreational path popular with lovers, joggers, bicyclists, and city-dwellers walking their dogs. You can rent bicycles and in-line skates at **Bicicletas Ralí** *(tel 220-3844)*. Walking the calzada is especially pleasurable at dawn and dusk. While beloved of locals, the tempting sands of **Isla Naos** can't be recommended due to health hazards washing in off the bay.

Connecting Balboa to the islands of Naos, Culebra, Perico, and Flamenco, the causeway was constructed of rock removed during construction of the canal. It extends 3 miles (4.5 km) across tidal mud flats to block silt-bearing currents that might clog the canal's southern entrance. After its completion in 1913, the entire causeway became a mighty U.S. military complex—Fort Grant (later Fort Amador)—established to guard the approaches. Two formidable 14-inch (36 cm) cannons were mounted there on railway carriages and could be transported across the isthmus to protect either approach to the canal.

During World War II, **Isla Flamenco** was a bombproof strategic command center. Today it is the setting for the **Fuerte Amador Resort & Marina** *(tel 314-0932, www.fuerteamador.com)*, with a cruise ship terminal, major shopping mall, and a marina full of sleek yachts straight out of a James Bond movie. You can charter boats at the **Flamenco Yacht Club** *(tel 314-0665)*. By night, Fuerte Amador's two dozen or so cosmopolitan restaurants, bars, and nightclubs thrum to a South Beach–style *vida loca* vibe.

Nearby, **Panamá Canal Village** *(tel 314-1414, www .panamacanalvillage.com)* holds the neo-colonial styled **Figali Convention Center,** which opened just in time to host the 2003 Miss Universe pageant. It forms a venue for many of the city's biggest concerts, from classical to rock. Nearby, the **Parque Torrijos-Carter** contains the Monumento Histórico Mausoleo del General Omar Torrijos Herrera, beneath which the former dictator-president slumbers.

CENTRO DE EXHIBICIONES MARINAS

Sharks, turtles, and crabs! The Smithsonian Tropical Research Institute has a marine research station that occupies former military bunkers atop rocky Punta Culebra. Visitors are welcome at the Marine Exhibitions Center, an open-air museum with six aquariums dedicated to marine coastal environments. One aquarium displays species of the Pacific, while Caribbean species inhabit another. Children will especially enjoy the sharks and turtles and the pond where they can touch sea stars and other marine invertebrates.

Two trails meander through a rare patch of Pacific tropical dry forest, a Central American ecosystem that is almost extinct today. Sloths can be seen feeding languidly or snoozing. Iguanas abound. And the forest is a refuge for armadillos and birds of all kinds: cormorants, frigate birds, brown-footed boobies, and even the rare blue-footed booby. A sheltered sandy beach is fringed by white mangrove forest.

Waves crash against the tip of the peninsula, causing crabs to scurry back and forth. Here, a viewing veranda has a telescope and educational profiles on various types of vessels, permitting visitors to identify many of the ships waiting nearby to transit the canal. ■

Museo de la Biodiversidad

Panama: Bridge of Life Museum of Biodiversity (tel 314-1395, www.biomuseo panama.org) is scheduled to open in the next few years as a joint effort of the Smithsonian Tropical Research Institute, the University of Panama, and the Interoceanic Regional Authority. Designed by Frank Gehry (1929–), creator of the futuristic Guggenheim Museum in Bilbao, Spain, the museum is being touted as an icon for Panama, much as the Opera House is for Sydney. To be located at the entrance to the causeway, the controversial structure will be faceted like quartz crystals and topped by a roof with a twisting silhouette meant to represent the forces of nature. Its eight halls will feature multimedia exhibitions showcasing Panama's astonishing biodiversity, from its oceans to its cloud forests. ■

Full of chic restaurants, the exclusive Fuerte Amador Resort & Marina boasts lovely views across the bay toward Panama City.

Centro de Exhibiciones Marinas
www.stri.org
✉ Calzada de Amador
☎ 212-8820
🕐 Closed Mon.
💲 $

Balboa & Ancón

Spinning a heroic tale, the Panama Canal murals in the Panama Canal Administration Building depict the monumental canal-building effort.

SPIRALING AROUND CERRO ANCÓN, THE CITY'S HIGHEST point, are three contiguous communities laid out a century ago as the "capital" of the former Canal Zone and U.S. military command. Stately royal palms rise like silver Corinthian columns here; broad-canopied mango trees and jacarandas cast pools of cool shadow on streets lined with buildings from grandiose to quaint, all in tropical vernacular style with red-tile roofs and broad eaves.

Balboa & Ancón

🅰 58 A1 & B1

Panama Canal Administration Building
www.pancanal.com

🅰 58 A1

✉ 101 Heights Rd., Balboa

☎ 272-1111

🕓 Closed Sat. & Sun.

Museo de Arte Contemporaneo
www.macpanama.org

🅰 58 B2

✉ San Blas Place, Ancón

☎ 262-6282

🕓 Closed Mon

💲 $

BALBOA

Occupying the sloping land immediately east of the Pacific terminus of the canal, Balboa, between Cerro Ancón and the east side of **Cerro Sosa,** still houses the operating headquarters for the Panama Canal. The town was named for Vasco Núñez de Balboa, the first Spaniard to see the Pacific Ocean.

The monumental E-shaped **Panama Canal Administration Building,** at the northwestern foot of Cerro Ancón, was inaugurated on July 15, 1914, on a hilltop overlooking Balboa township. Visitors are welcome to enter 24 hours a day to admire the high-domed rotunda, with its stately marble columns (the eight columns were accidentally installed upside down) and alcoves

containing busts of Ferdinand de Lesseps, Theodore Roosevelt, and Emperor Charles V. Drawing your eyes upward is a cupola framed by Panama Canal murals. Graphic in detail, enormous in scope, the murals, painted by New York artist William B. Van Ingen (1858–1955), record the monumental achievement in four main scenes depicting the Gaillard Cut, the building of the Gatún Dam spillway, construction of a lock miter gate, and the Miraflores Locks. The mahogany and Tennessee marble staircase leads up to an art gallery of canal-related paintings by U.S. artist Al Sprague and, above, relief maps from the construction era.

To the rear (west) of the building, a flight of 110 steps leads down

to **El Prado,** a palm-lined boulevard with a grassy median built to
the exact dimensions of a lock
chamber (110 feet/34 m wide by
1,000 feet/305 m long). Concerts
are held on the lawns near the steps
on Tuesday and Thursday evenings
in dry season. At the base of the
steps stands the **Goethals Monument,** a gray marble monolith
erected to honor George W.
Goethals, chief engineer of the
canal project from 1907 to 1914.
About 100 yards (91 m) west,
across Avenida Roosevelt, a 95-ton
(86 metric ton) **Bucyrus steam
shovel** (one of dozens employed
during canal construction) is ex-
hibited roadside.

Between the monument and
shovel stands the former Balboa
High School, now the **Centro de
Capacitación Ascanio Arosemena** *(Edificio 704, tel 272-8182,
closed Sat. & Sun.),* the training center for canal employees. The breeze-
way entrance hosts the **Monumento a los Mártires,** dedicated
to the 21 Panamanians killed during
the January 9, 1964, "Flag Riots,"
known in Panama as the "Day of the
Martyrs." The names of those killed
are inscribed on 21 slender pillars
surrounding the location of the original flagpole—long gone—that inspired the fatal riots. Inside, hallways
on two levels exhibit memorabilia
relating to the canal construction.

Midway down El Prado (for-
mally Avenida 9 de enero), the
**Centro de Información Pro-
puesta Tercer Juego de Esclusas** *(Edificio 714, tel 272-2278,
closed Sat. & Sun.)* has state-of-the-
art exhibits and audiovisual presentations on the proposed third set
of Panama Canal locks, soon to
be constructed to permit passage
of megaships. **Stevens Circle,**
at El Prado's south end, is a small
rotunda with a monument to
John Stevens (chief engineer

1905–1907). To your left, note the
single-story **Balboa Post Office**
and, ahead, the **Teatro Balboa** *(tel
228-0327),* an art deco jewel built in
1946 as the Electric Theater movie
house and still functioning as a
concert hall. The voluptuously
adorned lobby gleams with mosaic
tilework. **Niko's Café** *(tel 228-
8888),* in a former bowling alley on
the northeast side of Stevens Circle,
has black-and-white period photos
of old Panama.

Avenida Arnulfo Arias Madrid
(formerly Balboa Road) leads east
from the circle past the ecumenical
Union Church *(tel 314-1004),* a
soaring Gothic-style edifice dating
from 1917. Immediately beyond
is the rather incredible **Monumento a la Democracia,** featuring a circular fountain pierced by
a long, spearlike sliver of bronze.
The sculpture by Colombian artist
Hector Lombana (1930–) was
dedicated in 2002 and honors
three-time Panamanian president
Arnulfo Arias Madrid (1901–1988),
shown standing at the pointy tip
and waving at Panamanian people
rushing to greet him.

On the monument's north side,
the **Panama Canal Pilots headquarters** *(tel 228-4868)* displays a
9-foot-long (3 m) scale model of
the M/V *John Constantine* four-
masted barque in the board room.
The receptionist may let you in to
see it. Facing the monument from
the east is the **Centro Artesanal**
adjoining the old YMCA building
with craft shops.

QUARRY HEIGHTS

Quarry Heights, northeast of Balboa, was headquarters of the U.S.
Southern Command and of the
U.S. military in Panama from 1916
to 1999. Noted for their architectural significance, the homes of this
leafy district (today renamed Altos
de Ancón) were built on two ter-

races quarried from Cerro Ancón and were mostly occupied by military officers and by doctors who practiced at nearby Gorgas Hospital. Lined with mahogany trees, bamboo, and palms, the beauty of its bucolic streets recalls the days when the atmosphere within the Zone was that of an affluent country club.

The two-story **Administrator's House** *(107 Heights Rd.)*, standing at the junction of Heights Road and Quarry Road, was the palatial quarters of the chief engineer during construction and until 1997 of the U.S. commanding general. It originally overlooked Culebra Cut so that the administrator could keep an eye on the excavation; in 1914, the house was loaded onto a train and rebuilt at its present site. Today it is used as a guest house for foreign dignitaries.

Quarry Road grants access to forested 654-foot-high (198 m) **Cerro Ancón,** once topped by fortified guns but today marked by a flagstaff from which flutters a giant Panamanian flag. Panamanian poet Amelia Denis de Icaza (1836–1911), sitting in bronze effigy beneath the flag, gazes serenely over the views of the city. The woodsy hill is today a nature reserve teeming with monkeys, agoutis, and sloths. It's a stiff 20-minute hike to the summit along the asphalt road that coils up from the headquarters of **Asociación Nacional para la Conservación de la Naturaleza** (ANCON, *Bldg. 153, Calle Amelia Denis de Icaza, tel. 314-0050, www.ancon.org).* Police are usually present at the summit, where muggings have been reported; it is best not to hike alone.

East of ANCON, as you begin to ascend Cerro Ancón, you look down upon **Montague Hall** *(Bldg. 88, Andrews Rd.),* a nondescript concrete oblong that was until 1999 the unlikely headquarters of the entire U.S. Southern Command. Inset in the rock face is the entrance to a bombproof 40-room command post tunneled deep inside Cerro Ancón in 1942. It still serves as a communications and intelligence center for the Strategic Plan of National Security, for which reason the area is off-limits to visitors.

ANCÓN

The hill's northeast side was the setting for the original French settlement, centered on Ancón Hospital, founded in 1881 as L'Hôpital Notre Dame du Canal. By 1907 Ancón Hospital had 96 buildings. In 1928, the main building—fronted by a two-story neoclassic portico and topped by green copper domes—was renamed **Gorgas Hospital** after the chief sanitary officer who conquered yellow fever and malaria. Part of the sprawling hillside facility today houses the **Corte Suprema de Justicia** *(Gorgas Rd., tel 212-7300),* Panama's Supreme Court.

At the base of Gorgas Road, the Romanesque **Cathedral of St. Luke** *(tel 262-1280),* fronted by a row of Corinthian columns, dates back to 1923. Another church—**Parroquia Sagrado Corazón de Jesús** *(Ancon Blvd. at Chame St.)*—in Spanish colonial vernacular is tucked away 200 yards (183 m) to the northwest.

Culture vultures may thrill to the nearby **Museo de Arte Contemporáneo,** occupying a former Masonic hall from the 1930s. Privately owned and relying on donations by working artists, the twin-tier museum displays more than 400 contemporary ceramics, paintings, photographs, and sculptures by prominent artists from Panama and around the world. The museum hosts art and serigraphy classes, informal lectures, and music recitals. ■

Panama Viejo

FOUNDED ON AUGUST 15, 1519, AS THE FIRST CITY ALONG the Pacific shore, Panama Viejo is today a national monument and an archaeological treasure. A restoration project has resurrected parts of the ancient enclave, allowing visitors to appreciate what was once one of the wealthiest cities of its time.

Built atop a pre-Columbian burial ground on a promontory overlooking the sea, the original city was protected to the north by a marshy inlet. For a century and a half, it prospered as a clearinghouse and marshaling point for the Camino Real, the treasure trail that linked Panama to the Caribbean port at Nombre de Dios and, later, Portobelo. Panama became a city of more than 5,000 houses built mostly of cedar, with a mint, a hospital, eight convents, and a splendid cathedral. Most buildings were consumed in the conflagration of 1671 that followed pirate Henry Morgan's attack; the city was then abandoned.

In recent decades, slums have arisen atop much of the former city, which remains mostly in ruins. The site was named a national monument in 1976 and a restoration project begun under the auspices of the Patronato Panamá Viejo *(tel 226-8915),* which has administered Panama Viejo since 1995. The busy Vía Cincuentenario highway cuts through the heart of the old city. A walking tour should take about two hours.

WEST SIDE
The entrance to the city in colonial times was the still-extant **Puente de Matadero** (Bridge of the Slaughterhouse), an arched stone bridge spanning the Río Algarrobo. It was guarded by the **Fuerte de la Natividad** (Nativity Fort), its gun emplacements now covered with creeping vines. Immediately

A concrete counterpoint to the raw stonework of yesteryear, the modern city forms a backdrop for the ruins of Panama Viejo.

Panama Viejo
🗺 59 G2

Visitor information
✉ Vía Cincuentenario
☎ 226-4419

Museo de Sitio de Panamá Viejo

www.panamaviejo.org

59 G2

4 miles (6.4 km) NE of downtown

226-8915

Closed Mon.

$

east is the modern **Centro de Visitantes de Panamá Viejo** (visitor center). The center's excellent **Museo de Sitio de Panamá Viejo** displays musket balls, coins, surgical knives, and other pieces unearthed at the site. A scale model shows the city as it was in 1671. Signs are in both Spanish and English, and an English-language taped narration is offered.

A walking trail shaded by wide-spreading trees leads from the visitor center to a series of historical sites, beginning with the **Iglesia y**

Magnificent pre-Columbian artifacts spotlight the ancient past at the Museo de Sitio de Panamá Viejo.

Opposite: Newly restored, the bell tower of La Catedral de Nuestra Señora de la Ascunción provides a glimpse into the past.

Convento la Merced. This church was spared during Morgan's attack and was thereafter disassembled and reconstituted in the new city. Beyond stood the **Iglesia y Convento de San Francisco,** completed by the Franciscans in 1603, and the **Hospital de San Juan Dios,** erected in 1521. Only remnants of these sites remain.

Among the best preserved structures is the **Iglesia y Convento de las Monjas de la Concepción,** built by the Concepción order of nuns. It retains its bell tower and an *aljibe* (well). Adjoining it to the east, the **Iglesia y Convento de la Compañía de Jesús** was completed in 1582.

EAST SIDE

The city's ancient heart was the **Plaza Mayor,** the main square, today a grassy swathe. To its east stood the two-story **Cabildo de la Ciudad,** the city hall, and the **Casas Reales,** guarded by a moat. This center of power housed the governor and nobles, plus the court and city dungeons on land protected on three sides by water.

Rising over Panama Viejo, the enormous bell tower of **La Catedral de Nuestra Señora de la Asunción** (built between 1619 and 1626) gives the best impression of the city's former glory. Restoration was completed in 2006. The 90-foot (27 m) tower contains a modern staircase that you can ascend for views from the lookout. The rest of the cathedral remains in ruins. To the north are the skeletons of the **Casa del Obispo** (Bishop's House) and **Casas Terrín,** built about 1640 for a nobleman. The Dominicans' **Iglesia y Convento de Santo Domingo,** founded in 1571 farther north, stood within earshot of slaves being brought ashore at the wharfside **Casa de los Genoveses** to the east.

The famous Altar de Oro originally graced the **Iglesia y Convento de San José** at the extreme north end of Panama Viejo. Both church and altar survived the pirate attack. The altar was later relocated to the new city (see p. 70); the Augustine church, with its two vaulted chapels, went to ruin. The northern entrance to the city and gateway to the Camino Real was the **Puente del Rey** (King's Bridge), completed in 1634 and arching over the Río Abajo (former Río Gallinero).

After exploring the ruins, you might browse the **Mercado Nacional de Artesanías** (Crafts Market) to the south of Plaza Mayor, staffed by indigenous peoples selling their specialties. ∎

More places to visit in Panama City

MI PUEBLITO

Comprising three stereotypical villages, "My Little Village," at the eastern foot of Cerro Ancón, serves as a museum of Panamanian culture and traditions. The main exhibit replicates a colonial-era country village; around its cobbled plaza are a mission-style Spanish church, mayor's office, telegraph office, and a museum dedicated to the colorful national costume, the pollera dress. The Antillean–West Indian village, with its gaily painted two-story wooden structures, includes La Casa del Café, offering dozens of coffee brands. Set against the forested hills, the Indian village represents various indigenous cultures, with thatched huts and artifacts honoring the Kuna, Emberá, and Wounaan ways of life. There are restaurants and souvenir stores. Folkloric groups perform on Friday and Saturday evenings. 🅰 58 A1 ✉ Ave. de los Mártires 🕐 Closed Mon. 🛈 $

An emerald set in gold steals the limelight at the Museo de la Esmeralda.

MUSEO ANTROPOLÓGICO REINA TORRES DE ARAÚZ

Celebrating the nation's pre-Columbian heritage, this museum opened in late 2006. Only a small selection of its 14,000-piece collection is on view, including stone *metates* (curved ceremonial tables), grinding tools, and stone figurines. Most exhibits relate to the Barriles culture. Glittering under spotlights are gold figures, amulets, half-moon-shaped nose pieces, and other ancient treasure—collectively called *huacas*—excavated from the tombs of *caciques*. Guided tours are given in Spanish. 🅰 58 C3 ✉ Calle 4 Este & Ave. Ascanio Villalaz, Llanos de Curundú ☎ 232-7644 🕐 Closed Mon. 🛈 $

MUSEO DE LA ESMERALDA

To learn all about the creation and mining of emeralds, step inside this museum featuring life-size representations of miners at work, plus a large collection of raw stones, polished emeralds, and fine jewelry. The museum is associated with a commercial jewelry store and visitors can expect a strong sales pitch. 🅰 59 D2 ✉ Vía Italia, 50 yards (46 m) E of Ave. Balboa ☎ 262-1665, www.museodelaesmeralda.com

PARQUE RECREATIVO OMAR

An oasis of tranquility on the city's northeast side, Omar Recreation Park is Panama City's second largest metropolitan park. This green swathe, in the middle-class San Francisco district, is considered one of the city's best venues for picnics. Originally Panama's first golf course, it was renamed to honor Gen. Omar Torrijos, who ruled Panama from 1968 to 1981; his bust stands by the main gate. Facilities include a jogging trail, a swimming pool, and children's play areas, plus baseball, soccer, and tennis courts. The park is also home to the country's largest library, **Biblioteca Nacional Ernesto J. Castillero** (*tel 221-8360, www.binal.ac.pa, closed Sun.*). 🅰 59 E3 ✉ Ave. Belisario Porras & Calle 74

PUENTE DE LAS AMÉRICAS

The cantilevered Bridge of the Americas was completed in 1962 at a cost of 20 million dollars as the first bridge spanning the canal, replacing a ferry that had been the sole means of crossing the waterway at this point. It rises 384 feet high (118 m) and is 5,425 feet long (1,654 m) in 14 spans. You can take the pedestrian sidewalks to the bridge's western side, where a lookout station offers a fine, albeit foreshortened, perspective. 🅰 58 inset ✉ Via Interamerican Hwy., 0.5 mile (1 km) W of Calle Amador ∎

Richly forested, the zone bordering the Panama Canal offers world-class birding, hiking, and white-water rafting, while ancient fortresses, Emberá Indian communities, and excursions on the canal are other attractions.

Central Caribbean & the canal

Tropical fish at Miraflores Locks Visitor Center

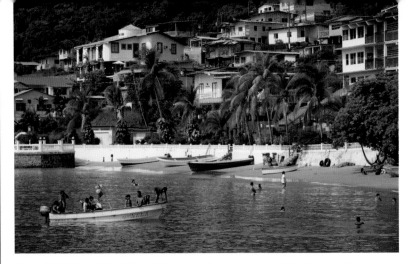

Sleepy San Pedro, on Isla Taboga, offers a calming contrast to bustling Panama City.

Central Caribbean & the canal

THE ROUTE THAT CHANGED THE WORLD, THE PANAMA CANAL IS THE nation's most visible and recognized symbol. Extending from the city of Colón on the Caribbean Sea to Panama City on the Pacific Ocean, this 51-mile-long (80 km) umbilical cord linking two oceans is both a feat of astonishing engineering and Panama's main tourist draw. The lush hinterlands swarm with wildlife, while fortress ruins scattered along the Caribbean shores hark back to the days when Sir Francis Drake wreaked havoc along the Spanish Main.

Topping every visitor's list of things to see, the canal is both grand and tourist friendly. Viewing the passage of enormous cruise ships and cargo vessels is easy at the Miraflores and Gatún Locks, where spectator stands provide an intimate perspective. The Miraflores Locks Visitor Center even features world-class exhibition halls. Nor do you need to book yourself on a major cruise ship to experience the thrill of a canal passage: Excursion vessels operate weekly.

This narrow isthmus separating two oceans has served for centuries as a commercial route between the Old and New Worlds. Four centuries before the canal was built, millions of pounds of silver and gold were transported across the isthmus via the Camino Real and, later, the Camino de Cruces. Built by Indian slaves, the ancient trails are remarkably well preserved and today are popular as hiking trails, delving into cathedral-like naves beneath moss-laden branches draped with air plants.

The official Canal Zone that extends 10 miles (16 km) to either side of the canal serves as a biological corridor of astonishing wealth. The need to guarantee a water supply for the canal has ensured that the forests have been protected. The watershed is enshrined within national parks whose lush rain forests provide hikers and birders with rewards aplenty (pick up a copy of *The Panamá Canal Birding Trail* map and guide, published by USAID and the Panama Audubon Society). Just minutes from Panama City, visitors can park by the highway and view wildlife with ease. Parque Nacional Soberanía, Parque Nacional Chagres, and Parque Natural Summit Panama are linked by smaller enclaves of primeval forest to form La Ruta Ecológica entre dos Océanos—the Ecological Route Between Two Oceans. Capybaras, monkeys, ocelots, kinkajous, sloths, and an encyclopedic assortment of feathered friends call these forests home.

Communities of Emberá Indians also live deep in the mountainous interior, where effervescent rivers provide white-water thrills. Welcoming visitors with ceremonial dances, the Emberá villages are easily accessed by boat or on package excursions from Panama City. By contrast, the Caribbean communities of Colón, Portobelo, and Nombre de Dios murmur with an Afro-Antillean beat. The cuisine and clapboard houses of the coast known as the Costa Arriba hint at a Caribbean potpourri. Portobelo's fortress ruins echo to the footsteps of Spanish defenders and marauding pirates, while the town flickers to life every October during the Black Christ Festival.

On the Pacific side, Isla Taboga lies a mere 30-minute boat ride from Panama City. A century ago, the cozy charm of this Pacific Ocean isle was a favored idyll for day-trippers (among them Paul Gauguin) escaping the mainland heat and humidity. It still lures city-dwellers who come for beach time with ocean breezes. Farther out, the Archipiélago de las Perlas studs the aquamarine seas like coral jewels. The isles' white-hot blazing beaches are stunners, shelving gently into shimmering waters. Only two islands have resort facilities (a third—Isla Viveros—is slated for major touristic development). The rest of the archipelago is left to nature and the fishing and pearl-diving community. ■

Isla Taboga

NICKNAMED THE "ISLAND OF FLOWERS" FOR THE HIBISCUS, bougainvillea, jasmine, and Taboga roses that bloom in riotous abundance, this laid-back island is almost Mediterranean in flavor and understandably popular with day-trippers escaping the heat and bustle of Panama City.

Bearing Santa Carmen through the streets, locals honor the patron saint of fishermen every July.

Isla Taboga
🔺 91 B2
Visitor information
www.taboga.panamanow.com

Refugio de Vida Silvestre Islas Taboga y Urabá
www.anam.gob.pa
🔺 91 B2
✉ Ranger station 1 mile (1.75 km) S of Iglesia San Pedro
☎ 250-2082 or 500-0855

Cooler and less rainy than Panama City, the 568-acre (230 ha) isle, 11 miles (18 km) south of the city, was first settled by the Spanish in 1524 and later served as a base for Francisco Pizarro's conquest of the Inca Empire and for piratical predations on Spanish shipping.

The quaint village of **San**

Gauguin & Isla Taboga

Painter Paul Gauguin (1848–1903) first escaped Europe in 1887 with plans to buy some land on Isla Taboga and live "on fish and fruit for nothing...without anxiety for the day or for the morrow." Alas, the land was priced beyond his reach. Penniless, he ended up laboring as a tropical tramp on the French canal project before sailing off for Martinique and, eventually, Tahiti. ∎

Pedro, tucked in a horseshoe cove between forested hills and sheltered beach, surrounds tiny whitewashed **Iglesia San Pedro,** founded in 1524 and acclaimed as the second oldest church in the Western Hemisphere. The adjacent flower-filled plaza is marked by a statue of Nuestra Señora del Carmen, the island's patron saint.

Colorful fishing boats bob at anchor off **Playa La Restinga,** a handsome little beach that sparkles on sunny days; avoid the crowded weekends. Aqua-bikes and kayaks can be rented, and at low tide you can walk across an exposed sand bar to **Isla El Morro.** Local fishermen can take you to good snorkeling spots and more reclusive beaches farther afield.

The narrow main street leads along the waterfront and ascends through forest past abandoned **World War II bunkers** and the ruins of a Spanish cannon embrasure. The trail ends atop **Cerro de la Cruz,** where you can survey the isle and the gulf.

Covering the entire western fringe of Isla Taboga, **Refugio de Vida Silvestre Islas Taboga y Urabá** protects the site where as many as 100,000 brown pelicans nest from January to July. To visit, get permission from ANAM beside the ferry dock.

The short ferry ride to the island aboard the *Calypso Queen (tel 314-1730),* departing from La Playita de Amador, is a treat. Keep your eye out for whales as you cross the glassy bay. ∎

Miraflores Locks

THE CLOSEST SET OF CANAL LOCKS TO PANAMA CITY AND in many ways the most impressive, these twin-flight locks at the Pacific entrance to the canal are an engineering marvel and justifiably the most visited site in the country.

Miraflores Locks Visitor Center

www.pancanal.com

 91 B3

✉ 5 miles (8 km) NW of Balboa via Ave. Omar Torrijos Herrera (Gaillard Hwy.)

☎ 276-8325

$ $$

Stretching for more than a mile (1.7 km) including the approach channel, the scale of the locks is humbling, reducing the visitor's perspective to an ant's as cruise ships and supertankers the height of a ten-story building ease past at fingertip distance. While the lift of the other two locks is fixed, the lift at Miraflores varies between 43 feet (13 m) and 64.5 feet (19 m) due to the extreme tides of the Pacific Ocean. Completed in May 1913, Miraflores, with only two flights linking the Pacific Ocean with Miraflores Lake, has the deepest chamber and tallest gates of the three locks.

It takes approximately ten minutes to pass through the locks. Locomotives shuttle back and forth as they maneuver the massive ships.

An 1887 Belgian locomotive abandoned during creation of Gatún Lake and raised in 2000 is displayed near the steps to the Miraflores Locks visitor center. Outside, the **Culebra Cut Rock**—dedicated "to the builders of the canal"—is inset with a plaque quoting Theodore Roosevelt's words to the workers.

MIRAFLORES LOCKS VISITOR CENTER

Enhancing the experience immeasurably, the state-of-the-art visitor center opened in December 2003 on the east side of the Miraflores Locks. Overlooking the locks and control tower, the four-story edifice has viewing verandas on three levels. Bilingual guides offer running commentaries as up

to four vessels transit the locks simultaneously.

The center has a 182-seat theater, plus four exhibition halls with dioramas, interactive displays, and video presentations themed by floor. Displays cover the history and ecology of the canal; the third floor features a scale model and a pilot-training simulator. After touring the center, you can dine alfresco on the third-floor restaurant terrace.

The visitor center is just off the Gaillard Highway, a 30-minute drive from the city center. Buses serve Miraflores from the "SACA" terminal at Plaza Cinco de Mayo. ■

Tethered by taut steel cables, a Panamax cargo ship is guided through Miraflores Locks by locomotive *mulas* **(mules).**

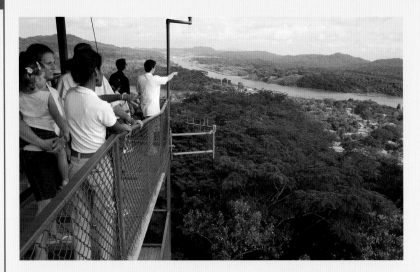

Visitors to the Rainforest Aerial Tram at Gamboa enjoy a panoramic view of the canal.

Panama Canal

Simple in conception, monumental in scale, and a work of genius in design and construction, the Panama Canal is a supreme triumph of humanity over nature. The largest and most costly human endeavor ever mounted to its day, the canal fulfilled a dream dating back to Balboa's first sighting of the Pacific in 1513. Its completion cut ten days off the sea passage around the Horn and elevated the nation to a position of supreme strategic importance. Today ships of every shape and size transit 24/7, maintaining a passage that has operated flawlessly for almost a century.

The canal's construction eventually spawned a revolution, toppled a government, and even gave birth to the Republic of Panama. A testament to U.S. ingenuity and will, it also heralded the arrival of the United States' unbridled power. Construction from 1906 to 1914 cost an unprecedented 375 million dollars. An unimaginable 500 lives (mostly black laborers) were lost per mile (1.6 km) of canal; the American effort claimed 5,609 lives, after another 20,000 or so had died during the failed French effort.

Cut through the narrowest and lowest saddle of the Central American isthmus, the canal runs through Panama north to south, connecting the Caribbean Sea (north) and Pacific Ocean (south). Approximately 50 miles (80 km) long, it features three sets of *esclusas* (locks), each with twin chambers side by side. Each chamber measures 1,000 feet (305 m) long by 110 feet (34 m) wide to accommodate the largest ships of the day. Upper chambers have double layers of paired miter gates to prevent catastrophic flooding if the first pair is breached. The largest permissible vessels—called Panamax ships—are 106 feet (32 m) wide and 965 feet (294 m) long.

A ship transiting from the Caribbean to the Pacific Ocean enters the channel at the Bay of Limón and sails 6 miles (10 km) to reach Gatún Locks (see p. 107). This triple-lock system raises ships 85 feet (26 m) to the level of Gatún Lake. The 27-mile (37.8 km) passage across the lake ends at the north end of the 8.5-mile-long (13.7 km) Gaillard Cut, named for Col. David Gaillard, the engineer in charge of blasting and excavating this passage through the continental divide. After passing through the Cut, ships enter the single-step lock at Pedro Miguel and are lowered to Miraflores Lake. At Miraflores Locks (see p. 93), ships are lowered two more flights to the level of the Pacific Ocean.

Navigational markers help guide the ships

through the channels and lake. Once in the locks, vessels move under their own propulsion but are tethered to electric locomotives called *mulas* (mules), working in tandem on narrow-gauge tracks to keep the ships tautly aligned. Still, every captain must relinquish control of his or her vessel to a pilot for the duration of every transit, which averages eight hours. Currently, northbound ships transit between midnight and noon, and southbound ships between noon and midnight (the canal has operated around the clock since 1963, when lighting was installed along the Gaillard Cut).

the center wall dividing the chambers and in each of the outer side walls. Valves at each end of the culverts control the ingress and egress of water. No pumps are involved. Sliding up and down on roller bearings like windows in a frame, the valves at the upper end of the chamber are opened while the valves at the lower end are closed to flood a lock. Water pours down the main culvert and through 20 smaller cross-culverts that run beneath the floor of each lock perpendicular to the main ones (ten culverts connect with the center-wall culvert and alternate with ten from the

Mulas **work in tandem to guide ships through the locks.**

With every ship's passage, 52 million gallons (197 million l) of fresh water are flushed out to sea: the canal accounts for some 60 percent of the nation's use of fresh water.

HOW THE LOCKS WORK

The entire system is powered by nothing more than the flow of fresh water (which prevents corrosion of lock mechanisms) under the force of gravity. Water from either Gatún Lake or Miraflores Lake fills the locks and raises the ships; water flowing from one chamber to the next or to the sea-level channels empties the locks and lowers the ships.

Water surges through three giant culverts (each up to 22 feet/6.7 m wide) embedded in

sidewall culverts). The water then boils up into the chambers through 70 well-like culverts that rise from the cross-culverts. The large number of wells, distributed evenly across the chamber floors, minimizes turbulence while permitting each chamber to be filled or emptied of 52 million gallons (197 million l) of water in as little as eight minutes. To empty a chamber, the valves at the upper end are closed and those at the lower end are opened.

Originally, the enormous metal gates (the heaviest, the lower chamber gates at Miraflores, weighing 745 tons/676 metric tons) were designed to be opened and closed with a huge connecting rod between each gate leaf and a massive horizontal "bull wheel."

This mechanism was replaced by hydraulic struts in 1998. The entire system was designed to operate electrically, with a water spillway at Gatún Dam generating the power for the 1,500 electric motors. Each set of locks is controlled from a central room resembling an airport control tower built atop the center wall of each upper lock. The original central control board in each featured a working scale model of the actual locks with moving components that mirrored the exact state of the actual lock components at any given moment. Every switch had to be operated in the correct sequence to function, providing a guarantee against human error. In recent years, a modern computer-based control system using fiber-optic cable has replaced the original electromechanical system, while the original valves are being replaced by computer-controlled hydraulics.

ADMINISTRATION & EXPANSION

After completion of the canal in 1914, responsibility for canal administration was vested in various U.S. government agencies. Following the Torrijos-Carter Treaty in 1977, Panama gained jurisdiction of the former Canal Zone and on December 31, 1999, the ACP, or Panama Canal Authority, assumed responsibility for the canal and its 2,134-square-mile (552,761 ha) watershed.

Since taking over operations in 1999, the ACP has invested more than 1 billion dollars in improvements, increasing both canal capacity and the average canal transit

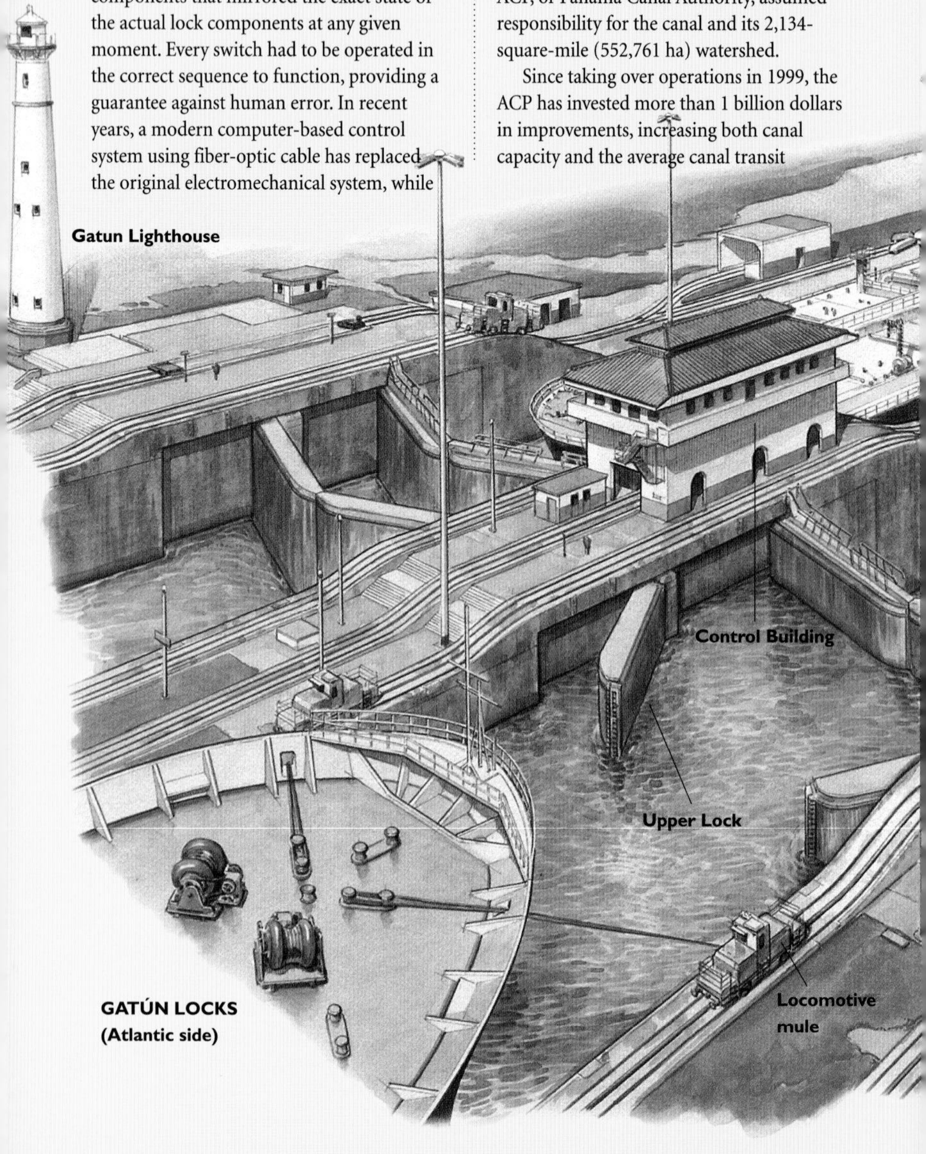

Gatun Lighthouse

Control Building

Upper Lock

GATÚN LOCKS
(Atlantic side)

Locomotive mule

time by 20 percent. Average daily traffic has been increased from 38 to 43 ships. More than 14,000 ships passed through the canal in 2005, paying an average toll of $54,000. The highest toll was $249,165, paid in 2006 by the Maersk Dellys container ship; the lowest fee—36 cents—was paid in 1928 by English adventurer and writer Richard Halliburton, who swam the canal in ten days. The canal currently operates at about 85 percent of its potential capacity, and the ACP has been deepening, widening, and straightening the canal to permit passage of longer and ever larger ships. Nonetheless, due to its inability to handle today's mega-size ("post-Panamax") ships, the canal has been losing market share to the Suez Canal.

In April 2006, the ACP announced plans for an ambitious 5.2 billion-dollar *ampliación* (expansion). The mammoth decade-long project will create a separate and parallel canal and lock system large enough for 150,000-ton (136,000 metric tons) post-Panamax vessels. Each new *esclusa* will be 1,400 feet (427 m) long by 180 feet (55 m) wide. The proposed designs call for locks with their own reservoirs from which vast volumes of water will be recycled. ∎

Lower Lock

Middle Lock

Lock Gate

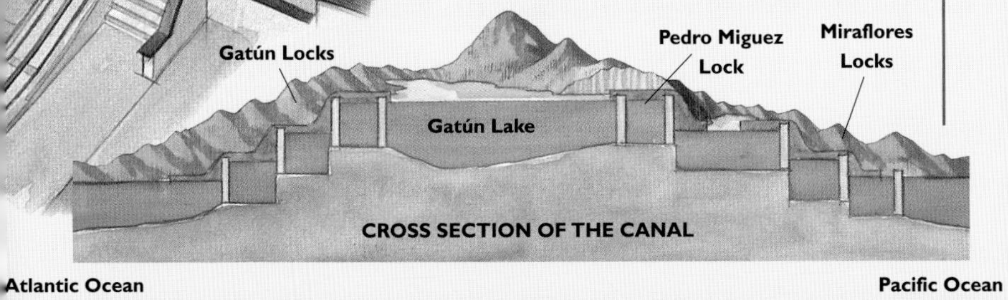

Gatún Locks

Gatún Lake

Pedro Miguez Lock

Miraflores Locks

CROSS SECTION OF THE CANAL

Atlantic Ocean

Pacific Ocean

Parque Nacional Soberanía

WITH A REMARKABLE DIVERSITY OF WILDLIFE CLOSE TO the capital city, this rain-forest park protects much of the Panama Canal watershed and teems with animals. Birds ranging from red-lored Amazons to harpy eagles have earned Parque Nacional Soberanía a reputation for some of Central America's finest birding.

A kinkajou (a member of the raccoon family) scurries along a branch at night.

Parque Nacional Soberanía
www.anam.gob.pa

 91 A3

✉ Gaillard Hwy., 16 miles (25 km) NW of Panama City via Madden Rd.

☎ 500-0855

$ $

Created in 1980 to preserve 54,597 acres (22,104 ha) of forest cover, Soberanía National Park extends south from the eastern shores of Gatún Lake to a few miles south of the Río Chagres. The terrain undulates gently like a great swelling sea and rises to 279 feet (85 m) atop **Cerro Calabaza.** Silk cotton trees, giant mahoganies, and smooth gray cuipo trees like silvery columns of light form a lush canopy over the forest, home to more than 100 mammal, 79 reptile, and 55 amphibian species.

It also has birds: crested eagles, keel-billed toucans, white-bellied antbirds, violaceous trogons. Renowned for its phenomenal birding, Soberanía vibrates with squawks, chirps, and screeches. Serious birders take to the 10-mile-long (16 km) Camino del Oleoducto, more famously known as **Pipeline Road** and considered among the best birding trails in the

world: More species of birds have been sighted there in a single day than anywhere else on Earth! Capybaras, the world's largest rodents, are frequently seen in early morning in the swampy area near the entrance to the trail. Opportunities also abound for sighting anteaters, coatimundis, kinkajous, and howler monkeys.

The broad 4-mile-long (6.4 km) **Plantation Road** also offers spectacular birding. With luck you might spot an army ant swarm attended by bicolored, ocellated, and spotted antbirds. The short **Sendero El Charco** trail begins roadside and leads to a small waterfall and refreshing pool, while **Sendero Camino de Cruces** follows the 16th-century Camino de Cruces (see sidebar p. 103). A section of cobbles has been reclaimed from the jungle and restored. In places you can detect hoof hollows etched by the metronomic march of multitudinous mules. The trail eventually leads to the Río Chagres—a five-hour venture for intrepid hikers—where **Comunidad Wounaan San Antonio** and **Comunidad Emberá Ella Purú** welcome visitors keen for an immersion in indigenous culture.

The ANAM office at the park entrance has maps and issues hiking and camping permits. Tour companies offer trips from Panama City and can arrange birding guides. Robberies have been reported; it is not considered safe to hike alone. ∎

Parque Nacional Chagres

The mighty Río Chagres provides most of the fresh water essential to the functioning of the Panama Canal.

CREATED IN 1985, CHAGRES NATIONAL PARK IS NAMED FOR a legendary Indian chief who ruled the region at the time of the conquistadors. Encompassing 500 square miles (1,295 sq km), the park protects the watershed of the Chagres River basin and is a veritable Noah's Ark of animals and birds.

The Chagres and its tributaries drain 1,300 square miles (3,367 sq km) and provide much of the drinking water for Panama City, as well as water for the canal. The upper reaches cascade in a violent torrent that spills onto lowland and slows to big lazy loops. Before construction of the Gatún Dam, the river flowed unimpeded into the Caribbean. Tamed, today it feeds Gatún Lake.

The terrain ranges from 200 feet (60 m) above sea level to 3,003 feet (915 m) atop **Cerro Jefe** in the southeast. Giant *cedro* trees tower more than 100 feet (30 m) above the lowland tropical moist forest, while rare elfin forest grows on the highest slopes. The park boasts more than 500 bird species, including the rare Tacarcuna bush tanager. Crocodiles and otters swim in the rivers. Five species of monkeys swing from the trees, while below jaguars prowl. Cerro Jefe and neighboring 2,529-foot (771 m) **Cerro Azul** are known for their birdlife; they are most

easily accessed from the Km 40 marker on the Interamerican Highway, 24 miles (39 km) east of Panama City (a four-wheel-drive vehicle is required).

The Chagres River was dammed in 1935 to form **Lago Alajuela,** which offers excellent fishing. Boats cross Lake Alajuela to **Comunidad de Emberá Parará Puru,** a friendly Emberá Indian community that provides an opportunity to learn about native lore. The **Emberá Drua** community is farther inland.

Hikers can try out the old **Camino Real treasure trail** (see sidebar p. 103), a narrow, overgrown, and rugged jungle path that follows the valleys of the Boquerón and Nombre de Dios Rivers. A guide is essential. The rocky upper Chagres provides a thrilling white-water run.

You can camp at Cerro Azul ranger station, and there are several simple hostels and inns near Cerro Jefe. Bring insect repellent, and keep a wary eye out for venomous snakes. ■

Parque Nacional Chagres

www.anam.gob.pa

🅰 91 B3

✉ Lago Alajuela: Carretera Transístmica & Carretera Calzada Larga

Cerro Azul: 16 miles (25 km) N of Tocumen via Interamerican Hwy.

☎ 500-0855

💲 $

A waterborne excursion through the canal locks

A passage through the canal is the dream of almost every visitor to Panama. The experience of transiting the locks, as opposed to merely viewing them from the sidelines, is one of the country's most thrilling and rewarding journeys. Two companies offer the opportunity to feel the surge of water filling and emptying the locks with small cruise vessels that operate "partial transits"; running narratives enhance the journey. The trip described here is for a northbound passage.

The Pacific Queen provides a thrilling excursion from its berth at Amador Causeway.

Canal & Bay Tours *(tel 227-2000, www.canal andbaytours.com, $$$$$)* offers trips every Saturday year-round from the Muelle de Amador dock aboard the intimate 90-passenger *Isla Morada,* a 1911 Prohibition-era rum-runner. **Panamá Marine** *(tel 226-8917, www.pmatours.net, $$$$$)* has similar trips aboard the *Pacific Queen* departing Flamenco Marina every Saturday, plus Thursdays in January through April (full transits of the canal are also offered once monthly). Apply plenty of sunscreen and have patience, as skippers must take on an ACP pilot before being permitted to enter canal waters.

Once under way, it is a five-hour journey to Gamboa. Arching over the canal entrance, the **Bridge of the Americas** ❶ (see p. 88) looms overhead as your vessel slides beneath its broad span. Within minutes, you pass the

bustling commercial port of **Balboa** on the eastern shore, beyond which the banks are cloaked in deep verdure. Crocodiles can often be seen on sunny days hauled out on the banks, soaking up the rays.

About 2 miles (3 km) from the bridge, you pass on your left the **Third Cut,** an unfinished canal dug in the 1940s to permit passage of U.S. battleships. In May 2006, the Panamanian government announced plans to complete the cut for its proposed Ampliación del Canal (Canal Expansion; see pp. 94–97). As you approach the entrance to **Miraflores Locks** ❷, you pass the former Fort Clayton U.S. military base on the east bank. Today the enclave is the **Ciudad del Saber** (see p. 88).

After bucking the current as the first lock is drained, the huge lock gates sweep open, your vessel eases into the chamber, the gates close, and the lock fills with swirling water. With the vessel tethered securely fore and aft, you can touch the massive walls. In less than eight minutes the lock has filled and you look *down* upon the chamber walls. The metal gates to the fore open, and you move into the second chamber, where the process is repeated. Larger vessels in adjoining locks levitate or fall around you as the electric trains called *mulas* guide them through the chambers.

Entering **Lago Miraflores,** you approach **Pedro Miguel Locks** ❸ for the third and final lock passage. Beyond, the canal narrows down through the **Gaillard Cut** ❹, spanned by the graceful twin-towered **Centennial Bridge,** opened in 2004 and linking Panama City to the town of Arraiján. Passing beneath this high-strung harp (beautifully illuminated at night), the stepped rock-face of **Contractor's Hill** looms on your left. Nature then closes in. With luck you might spot toucans and parrots bursting from the bottle-green forests that line the 8.5-mile (14 km) Gaillard Cut. Excavators continue to gnaw at

the cut, which today averages 630 feet (192 m) wide to permit the passage of ever larger ships.

Some 7.5 miles (12 km) beyond the bridge, the **Río Chagres** pours into the cut beneath a metal bridge. Note the black-painted **lighthouse** atop the north bank; dating from 1914, it has since been supplanted by modern navigational markers. Another 400 yards (366 m) brings you to the wharf at **Gamboa** ❺ and the end of your journey, where return transfers await. ∎

✚ See area map p. 91
▶ Muelle de Amador
↔ 15 miles (24 km)
🕐 5 hours
▶ Flamenco Marina, Gamboa

NOT TO BE MISSED
- Bridge of the Americas
- Miraflores Locks
- Gaillard Cut
- Centennial Bridge

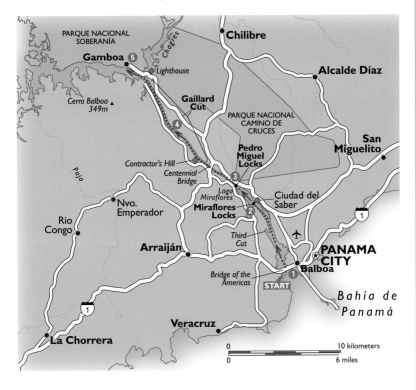

Visitors to the Rainforest Aerial Tram gain insights into tropical ecology as they glide through dense forest.

Gamboa & around

MIDWAY ALONG THE CANAL, GRACED BY COLORFUL duplex wooden houses in U.S. colonial style, the small community of Gamboa provides a fine base for exploring the surrounding tropical forests. Several nearby sites are five-star venues for wildlife viewing.

GAMBOA

Gamboa, 20 miles (32 km) northwest of Panama City, was built in the early 1930s and nuzzles up to forested hills where the Río Chagres pours into the Panama Canal. The Smithsonian Tropical Research Institute runs the **Gamboa Field Station** *(Gamboa, tel 212-8000, www.stri.org)* here. Madden Road ends a short distance beyond, where begins Pipeline Road (see p.

98) for the ultimate in birding.

Also inducing ornithological exhilaration is the 12-sided metal **Canopy Tower** *(Semaphore Hill Rd., tel 264-5720, www.canopytower .com)*, a former U.S. military radar station converted into an ecolodge. Poking up over the forest from atop Semaphore Hill, the observation deck over the Parque Nacional Soberanía is just the ticket for spying motmots, white-whiskered puffbirds, olivaceous flatbills, and

Treasure trails

The wealth plundered from the Inca Empire crossed the isthmus en route to Spain via two trails built by slave labor. Begun in 1516, the Camino Real linked Panama City to Nombre de Dios (and later to Portobelo). Traversing the continental divide, it was "eighteen leagues of misery and curses" in which mules laden with silver ingots often sank in quagmires or plunged down the mountainside. The Camino de Cruces—a far easier route—was begun in 1527 and linked Panama City to the port of Ventas de Cruces on the Río Chagres. Its paving stones were laid in the form of the Christian cross: hence "Trail of Crosses." To visit the Cruces trail, you park by Km marker 6.3 on Madden Road and start hiking. ∎

Parque Natural Summit Panamá

www.summitpanama.org

🅰 91 B3

✉ Madden Rd., 6 mi (10 km) NW of Miraflores

☎ 232-4850

💲 $

Gamboa Rainforest Resort

www.gamboaresort.com

✉ Gamboa, 12 miles (20 km) NW of Panama City

☎ 314-9000

🕐 Rainforest Aerial Tram: 9:15 a.m., 10:30 a.m., 1:30 p.m., 3:00 p.m. Closed Mon.

💲 $$–$$$$$ depending on activity

other dazzling species. Howler and tamarin monkeys frolic nearby, and agoutis, anteaters, and coatis are commonly seen on Semaphore Hill Road. Day visitors are welcome, but an overnight stay is recommended.

PARQUE NATURAL SUMMIT PANAMÁ

Considered Panama's national botanical garden and zoo, this city-owned park has more than 150 species of trees, palms, and shrubs from around the world shading sprawling lawns good for picnicking. Fenced exhibits enclose such elusive creatures as margays, ocelots, peccaries, and jaguars. For birders, a highlight is the large harpy eagle breeding enclosure.

GAMBOA RAINFOREST RESORT

Welcoming day visitors, this luxury hotel and spa enjoys an incredible setting overlooking the Río Chagres. It specializes in nature-themed activities, including wildlife safaris by boat and guided birding hikes. Go-it-aloners can follow the resort's easily hiked **Sendero de la Laguna,** a gravel-lined mile-long (1.6 km) trail.

To learn about rain forests, take a guided tour at the **Interpretative Park,** 250 acres (101 ha) of lowland tropical forest and marsh. Also here: an orchid nursery; a butterfly exhibit; a model Emberá village; and a serpentarium. A resort highlight is a ride on the **Rainforest Aerial Tram,** with18 carriages that rise 367 feet (112 m) to a *mirador* offering superlative 360-degree vistas. ∎

Lago Gatún

Monumento Natural Isla Barro Colorado

www.stri.org

🗺 91 A3

✉ Southern Gatún Lake

☎ 212-8026 or 212-8951 for reservations

🕐 Boat departures from Gamboa 7:15 a.m. Mon.–Fri., 8 a.m. Sat.–Sun.

💲 $$$$

AN INTEGRAL PART OF THE CANAL, THIS 166-SQUARE-MILE (423 sq km) freshwater lake provides the 52 million gallons (197 million l) of water necessary to operate the locks every time a ship passes through the canal. It is dotted with islands and surrounded by lush green tropical vegetation.

First conceived by French engineer Godin de Lépinay (1821–1898) in 1879, Gatún Lake was formed by damming the Río Chagres at Gatún, near the river's mouth, to create a body of water to bridge the isthmus. Flooding took four years (1910–14) to bring the lake to its full depth, with the surface 85 feet (26 m) above sea level.

witches' fingers. Ships follow the course of the now-submerged riverbed—the deepest part of the lake—traveling 23 miles (37 km) between the Gatún Locks and Gaillard Cut. The navigational channel is currently being deepened to permit the passage of vessels of greater draft and to increase water storage capacity, providing enough

At the time of its creation, Gatún Lake was the world's largest artificial lake. The water inundated much of the Panama Railroad (a new railroad had to be built on higher ground) and dozens of villages and impoverished local communities, few of whose occupants received compensation. Giant trees that could form submerged hazards to shipping were cut down and the trunks dynamited. Gnarled trunks still protrude from the cobalt waters like

Mighty Gatún Lake feeds the locks and provides electric power for the Panama Canal system.

water for an additional six transits per day.

Nature tours by canopied boat are offered by Aventuras 2000 *(tel 227-2000, www.colon2000.com/tours.html, $$$$)*. Panamá City Tours *(tel 263-8918, www.gatunexplorer.com, $$$$)* also offers boat tours aboard the *Gatun Explorer*. Expect to see snail kites, Panama flycatchers, anhingas, monkeys, and sloths. The lake is also popular for water-skiing and even scuba diving, although an expanding population of crocodiles makes these pursuits increasingly hazardous. Scubapanama *(tel 261-3841, www.scubapanama.com, $$$$$)* takes divers into the murky waters. There are even drowned villages to explore. Anglers rave about the lake's feisty peacock bass (known locally as *sargento*), an Amazonian species that was introduced to Gatún Lake decades ago and has since proliferated, to the benefit of the crocodiles. Fishing boats and kayaks can be rented at the village of Escobal, 10 miles (18 km) southwest of Gatún; Panamá Fishing & Catching *(tel 6622-0212, www.panamafishingand catching.com)* offers fishing trips.

MONUMENTO NATURAL ISLA BARRO COLORADO

Isla Barro Colorado rises from the waters of southern Gatun Lake. The largest island in the canal system, it is also the centerpiece of the namesake 13,800-acre (5,600 ha) nature monument incorporating the 4,000-acre (1,500 ha) island, plus five surrounding mainland peninsulas (Bohío, Buena Vista, Frijoles, Gigante, and Peña Blanca). The area was established as a biological reserve in 1923 and today functions as an open-air laboratory for scientists from around the world. Since 1946, it has been managed by the Smithsonian Tropical Research Institute (STRI), which operates an intensive study program of tropical ecosystems.

Smothered in lowland tropical moist forest, the island is home to 122 mammal species (including agoutis, coatimundis, ocelots, peccaries, sloths, tapirs, five monkey species, and 72 species of bats), plus 381 kinds of birds and innumerable insect species that include more than 200 varieties of ants. More than 35 miles (56 km) of trails lace the island, although visitors are restricted to a single 1.5-mile (2.4 km) nature trail that weaves beneath massive strangler figs, palms, and ceibas, including one specimen so stupendous and ancient that other trees have sprouted from its branches.

Monkey islands

More than 7,000 simians—white-faced capuchins, mantled howlers, black-handed spider monkeys, rufous-naped tamarins, and night monkeys—inhabit the group of 42 islands collectively called Islas Tigre and Islas Las Brujas. The monkeys were all once captive (either as pets or for the illegal monkey trade) and were released here to prepare them for reintroduction into the wild. Begun in 1982, the Primate Refuge and Sanctuary of Panama (PRSP) grew to become the world's second largest primate sanctuary, with a mission of caring for and rehabilitating the mammals. In 2004 the Panama Canal Authority (ACP) ordered the refuge closed as part of enhanced security efforts that include limiting non-canal-related use of Gatún Lake. Visits are no longer allowed, but the monkeys still frolic. ■

The island is open to daytime visitors by prior arrangement through STRI or approved tour operators, with 45-minute transfers aboard the STRI launch from Gamboa. Ashore, a guided two-hour hike along the interpretative nature trail leads through soaring forest and ends at the visitor center in the Field Research Station. Reservations well in advance are essential; no children under ten are permitted. ■

Colón & around

BIRTHED WITH THE PANAMA RAILROAD IN 1850, THE country's second largest city is inextricably linked to the quests of trans-isthmian passage. Despite its size and moments of illustrious history, Colón (pronounced ko LOAN) is only now emerging from a long spell of depression and should be explored only with a guide or organized tour. Beyond the city await an ancient fortress, prime birding sites, and A-list coastal vistas.

Panoramic vistas are a highlight of the rail journey linking Panama City with Colón.

Colón
🗺 91 A3
Visitor information
✉ IPAT office, Comercial Colón 2000, Paseo Gorgas & Calle 11
☎ 475-2301

COLÓN

The sultry port city of Colón (pop. 45,000) was built by the Pacific Railroad Company on Isla Manzanillo at the Bahía de Limón's eastern tip. Most of the original structures were destroyed by a fire on March 31, 1885.

Avenida Central, the tree-shaded central boulevard colloquially called "El Paseo," makes a pleasant stroll. Among its many statues and monuments are the monument of John Stevens *(at Calle 16)*, the statue of Ferdinand de Lesseps *(between Calles 3 & 4)*, the Columbus monument *(between Calles 2 & 3)*, and the statue of El Cristo Redentor (Christ the Redeemer; *Calle 1*) with arms outstretched. Caribbean clapboard houses in faded tropical pastels line the boulevard. A sturdy contrast, the **Hotel Washington** *(Ave. del Frente & Calle 2, tel 441-7133)* boasts a Moorish facade and a surfeit of marble. The grand dame, established in 1913, counted presidents William Howard Taft and Warren Harding among its illustrious guests. Immediately to the west, the **Battery Morgan**

park displays various cannon.

Cruise ships dock at **Colón 2000** wharf *(Paseo Gorgas)*, close to the **Zona Libre** *(Ave. Roosevelt, Calle 13, tel 475-9500)*, which is the world's second largest free-trade zone after Hong Kong. Trading principally with international wholesalers, it generates 10 billion dollars annually.

OUTSKIRTS OF COLÓN

Highway 32 leads west from Colón past the old hilltop **Cementerio Monte de Esperanza** (formerly Mt. Hope cemetery), dating from 1908, with a section for U.S. servicemen maintained under treaty by the American Battlefields and Monuments Commission. Beyond, the **Gatún Locks** have a spectator stand permitting an eagle's-eye view of ships passing through the three-stage locks. Crossing beneath the massive mitered gates via a one-lane swing bridge, you pass a section of the old unfinished French canal to arrive at the **Gatún Dam,** once the world's largest earthen dam. Completed in 1913 and damming the Río Chagres about 6 miles (10 km) from its mouth, the dam measures 1.4 miles (2.3 km) along the top and 2,100 feet (640 m) thick at the base. Fourteen gates top its curvilinear spillway.

PARQUE NACIONAL SAN LORENZO

Created in 1997, San Lorenzo National Park spreads over 23,852 acres (9,653 ha) of coastal wetlands, cativo forests, and semideciduous and moist forest where U.S. forces and astronauts once learned jungle survival and combat techniques. Since 1999, the former Fort Sherman Jungle Operations Training Center (JOTC) is being developed for ecotourism; you need to present your passport to enter. Despite its small size, an astounding 430 bird species have been identified here, as well as 81 mammals, including jaguars and tapirs. Birders flock like breeding macaws to **El Camino de Achiote** and the **Sendero El Trogón** trail.

The park's highlight is **Castillo de San Lorenzo el Real de Chagres,** a fort looming magnificently over the mouth of the Río Chagres. Built in 1597 and rebuilt in 1680, its rusted cannon and timeworn walls recall the day in 1671 when Henry Morgan and his pirates stormed the ramparts. Today a UNESCO World Heritage site, it has excellent signage in English. It is reached by a poorly maintained dirt road.

Nearby, the U.S. Army's School of the Americas has been transformed into a luxury hotel, the **Meliá Panamá Canal** (see p. 243), from which boats set out for safaris on Gatún Lake (see p. 104). ∎

Parque Nacional San Lorenzo
www.sanlorenzo.org.pa
🅰 91 A3
Visitor center
✉ El Tucán, Achiote
☎ 226-6602 or 226-4529

Pillage & plunder

Pirates color Panama's chromatic past. Swashbuckling a blazing trail through the Indies, cutthroat privateers and pirates were the terrorists of their day, entirely lacking in compassion and scruples. For almost two centuries, these wild and ruthless sea rovers plundered the Spanish Main, the Spanish-controlled coastline running from Panama to the Orinoco River. No Spanish strongholds were as tempting as the ports of Nombre de Díos and Portobelo, the New World's main gateways for great galleons laden with treasure en route to Spain.

From the earliest days of Spain's discovery of the Americas, Panama served as the chief conduit for the continent's unsurpassed wealth. From pearls of the Archipiélago de las Perlas to Colombian emeralds and silver and gold pillaged from the Incas of Peru, treasure in mind-boggling quantities passed through the isthmus to await transshipment to Spain. Panama was a plump plum ripe for picking. Daring foreigners seized Spanish galleons at will, often with the official sanction of Spain's sworn enemies: England, France, and Holland licensed individual captains as privateers to attack Spanish ships and cities in the New World.

The most notorious privateer was Sir Francis Drake (1540–1596), who first sailed to the New World in 1567 with his cousin John Hawkins and a cargo of African slaves. Their fleet was attacked by the Spanish, filling Drake—a devout Protestant—with anti-papist hatred. In 1572 he returned and ransacked Nombre de Dios, captured several Spanish vessels, and waylaid a mule train on the Camino de Cruces. Drake sailed for England with the ships' holds groaning with treasure. Sanctioned by Queen Elizabeth I, in 1577 he set out again with five vessels and the purpose of plunder. After pillaging the Pacific coast of South America, Drake—reduced to one vessel, the *Golden Hind*—captured the *Nuestra Señora de la Concepción* treasure ship and returned to England in 1580 after circumnavigating the world. Drake (who was now so feared that the Spanish used the name *El Draque* to frighten

children) returned to Panama in August 1596 with a fleet of 26 ships. He died of dysentery on January 28, 1596, while preparing to attack Portobelo, and was buried at sea.

In the mid-17th century, a new breed of cutthroats appeared. The "buccaneers" began life as a motley group of seafaring miscreants of all creeds and nations who had coalesced off Hispaniola, where they hunted wild boar and raised livestock for sale to passing ships (the dried meat was called *boucan*). The Spanish resented their presence, however,

and drove them to sea. They formed the Brethren of the Coast and turned to piracy against the Spanish. Success swelled their numbers as they captured ships, grew vastly more powerful, and eventually were officially welcomed to Port Royal, Jamaica, which became their base.

Chief among them was Henry Morgan (1635–1688), a ruthless Welshman who led the brotherhood to unsurpassed heights of success and depravity: When Morgan sacked Portobelo in 1688, he used Catholic nuns and monks as human shields against Spanish fire. Morgan's ruinous rape of the Spanish Main was crowned in 1671 by the sacking and destruction of Panama City (in the chaos, the city burned down, denying Morgan much of his loot). Spain and England had just signed a peace treaty, however. Although Morgan was recalled to England to stand trial, he was exonerated, then knighted and even named governor of Jamaica. In 1697, Spain and England made peace and embarked on a crusade to suppress piracy. ■

Don Pedro de Valdés, admiral of the Spanish flagship *Nuestra Senora del Rosario*, surrenders his sword to Sir Francis Drake in 1588, following the defeat of the Spanish Armada.

Parque Nacional Portobelo

THIS PARK, COVERING 139 SQUARE MILES (360 SQ KM), IS A triptych protecting forested coastal mountains, 44 miles (70 km) of shoreline, and Caribbean waters that sustain precious mangroves and coral reefs. It encloses Spanish colonial ruins dating back five centuries to when the town of Portobelo was the most important treasure port in the Americas.

Parque Nacional Portobelo

🗺 91 B4

Visitor information

✉ Calle Principal Frente at la Alcaldía

☎ 448-2200

Portobelo and the wild and beautiful surrounding Caribbean region known as the Costa Arriba de Colón has seen only limited development since its 16th-century colonial heyday.

PORTOBELO

This somnolent town, 28 miles (45 km) east of Colón, lives up to the name—Beautiful Port—given to the setting by Christopher Columbus, when his worm-eaten ships limped into the bay on November 2, 1502, during the explorer's final voyage to the New World. Nestled within gently folded hills, the town enjoys an exquisite setting when seen from the sea.

Founded in 1597 following Sir Francis Drake's sacking of Nombre de Dios, Portobelo became the departure point for the annual treasure fleets carrying the plundered wealth of South America back to Spain. Although the town had a permanent population of fewer than 1,000 people, more than 10,000 traders flocked in every year for the trade fair that coincided with the arrival of the Spanish fleet. Although Portobelo remained unwalled, castles went up and Portobelo, with Havana and Veracruz, was the most heavily fortified town in the Americas. The first two fortresses—Todo Fierro (Iron Castle) and Fortaleza Santiago de la Gloria—were completed in 1620 but destroyed in 1738 by English naval commander Sir Edward Vernon.

The 18th-century fortress ruins seen today are second generation and smaller than their precursors, since they protected a port that had lost its importance as trade waned. Built into the rugged hills on each side of the bay, their *baluartes* (watchtowers) peek out from between palms atop walls slowly yielding to the encroaching jungle.

Entering town, you pass the **Batería de Santiago,** with cannon in embrasures; a stepped trail that begins on the right-hand side of the road leads uphill to another battery offering spectacular views. The former Castillo de Santiago de la Gloria, 150 yards (137 m) farther along, is now built over, but steps on the right lead up to the **Mirador El Perú** lookout. Across the harbor, the twin batteries of the **Fuerte de San Fernando** were intended to catch invaders in a cross fire.

Castillo de San Jerónimo guards the harbor in the center of town and points its rusting cannon toward the ghosts of pirates past. On its south side, the recently restored twin-story **Real Aduana,** the customhouse, hosts a small museum welcoming you with an excellent English-language video on the history of Portobelo, an illuminated map of the treasure fleet routes, plus cannonballs and 3-D models of the castles.

A stone's throw east, the **Iglesia de San Felipe** features a two-tier campanile rising over the town. Birds swoop around the simple altar of gilt mahogany and statue of the Black Christ. Time your visit for the last Sunday of the month, when a special 11 a.m. Mass incorporates African-based congo traditions. Tucked away to the rear of the church, the tiny former church-hospital of **San Juan de Dios** contains the **Museo del Cristo Negro de Portobelo** *(tel 448-2024, $),* displaying festival robes.

Twin islands stand guard at the entrance to the deepwater bay. Supposedly the pirate Sir Francis Drake was buried off **Isla Drake** on January 28, 1596, after he died in these waters following an attack on Portobelo.

The former counting house for the wealth of an empire, the recently restored Real Aduana today houses a museum.

NATURAL HIGHS

The rivers that rise inland of Portobelo snake down to Portobelo Bay in long, lazy loops perfect for boating tours into the mangroves and lowland moist forest. You can hire a local boatman to take you on a wildlife safari along the **Río Cascajal** and **Río Claro.** Sloths, howler monkeys, river otters, and even crocodiles and caimans are possible wildlife treats. Selvaventuras *(tel 442-1042, www.geocities.com/selvaventuras/)*

French in 1893 tops the isle. **Bananas Village Resort** *(tel 263-9510, www.bananasresort.com)* admits day visitors and has water sports. Nearby **Isla Mamey** is also good for snorkeling. Water taxis for Isla Grande and Isla Mamey depart the waterfront village of La Guayra, 13 miles (21 km) east of Portobelo.

Farther along, the serpentine coast road provides a roller-coaster ride through picturesque countryside framed by the mountains of Parque Nacional

Black Christ festival

Every October 21, as many as 40,000 people throng Portobelo for the Festival del Nazareno, which honors the life-size wooden figure of a black Christ thought to have answered Portobelo's prayers for salvation from a cholera epidemic. Pilgrims petition favors, while others are drawn to witness the colorful spectacle. Each *peregrino* (pilgrim) wears an ankle-length velvet toga of deepest claret edged with lace and aglitter with faux jewels, gold braid, and sequins. Secular tokens are often pinned to the toga. At night the effigy is borne from the church atop a litter carried by as many as 40 men robed in purple. Barefoot and with heads freshly shaved, they snake through Portobelo—three steps forward, two steps back—waying side-to-side in unison with lively music. The penitents follow, some crawling on their knees or bellies. At midnight, the litter is returned to the church, pilgrims cast off their robes, and Portobelo explodes in an irreligious bacchanal. ■

The statue of the Black Christ bears a cross atop his pedestal in Iglesia de San Felipe, Portobelo's main church.

offers guided nature trips, including hikes into the nearby mountains.

The wrecks of Spanish galleons will tempt divers near **Arrecife Salmedina,** a fine coral reef also blessed with the remains of a Beech C-45 warplane 75 feet (23 m) down. Scuba Portobelo *(tel 448-2147, e-mail: info@scubapan ama.com)* offers trips.

Isla Grande, 3 miles (5 km) northeast of Portobelo, is a popular weekend retreat for urbanites from Panama City. Reggae rhythms drift down the frost-white sand, and surf washes over a coral reef a short distance beyond calm turquoise shallows. A lighthouse built by the

Chagres (see p. 99). Some 15 miles (25 km) east of Portobelo, you arrive at **Nombre de Dios,** a funky fishing village spanning a river of the same name. First settled in 1509, for 77 years the town served as the treasure port of the isthmus. However, the harbor proved unsafe in storms (in 1525 an entire fleet of 25 ships was sunk) and was superseded by Portobelo. A wreck thought to be Columbus's *Vizcaína,* which sank hereabouts in 1502, was discovered in 1998 off Playa Damas. Though declared a national monument, the ship still lies in archaeological limbo five fathoms down. ■

Archipiélago de las Perlas

COMPRISING MORE THAN 200 ISLANDS AND CAYS JUST A two-hour boat ride or 20-minute plane trip from Panama City, these emerald jewels are made complete by their exquisite setting in waters of mesmerizing blues and greens. Humpback whales frequent the warm waters in winter and can even be seen from shore.

Archipiélago de las Perlas

🄰 91 C1 & C2

Visitor information

☎ IPAT, 526-7000

The island group, between 40 miles (65 km) and 68 miles (110 km) southeast of Panama City, is named for the pearls found there. After wiping out the indigenous population, the early Spanish set up a pearl trade. Communities on **Isla Casaya** and neighboring **Isla Casayeta** still live on the profits of pearl diving.

Las Perlas were boosted to recent world fame as a setting for the TV series *Survivor,* filmed on uninhabited **Isla Mogo Mogo** and **Isla Chapera,** whose charms are typical of the isles. They feature beaches with sands like pulverized sugar, coral reefs patrolled by a kaleidoscope of fish, and lush forests roamed by anteaters, iguanas, sloths, and peccaries.

Tiny **Isla Contadora,** named for its role as the counting house for the Spanish pearl trade, is the most developed isle and is served by an airstrip. Multimillion-dollar vacation houses are nestled along Contadora's 11 gorgeous beaches. The largest and most developed of the beaches is **Playa Larga,** while nearby **Playa de las Suecas** offers good snorkeling. Golfers can get into the swing on a nine-hole course, and **Las Perlas Sailing** *(tel 250-4134)* offers scuba diving, sportfishing, and whale-watching trips.

The largest isle, 93-square-mile (240 sq km) **Isla del Rey,** has the sole town, San Miguel. The clear waters around the island offer some of Panama's best sportfishing, scuba diving, and whale watching, all

offered from **Kingfisher Bay Resort** *(tel 200-1122, www.kingfisherbay.net).* To the west, **Isla San José** hosts the island's most upscale hotel, the **Hacienda del Mar** *(tel 269-6634, www.haciendadelmar.net;* see p. 241), which offers ATV tours, mountain biking, and a panoply of other activities. ∎

Pretty as pearls, the white sand beaches of Isla Contadora are launch pads for latter-day pearl hunters.

La Peregrina

The plump, pear-shaped "Peregrina Pearl," weighing more than .03 ounces (10 g), was discovered in the archipelago in the 16th century. Vasco Núñez de Balboa presented it to King Ferdinand V of Spain. It was later given as a gift to Mary Tudor (daughter of Henry VIII). In 1969 actor Richard Burton bought it for $37,000 for Elizabeth Taylor, who still owns it. ∎

More places to visit in the central Caribbean & the canal region

CIUDAD DEL SABER

Spanning 297 acres (120 ha) of the former Fort Clayton U.S. Army base, the City of Knowledge comprises a broad-ranging number of Panamanian and international institutions dedicated to research in the sciences, education, and societal and human development. Initiated in 1999, the site today hosts such entities as the Smithsonian Tropical Research Institute, the Meteorological Center of Panama, and the Organization of American States. Computer-based and high-tech entities are located in the **Tecnoparque Internacional de Panamá.** A highlight for visitors is the **Fondo Peregrino Panamá** (Peregrine Fund of Panama; *tel 317-0350, www.fondoperegrino.org*), which breeds harpy eagles for reintroduction into the wild; visitors can even hold a "tame" eagle.

🗺 91 B3 ✉ Clayton, 5 miles (8 km) NW of Balboa ☎ 317-0111, www.cdspanama.org

ECOPARQUE PANAMÁ

This ecopark, on the west side of the canal near Arraiján, was opened in 2005 and is a mere ten-minute drive from Casco Viejo. Still in evolution, the park is intended to provide an all-round introduction to tropical forest environments, with trails that offer fabulous vistas toward Panama City, plus elevated walkways through the treetops. Red-eyed tree frogs are frequently spotted perched atop leaves. The park hosts almost 200 bird species, plus such mammals as squirrel monkeys, jaguarundis, and sloths. A visitor center is planned, as are a botanic garden, a butterfly garden, and a **Centro de Vida Silvestre** (Wildlife Center). 🗺 91 B3 ✉ Carretera Brujas, 2.5 miles (4 km) W of Puente de las Américas ☎ 226-4922, www.ecoparquepanama.org

GALETA ISLAND MARINE EDUCATION CENTER

The Smithsonian Institution operates **Galeta Marine Laboratory,** a science and marine education center created in 1997 on the site of a U.S. Navy satellite communications system.

The facility has a visitor center where exhibits include a whale skeleton. Aquariums and marine pools display moray eels, sea stars, stingrays, and turtles—many in touching pools. A boardwalk leads into the mangroves, where long-billed shorebirds pick for tasty morsels in the mudflats. 🗺 91 A1 ✉ Isla Galeta, 3 miles (5 km) NE of Colón ☎ 212-8191, www.stri.org 🕐 Closed Sat. & Sun. 💲 $$

PARQUE NACIONAL CAMINO DE CRUCES

Established in 1992, the 18-square-mile (46 sq km) national park connects Parque Nacional Soberanía (see p. 98) to the north and Parque Natural Metropolitano (see p. 71) to the south. Predominantly moist tropical forest, it also preserves portions of the eponymous treasure trail (see sidebar p. 103), which awaits excavation. The roots of fig trees and giant ceiba curl along the forest floor, while guayacán blooms spectacularly in spring. The park hosts many of the same species as its neighbors, including crested eagles, red and green macaws, and slaty-tailed trogons. 🗺 91 B3 ✉ Pedro Miguel, 7 miles (14 km) N of Balboa ☎ 500-0855, www.anam.gob.pa

SIERRA LLORONA

Popular with birders, this 494-acre (200 ha) tropical forest reserve is centered on a modern ecolodge offering cozy accommodations. More than 210 bird species have been spotted here and are easily seen along 2.5 miles (4 km) of trails that wind through the lowland and mid-elevation rain forest. Poison dart frogs, kinkajous, and various monkeys are commonly seen; you might even spot ocelots and jaguarundis, plus snakes such as the cat-eyed snake and eyelash palm pit viper. Predawn birding tours are offered. Observation platforms offer bird's-eye views of the canopy. A four-wheel-drive or high-chassis vehicle is essential for the bumpy, muddy road.
🗺 91 A1 ✉ 2.8 miles (4.5 km) N of La Sabanita, 9 miles (14.5 km) SE of Colón ☎ 442-8104, www.sierrallorona.com 💲 $$$ ■

The island beauty of the Comarca de Kuna Yala, which comprises the Archipiélago de San Blas along Panama's Caribbean coast, is exceeded only by that of Kuna Indian women and children exotically clad in traditional, brightly colored attire.

Kuna Yala

Detail of a reverse-appliqué *mola,* a Kuna specialty

Kuna children enjoy simple pleasures at play on Isla Corbisky.

Kuna Yala

THE BEAUTIFUL ARCHIPIÉLAGO DE SAN BLAS IS A SEAGIRT WILDERNESS OF sandy coral islands, sun-bleached jewels in a sapphire sea, that stretches for almost 140 miles (226 km) along Panama's Caribbean coast. The islands' prime colors seem to pulsate in the dazzling Caribbean light. Together, the island chain and a narrow mainland strip comprise the Comarca de Kuna Yala, a district created in 1938, administered autonomously, and exclusively populated by Kuna people. Few among the 365 isles are inhabited or even accessible. Most Kuna live in 40 communities on palm-fringed islands—the majority no more than dots on a map—spread throughout the archipelago. Another 10,000 or so live in 12 fishing communities on tribal mainland territory along the Caribbean coast, none of which is set up with facilities for tourism.

The *comarca* covers 2,151 square miles (5,570 sq km), extending from the ridgeline of the continental divide to the continental shelf offshore. The pencil-thin district stretches almost from Punta Cocoye in the west to Cabo Tiburón and the Colombian border. Close to half is marine territory speckled with coral cays and lush isles protected by an offshore coral reef.

The narrow mainland coastal strip is farmed with coconut palms and provides a hunting and agricultural ground for Kuna, who conscientiously preserve the virgin forests that shawl the Serranía de San Blás and Serranía del Darién mountains inland. In all these miles, only one road—a treacherous affair suitable only for the most rugged vehicles—penetrates the mountains

to link the comarca to the rest of Panama. The Kuna wish to keep it that way and have named the entire western mainland comarca a nature reserve to guard against loggers and *waga* (outsiders).

These self-governing people protect their cultural identity and bloodlines with vigor. Foreigners are subject to Kuna local law and visitation by tourists is strictly regulated. Alcohol is banned on many islands, and this is one place where the peace hasn't yet been violated by boom-box music. Kuna even restrict who may fish in their waters, as well as what may be caught. Despite the beauty of the reefs, scuba diving is not permitted. The snorkeling, however, is unsurpassed.

The reception offered to tourists varies from isle to isle: welcoming and open on some, but reticent and wary on others. Visitors are expected to show respect for Kuna culture. Dress modestly away from the beach. Most villages are tightly packed warrens of humble bamboo-walled huts. Their sole appeal is the chance to experience an indigenous lifestyle close at hand and to photograph the exuberantly costumed women (the men dress Western fashion). The populated isles tend to be polluted with trash, and over-the-water toilets make swimming here a risky business. Still, you can paddle out in dugout canoes to any of dozens of uninhabited private islands to leave your Man Friday footprints in the frosted sands. Always, you'll be accompanied by one or more Kuna custodians, who will usually be happy to make you a meal of fresh fish between bouts of snorkeling and lazing in a hammock.

Access requires boat or air travel. Air Panama *(tel 316-9000, www.flyairpanama .com)* and Aeroperlas *(tel 315-7500, www.aeroperlas.com)* serve airstrips throughout the archipelago with light aircraft; reserve well in advance. Boats can whisk you to smaller islands farther afield. With long distances between each island cluster, it is best to concentrate on one area. The few hotels that exist are rustic (extremely so, in most cases) and, like all businesses in the comarca, are owned and operated exclusively by Kuna, who serve simple meals. There are few freestanding restaurants. A registration fee (usually $3 to $5) is charged for each island visit (yachters must also pay a $5 anchorage fee at each isle). If traveling independently, you will need your passport, which must be presented immediately to local Kuna police.

Travel is made easier by booking travel and accommodations in advance through a tour operator in Panama City (see p. 264). Day trips are available. Kuna Yala is a cash-only society (there is only one bank in the comarca).

Yachters, take heed: These waters are notoriously tricky, and drug-trafficking is common. A copy of *Cruising Guide to the Isthmus of Panamá* by Nancy and Tom Schwalbe Zydler is a must. ■

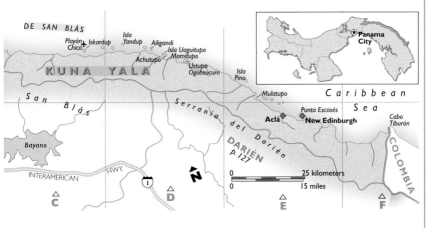

El Porvenir & western isles

El Porvenir
🗺 116 A2

**Museo de la
Nación Kuna**
www.congresogeneralkuna
.org/nacion_kuna.htm
✉ El Porvenir
☎ 314-1293
$ $

WITH DOZENS OF EASILY ACCESSED ISLANDS TO CHOOSE from, visitors typically pick the western group speckling the Golfo de San Blás. Cruise ships disgorge passengers en masse around the two hot spots of El Porvenir and Cartí. Each cluster offers fantastic snorkeling, while the Cayos Holandeses even boasts a number of wrecks.

AROUND EL PORVENIR

Lying about 1 mile (1.6 km) east of Punta de San Blas, the small island of **El Porvenir** (known to the Kuna as Gaigirgordup) is the main gateway to the western islands, as well as capital of the entire comarca, despite its minimal populace and facilities. The isle hosts an airstrip, a few bamboo-walled houses, a police station, a Kuna administrative post, and the **Museo de la Nación Kuna.** Opened in 2005, the small, two-story museum exhibits ceramics, kitchen utensils, musical instruments, baskets, and an example of a Kuna grave. Several nearby islands are within a few minutes' travel by boat.

Nearby **Wichub-Huala** is one of the most popular islands. Large cruise ships often anchor offshore and disgorge as many as 1,000 passengers into the narrow village streets extending from one end of this tiny isle to the other. Almost every square inch seems taken up by Kuna women hawking exquisite *molas.* Barely a stone's throw north of Wichub-Huala, **Ukuptupu** is a rocky speck of an isle with a warren of wooden boardwalks connecting a hodgepodge of simple houses and a hotel that until 1998 served as a Smithsonian Tropical Research Institute facility.

Completing this small island grouping, beachless **Nalunega,** immediately southwest of El Porvenir, is cleaner and more endearing than neighboring and heavily polluted Wichub-Huala,

thanks to the efforts of the savvy Kuna owner of the local hotel, who organizes local cleanups. About 400 Kuna live here, surviving on fishing from sleek *ulus* (dugout canoes).

To escape the throngs, hire a local boatman to take you to **Isla de los Perros.** Sometimes called Achutupu (not to be mistaken with another Achutupu farther east), this exquisite cay represents everything that an idyllic tropical island should be. Isla de los Perros is perfect for snorkeling, with coral reefs edging right up to the whiter-than-white beach that rings the isle; a small shipwreck lies off the south shore. Jet-skiing and waterskiing are not allowed. The silence is absolute except for the soft music of ripples washing ashore. A single family owns the coconut palms (though not the land) and is in attendance when visitors are present. There's a bench and table under palms, and the Kuna caretakers will sometimes cook up a meal by request.

CARTÍ & AROUND

The island town of **Cartí Sugtupu,** one of the largest settlements in the Kuna comarca, lies a stone's throw from the mainland airstrip. A post office, public library, and other key services for the western isles are concentrated here, although the sole accommodation is a rustic dorm, and the trash littering the streets and shores is an eyesore. Favored as a port of call by cruise ships, Cartí can be congested with swarms of tourists. The highlight is

Opposite: Silken waters ring the picture-perfect isles of San Blas, such as Isla Pelicana.

the small **Kuna Museum of Culture,** honoring local culture and mythology. Bilingual guides are on hand to explain the artifacts. Water taxis serve the mainland wharf, which can be accessed by a

Suspended above rippling waters, the simple Dad Ibe Island Lodge (see p. 243) occupies a private island the size of a basketball court.

Cartí Sugtupu
 116 A2
✉ Cartí Sugtupu

Kuna Museum of Culture
✉ Cartí Sugtupu
☎ 299-9002
$ $

horrendously muddy road that connects to the Interamerican Highway (see sidebar below).

A hop, skip, and jump across the waters, **Isla Aguja** offers a

---

Stick in the mud

The dirt road linking Cartí with the Interamerican Highway (the junction is at El Llano, 11 miles/18 km east of Chepo) is not for the fainthearted. It's a brutal drive, especially in rainy season, when sinking deep into vacuumlike mud is likely. Even in dry season, the route is usually impassable to all but the biggest high-clearance, four-wheel-drive vehicles. Bring a chain for winching yourself out of the mud; you don't want to get stuck in the rain forest. Exotics Adventures (tel 223-9283 or 6673-5381, www.panamaexoticsadventures.com) offers a three-day Cartí–El Llano hike and kayak trip. ∎

---

strikingly pristine contrast and is perfect for lazing all day on the beach beneath the shade of palms.

CAYOS LOS GRULLOS & HOLANDESES

The densely populated twin communities of **Río Sidra** and neighboring **Nusatupo,** 9.5 miles (15 km) east of Cartí, are served by a mainland airstrip and are the main gateway to **Cayos Los Grullos,** a dozen or so tiny cays grouped together some 6 miles (10 km) northeast of Nusatupo. Devoid of tourist facilities, the Los Grullos cays are prime snorkeling spots, with calm bays that provide secure anchorage for yachters.

Competing for diamond-dust beaches and transparent blue waters, **Narasgandup Pipi** (sometimes called Naranjo Chico), 2 miles (3.5 km) northwest of Nusatupo, is another perfect spot in which to laze in a hammock beneath palms. It has crude accommodations.

Looking like it dropped from a picture postcard, **Kuanidup** is a diminutive, exquisite palm-shaded isle midway between El Porvenir and Río Sidra.

Recognized for its mola-making tradition, **Isla Maquina,** about 2 miles (3.2 km) from Río Sidra, is less polluted and more laid-back than the latter and makes for delightful strolling. On Río Sidra, local Kuna transvestite and master mola-maker Lisa Harris has a small museum of outstanding molas.

Sprinkled like pieces of eight over the edge of the continental shelf, the **Cayos Holandeses** comprise a cluster of deserted isles about 19 miles (30 km) from shore. Surf crashes up against the jagged reef edge there. **Wreck Reef** is named for the Spanish galleons and other ships that foundered there. Sublime snorkeling awaits. ∎

Narganá & central isles

HUGGING THE COASTLINE OF THE CENTRAL COMARCA, with the Serranía de San Blas rising tight behind like a frozen sea of billowing waves, these widely dispersed isles are less traditional, for the most part, than islands to west and east. Nonetheless, you'll leave bearing a treasure of colorful memories.

Narganá

⚠ 116 B2

NARGANÁ & AROUND

Narganá is an administrative center joined by a long, arching footbridge to **Corazón de Jesús,** a small peninsula with an airstrip. These twin isles have little appeal, with mostly concrete houses, no shortage of TVs and satellite dishes, and comparatively little display of traditional clothing, the community having been sucked into the vortex of Western modes and mores. Still, Narganá has the only bank in Kuna Yala, plus a hospital. A bronze **statue of Carlos Inaediguine Robinson** (an educator and leader of the 1925 Kuna Revolution) marks the village square; his birthday is celebrated each August 20 with music, dance, and excessive drinking.

Río Azúcar, 3 miles (5 km) west of Narganá, is another crowded island with telephones, a medical center, and other services that draw yachters. It has been a focal point for missionary work in recent years, despite which it hosts a Carnival bacchanal at Easter.

Culturally perhaps the most vibrant and intriguing of all the San Blas islands, **Isla Tigre,** 4.5 miles (7 km) east of Narganá, is kept spic and span, its streets swept clean by conscientious Kuna. Local pride is so strong that even children are encouraged to pick up and dispose of detritus. Uniquely, too, the local Kuna go about their traditional lives with little regard for tourists. Visitors can roam freely without being badgered to buy, though you must still report upon arrival to the local tourism commission. A dramatic reenactment of the Kuna Revolt of 1925 is held each February 25, and every mid-October the island hosts a weeklong festival of music and dance.

Small planes serve **Playón Chico,** another crowded modern community that serves as a jumping-off point for forays to neighboring isles such as tiny **Isla Yandup** (*visitor information: www.yandupisland.com*), a coral-fringed cay good for snorkeling; it has a small hotel. Pinprick-size **Iskardup** boasts fine accommodations with the **Sapibenega Kuna Lodge** (see p. 244). The English-speaking hotel owner leads jungle hikes into the mainland mountains, including to the **Ibe Igar** waterfall and a Kuna burial ground. There, the deceased slumber inside earth coffins topped by keepsakes from their earthly lives. ∎

Kuna children on Isla Playon Chico

Kuna culture

Kuna women paint their noses as marks of beauty.

Fierce defenders of tribal tradition, the Kuna people cling tightly to an indigenous culture that is one of the most colorful and intact in the New World. Whether in Panama City, Penonomé, or the islands of their *comarca* (autonomous district), Kuna women are instantly recognizable in their colorful skirts and blouses adorned with *molas* in primary colors.

According to their oral tradition, the Kuna (or Tule, as they sometimes refer to themselves) originally lived in the forests of Darién. Around the time of the Spanish arrival, warfare with the encroaching Emberá-Wounaan and, possibly, with the Spaniards forced the Kuna northward into the Serranía de Panamá and Caribbean plains and, later, to the islands offshore. About 70,000 Kuna survive today, of whom about 32,000 inhabit the islands and as many as 30,000 occupy the Panamanian diaspora.

A diminutive people averaging about 5 feet (150 cm) in height—only the Pygmies of Africa are smaller—the Kuna have slender, sinewy limbs and disproportionately large heads, with aquiline noses esteemed as a sign of beauty. They speak *dulegaya,* the Kuna language, and protect their tribal bloodlines assiduously: Anyone marrying outside the tribe is expelled. Insularity promotes inter-breeding; perhaps as a result of this, rates of albinism here are the highest in the world. The ancient tradition of killing albinos at birth has given way to reverence. Today albinos are considered specially chosen and gifted "Moon children," born after a pregnant women is supposedly exposed to the full moon. Albino boys are trained in the ways of women and can often be seen stitching or selling molas in the cool shade.

Kuna society is matriarchal. Women control the local real estate, mostly comprising simple thatched huts walled with stiff reeds or cane and with bare earth for floors. The ground beneath their feet, however, is owned in common by the community and has prevented the division of Kuna society into "haves" and "have nots." A man moves into his lover's home to signal marriage and simply moves out again to enact a divorce. While the men don mask and flippers to dive for lobsters for sale to passing yachts and to tourists, it is the women who fill the family coffers stitching and selling their colorful molas to an appreciative international market.

A girl's passage into womanhood is cele-brated by the entire community, when a surfeit of chicha is drunk. At puberty, women cut their hair short and henceforth cover their head with a blood-red muswe (shawl). Their daily attire is a saburet (skirt) worn over a bicha (petticoat) held by a mudub (belt). Although Western lipstick has made inroads, many women still paint their cheeks with achiote, a natural rouge obtained from the achiote seed, and paint a black line of tagua dye down the length of their nose. The ensemble is completed by large gold earrings and nose rings, plus necklaces of colored beads, used also to cre-ate beaded bracelets to decorate their fore-arms and ankles. By contrast, the men go unadorned in Western clothing.

Both women and men are skilled in their

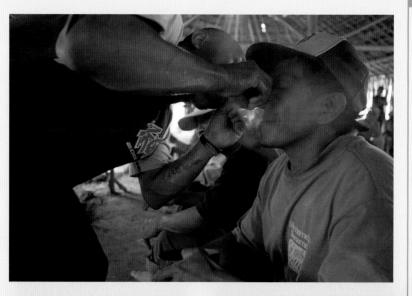

A Kuna blows smoke in the nostril of a village elder during a council meeting (top). Beaded calf adornments are meant to draw attention to a woman's slender legs (above). Kuna women in colorful *molas* prepare a potent *chicha* brew made of fermented corn in celebration of the bloody 1925 revolution that led to autonomy (right).

A fisherman heads to work in a traditional Kuna sailcraft as the sun rises over the Caribbean Sea near Achutupu in the San Blas archipelago.

use of dugout *cayucos* or *ulus* (canoes), ferrying between islands propelled by paddle or urged along by a single triangular sail. At daybreak, some men set sail to go lobstering and fishing, while others head to the mainland to fetch water, attend to subsistence lots, and collect coconuts for sale or barter to Colombian schooners. As many as 30 million coconuts may be harvested in a good year and sold at a price fixed (and strictly enforced) by community elders. Although the beauty of Kuna women hides the economic plight of most Kuna families, they are not at all preoccupied with the fact that they are poor economically. In fact, the Kuna are rich in spirit and resourcefulness.

The Kuna comarca is divided into four districts, each presided over by an elected chief, or *sahila,* under a supreme sahila who chairs a six-monthly *congreso,* or *onmaket nega,* of village heads. Every village has its own daily congreso headed by its own sahila versed in Kuna traditions; all males over 18 years

of age must attend the Sunday sessions or face a fine. Custodians of sacred rites, the village *absoguedi* (chanter) and *nele* (shaman) employ spiritually alive wooden human figures called *nuchus* to divine and cure human sickness. Like scribes in a Dickensian novel, an army of secretaries maintains records and writes countless permits issued (for a fee) to individuals wishing, for example, to visit another village or travel outside the comarca.

The Kuna are deep believers in a spirit world, in which every natural thing is possessed of a positive guardian spirit. *Poni*— evil spirits—also roam the land; to guard against them, the Kuna use nuchus carved of balsa. The Kuna practice a kinship with the forests and land; to deforest the land, for example, will bring harm to the community. Nonetheless, the Kuna fish indiscriminately. The lobster population has suffered greatly, and marine turtles are now rarely seen in these waters. ■

Eastern isles

THESE DARK GREEN CAYS RISING OUT OF THE WATER IN A long line like a Spanish flotilla are beyond the reach of easy boat travel from points farther west. Airstrips serve the main islands. Boasting some of the most exquisite of all the San Blas islands, this part of the world offers visitors a chance to see Panama through the eyes of an explorer.

Eastern isles
117 D2, E2, & F2

Lacking an offshore coral reef, in inclement weather these isles are subject to battering by high seas. Ocean passage is a comparatively tricky and even risky affair. Colombian drug-smuggling boats run these waters, while paramilitary and guerrilla groups occasionally infiltrate the coastal strip close to the Colombian border.

The main airstrip for the isles is in densely populated **Achutupu,** centered on a large thatched community hall. A mere 200 yards (183 m) west of Achutupu, the more intimate **Isla Uaguitupo** (aka Uaguinega) is almost entirely taken up by the **Dolphin Island Lodge,** one of the best hotels on the isle (see p. 243); tours are offered from here.

Ailigandi, 3 miles (5 km) west of Achutupu, crams 1,200 Kuna into its impossibly small compass. The isle is studded with statues and painted with political murals commemorating the 1925 Kuna revolt; the **Instituto Nacional de Cultura** teaches mola techniques. Ailigandi is welcoming to tourists, in contrast to nearby **Mamitupu,** where the sahila bars photography. Worldly-wise local Kuna Pablo Núñez Perez acts as an informal tour guide and will paddle out to greet you in his dugout canoe if you arrive by yacht at Mamitupu.

Farther east, **Mulatupo,** with one of the largest populations in the San Blas chain, is a stepping-stone to the mainland coast. From here you can visit **Aclá,** founded in 1515 as the first Spanish settlement on the Spanish Main and, at **Punta Escocés,** New Edinburgh, founded in 1698 (see p. 28). ■

A domesticated parrot takes in village life from its window perch in Ailigandi.

Shutter-happy etiquette

Kuna children with a photogenic smile and parrots on their shoulders will have you reaching for your camera posthaste. First, be sure you have plenty of dollar bills at hand. The rarely waived rule is $1 per photo. The rate usually doesn't apply to scenics or group shots, such as ceremonial dances, although pointing a camera at a group of Kuna women usually causes most of them to cover their faces. Never photograph without asking permission. Kuna village elders enforce the rules, and merely carrying a camcorder can result in being charged $10 to $50 or more. Some islands are more tolerant than others. ■

More places to visit in Kuna Yala

ÁREA SILVESTRE CORREGIMIENTO DE NARGANÁ

The mountainous Narganá Magisterial Wilderness Area—a 230-square-mile (596 sq km) swathe of virgin rain forest inhabited solely by wild animals—serves as a barrier intentionally isolating the comarca from the rest of the country. It is also a buffer zone against intrusion by non-Indians and by loggers with their eyes on deforestation. The park merges with Parque Nacional Chagres to the west and extends from the continental divide to the Caribbean coast. The birding is equal to anywhere in Panama. More than 400 species have been seen here: keel-billed

Molas

Layered in textured tradition, brightly colored molas are world-renowned symbols of Kuna culture. Originally decorative blouse panels, these oblong works of art averaging about 18 inches (46 cm) wide are made of several layers of cotton cloth of contrasting colors. Patterns are cut into the separate layers, which are then hand-stitched together along the curve of the cut—a process called reverse appliqué. The basic designs usually represent parrots, butterflies, and other natural organisms, although abstract patterns can also be found. The end result is enhanced by a 3-D effect produced by the multilayered technique. ∎

toucans, black-crowned antpittas, sulphur-rumped tanagers, blue-headed parrots, and more. Birding is best from December to June. **Burbayar Lodge** *(tel 261-1679, www.burbayar.com;* see p. 244) is a Kuna-run ecolodge on the edge of the reserve at a springlike 1,200-foot (375 m) elevation. Six trails (including the Kuna Medicinal Forest Trail) of varying difficulty lead into the lodge's own 122-acre (50 ha) rain-forest reserve, good for spotting poison dart frogs, vine snakes, bats, iguanas, families of monkeys, pumas, jaguars, and tapirs. You can even hike to Cartí (6 to 10 hours). Access to Burbayar is easy by four-wheel-drive; beyond Burbayar, the road deteriorates rapidly.

🗺 116 A2 ✉ Nusagandi, 12.5 miles (20 km) N of El Llano, on the Interamerican Highway ☎ 390-6674, www.burbayar.com

BAHÍA DE ESCRIBANO

This serene bay, just outside the Kuna Yala comarca, about 10 miles (16 km) west of El Porvenir, is protected by an offshore barrier reef called Baja Escribano, 3 miles (4.8 km) out. Gin-clear waters wash onto beaches of pure white radiance. The pristine coral reefs offer breathtaking diving. Almost 70 species of hard corals and more than 60 species of sponges provide a pelagic playground for a star-studded cast: barracudas, giant groupers, manta rays, harmless nurse sharks, and moray eels peering out from their coral crevices at the dizzying array of damsels, tangs, wrasses and an extravaganza of other rainbow-hued fish. In 1501, Spanish explorer Rodrigo de Bastidas became the first European to land in Panama when he stepped ashore here. Later, pirates Henry Morgan and Sir Francis Drake used the bay as a staging ground to ambush Spanish galleons. For years the bay has drawn yachters to its white sands. In 2006, the first hotel opened. **Coral Lodge Resort** *(tel 317-6754, www.corallodge.com;* see p. 244), accessible solely by plane and boat, offers diving and kayaking. 🗺 116 A2 ✉ By yacht or by boat transfer from Porvenir ∎

Precise geometric patterns are a staple design for vibrant traditional molas.

A biological Eden in the largest pristine wilderness habitat in Central America, this eastern province is a birder's and nature lover's dream. Encounters with Emberá indigenous communities guarantee a spectacular cultural experience.

Darién

A launch near Punta Patiño

Darién

NAMED FOR AN INDIAN CHIEF WHO RULED HERE DURING THE SPANISH conquest, this vast eastern third of the country is renowned for rain forests so thick that the last leg of the Interamerican Highway still has not come through. A mother lode of biodiversity, sparsely populated Darién Province contains the largest tract of pristine rain forest in Central America. Birding and wildlife viewing is unexcelled in the country. However, relatively few places are accessible, amenities for tourists are few, and much of the region resembles a war zone and is thereby off-limits.

The Río Sambú snakes through the forests and clear-cut fields of Darién.

The Interamerican Highway, unfurling east as far as Yaviza, is the sole highway access to this region. Completed to this point in 1977, the road brought a rapid influx of *mestizo* settlers and massive deforestation. Today there are two Dariéns: the wounded western half speckled along the highway with recently established, albeit tiny, townships; and eastern Darién, still smothered in virginal rain forest enshrined within 2,236-square-mile (5,791 sq km) Parque Nacional Darién. Virtually uninhabited, this creepered Amazonian world of throttling greens is accessed by airstrips and by long narrow dugout *cayucos* (canoes). Up the black tannic rivers are remote Emberá and Wounaan Indian villages predominantly found in two semiautonomous districts, the Comarca Emberá Cemaco and Comarca Emberá Sambú. Bodies and limbs blackened

with jagua juice, the Emberá-Wounaan embrace tourists with smiles to melt gold. Although creeping Westernization is subtly altering Emberá-Wounaan lifestyles, many ancient traditions endure, including hunting with *boroquera* (blow gun) and poison-tipped darts.

Framing the region to the northeast, the rugged Serranía del Darién coastal mountain range separates Darién from the Comarca de Kuna Yala. The long and lonesome western shoreline is also backed by the Serranía del Sapo and Serranía de Jungurudó, winding southward into the Colombian Andes. The mountains rise to heights exceeding 6,000 feet (1,800 m) and ethereal mists swirl through the treetops of classic montane cloud forest—one of Parque Nacional Darién's five distinct life zones. Countless rivers cascade onto

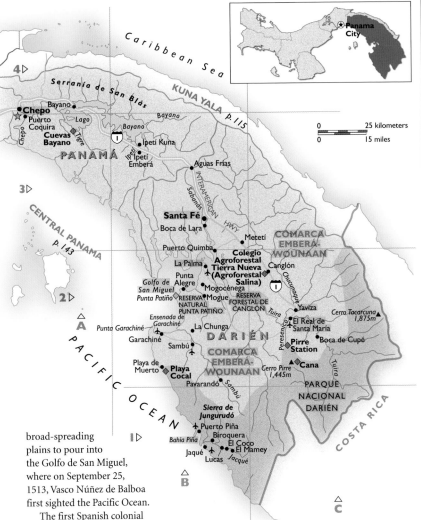

broad-spreading plains to pour into the Golfo de San Miguel, where on September 25, 1513, Vasco Núñez de Balboa first sighted the Pacific Ocean.

The first Spanish colonial settlements in Panama were established in Darién, spawned by discovery of the Cana gold mines that once provided the Choco Indians with the raw material for their ancient finery. The precious metal was ferried downriver in canoes and loaded on larger ships to be carried north to the Camino Real; Spanish forts built to guard the port at the mouth of the Río Tuira peer out from the luxuriant biomass. Today, Cana is a gold mine for hikers and birders. Punta Patiño Nature Reserve offers an alternative wildlife experience and is a

short boat ride from La Palma, the provincial capital, in the Golfo de San Miguel.

Many settlements are guarded by heavily armed police, a reminder that parts of the national park and the Comarca Emberá Cemaco are a hideout for a variety of outlaws spilling over the uncontrolled Colombian border. The best way to explore these zones is with an accredited guide or reputable tour company (see pp. 263–264). ∎

Along the Interamerican Highway

Villages along the Interamerican Highway such as Santa Fé (below) provide glimpses into local Kuna and Emberá life.

PART OF THE PAN-AMERICAN HIGHWAY STRETCHING FROM the tip of Alaska to Tierra del Fuego, the 3,400-mile (5,470 km) Interamerican Highway links the Central American nations from Nuevo Laredo, in Mexico, to Yaviza, 172 miles (276 km) east of Panama City. Forested mountains rise above the deforested landscape, providing a setting for welcoming Kuna and Emberá hamlets.

Interamerican Highway

⬛ 129 A3, A4, B3, & C2

Visitor information
www.anam.gob.pa

☎ ANAM (Autoridad Nacional del Ambiente) 299-6183

CHEPO TO IPETÍ

The gateway to Darién Province is **Chepo,** 33 miles (53 km) east of the heart of Panama City. While the town, which lies 2 miles (3.2 km) south of the highway, is within eastern Panamá Province, Panamanians consider this to be the Darién frontier, as until the early 1970s it was here that the highway ended and the jungle began. Onward travel was by dugout canoe from **Puerto Coquira,** where *cayucos* still set out down the mangrove-lined Río Chepo, roosting site for white

ibis, anhingas, and the largest colony of cattle egrets in Panama.

East of Chepo, **Lago Bayano** spreads across the valley like a pool of silver-gray mercury. Covering 86,000 acres (35,000 ha), the U-shaped lake was created in 1975 when the Ascanio Villalaz hydroelectric dam was built across the Río Bayano. The lake, one of Panama's few breeding sites for the Cocoi heron and neotropical cormorant, is named for a warrior leader of *cimarrones*—escaped African slaves—who led a fierce resistance to Spanish rule. According to local belief, a Loch Ness–like monster inhabits the lake. You can hire a boat (local guide Mateo Cortéz, *tel 297-0157,* is recommended) at **Bayano** for a 45-minute ride to **Cuevas Bayano,** bat-filled caves that lie along the Río Tigre. Feeling like Indiana Jones, you can explore the chambers—often up to your chest in cold water—lined with stalactites, stalagmites, and calcareous sheets.

Most of the lake lies within the **Comarca de Kuna de Madugandi,** an 800-square-mile (2,073 sq km) semiautonomous region created in 1996 and adjoining the Comarca de Kuna Yala. Approximately 5,000 Kuna inhabitants in 12 communities struggle to maintain their cultural identity against the tide of non-Indian peoples, logging companies, and mercantilism washing in since the opening of the Interamerican Highway. The community of **Ipetí Kuna,** tucked 1 mile (1.6 km) north of the highway, welcomes visitors with ceremonial dances and offers insights into traditional crafts and medical practices. Local guide Igua Jiménez *(tel 6595-9500, e-mail: iguat28@yahoo.com)* leads tours. The villagers of neighboring **Ipetí Emberá,** 0.6 mile (1 km) south of the highway, also perform traditional ceremonial dances, sell crafts, and offer trips by *piragua* along the Río Ipetí. The village has simple thatched lodging in a characteristic open-walled house raised on stilts. **Panamá City Tours** *(tel 263-8918, www .panamacitytours.com)* offers cultural tours.

SANTA FÉ TO YAVIZA

Santa Fé, 32 miles (51 km) east of Ipetí and 2 miles (3.2 km) west of the highway, is a river town on the east bank of the Río Sabaná. Here, **ECODIC** is a community development project that makes natural scented soaps, medicinal products, and colorful murals for sale; you can hike forest trails and learn about organic production of pineapples and other fruits at agricultural station **Finca Sonia.** At high tide, piraguas travel 5 miles (8 km) downriver to **Boca de Lara,** a Wounaan community also accessible from the Interamerican Highway by four-wheel-drive. Here you can sleep local fashion in a thatched open-walled lodge. Exotics Adventures *(tel 223-9283 or 6673-5381, www.panamaex oticsadventures.com)* offers trips to Boca de Lara.

Metetí, the major settlement between Chepo and Yaviza, has spartan hotels. A paved road leads west 12 miles (20 km) to ramshackle **Puerto Quimba,** bustling with water traffic to-ing and fro-ing between destinations in the Golfo de San Miguel (see pp. 138–139). Farther east, the settlement of Canglón holds the **Colegio Agroforestal Tierra Nueva** *(tel 202-1421, www.tierranueva.org),* with trails through the primary rain forest of its private reserve, **Agroforestal Salina,** taking you past poison dart frogs, monkeys, and scores of tropical bird species.

Sordid accommodations fit the melancholy mood of **Yaviza,** at the end of the road 165 miles (266 km) from Panama City. Journeying solo beyond Yaviza is ill-advised. After registering your arrival at the police station, take time to scout the ruins of the **Fuerte San Jerónimo de Yaviza,** an 18th-century Spanish fortress overhanging the Río Chucunaque. ∎

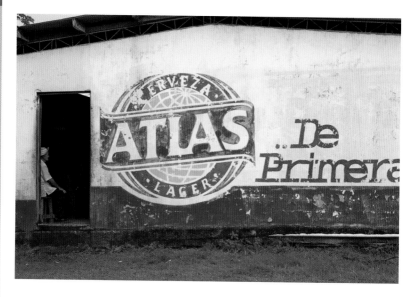

Simple roadside cantinas, such as this one in Canita, provide gathering spots for locals.

Driving the Interamerican Highway

A single road probes the vastness of Darién Province. This journey, an adventurous escape along perhaps the most famous highway in the world, delivers you quite literally to the end of the road. Beyond that, a 70-mile (106 km) swathe of dense rain forest spanning the country coast to coast comprises the infamous "Darién Gap"—the only unbridged section along the entire 16,000-mile (25,800 km) route of the highway between the tips of Alaska and Argentina. Although the road is paved for the first three-quarters of the trip, conditions then deteriorate markedly and you will need a four-wheel-drive vehicle to proceed. Even so, reaching Yaviza, where the road peters out, may prove impossible in wet season.

The journey is mostly flat as the highway unfurls along a broad valley hemmed by the Serranía de San Blas and Serranía de Majé mountains. Cut into the virgin jungle in the 1970s, the highway's construction ushered in an era of deforestation. Fortunately the Panamanian government is resisting efforts by loggers and other commercial interests to extend the Interamerican Highway to the Colombian border—a guaranteed recipe for ecological disaster. The few sites of interest are separated by long stretches of cattle pasture. Accommodations along the route are few and mostly dismal, and militarized police checkpoints are reminders that venturing beyond Yaviza is a foolhardy

notion. Plan on a same-day, round-trip journey, setting out in early morning. *You will need your passport.*

Begin in **Chepo ❶**, a quiet, colorful town discreetly hidden 2 miles (3.5 km) south of the Interamerican Highway, 33 miles (33 km) east of Panama City. A police checkpoint and a statue of St. Christopher with a child on his shoulder mark the junction, east of which the highway undulates along the southern lee of the Serranía de San Blás. After 24 miles (39 km), silvery **Lago Bayano ❷** (see pp. 130–131) comes into view. You'll need to present your passport at the police checkpoint in the community of **Bayano,** where Kuna women in traditional costumes add bright notes of color. Crossing over the lake on an iron bridge, you enter the Comarca de Kuna de Madugandí tribal territory. For the next 20 miles (32 km) the road is fringed by forest and is a veritable freeway for butterflies and parrots.

The forest fades beyond **Quebrada Calí,** opening the vistas southward toward the sawtoothed Serranía de Majé. Farther east, the tiny community of **Ipetí Kuna** ③ (see p. 131) sells molas. After visiting this village and the nearby Emberá village of **Ipetí Emberá,** your route is now lined with pastures studded with freestanding mahoganies and other sky-reaching trees. The roadside community of **Tortí** is known for its *feria* featuring rodeos and bull-taunting in late March, and for the manufacture of handcrafted saddles; the *talabarterías* (leather workshops) face each other across the street. Passing teak

plantations, you arrive at **Aguas Frías** ④, with a police checkpoint and billboard that reads "Welcome to Darién." Some 13 miles (20 km) farther, take a break at **Emberá Arimae** (aka Los Monos), known for its artistic traditions; the community sells crafts and welcomes visitors with traditional dances.

The asphalt that begins in Alaska ends at the Afro-Antillean community of **Zapallal** ⑤. From here on, you'll kick up dust or mud as you slingshot (or slog) south to **Metetí,** where police at the fortified checkpoint may discourage your onward passage. Metetí has a gas station and bank.

East of Metetí the highway becomes an embarrassment to road engineers; in wet season, you should call a halt here. Your speed is halved and then quartered as the going deteriorates with every mile until it fizzles out in **Yaviza** ⑥, a dilapidated, vaguely menacing frontier town beyond which the fur-thick jungle takes over. ■

See area map p. 129
► Chepo
↔ 127 miles (204 km)
⊙ 5 hours one way
► Yaviza

NOT TO BE MISSED
- Lago Bayano
- Ipetí Kuna
- Ipetí Emberá
- Zapallal

Parque Nacional Darién

Parque Nacional Darién
www.anam.gob.pa
🅰 129 C1 & C2
✉ El Real de Santa María
☎ 299-6579 or 299-6183
💲 $$, permit compulsory

OUTSIZING ALL OTHER NATIONAL PARKS THROUGHOUT Central America, Darién has earned a reputation for some of the region's best wildlife viewing. From tiny poison dart frogs to the world's largest eagle, this foreboding mini-Amazon is a crown jewel of rain forest and wetland biota whose enormous appeal is well worth the discomforts of sodden humidity and rains.

A vast oasis of biodiversity, the park was established in 1980 to protect 2,236 square miles (5,791 sq km) of lowland rain forest, as well as a range of other life zones extending from mangrove and cativo swamps to premontane rain forest atop 6,150-foot (1,875 m) **Cerro Tacarcuna.** Stretching virtually the length of the Panamanian-Colombian border, entire sections of the park are infiltrated by guerrillas, narco-traffickers, and bandits, and travel outside established secure zones is dangerous. Under all circumstances, travel should be only with a knowledgeable guide and/or reputable tour company. The only facilities for overnighting are at Pirre and Cana (see below).

The National Authority for the Environment (Autoridad Nacional del Ambiente, or ANAM) park headquarters is at the riverside town of **El Real de Santa María** (see p. 142), from which you can hike (four hours; dry season only) or travel by canoe to ANAM's **Pirre Station,** on the banks of the Río Peresenico in the heart of the lowland rain forest. Pirre has a dormitory with meager facilities. Bring your own food and flashlight; there is no electricity.

Set deep in the heart of the park, **Cana,** at a 1,500-foot (457 m) elevation on the eastern slopes of **Cerro Pirre,** offers more comforts and is an exhilarating

The lush rain forests of Darién are a treasure house of fabulous flora.

site for birding. It is accessible only by foot. This biological research station run by the Asociación para la Conservación de la Natureleza (ANCON) also serves as an ecolodge operated by Ancon Expeditions (tel 269-9415, www.anconexpeditions.com). Remarkably, given its isolation, Cana was founded in the 16th century and grew to become a large town from the wealth of the Espíritu Santo gold mines. Abandoned about 1727, Santa Cruz de Cana was soon overwhelmed by vegetation. The mines were briefly revived in the late 19th century; rusting relics of a railroad still litter the forest, evoking *Heart of Darkness.*

STUPENDOUS WILDLIFE

Declared a UNESCO World Heritage site in 1981 and a Biosphere Reserve in 1982, this lush biological Eden boasts wildlife in astounding abundance. Darién hosts viable populations of 56 species endangered elsewhere in the continent. Harpy eagles are commonly sighted, as are tapirs, while jaguars have even been seen sauntering along Cana's airstrip. Chances of seeing any of the five big cat species are greater here than anywhere else in the nation. So, too, white-lipped peccaries, tamanduas, both two- and three-toed sloths, and a variety of monkeys.

Exotically painted poison dart

frogs hop about on the dank forest floor, secure in their toxic-warning liveries from predation by Darién's abundance of snakes. Crocodiles and caimans splash about in the rivers. More than 450 bird species have been recorded here, including blue-and-yellow, great green, and red-and-green macaws.

(2 km) trail leads to a series of exquisite cascades; for safety, avoid the temptation to climb the falls. The steep **Sendero Cerro Pirre** offers a greater challenge going up Cerro Pirre but pays off with views over the river valley from a mountain ridge.

Five trails originate at Cana. One, a short and easy hike along

HIKING

You need not venture far from Pirre or Cana to get close to the wildlife. Bring waterproof hiking shoes for the muddy trails, plus bug spray and water. Watch out for venomous snakes, not least for fer-de-lances, large, well-camouflaged pit vipers with brown-and-black backs whose bite can be fatal in minutes. *Do not hike without a guide.* If you get lost or are injured in the forests of Darién, your odds of survival are slim.

From Pirre, a 1.5-mile-long

the **Sendero Maquina,** leads to rusted 19th-century steam locomotives. Six-mile-long (9 km) **Sendero Cerro Pirre** ascends Cerro Pirre to a mist-shrouded tent-camp swaddled in high-elevation cloud forest; from here the **Sendero Bosque Nuboso** offers opportunities for spotting the rare golden-headed quetzal.

Trails also lead from the ANAM ranger station at **Rancho Frío,** a three-hour walk from El Real; one leads to the summit of Pirre. ■

A hut with a view at Cana, deep in the heart of Parque Nacional Darién

Poison dart frogs

Breathtaking in their beautiful coloration, poison dart frogs inhabit the warm moist forests of the neotropics of Central and South America. Most are no bigger than a thumbnail, though a few grow to 2 inches (5 cm) long. Notwithstanding their diminutive size, these tiny critters produce some of the deadliest toxins known to science.

The vividly colored frogs are members of the Dendrobatidae family. New species are still being discovered, such as *Dendrobates claudiae,* first identified on Panama's Isla Bastimentos in 2000. Of the 170 or so recognized species, only one-third are known to be toxic.

Poison dart frogs produce bitter-tasting alkaloid compounds that are stored in microscopic mucous glands beneath the frog's skin; they cause any hungry predator to instantly gag. The most potent toxin of all is batrachotoxin (from *batrachos,* the Greek word for frog), produced uniquely by the three extraordinarily lethal species of *Phyllobates* genus. Found only in Darién and Colombia's Andean lowlands, these are the true "poison dart" frogs after whom the entire family is named. Emberá-Wounaan Indians have traditionally used *Phyllobates'* secretions to coat the tips of the blow darts they use to hunt monkeys and other game. The frogs typically secrete their deadly potions when they feel stressed or threatened. However, the silvery yellow, 2-inch-long (5 cm) *Phyllobates terribilis* even without being agitated is lethal to the touch for humans—the Emberá-Wounaan need do no more than wipe their darts along its back. This frog's rare neurotoxin, 250 times more potent than strychnine, is so deadly that a toxin-tipped dart can remain lethal for more than a year.

The frogs derive their specific toxicity from their diets. The *Phyllobates'* batrachotoxin, for example, is ingested from a little-known group of tiny beetles of the *Choresine* genus that contain high concentrations of the neurotoxin. When placed in captivity and removed from their natural diets, the amphibians gradually lose their toxicity.

Nature's neon touch-me-nots advertise their toxicity through brilliant coloration that serves as a warning to potential predators. While some are uniform in coloration, typically they have a predominant Day-Glo color on top (usually bright red, orange, green, or blue) and a secondary color (usually yellow, red, white, blue, or black) underneath, often appearing as spots or speckles. Species vary from island to island. For example, the frogs of Bocas del Toro archipelago are green on Isla Popa, green-and-black on Isla Taboga, dark blue on Cerro Brujo, yellow with black dots on Isla Bocas, and ripe-strawberry red on Isla Bastimentos.

Most poison dart frogs are ground dwellers, looking like little enameled porcelain figures on the moist forest floor. Boldly diurnal, they hop around by day secure from predation. Males aggressively defend their territories against rivals and can often be seen wrestling chest-to-chest like miniature sumos. Uniquely immune to the frog's toxin, the fire-bellied snake (*Leimadophis epinephelus*) is the amphibians' only natural predator.

Poison dart frogs lay their eggs among the leaf litter and go to great lengths to safeguard their precious offspring, who lack toxins. Once the eggs hatch, one parent (either female or male, depending on the species) loads the tiny tadpoles on its back and carries them one at a time into the trees, where it deposits them in water-filled leafy funnels of bromeliads. While most other frog species typically abandon the young tadpoles, female poison dart frogs visit their babies every few days to feed them by depositing unfertilized eggs in the water. ■

Dendrobates azureus comes in various shades of blues, from powder to cobalt, although poison dart frogs can also be red, green, or yellow.

The colorful wooden houses of *afrodarienitas*—Afro-Antillean Panamanians—enliven La Palma.

La Palma & Golfo de San Miguel

THE GOLFO DE SAN MIGUEL FORMS THE WATERY GATEWAY to Darién. Humpback whales can often be seen frolicking in the ultra-warm waters into which Vasco Núñez de Balboa waded in 1513, sweating and laden with armor, after stepping from the jungle to claim the Pacific for Spain.

La Palma

⚠ 129 B2

Visitor information

☎ ANAM, 299-6183

La Palma, the region's ugly duckling provincial capital, occupies the tip of a crocodile-shaped peninsula at the mouth of the Río Tuira, with the Golfo de San Miguel spreading westward like a Spanish fan. Served by an airstrip and connected to the Interamerican Highway by boat via Puerto Quimba (water taxis leave every 30 minutes for a 20-minute journey), La Palma is primarily a base for exploring inland along the **Río Tuira** (see p. 140) and west along the coast and up the Río Sambú into the **Comarca Emberá Sambú** (see pp. 140–141). Its small harbor is a hive of activity. During early Spanish colonial days the port

served as a transshipment point for gold extracted upriver at the Cana gold mines. The ruins of 16th-century **Fuerte San Carlos** peer out from beneath a writhing sarcophagus of strangler vines on **Isla Boca Chica,** five minutes by boat from shore.

The local population is predominantly Afro-Antillean. These *afrodarienitas*—descendants of African slaves imported to work the Espíritu Santo mines of Cana—are renowned for their musical traditions, considered to reach a zenith in the impoverished fishing village of **Punta Alegre,** 14 miles (22 km) southwest of La Palma. Linger awhile and people are sure to break out guitars, bongo drums, and maracas while dancers perform a sensual *bullerengue*, a dance whose roots can be traced to the Batá region of Africa's Spanish Guinea.

Beyond **Punta Patiño,** the huge sweep of **Ensenada de Garachiné** curls around to Punta Garachiné and the open Pacific. Boats to **Playa de Muerto** (see p. 141) can be hired in the Afro-Antillean community of Garachiné, from which a road unfurls into the valley of the **Río Sambú** (see p. 141).

RESERVA NATURAL PUNTA PATIÑO

Capybaras munch the marshy grasslands a short distance from the cozy nature lodge at Punta Patiño, a 117-square-mile (303 sq km) nature reserve owned by ANCON. These blunt-nosed rodents the size of small pigs are commonly seen as you hike the trails that lead through mangroves, coastal wetlands, and tropical dry and moist forests occupying a peninsula jutting out into the Golfo de San Miguel. Much of the reserve is a former coconut plantation and cattle ranch that is being reforested. Amazingly diverse for such a small area, it claims 10 percent of

the animal and bird species in Panama, including harpy eagles, great curassows, jaguars, ocelots, and pumas. The easy **Sendero Piedra de Candela** trail loops through coastal forest and is a good place to spot poison dart frogs (and red-eyed tree frogs at night).

The reserve has a private airstrip and is a one-hour boat journey west from La Palma; a tractor pulls arriving boats ashore through the muddy flats as mosquitoes whine about your ears. Overnight visits must be reserved through Ancon Expeditions *(tel 269-9415, www.anconexpeditions.com),* which offers package tours. ∎

Ibises are among the many bird species easily seen along the shores of the Golfo de San Miguel.

Reserva Natural Punta Patiño
www.anconexpeditions.com
 129 B2
✉ 9 miles (14.5 km) SW of La Palma by boat
☎ 269-9415. Fax: 264-3713

Vasco Núñez de Balboa

In 1510, conquistador Vasco Núñez de Balboa founded Santa María la Antigua del Darién, the first permanent settlement in the New World. Local *caciques* (Indian chiefs) told him of the Inca wealth of Peru and of a new sea. On September 1, 1513, he set out with 190 Spaniards and 800 Indians and on September 22 sighted the Pacific from a mountaintop. Three days later, Balboa arrived at the shores of the Golfo de San Miguel and claimed the Mar del Sur for the King of Spain. He fashioned ships, took over the Pearl Islands, and was named Adelantado of the South Sea (Admiral of the Pacific) and governor of Panama. A jealous rival, Don Pedro Arias de Ávila, schemed against Balboa and had him tried for treason; Balboa was executed in January 1519. ∎

Emberá & Wounaan villages

**Comarca
Emberá–Wounaan**
🗺 **129 B2, C2, & C3**

SPINNING A MAGICAL MYSTERY TOUR OF HOMESPUN ART and tribal traditions, river trips into Darién's interior provide an intriguing insight into the region's rich indigenous culture, while the fantastic journeys also guarantee astonishing wildlife viewing. The experience is one of the most rewarding to be had in the country.

Emberá youngsters beat the heat by leaping into the Río Mogue.

The Emberá-Wounaan peoples originated in Colombia and have lived in the forests of Darién for at least two centuries as hunter-gatherers. Only in recent decades have they begun to settle in villages scattered throughout the province. Their territorial rights were recognized in 1983 with formation of the Comarca Emberá-Wounaan, home to some 17,000 people, mostly Emberá with a Wounaan minority. Covering a quarter of Darién Province, it comprises two separate comarcas.

The 1,112-square-mile (2,880 sq km) **Comarca Emberá Cemaco,** with 28 native communities, occupies the Chucunaque-Tuira river basin in

the northeast. The wide **Río Tuira** twists in great loops, linking isolated communities of Emberá, Wounaan, and *afrodarienitas.* Travelers must register at every police checkpoint. Travel beyond (and sometimes to) **Boca de Cupé,** erstwhile headquarters for the Cana gold mines, is off limits due to guerrilla infiltration, as is the trail from Boca to Cana. Boca once boasted almost 20,000 inhabitants and was connected to the mines by a railroad; today it is a virtual ghost town.

The 502-square-mile (1,300 sq km) **Comarca Emberá Sambú,** in the southwest, is safer and easily accessed by river. The comarca's 12 major villages are all set up to receive tourists. Most villages offer basic accommodations and meals and are protected by heavily armed police brigades. **Mogue,** 3 miles (5 km) up the murky Río Mogue, midway between La Palma and Punta Patiño, is the most accessible community. It's a 20-minute walk from wharf to village, the sodden air hanging heavy around you. Trails lead into primary rain forest.

RÍO SAMBÚ

The Río Sambú, a 90-minute boat ride from La Palma, is plied by cayucos and piraguas that follow the river as it snakes deep into the heart of Darién as far as **Pavarandó,** the easternmost Emberá village. Crocodiles slither down the muddy banks; swimming is best avoided.

La Chunga, on the Río Chunga tributary, is relatively touristy. Farther upriver, **Sambú**—part Emberá, part Afro-Antillean—provides a study of diverse ethnic groups living in harmony with each other and their environment. The **Sambu Hause B&B,** a spacious wooden lodge, is the perfect base for cultural and nature explorations (see p. 245). Guides lead forest hikes, including to a rock covered with **pre-Columbian petroglyphs.** The nearby community of **Werará Perú** has an artisan's workshop.

Travel farther upriver is a day-long affair. The journey can be arranged through Ancón Expeditions *(tel 269-9415, www.anconexpeditions.com).* Bring plenty of insect repellent.

PLAYA DE MUERTO

This unique coastal community is difficult to reach but well worth the effort. An early morning

---

Emissary of Darién

The Emberá-Wounaan can produce more income from a single tree in the rain forest than from 40 acres (16 ha) of cattle grazing, claims Jim Brunton, founder of the Pajaro Jai Foundation (420 Post Rd., West #202, Westport, CT 06880, USA), which works to promote the self-sufficiency and maintain the strength of Darién indigenous culture. Centered on the village of Mogue, PJF fosters eco-sensitive projects such as native crafts for export, the opening of jungle lodges for ecotourism, and small-scale furniture factories that produce dowels, frames, and furniture of blood-red nazareno, fiery-gold pino amarillo, and coral-hued almond. PJF's primary educational tool is the *Pajaro Jai* (Enchanted Bird). The result of 15 years' labor by the Emberá, this sleek, 92-foot-long (28 m) ocean-going ketch was hand built and is crewed by Emberá-Wounaan in native dress. ■

---

departure is best for the two-hour boat journey from Garachiné (you must register with the police before leaving), which lands you on a miles-long black sand beach fronting the Emberá village. It's a staggering setting against darkly brooding mountains. The 225 inhabitants perform native dancing, sell exquisite artwork, and demonstrate medicinal plants. Guides lead hikes to **Playa Cocal,** where a trail leads through rain forest to a waterfall. Playa de Muerto has simple accommodation with the stentorian roar of howler monkeys for reveille (see p. 245). ■

More places to visit in Darién

BAHÍA PIÑA

Midway between Punta Garachiné and the Colombian border, this small bay pincered by narrow promontories boasts a setting of magnificent beauty. Waves crash against rocky cliffs backed by emerald forests spilling down the Sierra de Jungurudó. Humpback whales and bottlenose dolphins frequent the bay. An airstrip serves the hamlet of **Puerto Piña,** where Emberá often welcome visitors with traditional dances. The bay is the setting for **Tropic Star Lodge** (see p. 245), a fishing lodge known for its hundreds of International Game Fish Association world-record catches culled from the churning waters of **Zane Grey Reef,** an underwater mountain 15 miles (25 km) from shore. A mountain trail leads to talcum-white **Playa Blanca,** shelving into turquoise waters protected by a coral reef good for snorkeling.
🗺 129 B1

Harpy eagles

The endangered *Harpia harpyja*—Panama's national bird and the world's largest eagle—has a wingspan of 7 feet (2.1 m). With deadly talons the size of grizzly bear claws, this powerful raptor lords it over the lowland rain forest, where it seizes tree-dwelling prey such as monkeys and sloths. Its range is now limited to pockets of Central and South America. ∎

JAQUÉ

The southernmost settlement in Panama, 5 miles (8 km) south of Bahía Piña, is served by twice-weekly flights from Panama City. Many occupants are Colombian refugees. **Bridges across Borders** (*U.S. tel 352-485-2594, www.bridgesacrossborders.org*) sponsors a women's cooperative that makes cards from recycled paper and natural fibers. Village elder Don Pininin metamorphoses balsa logs into exquisite drums. And villagers gather and tend the eggs of leatherback turtles, which nest on the miles-long black-sand beaches; the community has released thousands of baby turtles back to sea. Simple accommodations are available. You can journey up the Río Jaqué to **Biroquera,** a Wounaan village, and to the Emberá villages of **Lucas, El Coco,** and **El Mamey**. However, venturing beyond Biroquera is foolhardy (in January 2006, an armed group kidnapped two Spanish citizens).
🗺 129 B1

EL REAL DE SANTA MARÍA

This ramshackle frontier town, with an airstrip ringed by jungle, is the main gateway to Parque Nacional Darién (see pp. 134–135). Solo travelers intent on visiting the park must register with ANAM (tel 299-6965). Situated on the Río Tuira, 40 miles (65 km) upriver from La Palma and 4 miles (6.4 km) downriver from Yaviza, the village dates back to the early 17th century, when it served as a stopover for gold from the Cana mines; the treasure was stored here before being shipped north for passage to Portobelo via the Camino Real. The barely discernible ruins of a Spanish-built fort are overgrown by a fantasy of thick foliage. The town has accommodations for hardened stoics.
🗺 129 C2

RESERVA FORESTAL DE CANGLÓN

On the north bank of the Río Tuira, midway between La Palma and El Real de Santa María, this 122-square-mile (316 sq km) wetland—also known as Humedal de Matusagaratí—protects a vital network of mangroves, riverine marshes, and tropical humid forest. Egrets, herons, and ibis pick among the sedge wetlands, where jacanas can be seen tiptoeing across lily pads, using the ultrawide span of their toes to disperse their weight. With luck you may spot capybaras also, as well as crocodiles lurking in the river or sunning on the riverbank, motionless as logs.
🗺 129 C2 ☎ 299-6183, www.anam.gob.pa ∎

Riding the hub of a rugged mountain complex, central Panama has magnificent hiking and a coast lined with beaches and precious wetlands. Colonial antiquities and an offshore island with stupendous scuba diving and whale-watching add to the well-rounded appeal.

Central Panama

Detail of a 1,200-year-old ceramic, Museo de Veraguas, Santiago

Mists shroud mountaintops in Parque Nacional Omar Torrijos.

Central Panama

THIS REGION IS BLESSED WITH TOURIST ATTRACTIONS OF EVERY SORT—FINE beaches, magnificent mountain scenery, forests teeming with wildlife, even pre-Columbian sites and important colonial architecture. All are within a few hours' drive of Panama City. It's easy to understand why the provinces of Coclé and Veraguas—the only Panamanian province that extends between Caribbean and Pacific shores—have together become the premier vacation destination for residents of Panama City, drawing visitors to their multiple splendors.

The region is bounded to the north by the rugged mountains of the continental divide. Isolated Ngöbe-Buglé communities dot the mountains, and the coast is sparsely populated by Afro-Antillean communities. No roads penetrate the Caribbean region that, with the "Darién Gap," constitutes Panama's final frontier.

On the Pacific side, the rivers that tumble out of these steep mountains flow down to rolling flatlands and empty through swampy wetlands into the Bahía de Parita. East of the bay, 40 miles (64 km) of sun-kissed beaches with taupe sands stretch along the Pacific shore from Farallón to Punta Chame and the Bahía de Panamá (Bay of Panama). Though

Panamanians flock to this coast, relatively few foreign tourists know of these beaches, which begin about one hour west of Panama City and are are marked by signposts on the Interamerican Highway.

Most beach communities are loosely organized agglomerations of second homes and vacation rentals. Large all-inclusive resort hotels have recently opened (one has a golf course), appealing mainly to Panama's middle class. Other accommodations are limited; beach restaurants are even fewer.

The hilly interior invites cooler pleasures. The mountain settlement of El Valle de Antón, spread out in a leisurely fashion in an ancient volcanic crater, basks in a springlike

Map labels:

0 — 25 kilometers
0 — 15 miles

4▷

Golfo de los Mosquitos

COLÓN

Coclé del Norte

CANAL ZONE p. 89

Belén

COCLÉ

Molejón

Calovébora

PARQUE NACIONAL OMAR TORRIJOS

PARQUE NACIONAL ALTOS DE CAMPANA

Capira

Sertanía del Escaliche

Cerro Trinidad ▲968m

Campana Isla

La Rica

Cerro Marta 1,046m

Cerro Chame ▲1,007m Cerro Campana Taborcillo

BOCAS DEL TORO p. 209

Cerro Peña Blanca 1,314m

Cerro La Vieja ▲

Cerro Gaital 207m Bahía de Punta

Barrigón

Cerro Negro 1,518m

El Copé

La Pintada

Cerro ▲ 1,185m

Bejuco Chame Chame

Cerro Cabeza de Toro 1,412m

PARQUE NACIONAL SANTA FÉ DE VERAGUAS

Predregosa

Cerro La India Dormida

El Valle de Antón

Tanglewood Wellness Center

Santa Fé

Cerro Tute

Penonomé

Playa Coronado

Playa Gorgona

VERAGUAS

Parque y Museo Arqueológico del Caño

El Caño

San Carlos

Playa El Palmar

Playa Río Mar

Nata de los Caballeros

Río Hato

Santa Clara

Playa Santa Clara △

San Francisco

Playa Farallón

D

Aguadulce

Bahía de Parita

Las Palmas

Santiago de Veraguas

RESERVA FORESTAL EL MONTUOSO

Panama City

INTERAMERICAN HWY

Soná

HERRERA

△ C

2▷

Puerto Mutis

Playa Santa Catalina

Golfo de Montijo

Mariato

1▷

Playa El Estero

PARQUE

Isla Coibita

Isla Cébaco

NACIONAL

ISLA

Bahía Damas

△ B

COIBA

Isla Coiba

El Varadero

PARQUE NACIONAL CERRO HOYA

△ A

---

temperate climate year-round. You can delight in hiking and horseback rides, plus get a close look at creatures you miss in the wild by visiting one of the country's two zoos. Wildlife is also the name of the game in rugged Parque Nacional Altos de Campana—starkly beautiful high country from which all Panama seems to explode into view—and Parque Nacional Omar Torrijos. Together they offer some of the most spectacular mountain hiking in Panama, with lush forests bursting with epiphytes, orchids, and birdsong. Birders and orchid fans flock, too, to the end-of-the-road highland hamlet of Santa Fé.

The region is cut through by the Interamerican Highway, which grants easy access to every sight. The highway itself is a fast, rather unexciting drive, two lanes in each direction, and well maintained. Keep to the speed limit, as the road is heavily patrolled. The route is dotted with towns abuzz with modern vitality yet containing time-warp Spanish-village centers. Penonomé is one such, living in another century entirely at its core. Natá is graced by the oldest Catholic church in the Western Hemisphere. Nearby El Caño offers Panama's most important pre-Columbian site. And Santiago boasts a fine museum brimming with dusty archaeological relics.

West of Santiago, the Interamerican Highway narrows down to one lane in each direction and after about 25 miles (40 km) climbs over mountain ridges that separate Veraguas and Chiriquí Provinces. There are few settlements, nor even gas stations or hotels, along this long stretch of road, and it holds only a fistful of basic restaurants. Surfers and sportfishers typically divert south to the Golfo de Montijo for some of the best waves and angling thrills in the country. And Parque Nacional Isla Coiba is, not least, world-renowned for its stupendous diving. ∎

Parque Nacional y Reserva Biológica Altos de Campana

Parque Nacional y Reserva Biológica Altos de Campana
🗺 145 D3
Visitor information
www.anam.gob.pa
✉ 2.8 miles (4.5 km) W of the Interamerican Hwy., at Capira
☎ 997-7538

THE WILD, BARREN HEIGHTS OF ALTOS DE CAMPANA more closely resemble the whiskey-brown crags of the Scottish Highlands than the torrid tropics. The 12,170 acres (4,925 ha) of mountainous wilderness include severely deforested lower slopes, yet the breeze-swept heights are lush and lovely, with a large concentration of endemic species atop the highest peaks.

Established in 1966 as the country's first national park, Altos de Campana is shaped like a barbell. The dramatic mountain formations reflect the area's tormented volcanic origins. Lava fields and volcanic tors—gnarly, sheer-sided, freestanding boulders—stipple the steep slopes, which range from about 1,300 feet (396 m) elevation to 3,304 feet (1,007 m) atop **Cerro Chame.**

The main access road to the southerly Cerro Chame section begins 2 miles (3 km) west of Capira (on the Interamerican Highway), from which a paved road with more curves than the girl from Ipanema winds its way 3 miles (5 km) up to the park entrance on the western side of the mountains. The road offers fantastic views over the coastal plains, best enjoyed from the *mirador* (lookout point) 200 yards (183 m) beyond the ranger station. Though much of the western and southern slopes is entirely denuded, forests await above. The well-maintained, 3-mile-long (5 km) **Sendero La Cruz** begins on the right about 3 miles (5 km) above the ranger station and ascends to the summit of **Cerro Campana,** topped by a cross. The more demanding **Sendero Cerro Campana** offers an alternate route.

The park has four distinct forest types, including tropical pine forest on the drier Pacific slopes. The more lushly clad Atlantic slopes resound with chattering birds: bronze-tailed plumeleteers, scale-crested pygmy tyrants, and a variety of trogons are among the 267 species recorded. The area is known for its large numbers of reptiles and amphibians, including Panama's endangered golden frog, restricted to the northwest corner near El Valle de Antón (see p. 147).

Rugged 3,176-foot (968 m) **Cerro Trinidad,** an imposing triptych peak often swaddled in clouds, offers a steep and sometimes slippery three-hour hike to the summit, which rewards the visitor with 360-degree vistas as spectacular as any in Panama. From Capira, a four-wheel-drive track claws its way up the eastern slopes to the trailhead. Simple huts *(refugios)* are available for overnights. ■

The golden frog

A national symbol of Panama, the golden frog *(Atelopus zeteki)* is found only in a small area of these mountains and nowhere else. It was revered by pre-Columbian Guaymí, who made gold frog talismans *(huacas)* representing fertility. According to legend, the frogs turn into huacas when they die; local belief holds that seeing or possessing a live frog will bring good luck. ■

El Valle de Antón

TUCKED IN A VALLEY AT ABOUT 1,975 FEET (602 M) WITH mountains all around, the breathtaking beauty of the town and region known as El Valle is equaled only by its sublime climate, while golden frogs, square trees, market, exhilarating hikes, and thrilling zipline ride through the forest canopy count among its attractions.

El Valle de Antón
🗺 145 C3
Visitor information
✉ Mercado Artesanal, Ave. Central
☎ 983-6484

Flat as a billiard table and just as green, the valley floor after which El Valle is named was once a lakebed occupying the vast crater of a volcano that literally blew its top about three million years ago. A veritable Shangri-La, this jewel of a vale 16 miles (25 km) north of the Interamerican Highway at Las Uvas is a popular weekend retreat for Panama City's wealthy. The tranquil town is laid out on the east bank of the Río Antón, which sparkles like frothy champagne.

Trails lead up the mountain known as **Cerro La India Dormida** (Sleeping Indian Woman), resembling a woman sleeping on her back. Look for exquisite orchids blooming in shady niches. The Panama Explorer Club *(tel 215-2330, www.pexclub.com)* offers guided hiking and more.

Every Sunday, Ngöbe-Buglé Indians flock to the traditional **market** *(Ave. Central at Calle del Mercado)* to sell crafts, including figurines of *ranas doradas*—the endangered yellow-and-black poison dart frogs synonymous with El Valle. To see the real thing, head to **Hotel Campestre** *(tel 983-6146; see p. 246),* an alpine lodge backed by thickly forested 3,888-foot (1,185 m) **Monumento Natural Cerro Gaital.** The mountain reserve is accessed by a trail that begins near the hotel. Another trail behind the hotel leads to a cluster of *árboles cuadrados* (square trees), although only a vivid imagination can discern the quadrangular form.

El Níspero, a botanic garden and zoo, also displays ranas doradas, plus monkeys, agoutis, parrots, kinkajous, ocelots, and even ostriches. **El Valle Amphibian Conservation Center,** an exhibition center and laboratory, breeds ranas doradas.

Canopy Adventure *(tel 983-6547, www.panamabirding.com /adventure, $$)* lets you whiz Tarzanlike between treetops on a zipline. The highlight is gliding over the **Chorro Machoa,** a 150-foot (46 m) waterfall also accessed by good birding trails. Nearby, the **Piedra Pintada**—a boulder the size of a truck—is carved with pre-Columbian symbols thought to represent an ancient map. Adjoining the tiny **Iglesia de San José** *(Ave. Central at Calle la Compaía),* the tinier **Museo El Valle** has simple displays of pre-Columbian petroglyphs, ceramics, and folkloric costumes. ∎

A colorful farmers' market is held weekly in El Valle.

El Níspero
✉ 0.75 mile (1.2 km) N of the police station, Ave. Central
☎ 983-6142
$ $

Museo El Valle
✉ Ave. Central
☎ 6486-5194
$ $

Local youth show off their soccer skills on Playa Santa Clara.

The beaches

UNRAVELING LIKE A STRING BIKINI ALONG THE CURVACEOUS coast of western Panamá Province and Coclé Province, silvery beaches run one into the other for 40 miles (64 km). Less than a two hours' drive from Panama City and thereby extremely popular with the city's middle class, the beaches can get packed on weekends and during fiestas. Ramshackle fishing hamlets speckle the shore, where marine turtles haul out to deposit their eggs above the high-water mark.

The beaches

🅜 145 C3 & D3

Visitor information

✉ IPAT, Río Hato, Farallón mainstreet

☎ 993-3241

🕐 Closed Sat. & Sun.

Most of the beaches are indicated by signposts on the Interamerican Highway, which runs inland of the shore. The sands—in colors from chocolate and taupe to black—are easily accessible by public bus from Panama City's Gran Terminal. Taxis ply the highway or await at the bus stops, ready to shuttle you to your beach.

PUNTA CHAME & AROUND

Curling north like a fishhook around the eastern flank of the **Bahía de Chame,** the needle-thin sandspit called **Punta Chame** divides two unique worlds. You'll thrill to gorgeous views as you follow the potholed, roller-coaster road to the tip of the point. The bayshore, lined with shrimp farms and mangroves, rings with the sounds of shorebirds and forms a vital nursery for caiman, turtles, and juvenile fish. Dolphins frolic in the blue-gray waters and kite-surfers scud across the bay. The nondescript community of Punta Chame is the capital of kite-surfing in Panama. To try your hand at the sport, contact Machete Kiteboarding *(tel 6674-7772, www.machetekites.com).*

The bay's lush boomerang-shaped **Isla Taborcillo** (see p. 247) is commonly known as Isla de John Wayne, who bought it after filming *Rio Bravo* in Panama in 1959. New owners have built a family-oriented hotel and entertainment complex in mock-Western fashion, staffed by live actors re-creating Wayne's swaggering cowboy aura. The isle is also an important nesting site for tricolored herons and yellow-crowned night-herons.

Punta Chame's oceanside beach glitters in the sunlight like silver coins washed ashore from a Spanish galleon. The waters are subject to undertow and stingrays congregate here, burrowing down into the sandy shallows; wading is a hazard. Three species of marine turtles waddle ashore at full moon. Floating 9 miles (15 km) offshore, craggy **Islas Otoque, Bona,** and **Estivá** are important breeding sites for pelicans, frigatebirds, and brown- and blue-footed boobies.

The black sands of **Playa Gorgona,** west of Punta Chame, sizzle tender soles underfoot and are thronged by music-loving family hordes from the city on weekends. A better bet, **Playa Coronado** is speckled with the second homes of wealthy Panamanians and draws a more upscale crowd. Many come to practice their swing at Coronado Golf & Beach Resort *(tel 264-3164),* which has a championship 18-hole golf course. Bring your ID to gain access.

PLAYA SAN CARLOS TO FARALLÓN

Playa El Palmar, reached via San Carlos on the main highway, pulls in winds off the open sea. Its 10-foot (3 m) waves are nirvana for surfers; the **Palmar Point Surf Hotel** *(tel 240-8004; see p. 249)* doubles as a surf school. For a taste of laid-back fishing community culture, head to **Playa San Carlos** or **Playa Río Mar.** Southward,

Playa Santa Clara is one of the prettiest beaches and is well served by modest accommodations and seafood restaurants where you can dine beneath palms with your feet practically in the water.

Thrusting the gray sands of **Playa Farallón** into the "hot beach" limelight when it opened in 2000, the all-inclusive Royal

Taking out Noriega

The Decameron resort stands beside an abandoned U.S. airfield between the towns of Santa Clara and Río Hato, on the same beach as Gen. Manuel Noriega's erstwhile beach home. On December 20, 1989, U.S. Army Rangers dropped from the sky and gunships riddled the airfield as Operation Just Cause got under way. Two 500-pound (227 kg) bombs were dropped near the barracks to frighten Noriega's infamous Panamanian Defense Force into submission. (Later, the U.S. military announced the discovery of more than 110 pounds (50 kg) of "cocaine" in Noriega's home: It turned out to be a ground corn powder for making tamales.) The dictator's home is still derelict and riddled with bullet holes. ■

Decameron Beach Resort & Casino (see p. 261) is beloved of monied Panameños on weekends; day passes can be purchased. Beyond the resort, the sandy coastal track threads between rustic fishermen's shacks. Colorful *piraguas* are drawn up on the beach and fishing nets drape tree branches. Bubba Shrimp Fishing Tours *(tel 993-2740 or 6615-4740)* offers sportfishing aboard a converted shrimp boat from Playa Farallón. ■

Playa Farallón
⚠ 145 C3
Visitor information
✉ ANAM, Centro de Desarrollo Sostenible, Playa Farallón
☎ 993-3585

Penonomé's graceful Iglesia San Juan Bautista dominates the town's central plaza.

Penonomé & around

STRIKING FOR ITS CHARMING COLONIAL PLAZA PROVIDING a whitewashed waystation at the base of the Cordillera Central, otherwise hurly-burly Penonomé is a handy springboard for exploring the mountain parks that rise north and east.

Penonomé
 145 C3
Visitor information
☎ Autoridad Nacional del Ambiente (ANAM), 997-7538

Museo de Penonomé
✉ Calle San Antonio
☎ 997-8490
$ $

The provincial capital of Penonomé (pop. 16,000) was founded in 1581 as a *reducción de indios,* an area where Indians were resettled to form a pool for forced labor. Following destruction of the original Panama City in 1671, Penonomé—the name derives from Indian chief Nomé, executed by the Spaniards here—served as the capital of the isthmus until today's Casco Viejo (see p. 60) was built.

This prosperous agricultural town is known for its *sombreros pintados* (straw hats), which can be bought for $10 to $200, depending on quality, at the **Mercado de Artesanías Coclé** *(19 miles/31 km NE of Penonomé via Vía Sonadora)*—itself built in the shape of a *sombrero montuno.* Though the town whirls in a contemporary commercial vortex, it retains an exquisite colonial plaza: **Parque 8**

de Diciembre, shaded by blossoming flame trees and with a bandstand at its heart. The modest **Iglesia San Juan Bautista,** on the plaza's north side, boasts beautiful stained glass. Rising over the west side are the Gobernación (municipal government building) and a handsome police station in quasi-medieval style. A life-size bronze statue of Simón Bolívar gazes over the park, which extends south into an elongated plazuela studded by monuments and busts of former homeboy presidents Ramón M. Valdez (1867–1918), Harmodio Arias Madrid (1886–1962), and three-time president Arnulfo Arias (1901–1988).

The small **Museo de Penonomé,** in a row of four charming blue-and-white 18th-century cottages, has pre-

Columbian ceramics, colonial religious icons, and exhibits on local architecture and archaeology.

LA PINTADA

Fifteen miles (24 km) northwest of Penonomé, the agricultural town of La Pintada revolves around a pretty main square fringed by pines. Heady aromas emanate from **Cigarros Joyas de Panamá** *(tel 991-0013),* a simple hillside facility where 20 rollers use locally grown tobacco to produce 12 types of cigars. It's best to call a day or two ahead to arrange a tour. The factory, 400 yards (366 m) southwest of the plaza, has signposts in town.

In the center of town, the **Mercado de Artesanías de La Pintada** sells straw hats and *muñequitas* (dolls) dressed in folkloric clothes. Many of the hats originate in neighboring **Pedregosa**, where the entire community conjures magnificent sombreros from straw.

A rough road leads northwest from La Pintada to **El Copé,** gateway to rugged, remote **Parque Nacional Omar Torrijos** (see pp. 154–155). Continuing due north from La Pintada across the continental divide into Ngöbe-Buglé territory leads to **Molejón,** site of a huge gold-mining project opening veins once tapped by conquistadors.

TRINIDAD SPA & LODGE

Part of a macadamia farm and reforestation project now two decades old, this hilltop lodge (also known as Posada Ecológica del Cerro la Vieja; see p. 247) welcomes day visitors for birding, hiking, and soaks. The spa has stone-walled rooms with deep whirlpools filled with healing mineral waters. Its superlative setting in the **Serranía del Escaliche**—studded with soaring forest-tipped limestone peaks—is one of the finest birding sites in the country. Oropendolas… toucans…sparrow hawks… rufous-winged tanagers: Every blink of an eye brings something new.

The 800-yard-long (0.75 km) **Sendero Pozo Azul** winds through lush grounds full of native and exotic plants to a fish-filled lake and the *pozo azul* (blue well), where you can soak in cool mineral waters. A more

Woven from black and white palm fibers, locally made *sombreros montunos* range from coarse to so fine as to hold water.

demanding hike leads to the **Tavida waterfall,** tumbling 92 feet (28 m) into a natural pool; en route, you'll pass a huge rock carved with pre-Columbian pictographs. You can even hike or ride a mule through the mountains to El Valle de Antón (see p. 147). Armadillos, ocelots, white-faced monkeys, and poison dart frogs are among the creatures that scurry through the forests.

It's best to overnight here to fully appreciate the serenity broken only by a calliope of birdsong. That strange metallic *bonk?* The call of a three-wattled bellbird. You awaken to views of **Cerro La Vieja** peeking out from beneath its own blanket of mist. ■

Trinidad Spa & Lodge
www.posadaecologica.com
✉ 17 miles (27 km) NE of Penonomé via Carretera a Chiquirí Arriba
☎ 983-8900
$ $$–$$$$ depending on activity

Penonomé to Trinidad Spa drive

Break out your camera for this 32-mile-long (52 km) drive through the foothills of the Cordillera Central. It's a magnificent journey, with the scenery unfolding like a series of Hollywood stage sets. Dramatic mountains stud the landscape, their sheer-sided, often cloud-shrouded summits bewigged in riotous greens.

The small, whitewashed church next to a park in La Pintada is typical of the many *iglesias* that line this route.

Much of this journey is along a well-worn road that is badly potholed and even washed out in places. Though easily attempted by sedan, your backside will be glad for the more robust suspension provided by a four-wheel-drive vehicle.

Begin in the charming main plaza of **Penonomé ❶** (see pp. 150–151), departing via the road that begins on the square's northwest corner. Following the level valley of the Río Coclé, this wide, well-paved section gives a foretaste of the beauty that awaits as you pass through cattle country with sensuously rounded peaks in the distance to east, west, and ahead. After 9 miles (15 km) you arrive in **La Pintada ❷** (see p. 151), a small agricultural town lent beauty by the gleaming white **Iglesia de Candelaria.** A side road that begins beside the church leads east a short distance to **Charco Las Lavanderas,** natural pools whose waters are said to have healing powers.

Alternately, at the church plaza turn left and follow the signs that lead you 400 yards (366 m) southwest along a winding road to **Cigarros Joyas de Panamá** (see p. 151), a cigar factory selling quality smokes for a pittance.

Retrace your route to the center of La Pintada. Turn right in the center of town toward **Las Minas ❸** and follow the partially paved road as it bores into ever more rugged terrain. As you ascend eastward you might stop to admire the view west toward **Cerro Orari,** a flat-topped, sheer-walled mesa. The next few miles provide a stop-and-go selection of magnificent panoramas over forest-clad valleys and mountains—more than adequate compensation for the deteriorating state of the road.

Arriving in the community of **Toabré,** turn left at the crossroads for **Tambo ❹,** a twee village flanked on its west side by citrus plantations. Turn right beside the church in

Tambo. Less than 2 miles (3.2 km) along, you'll pass a charming **cemetery** (on the left) against a backdrop of scalloped mountain ridges. Dominating the scene is **Cerro Chichibalí,** a free-standing nipple of volcanic rock rising majestically to the northeast. The peak lords it over the community of **Miraflores ⑤,** with its lovely church—the **Iglesia de San José**—enfolded by pines.

The road (unpaved in places) descends through conifer forest and cattle pasture to **Churuquita Grande ⑥.** En route, the vistas open up through the trees, revealing lush valleys studded with spectacular limestone formations. Turn left at the junction with the paved road in Churuquita Grande. Coiling gradually upward, the road ascends a spur ridge to **Caimito,** graced by the charming little **Capilla Católica de la Medalla Milagrosa.** For the next few miles, the ridgetop route delivers an array of

views to leave you breathless. The road narrows and grows steeper. After 32 miles (52 km), you arrive at your destination, **Trinidad Spa & Lodge ⑦** (see pp. 151 & 247), hanging on the hillside with wide-angle views. ■

⊕ See area map p. 145
▶ Penomomé
⟳ 32 miles (52 km)
⏱ 2 hours
▶ Trinidad Spa & Lodge

NOT TO BE MISSED
- Iglesia de Candelaria, La Pintada
- Cigarros Joyas de Panamá
- Capilla Católica de la Medalla Milagrosa, Caimito
- Trinidad Spa & Lodge

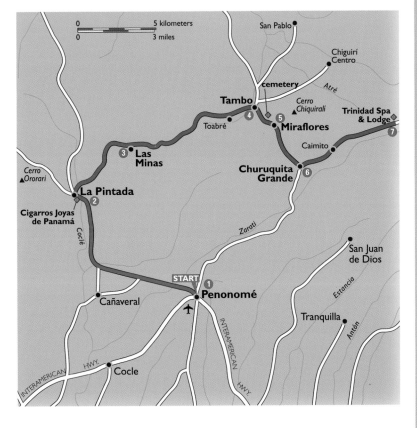

Parque Nacional Omar Torrijos

Parque Nacional Omar Torrijos
www.anam.gob.pa

🗺 145 B3 & C3

✉ 31 miles (50 km) NW of Penonomé; 5 miles (8 km) NW of El Copé

☎ 997-9089, 997-7538 (in Penonomé)

💲 $

SWADDLED IN MONTANE CLOUD FOREST ON ITS UPPER slopes, this rugged park teems with wildlife and, though facilities are meager, hikers and birders are amply rewarded with the chance of rare species sightings. A spiderweb of trails is well maintained by the U.S. Peace Corps.

Known commonly as El Copé (for the *copé* tree) and officially as Parque Nacional General de División Omar Torrijos Herrera, the 62,454-acre (25,275 ha) national park straddles the continental divide. Created in 1986, it is named for Panama's populist military leader Maj. Gen. Omar Torrijos, who fell in love with the area, sponsored local community programs, and was killed when his plane crashed here in foul weather on July 31, 1981 (remnants of the wreck can still be seen, a somber curiosity for bush-whacking hikers; it's a five-hour hike from the ranger station).

Tapirs

Mate an elephant with a pig and the result might resemble Baird's tapir (*Tapirus bairdii*), a corpulent mammal with short legs and a nose like a miniature trunk. This plant-eating forest dweller—the largest ter-restrial mammal in Central America—prefers to live near still water and can often be seen bathing in swamps. It has a keen sense of smell and good hearing. Adults have tough, bristly gray-brown skin; chestnut-brown calves are spotted and striped with white for camouflage. Their meat is considered a delicacy by hunters, who have brought the tapir to near extinction. ∎

The park protects the watersheds of the Bermejo and Marta Rivers on the Pacific slopes and those of the Blanco, Guabal, and Lajas Rivers on the Caribbean, which are deluged in rains. Mists that rise from the Caribbean Sea swirl ethereally through the forests that envelop the cool highland slopes—a habitat for the endangered immaculate antbird, golden-olive woodpecker, red-fronted parrotlet, and bare-necked umbrellabird, boasting a coiffure that would do Elvis proud. Panama's endangered golden frog hops around the forest floor. El Copé is also one of the last refuges in central Panama for the jaguar, puma, and tapir.

Parque Nacional Omar Torrijos can be reached from the Interamerican Highway, 10 miles (16 km) west of Penonomé. The paved road rises 16 miles (26 km) northward to the village of El Copé, from which a rugged track leads uphill to the **ANAM ranger station.** A four-wheel-drive is essential. A half-mile (0.7 km) hike beyond, the simple breeze-swept **Altos del Calvario Visitor Center** (with basic explanations on local ecology) is poised on a ridge with a vista toward the Caribbean through glass walls.

An easily hiked **interpretative trail** begins at the visitor center and takes about one hour round-trip; another short trail leads to a mountaintop mirador with magnificent vistas. More rugged trails lead to the remote hamlet of **La Rica,** the **Chorros de Tife** cascades, and the summits of **Cerro Marta** and **Cerro Peña Blanca.** Seasoned hikers can even trek to the Caribbean (a guide and sufficient provisions are essential).

A simple dorm with kitchen, lounge, and bunks is available, and camping is permitted. Bring warm clothing for chilly nights. The local Asociación de Guías can provide guides ($5 to $10 per person).

Midway between El Copé and the park entrance, the local community of **Barrigón** has established the Barrigón Grupo Boca, which offers bird guides and simple accommodations. ■

Torrential rainfall feeds magnificent cascades in Parque Nacional Omar Torrijos.

Aguadulce
 145 C2

Ingenio de Azúcar Santa Rosa
✉ 1 mile (1.6 km) N of El Roble, 15 miles (24 km) W of Aguadulce
☎ 987-8101
🕐 Closed Sat., Sun., & Mon.; 24-hour notice required

Aguadulce & around

LONG KNOWN AS A CENTER FOR SALT AND SUGAR production and for shrimp farming, Aguadulce occupies the flatlands of Coclé Province. Birders will thrill to migratory whimbrels and other waders in coastal wetlands, while the nearby Natá and El Caño hark back to the colonial and pre-Columbian past.

An important industrial town in the midst of an otherwise semiarid plain, Aguadulce, 115 miles (185 km) west of Panama City, is surrounded by lime-green sugarcane fields dusted by delicate white blossoms in spring. During the December-to-April sugar harvest, smoke-smudged field-hands in rough straw sombreros slash at the charred stalks with glinting machetes, and trucks trundle down the highway, dropping longs stalks of cut cane as they go. Then, too, **Ingenio de Azúcar Santa Rosa,** the Santa

Rosa Sugar Refinery, operates around the clock and black smoke rises in twirling tornadoes, tainting the air with the stench of molasses. Visitors may take a tour, which includes the original mill-owner's home with period furniture.

In town, the heart of affairs is **Plaza 19 de Octubre,** an unassuming square with the **Iglesia de San Juan Bautista** on its north side. The **Museo Regional Stella Sierra** (formerly the Museo de la Sal y el Azucar), in a quaint two-story mansion dating from 1925, contains period

furniture, stone axes, and other pre-Columbian artifacts, plus a tiny sugar press and other simple exhibits relating to the salt and sugar industries. The main drag has a median with a **monument of Rodolfo Chiari** (1869–1937), a local boy and president of Panama 1924–28, at its north end.

East of town, salt pans (*salinas*) abandoned a decade ago recall the days when Aguadulce was a major salt producer. Adjoining shrimp ponds deliver juicy plump jumbo shrimp to restaurants throughout the country. The pans and ponds merge into brackish marshes and mangroves lining the shore of the **Bahía de Parita.** The **Aguadulce wetlands** are an important breeding ground for herons, wood storks, roseate spoonbills, and other stilt-legged waders jabbing with long beaks for exposed bugs. At high tide, locals love to splash

around in four pools—**Las Piscinas**—built into rocks surrounded by the oozy mudflats.

NATÁ DE LOS CABALLEROS & NEARBY

Exquisite in the quietude of its central colonial plaza, Natá, founded in 1517 and named for a local Indian chief of the time, lures visitors to its lovely church in the leafy main square. Begun in 1522, the **Basílica Menor de Santiago Apóstol** is the second oldest church in the Americas. Its simple, whitewashed facade ripples like notes in a fugue. Within, the main altar is adorned with fruits and flowers crawling with feathered serpents, the work of Indian carvers. Note, too, the simple beamed ceiling, the painting of the Holy Trinity, and the statue of the patron saint holding a Spanish flag in his hand. If the church is locked, ask around and the caretaker can usually be found to open up; he may even let you ascend the single bell tower for a Quasimodo-style view over town.

The **Parque y Museo Arqueológico El Caño,** 5 miles (9 km) northeast of Natá, is worth a quick browse. Site of the nation's most abundant concentration of pre-Columbian discoveries, this ancient ceremonial center and burial ground found in 1924 covers 20 acres (8 ha) and dates back 5,000 years. A row of Stonehenge-like stone stellae that rise from the meadow march enigmatically into the past. A burial site displays five skeletons in situ, curled in fetal positions and even stuffed into jars. Blocks of stone inscribed with anthropomorphic images, a reproduction of a *cacique*'s hut, and a small colonial-era-style museum displaying ceramics, stone axes, and so forth, are among the attractions. ■

Museo Regional Stella Sierra

✉ Calle Fábrica Final, Aguadulce

☎ 997-4280

⊕ Closed Sun. & Mon.

$ $

Parque y Museo Arqueológico El Caño

http://ciudad.latinol.com /chicasusma/

✉ 2 miles (3.2 km) N of Interamerican Hwy., 17 miles (27 km) W of Penonomé

☎ 987-9352

⊕ Closed Mon.

$ $

Santiago de Veraguas

Santiagao de Veraguas

 145 B2

Visitor information

http://visitpanama.com

✉ IPAT, Ave. Héctor A. Santa Coloma, Plaza Palermo

☎ 998-3929

Museo Regional de Veraguas

✉ Calle 2da at Ave. Juan Demóstenes Arosemena

☎ 998-4543

🕒 Closed Sat. & Sun.

$ $

Pilgrims flock to the Iglesia Atalaya in Atalaya, southeast of Santiago, during the first Sunday in Lent to beseech miracles of a wooden Christ figure.

A BUSTLING COMMERCIAL HUB MARKING THE MIDWAY point between Panama City and Costa Rica on the Interamerican Highway, Santiago delivers a trio of appealing sites.

Santiago, 155 miles (249 km) west of Panama City, was founded in 1632. Today it is a thriving commercial and agricultural center. Broad Avenida Central unrolls past the **Mercado Artesanal de la Peña**—a good place to choose your *sombrero pintado*—to **Parque Juan Demóstenes Arosemena.** The plaza is graced by a bas-relief monument to the Santiago-born writer and politician (1879–1936) who died the year he was elected president of Panama.

Occupying a reproduction of the town's former jail, the **Museo Regional de Veraguas** has exhibits ranging from fossils of giant sloths to a re-creation of a pre-Columbian excavation site.

Santiago's crown jewel is the **Escuela Normal Superior Juan Demóstenes Arosemena** *(Calle 6ta, tel 998-4295)*, a teacher-

training facility from the 1920s. This historical monument features an elaborate plateresque portal and masterful murals in the main hall by local artist Roberto Lewis.

BEYOND TOWN

The quiet little village of **San Francisco de la Montaña,** 10 miles (16 km) north of Santiago, was founded in 1671 and draws pilgrims nationwide to the **Iglesia San Francisco de la Montaña.** This simple stone church, erected in 1727 and recently restored, contains exquisite frescoes and statues. The baroque altar is ornately carved with scenes from the Scriptures fused into elements of Indian folklore. Another delightful church, the **Igleslia Atalaya** in Atalaya, 5 miles (8 km) southeast of Santiago, is remarkable for its painted windows and vaulted ceilings. ■

Santa Fé & around

A ROLLER-COASTER ROAD ASCENDS FROM SANTIAGO INTO a dramatic mountain world of tumbling streams and rivers suitable for white-water rafting. Superlative birding and hiking originate from the delightful end-of-the-road hamlet of Santa Fé, known for orchids, fine coffee, and vibrant Ngöbe-Buglé peoples.

Santa Fé
🗺 145 B3

Tucked into a valley at a crisp 1,542 feet (470 m) of elevation in the shadow of **Cerro Tute,** only a few miles below the continental divide, sleepy Santa Fé has a springlike quality. Pines scent the alpine air. The climate is refreshing. And nature is never far away. This simple hamlet is laid out higgledy-piggledy, with a warren of narrow lanes snaking up and down the pine-studded hillsides without any semblance of order. (Note that there's no gas station between Santiago and Santa Fé, a distance of 33 miles/53 km).

The settlement was founded in 1557 by conquistador Francisco Vásquez to be near the gold mines. The Spanish met fierce resistance from Indians led by warrior chieftain Urracá, commemorated today on Panama's 1 centavo coin. The indigenous presence is still strong. Ngöbe Indian women in their bright dresses can often be seen gathered around the grassy pine-fringed plaza or selling their *chácaras*, plus hand-stitched clothing and other handicrafts, at the nearby **Mercado Agrícola y Artesanal Santa Fé.**

The hamlet is known for its orchids, grown enthusiastically by local amateur gardeners. Village mayor Berta Castrellón, former president of the Asociación de Orquideología de Panamá, opens her garden—**Orquideario y Cultivos Las Fragrancias de Santa Fé**—to visitors. You're welcome to push open the gate to her ridgetop home on the northeast

side of town. Dogs dance at your feet as you peruse the more than 260 species blooming on every branch and hanging in coconut shells from trellises. August is the best time to visit; the flowers are in their most riotous bloom and Santa Fé hosts an annual three-day orchid festival. The road past the orquideario leads down to the **Río Mulabá,** where inner tubes can be rented for idle float trips.

Aromas of fresh-roasted coffee draw you to **Café El Tute** *(980 feet/300 m N of the plaza, tel 954-0801, closed Sun.),* a tiny *beneficio* (roasting plant) where you can watch organically grown coffee fresh from the fields being sun-dried, husked, and roasted. Run as a local *campesino* (peasant) cooperative, Esperanza de los Campesinos employs mostly indigenous families on land once owned by wealthy absentee landlords. (The Colombian priest

Workers bag fresh coffee at Café El Tute in Santa Fé.

Orquideario y Cultivos Las Fragrancias de Santa Fé
✉ 100 yards (91 m) N and 400 yards (366 m) E of the plaza
☎ 954-0910
💲 By donation

Surrounded by pristine mountains, bucolic Santa Fé is a magnet for birders, hikers, and lovers of orchids.

Parque Nactional Santa Fé de Veraguas

🗺 145 B3

Visitor information

www.anam.gob.pa

☎ 998-4271 or 500-0855

who established the cooperative in the 1960s was murdered for overturning this feudal system.)

PARQUE NACIONAL SANTA FÉ DE VERAGUAS

The town is surrounded by mountains that tempt hikers and birders to seek out trails through the montane wet forest and cloud forests of this 280-square-mile (725 sq km) national park, created in 2001 to protect a vital corridor for a wealth of wildlife: agoutis, anteaters, deer, and even jaguars and tapirs. The more than 400 bird species recorded here include olivaceous woodpeckers, spectacled ant-pittas, slaty-capped flycatchers, and others whose names you may forget but whose beauty you will forever remember. The **Panama Audubon Society** *(tel 232-5977, www.panamaaudubon .org)* runs birdwatching trips. Dedicated birder Berta Castrellón acts as a guide (contact the Audubon Society).

A trail up **Alto de Piedra** is signed in town; the track (accessible to four-wheel-drive vehicles) is usually muddy but the effort is well rewarded as you ascend past *cafetales*—coffee farms—into forest full of birdsong. Another trail ascends to the summit of **Cerro Tute,** where mists play amid cloud forests. (This once made a perfect cover for a band of revolutionary guerrillas that, inspired by the success of the Cuban revolution, aimed in 1959 to topple the Panamanian government.) You can even cross the continental divide via the saddle between 4,633-foot (1,412 m) **Cerro Cabeza de Toro** and 4,980-foot (1,518 m) **Cerro Negro,** then drop down through the bejungled valley of the Río Calovébora to the Caribbean hamlet of Calovébora. However, this two-day hike is no piece of cake; a knowledgeable guide is essential. These trails can also be tackled on horseback by arrangement at the Hotel Santa Fé (see p. 249).

The area is threatened by plans to build a hydroelectric dam, while a wind turbine farm is slated for Cerro Tute. ∎

Golfo de Montijo

A MARVELOUS REPOSITORY OF AVIAN FAUNA AT THE MOUTH of the San Pablo and San Pedro Rivers, the watery world of the Montijo Gulf supports not only large flocks of waterfowl but also crocodiles and mammals. Waves crashing onto beaches along the southern shores are nirvana to surfers. This region is as poor as any in Panama, and simple fishing villages eke out a living from the sea.

Golfo de Montijo

🗺 145 A1 & B1

Wrapped in mangroves and marshy wetlands, the isle-studded gulf encompasses the **Humedal Golfo de Montijo** (Gulf of Montijo Wetlands), approximately 541 square miles (1,401 sq km) of coastal maritime ecosystems that include extensive tidal mudflats and the gulf waters between the east and west shores. The area—declared an Internationally Important Wetland under the Ramsar Convention—is a vital wintering area for whimbrels, short-billed dowitchers, willets, and other migratory shorebirds. Such nationally threatened species as bare-throated tiger herons, black-bellied whistling ducks, and muscovy ducks wade and waddle in large numbers, and pelicans and frigate birds are among the high roosters. Crocodiles and caimans bask motionless on the mud.

Access to the east-shore wetlands is by a new all-weather road running south via **Mariato** to the tiny fishing hamlet of **El Varadero,** gateway to Parque Nacional Cerro Hoya (see p. 185). Surf crashes into scalloped bays: **Playa Morrillo** has one of the most powerful beach breaks. Behind, copper-colored mountains loom massively over the dancing blue sea. The road climbs over headlands, drops into secret valleys, and offers magnificent views westward over the Pacific Ocean and **Isla Cébaco.**

The gulf waters boil with bonito and billfish. **Río Negro Sport**

Fishing Lodge (see p. 247), at Mariato, focuses on fishing around Isla Cébaco and Punta Mariato. Coiba Adventure Sportfishing *(tel 999-8108, www.coibadventure .com)* offers fishing trips to Isla Coiba and the Hannibal Banks from **Puerto Mutis,** a small, flyblown port at the head of the gulf 18 miles (29 km) southwest of Santiago.

On the west shore, a rolling road penetrates to **Playa Santa Catalina.** A funky favorite of the backpacking, surfing crowd, Santa Catalina has the buzz of a region that is on the cusp of realizing its tourism potential. Santa Catalina Boat Tours *(www.santacatalinaboattours.com)* offers surfing and snorkeling tours. Buses run twice daily from Soná on the Interamerican Highway. Immediately east, **Playa El Estero** edges to the tip of the peninsula at **Punta Brava.** ∎

Dawn breaks over fishing boats in Puerto Mutis, a launch point for vessels setting out for Isla Coiba.

Parque Nacional Isla Coiba

**Parque Nacional
Isla Coiba**

www.anam.gob.pa

⚠ 145 A1

✉ By private charter
flight or boat
from Puerto Mutis
(3 hrs.)

☎ 998-4871 ext. 15

$ $$

CENTRAL AMERICA'S LARGEST MARINE PARK ENCIRCLES rain-forest-clad Isla Coiba and offers spectacular snorkeling, diving, and sportfishing in warm waters. Renowned until recently as a remote penal colony, the isle has a new focus on ecotourism.

Coiba National Park encompasses 39 islands, including ox-jaw-shaped, 194-square-mile (502 sq km) Isla Coiba, the largest island in Panama. (The island is reachable only by boat from Puerto Mutis, by cruise ship, or by charter plane.) Virgin rain forest smothers 85 percent of the isle—a Noah's Ark where crocodiles slosh about in the estuarine muds and howler and white-faced monkeys cavort in the trees. This howler monkey is a sub-species endemic to Coiba, as are 21 of its 147 bird species, including the brown-and-white Coiba spinetail. Coiba is a last refuge for the endangered crested eagle. And Panama's largest nesting colony of scarlet macaws congregates at **Barco Quebrado.** You're sure to see them flying at night in pairs, squawking to their mates.

In 1918 the Panamanian government converted Isla Coiba into a Panamanian version of Devil's Island. The unfenced prison has been phased out, although a few dozen prisoners remain and hiking unescorted isn't wise. Hiking is currently limited to the vicinity of the **ANAM ranger station** and **biological research station,** tucked into a sandy cove in the island's northeast; a small natural history exhibit features pickled snakes and even the skeleton of a humpback whale. Duplex cabins can be rented by reservation. **Sendero del Observatorio—** a 20-minute amble—leads to an elevated mirador, with views toward Isla Coibita. **Sendero de**

los Monos (Monkey Trail), accessed by a 20-minute boat ride from the ranger station, is good for monkey sightings and provides an exhilarating one-hour loop as howlers and capuchin monkeys charge along branches overhead.

At **Granito de Oro,** you can wade in off a golden beach beneath rocky headlands to snorkel with green and hawksbill turtles and harmless nurse sharks. Local tour operators in the Golfo de Montijo (see p. 161) offer visits.

On the east side of the main island, the reefs of **Bahía Damas** spread across 334 acres (135 ha), making them the largest reef system in Central America. A kaleidoscope of dotted, dappled, and zebra-striped fish dart in and out of spectacular coral reefs encircling jagged undersea pinnacles. Humpback whales, Cuvier's beaked whales, pilot whales, sperm whales, and even orcas slice through these waters. Giant manta rays and sharks—hammerhead, tiger, white-tip, and harmless whale sharks—are also common, as are marlin, sailfish, and tuna. Sportfishing is permitted, and the **Hannibal Bank,** between Isla Coiba and Isla Montuosa, is especially favored.

The small, uninhabited **Islas Contreras,** northwest of Isla Coiba, are beloved of yachters in search of untamed places. Coconut palms shade sheltered coves with blazing white sands backed by dense forest. A submerged rock called **Sombrero de Pelo** is rated world-class for dives. ∎

**Opposite:
Warmly inviting,
the waters
around Isla
Granito de Oro
are a snorkeling
nirvana.**

Playground for whales

Panama's offshore waters have enough whale excitement to outdo Marine World. The warm tropical oceans and shallows draw dozens of species of dolphins and larger cetaceans. Some are seasonal visitors that can dependably be seen at predictable times of the year. Others are year-round dwellers.

Although humpback whales and, occasionally, other whale species can be seen off the Caribbean seaboard, the prime Panamanian habitats for cetaceans are the waters surrounding Isla Coiba and Las Perlas archipelago. The sweeping action of nearby Pacific equatorial currents scoops up oceanic nutrients from the deep, resulting in a rich supply of planktonic soup and shoaling fish. The warm, clear waters off Panama, Colombia, and Costa Rica are also perfect for breeding and calving.

Humpbacks from the southeast Pacific summer in the cold oceans off the south coast of Chile, where they gorge themselves on Antarctic krill. As winter approaches, they migrate north to their tropical breeding and birthing grounds in the gulfs of Panama and Chiriquí. The first animals begin arriving in June, their slow progress betrayed by explosive exhalations of breath. By October, they begin heading back to southern Pacific waters. Humpback whales—identifiable by their elongated jaws, white underbellies, and long pectoral fins—are felicitous lovers. Promiscuous, too. Males push and shove each other to mate with a female in heat, while the females commonly mate with several males in succession. Nonetheless, during copulation, much tender touching takes place. The subsequent year, pregnant females return to the same waters to give birth to their 2,500-pound (1,150 kg) offspring and about one month later are in estrus again.

Bryde's whales, fin whales, pilot whales, four species of beaked whale, and even blue whales—at up to 150 tons (136 metric tons), the largest creatures on Earth—are also seen in Panamanian waters. While they prefer deeper oceanic surroudings, North Atlantic blue whales have even been reported off San Cristóbal, near the eastern terminus of the Panama Canal. Pods of orcas can be seen at certain times of year around Isla Coiba and the Gulf of Panama. Like humpbacks, orcas (the largest members of the dolphin family) visit during annual feeding and breeding migrations. Almost always traveling in groups related by birth, these "wolves of the sea" come into Panamanian waters to hunt prey, such as smaller dolphins. They are easily distinguished

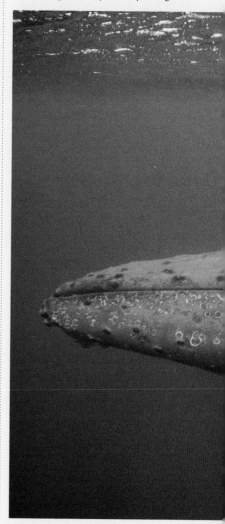

by their tall, sharply pointed dorsal fins, and black bodies streamlined for speedy attacks, with a distinctive white saddle and eye patch.

Close encounters of the first kind are virtually guaranteed on whale-watching trips, especially during summer months, when male humpbacks' songs haunt the oceans and resonate through the hull of your boat. A special thrill is the sight of a massive whale surging out of the water. Most whale species make Herculean leaps, even pirouetting midair like ballet dancers before crashing down with an explosive splash that echoes across the water like the boom of distant artillery. Experts are baffled by this spectacular behavior.

Panama's environmental authorities recently declared Las Perlas archipelago a marine corridor and have joined forces with the Smithsonian Tropical Research Institute (STRI) to protect the whales and draft appropriate whale-watching guidelines. ∎

Birthed in Panama's warm waters, this juvenile humpback will accompany its mother throughout its first year.

More places to visit in Central Panama

GOLFO DE LOS MOSQUITOS

One of Panama's last frontiers, the Caribbean coast of Veraguas borders the well-named Golfo de los Mosquitos. Isolated by thick jungle, the region is reachable only by boat or rugged jungle trails over the continental divide. Almost no one passes this way, and there are many miles of desolate coast between scant habitations populated by Afro-Antillean *playeros* (beach people)—descendants of Africans sent to work the 16th-century gold mines of Veraguas. It is possible to hike the coast from **Coclé del Norte** (site for **Las Bahías,** a nascent ecological tourism project) to **Belén** (with a statue of rebel Indian chief Quibián), and from there to **Calovébora.** Scrambling over rocks, trudging beaches, fording rivers—it is exhausting going, and only for well-provisioned Indiana Jones types with a guide armed with machete. The rugged, rain-sodden hinterland is cut through by rivers. Much remains unexplored. Trails that begin in Santa Fé (see p. 159), Parque Nacional Omar Torrijos (see pp. 154–155), and Molejón penetrate the jungled valleys to these isolated coast settlements, from which irregular supply boats connect to Colón. Tourist services are few. Las Bahías, at the remote hamlet of Coclé del Norte, offers simple accommodations and makes a good base for exploring. Boats connect Coclé del Norte to Gobea, in Colón Province. Alternately, take a bus from Penonomé (see p. 150) to Coclesito, then rent a cayuco for the five-hour journey downriver. January through March is best for traveling.

🗺 145 A4 & B4

LAS PALMAS

The sleepy village of Las Palmas in the hills of southwest Veraguas Province once lay along the old Pan-American Highway. Now a little-trafficked back road, the badly deteriorated route is a rolling ride offering magnificent scenery as it sidles south to **Soná** (a four-wheel-drive vehicle is recommended). One minute you're hanging onto the hillside looking down over verdant meadows; the next you're scrambling up a forested mountainside or bouncing along old metal bridges suspended over profound ravines. A dirt road leads from Las Palmas cemetery to a gorge where **El Salto,** a waterfall (accessed by an improved road), kicks up a fine spray and is perfect for cooling swims and a picnic. The cascade is the node of a 6,172-acre (2,498 ha) **Área Natural Recreativa,** although there are no facilities.

🗺 145 A2 ✉ 35 miles (56 km) W of Santiago via Interamerican Hwy., then 7 miles (11 km) S

TANGLEWOOD WELLNESS CENTER

A sanctuary for health-focused travelers, this health and fasting retreat on 17 acres (7 ha) of mountainside is surrounded by lush gardens and lawns opening to fabulous rock formations and stunning vistas. It's a magnificent setting to detoxify or simply relax, regroup, and rejuvenate. Health workshops and seminars are hosted here, and you can indulge in Reiki treatments (a Japanese technique for stress reduction and relaxation). A bed-and-breakfast hotel with zen touches is being added.

🗺 145 D3 ✉ Sorá, 9 miles (14.5 km) NW of Bejuco, off the Interamerican Hwy. ☎ 6671-9965 or U. S. 301-637-4657, www.tanglewood wellnesscenter.com ∎

Gold fever

When Columbus visited the Veraguas region in 1502, he met Indians who wore breastplates of gold. The gold fever that drew Columbus is still alive and well. Gold-bearing veins and fluvial gravels are common on the Caribbean slopes of Coclé Province, and the mines established by Spanish conquistadors have opened and closed over the centuries as the price of gold rose and fell. Small-time *oreros* still sift alluvial gravel at *lavaderos* in the soupy rivers, seeking their pot of gold at the end of the rainbow, while the mammoth Molejón Gold Project will tap a recently discovered vein containing an estimated 893,000 ounces of gold. ∎

Home to cowboy towns simmering with sentimental allure, the heartland of folkloric tradition beckons visitors to its festivals and pockets of colonial charm. Offshore isles are prime nesting sites for marine turtles, and coastal wetlands offer prime birding.

Azuero Peninsula

A *diablito* (devil) mask, Los Santos

Christian traditions remain strong throughout Panama in churches such as Santo Domingo in Los Santos.

Azuero Peninsula

AZUERO, COMPRISING LOS SANTOS AND HERRERA PROVINCES, HAS A beguilingly enigmatic appeal wholly unique in the nation. Remarkably overlooked by tourists, this 2,941-square-mile (7,616 sq km) trapezoid of land extending into the Pacific Ocean is considered the soul of the nation. Nowhere else in the country seems so antique as Azuero, with its creaky museums, whitewashed churches, and exquisite colonial homes in calming pastels. Life moves at a nostalgic pace. The clip-clop of horses' hooves echoes down streets lined with red-tile-roofed row houses, especially lovely at dawn and dusk, when sunlight gilds their timeworn facades.

This is Panama's dry quarter, hot as Hades in summer with the sun beating down hard as a hammer. Once a lush paradise, Azuero was deforested during the course of two centuries to make way for cattle. The barren wasteland of Parque Nacional Sarigua, in the extreme northeast, shows the ravaging long-term effect on the land. Mountainous western Azuero is much greener, but slash-and-burn agriculture still gnaws away at the forests. The peninsula is cowboy country par excellence. Men on *paso fino* horses, lassos at their sides, add an

intriguing appeal to the savanna landscape speckled by broad trees that in spring and summer explode in riotous colors.

Azuero is proud of its heritage. Almost every male above rap-appreciation age dons a *sombrero montuno* (see sidebar p. 186), the traditional straw hat that is an integral part of the national costume. Hat weaving is a local tradition, with Ocú the main center. Pottery is fired in old-fashioned adobe ovens in towns such as La Arena. And entire communities, such as Guararé and San José, keep *pollera* lace-making traditions alive.

The region is famed for its festive spirit: Azuero hosts more than 500 festivals yearly, when the streets are full of young ladies exquisitely dressed in polleras. Pre-Lenten Carnaval celebrations draw thousands of visitors from around the country. And every community devotes a day to its patron saint.

The inhabitants are almost wholly of Spanish heritage, with virtually no indigenous or African mixture. Despite this, the oldest archaeological sites in the nation are found along the eastern seaboard, where precious mangrove habitats gird mudflats that support profuse birdlife. A string of wildlife refuges protects the rookeries and feeding grounds. Farther east, Refugio de Vida Silvestre Isla Cañas is one of the hemisphere's prime marine turtle nesting sites. And snorkelers and scuba divers are rapturous about Refugio de Vida Silvestre Isla Iguana's coral reefs, which are surrounded by warm waters where

humpback whales gather to breed.

Two roads penetrate the peninsula from the Interamerican Highway. The easterly Carretera Nacional begins at Divisa and unfurls along a flat coastal plain, connecting one old-fashioned town to another. The more westerly route runs through the heart of Azuero, linking Ocú to Tonosí. Dipping and rising along the eastern flank of rugged mountains, this route passes through hamlets of simple rustic *bohíos* (huts) of adobe and thatch. No roads span the mountains, and the narrow coastal plain on the western side lies a world away in Veraguas Province.

There are relatively few tourist facilities or hotels and even fewer restaurants outside the towns. Reserve accommodations well in advance during festivals. Large-scale hotel investment has started near the beaches and there are plans to turn former president Mireya Moscoso's private airstrip near Pedasí into a public airport. ■

Worshipers receive communion at Santo Domingo church during the Corpus Christi festival in Los Santos.

Chitré & around

CAST IN A QUINTESSENTIAL COLONIAL TIME WARP, THE towns of northeast Azuero boast whitewashed churches and a miscellany of modest attractions. While the beaches—popular with locals—have limited appeal, the shoreline wetlands teem with migratory and nesting birds.

Chitré
🗺 169 B3
Visitor information
✉ IPAT, Circunvalación La Arena, Chitré
☎ 974-4532

Museo de Herrera
✉ Calle Manuel María Correa & Ave. Julio Arjona, Chitré
☎ 996-0077
🕐 Closed Sun. & Mon.
💲 $

CHITRÉ

The largest urban center, Chitré is a whirlwind of modern commercialism surrounding a colonial core. The town, founded in 1848 and named for an Indian *cacique,* is graced by row houses with red tile roofs, fronted by iron-studded doors and twirled wood window grills.

The leafy **Parque Unión** is highlighted by a *glorieta* (bandstand) and busts of local heroes. Casting cool shadows over the square, the **Catedral de San Juan Bautista** (built from 1896 to 1910) has a fabulous gilt-and-mahogany altar, plus lovely stained-glass windows adorning an otherwise simple interior. The building shows few hints of being a

postcolonial creation.

Housed in a merchant's mansion that later served as the town post office, the small **Museo de Herrera** traces the history of Azuero back to the antediluvian dawn. A mammoth fossil, pre-Columbian pottery and *huacas* (gold ornaments), and even a skeleton of a cacique buried with gold are among the highlights. The upstairs room displays polleras and devil costumes. Sala Herrera is dedicated to the history of Chitré.

Playa El Agallito, 4 miles (7 km) north of Chitré, is one of Panama's prime birding sites. Vast mudflats extending more than a mile out to sea are exposed at low tide, when spoonbills, terns, egrets, pharalopes, stilts, and other shorebird species flock in their thousands, long bills stabbing the silt for tasty morsels while humans poke in the mud for *concha negra* clams. Many of the birds migrate from as far afield as Alaska and Argentina. At high tide, the birds hop over to the adjacent pond-pocked salt marshes. Biologist Francisco Delgado *(tel 996-1725)* will happily guide you through the area—a tip is in order.

The Río La Villa marks the divide between Chitré and Los Santos Provinces and between their twin namesake towns.

VILLA DE LOS SANTOS

Founded in 1557, Los Santos—the "town of the saints"—is dear to Panamanians' hearts. The *grito de la Villa* ("Scream of Los Santos") emanated from here on November 10, 1821, launching the revolution that culminated 18 days later in independence from Spanish rule. The event is celebrated every year, and Panama's president flies in for the festivities.

The old town's compact main square, **Plaza Simón Bolívar,** features busts of the South American hero, as well as of José Vallarino (1792–1865), a local lad who rose to become General of the Royal Vault. The plaza is dominated by the **Iglesia de San Atanasio,** dating from 1782. Its simple wooden interior, painted white, features a baroque gilt altar and walls embedded with a plaque of former priests interred within, plus rococo altar screens and a retable that pre-date the church. The life-size wooden figure of Christ in the glass sepulcher is paraded by candlelight on Good Friday.

The jewel in the local crown is the **Museo de la Nacionalidad,** in an 18th-century building where the nation's Declaration of

Independence was signed in 1821. Painted in a delightful yellow, white, and turquoise combo, it is original in every regard, with walls of reed and adobe and well-worn terra-cotta floors. The charming gabled home opens to a beautiful courtyard with mortar and pestle, the remains of an old cart, and a reproduction of a traditional colonial country kitchen with clay *horno* (oven). Despite its diminutive size, this exquisite museum focusing on the quest for

independence from Spain and the eventual creation of a nation is the region's most appealing. Exhibits include a collection of pistols, sabers, and muskets. The Instituto Nacional de Cultura's **Centro de Estudios Superiores de Folklore Dora Pérez de Zárate** *(Calle Vallarino, Plaza Simón Bolívar, tel 966-8334)*—a school for students of folklore—can be visited by appointment.

The town is renowned for its festival of Corpus Christi (May/June, see sidebar p. 173), lasting two weeks and featuring more than 100 performers in various costume; *día del turismo* (tourism day) condenses all the festivities into one day.

Important archaeological finds are being unearthed at **Sitio**

Museo de la Nacionalidad

✉ Calle José Vallarino, Villa de Los Santos

☎ 966-8192

🕐 Closed Sun. & Mon.

💲 $

Pre-Columbian ceramics are prized exhibits at the Museo de la Nacionalidad in Los Santos.

Participants in the Corpus Christi festival, which takes place over two weeks in May and June, break for lunch.

Arqueológico Cerro Juan Díaz *(tel 966-7898, e-mail: cooker@naos.si.edu)* on a hill 3 miles (5 km) from Los Santos. The most important pre-Columbian burial site yet found in Panama, it dates back more than 2,000 years.

PARITA

This quintessential 18th-century colonial charmer, 6 miles (10 km) northwest of Chitré, takes you back in time. The streets are lined with single-story adobe dwellings, each painted in two-tone pastels. In the heat of mid-afternoon the village is surreally quiet.

At its heart is a small park where mock bullfights are held during the town's patron saint festival in early August. On its east side, the **Iglesia de Santo Domingo de Guzmán** dates from 1656; its steeple sparkles with mother-of-pearl. While otherwise appearing quite simple, its interior has an elaborately carved pulpit plus three lavish baroque altars, including a main altar supported by serpents. Silver candelabras and other religious icons gleam in the tiny **Museo de Arte Religioso Colonial** *(closed Sat. & Sun.)* in the adjoining chapel.

Devil dancers

The *danza de los diablos* (dance of the devils) is performed during Los Santos's Corpus Christi festival and is highlighted by the fight between *diablos sucios* (dirty devils), representing evil, and the *diablo blanco* (white devil, alias Archangel Michael), representing good. The diablos sucios don red-and-black-striped jumpsuits, red capes, and papier-mâché masks adorned with macaw feathers, usually representing demons or animals. Recalling pagan festivities, the dance can be traced back to Spain. ■

Parita
 169 B3

Parque Nacional Sarigua
www.anam.gob.pa
169 B3
6 miles (10 km) NE of Parita
996-7675
$

Refugio de Uso Múltiple Ciénaga de la Macana
www.anam.gob.pa
1.2 miles (2 km) of El Rincón, 12 miles (20 km) N of Parita

PARQUE NACIONAL SARIGUA

With lunar landscapes evocative of the Sahara, this park encompasses a dramatically sculpted arid environment that makes a stark contrast to the distant backdrop of lush green mountains. Tracts of rare dry forest pock the fragile ecosystem, a devastating legacy of slash-and-burn agriculture during the past 100 years. Stripped of vegetation for cattle farms, the thin tropical soils were soon blown and washed away, leaving an infertile wasteland of rocks, wind-tossed sands, and deeply eroded gullies.

Though terrestrial wildlife is scarce, more than 160 bird species (mostly migratory) flock to salty lagoons and mangroves that fringe the shore. Pre-Columbian settlements dating back 11,000 years (older than anywhere else on the isthmus) have been found, though there is no excavation site to explore. A mirador at the **ANAM ranger station** provides sweeping views. Time your visit for the cool morning hours; afternoons can be insufferably hot.

Fully 50 percent of the 20,000-acre (8,000 ha) national park comprises marine environment extending 6 miles (9.5 km) from shore. Commercial shrimp farms can be visited.

BIRDS OF A FEATHER

Take your pick from a fistful of nature reserves protecting vitally important bird habitats in the Bahía de Parita—second only to the Bahía de Panamá for the quantity and variety of migratory shorebirds. At 5,000 acres (2,000 ha), **Refugio de Uso Múltiple Ciénaga de la Macana** is the

Refugio de Vida Silvestre Cenegón del Mangle

www.anam.gob.pa

 4 miles (6 km) E of Paris, 6 miles (10 km) N of Parita

largest freshwater wetland in Azuero and the only known breeding site in Panama for fulvous whistling ducks and killdeer. Extending along the floodplain of the Río Santa María, its marshes surround a small lake covered with floating water hyacinths. Limpkins strut about, scavenging for snails,

Cerro Mangote, a shell midden, dates back at least 7,000 years. The enthusiastic and knowledgeable ranger offers guided walks (a tip is in order). The turnoff is marked by signs at the junction for Paris, 10 miles (16 km) south from the Interamerican Highway; a four-wheel-drive vehicle is useful.

Parque Nacional Sarigua shows the devastating effect of slash-and-burn agriculture.

Refugio de Vida Silvestre Peñón de la Honda

www.anam.gob.pa

169 C3

 1.5 miles (2.5 km) E of Playa Rompio

while snail kites watch from treetop perches. Birders in search of the glossy ibis should head to **Ciénaga del Rey,** a small marsh immediately west of Las Macanas and the bird's only known breeding site in Panama.

Refugio de Vida Silvestre Cenegón del Magle *(open 24 hours)* protects 2,063 acres (835 ha) of mangroves, brackish wetlands, and dry scrub at the mouth of the Río Santa María. Boardwalks permit easy viewing of birdlife; anhingas, black-crowned night herons, and boat-billed herons are its star draws. Snakes, caimans, and iguanas are commonly seen, and crocodiles are sometimes spotted. The mudflats bubble with pools— *los pozos*—of cool waters that locals believe have curative powers.

Farther south, **Reserva de Vida Silvestre Peñón de la Honda** spreads over 58 square miles (150 sq km). It centers on tiny, rocky Isla Peñón de la Honda (2.5 miles/4 km offshore), a nesting site for blue-footed boobies, black-crowned night herons, magnificent frigate birds, and white ibises. Also included is a narrow strip of beach, tidal mudflats, and coastal wetlands and mangroves at the mouth of the Las Monjas and Bayano Rivers. Sandpipers, short-billed dowitchers, willets, and whimbrels abound. More than three-quarters of the refuge protects inshore waters where marine turtles breed and females gather, waiting for the full moon before coming ashore to lay their eggs. ■

Central Azuero

FORSAKEN BY TOURISTS YET SUPERBLY SCENIC, THE Azuero interior is dominated by a broad mountain chain that runs clear down the peninsula. Twistier than a snake, the narrow highway through central Azuero steals away the hours as you coil along mountain ridges and curl through valleys whose traditional villages resound to the clip-clop of hooves.

Sleepy **Ocú** is known for its *sombreros ocueños*—the village's trademark straw hats trimmed in black and woven solely by women. Local seamstresses also make polleras with a unique *punto de cruz* (point of the cross) embroidered stitch. **San José,** 4 miles (7 km) west of Ocú, is another epicenter of *ocueño* traditions. Here, **Artesanía Ocueña** *(tel 974-1047),* a local women's cooperative, takes pride in its intricate hand-stitched linens.

Occupying a fertile plain, quaint **Pesé,** 15 miles (24 km) east of Ocú, is surrounded by fields of sugarcane. Facing the village church is the **Destilería Seco Herrerano** *(tel 974-9621, www.varelahermanos.com, closed Sun.),* founded in 1936 and producing Seco Herrerano cane spirit, Panama's national drink. The distillery, open to visitors, evolved from the first sugar mill in the country, established in 1908. The crushing mill is open during the January-to-March harvest; tours are granted with one week's notice.

South of Ocú, the deteriorated road takes you up to **Las Minas,** a charming pine-studded mountain village, before dropping down to **Macaracas,** with a *talabartería* (saddlery) on the main street. **Llano de Piedra,** 6 miles (9 km) south of Macaracas, is a trip back in time, its colonial houses fronted by well-trimmed lawns.

Southward, the road rises over the saddle between 3,271-foot (997 m) **Cerro Cacarañado** and 3,261-foot (994 m) **Cerro Quema**—a stupendously scenic switchback route. On the western flanks, **Reserva Forestal El Montuoso** covers 40 square miles (104 sq km) of tropical and premontane forest. A nature trail leads from here to the summit of 3,239-foot (987 m) **Cerro Alto Higo.** A bus from Las Minas serves **Chepo,** the reserve's gateway. ∎

Though largely deforested, the hills around Ocú spring to life in the wet season.

Central Azuero
🗺 169 A2, B2, A3, & B3

Reserva Forestal El Montuoso
www.anam.gob.pa
🗺 169 A2
✉ 7.5 miles (12 km) W of Las Minas

Polleras

Panamanian women are never more grace-ful than when *empollerada*—dressed in their polleras—for festive occasions. Evolving from humble origins, Panama's beautiful national costume is today worn with pride by the daughters of the peasantry and the aristocracy alike.

The exquisite *pollera de gala* consists of a short-sleeved ruffled blouse, two-tiered full-length skirt, and petticoat; it derives from a Gypsy dress worn in Spain at the time of the conquistadors. The simple white skirt, embroidered with floral designs, was perfectly suited to hot tropical climes. Society ladies, in their heavy brocades and satins, enviously eyed the lightweight garment worn by their maids and servants and then appropriated it, elaborating on the embroidery and decoration. In Panama, the large, lavish hairpins of Spain's Valencia and Salamanca

were enhanced by *templeques* (tremblers) of gold and tortoise shell embellished with pearls, while chains of gold coins and precious jewels were also added to the outfit.

Accepted as the national dress by the time of independence from Spain, the pollera and templeques have continued to evolve since that time, with several regional variations. However, the provinces of Herrera and Los Santos have jealously guarded their own tradition, and their elaborate polleras de gala have been adopted throughout the nation. The finest polleras can cost tens

Women display their polleras in Las Tablas's Festival Nacional de la Pollera (above) in July. A girl's pollera is completed by ribbons, chains, and templeques (top left), while traditional music is an essential part of festivities (below left).

of thousands of dollars and may take a year to complete.

A pollera may be made with cambric or fine linen, although the ground cloth must always be white. About 13 yards (12 m) of material is required. The blouse consists

While the Festival Nacional de la Pollera is a serious celebration of national heritage, the Panamanian love of color, and especially of devil masks, is integral to the festivities.

of two lace-edged ruffles and is worn off the shoulder, its neckline bordered with lace. The skirt is gathered on a waistband studded with gold buttons and consists of two or three ruffles that are raised to the sides, like a peacock's tail or mantilla fan. The ruffles of blouse and skirt are adorned with motifs of birds, flowers, or native designs finely executed in *talco en sombra* (hand-sewn appliqué) of a chosen color. Brightly colored wool is woven in and out of the neckline border, a large matching *mota* (pom-pom) is centered at both chest and back, and four matching *gallardetes* (graceful streamers) or ribbons hang from the waist at front and back.

Five *cabestrillos*—chains of gold coins—hang from the empollerada's neck to her waist. A gold cross or medallion on a black velvet ribbon is worn as a choker. And a *monedero* (silk purse) suspended from the waistline is fastened with gold brooches. To complete the outfit, the woman slips on satin slippers.

The hair, typically tied in a bun behind the ears, is held in place by three large gold combs

exquisitely filigreed, adorned with pearls, and worn like a crown. More fanciful still are the tembleques, elaborate "quivering pins" patterned after flowers or butterflies. Strung with pearls and sometimes with fish scales, the decorations tremble with the empollerada's every move. Finally come the *zarcillos* (earrings) of intricately ornamented gold or coral, and sometimes *dolores*—small gold discs tied to the hair at the temples.

The simpler *pollera montuna,* considered a daily dress, typically features a blouse with only one flounce, a skirt of solid color lacking embroidery, and a single gold chain and pendant earrings and perhaps an arrangement of natural flowers in the hair. In the *pollera montuna ocueña,* from Ocú, the hair adornments disappear altogether, replaced by a traditional straw hat. And the *pollera basquiña,* once daily attire among country women, replaces the shoulderless blouse with a fitted white jacket-style blouse with buttoned collar, shoulder pleats, and flared hem. ∎

Refugio de Vida Silvestre Isla Iguana

THIS WILDLIFE REFUGE ENCOMPASSES A BEACH AS WHITE as flaming magnesium, mangrove and tropical dry forest habitats that are roosts for a miscellany of seabirds, and coral reefs renowned for fabulous snorkeling and diving.

Created in 1981, Iguana Island Wildlife Refuge protects 131 acres (53 ha) of terrestrial and ocean realm that includes exotic fruit trees—the legacy of a self-styled Robinson Crusoe who briefly claimed the isle as his own in the 1960s.

The islet, 3 miles (4.3 km) offshore from **Playa El Bajadero** *(2 miles/3 km NE of Pedasí),* is home to the largest nesting colony of magnificent frigate birds in Panama. During the midwinter mating season, males—they're the one with inflatable red throat sacs—sit atop their nests, wings extended, puffing up their credentials as mates and ululating loudly as the white-throated females fly overhead. Brown pelicans also nest in certain years. Oystercatchers scurry along the beach, and five species of marine turtles arrive to nest between April and September.

Forty acres (16 ha) of coral reefs surround the isle. Twelve species of corals and more than 200 species of fish guarantee superb snorkeling with equally rewarding scuba diving farther out. Dolphins and harmless nurse sharks are commonly seen. Marine turtles flap by with leisurely sovereignty. And humpback whales migrate from colder waters to breed and give birth in the warm water shallows between June and November.

Boats for Iguana leave from **Playa El Arenal** and **Playa El Bajadero.** However, service is

fickle, and you need to clamber aboard through the surf. Trips can also be arranged through Buzos de Azuero *(tel 995-2405, www.dive-n-fishpanama.com).*

The 20-minute boat ride puts you ashore on gorgeous **Playa El Cirial,** where you are greeted by swarms of tiny hermit crabs. The beach has a ranger station and tiny **visitor center.** A nature trail connects El Cirial (on the west side) with **Playa El Faro** (on the ocean side), framed by rugged black rocks topped by a **lighthouse.** High waves sometimes crash on El Faro and swimmers should use caution.

Camping is permitted beneath a shelter at the ranger station, which also has a dorm. There is no electricity, and self-sufficiency is a must. Don't go wandering off the trails, due to the presence of unexploded ordnance (Isla Iguana was used for target practice during World War II). ■

The clear blue waters off Isla Iguana harbor a great variety of marine wildlife, including five species of turtles.

Refugio de Vida Silestre Isla Iguana

⚑ 169 C2
Visitor information
✉ 3 miles (4.3 km) offshore of Playa El Bajadero; boats leave from Playa El Arenal & Playa El Bajadero
☎ ANAM, Los Santos, 994-7313
$ $

A surfer searches for the sweet spot on Playa Venado (above). *Mejorana* guitars (below right) are made in Guararé.

Southeast Azuero

HEARTLAND OF PANAMA'S FOLKLORIC TRADITION, THIS arid quarter is known for its festivals and party spirit. The best embroidered lace skirts in the country are produced in colonial towns ablaze with bougainvillea, while lonesome beaches accessed by dirt roads and until now known only to surfers are on the cusp of development as hoteliers are rushing in.

Southeast Azuero

🅜 169 C1, C2, & B1

Visitor information

✉ ANAM, 0.75 mile (1 km) S of Las Tablas

☎ 994-7313

🕐 Closed Sat. & Sun.

Museo Belisario Porras

✉ Ave. Belisario Porras, Parque Central, Las Tablas

☎ 994-6326

🕐 Closed Sun. Guides available Tues.–Sat.

💲 $

LAS TABLAS & THE POLLERAS COMMUNITIES

The provincial capital of Las Tablas is an important center for polleras and hosts the Festival de la Pollera (as well as the nation's wildest Carnaval). Its most interesting sites are found around **Parque Porras,** dominated by **Iglesia de Santa Librada.** The church was completed in 1789, although most of what you see is a reproduction following a devastating fire in 1950. The red-and-gold retables decorated with angels' heads are originals; so, too, the cruciform Virgin. **Museo Belisario Porras** honors the three-time (between 1912 and 1924) president of Panama; it occupies the home where Porras (1856–1942) was born. Porras bought a simple

country house, built in 1889, which he used for cabinet meetings; today **Casa Museo El Pausilipo** contains exhibits relating to his life.

Northwest of Las Tablas, somnolent **Guararé** is a center for pollera production and for the distinctive five-string guitars known as *mejoranas* (note the giant mejorana at the northern entrance to town). The single-room **Casa-Museo Manuel F. Zárate** displays polleras from different regions alongside musical instruments and devil masks. Despite its small size and quietude, Guararé comes alive each September during the Festival Nacional de la Mejorana; the country's most important folkloric festival, held here since 1949. Then, ox-drawn wagons creaking with age parade through the streets bearing girls dressed in polleras.

PEDASÍ & AROUND

A sleepy fishing village at the southeastern tip of the Azuero Peninsula, Pedasí is a base for exploring beaches farther afield. Buzos de Azuero *(tel 995-2405, www.dive-n-fishpanama.com)* offers fishing and scuba-diving tours. Tuna fishermen set out from **Playa Punta Mala** to catch yellowfin and marlin; nearby, **Playa Los Destiladeres** tempts with its gorgeous long, palm-fringed brown sands washed by rollicking surf.

Beyond Destiladores, **Playa Venado** (aka Playa Venao) is also beloved of surfers. This vast, scalloped 2-mile-long (3.5 km) stretch of gray sand arcing south in a perfect half-moon is the setting for international surfing competitions. A large-scale resort is slated for development and the bay is the site of a Smithsonian Tropical Research Institute reforestation project. **Playita**

Carnaval!

Las Tablas's streets vibrate with festive color, and never more so than during Carnival, when the otherwise somnolent town explodes in party fever. For four days preceding Ash Wednesday, the town divides into Calle Arriba and Calle Abajo (High Road and Low Road). Each chooses a queen and competes to produce the best costume and music, while jesters toss tinted water at passersby. Each night after sundown, flamboyant floats with local beauties in sequined, befeathered bikinis lead Brazilian-style parades, fireworks explode too close for comfort, and partying spectators (many of them drunk) crowd into the plaza for the slightly salacious fun. Each night is themed, culminating on Tuesday with women dressed in polleras. ■

Resort, north of Venado, accepts day visitors but can be noisy on weekends, when day-trippers flock. Adjacent, the white sands of **Playa Achotines** gleam next to a cove; the headland is the setting for Laboratorio Achotines, a hatchery and laboratory (see p. 186). On the horizon, the twin **Islas Frailes del Sur** are the only nesting site in Panama for sooty and bridled terns; brown noddies and brown boobies also nest here.

Neotropic cormorants and black-crowned night herons roost at **Refugio de Vida Silvestre Pablo Arturo Barrios,** extending along 12.5 miles (20 km) of shoreline between the Purio and Caldera Rivers. It protects 37 square miles (96 sq km) of coastal wetlands and offshore waters contiguous with Isla Iguana. ■

Casa Museo El Pausilipo
✉ Las Tablas Abajo
☎ 994-6326
🕐 Closed Mon.
💲 $

Casa-Museo Manuel F. Zárate
✉ Calle 21 Enero, Guararé
☎ 994-5644
🕐 Closed Sun. & Mon.
💲 $

Refugio de Vida Silvestre Pablo Arturo Barrios
www.anam.gob.pa
✉ 1.2 miles (2 km) E of Pedasí

A drive through southeast Azuero

The rather ambitiously named Carretera Nacional (National Highway) runs inland of the eastern seaboard, skipping between a string of colonial towns and villages and facilitating the ease of sightseeing. Though paved the entire way, this journey is a form of time travel, taking you metaphorically back one year with every mile.

Villa Camilla, near Pedasí, is one of Panama's most inviting hotels.

Begin by turning south at **Divisa** ① on the Interamerican Highway. Follow the Carretera Nacional for 14 miles (23 km) and divert north to visit **Parque Nacional Sarigua** ② (see pp. 173–174) before continuing south to **Parita** ③ (see pp. 173–174) to stroll quaint colonial streets bolstered by a historic church of note. Opposite the Shell gas station as you enter town, stop at the home and mask-making studio of **Dario López** *(Carretera Nacional, tel 974-2015 or 6534-1958),* a world-famous maker of papier-mâché devil masks. A gracious host, Dario happily displays his works, plus *diablitos* in red-and-black striped costumes. This is a good place, too, to buy a Carnival mask—the perfect souvenir.

More shopping awaits in **La Arena,** a tidy colonial village famous for its ceramic workshops. The road is lined with artisans' stores displaying pottery pieces from reproductions of pre-Columbian images to wind chimes, vases, and folkloric motifs. Stop by **Cerámica Calderón,** where family patriarch Angel Calderón takes pride in showing his traditional spinning wheel and ovens.

Four miles (6.5 km) farther along the highway, the *carretera* delivers you to bustling **Chitré** ④ (see pp. 170–171), where you should peruse the **Museo de Herrera** and **Catedral de San Juan Bautista** on Parque Unión. From the southeast corner, follow Calle Aminta Burgos de Amado east, turn right onto Calle Carmelo Spadafora Abate (Carretera Nacional), and continue to **Villa de los Santos** (see pp. 170–171). After viewing the main sites, call in at the home of devil-mask maker **Carlos Ivan de León** *(Calle Tomás Herrera).*

Look for the roadside **La Casa de la Pipa** 5.5 miles (9 km) south of Los Santos; stop here for fresh coconut water from a husked *pipa* (unripe coconut). After 14 miles (22 km), you enter **Guararé** ⑤ (see p. 181). Visit the

Casa-Museo Manuel F. Zárate, then follow the dirt road north to La Enea. Here, on the east side of the town square, stop at the home of **Ildaura Saavedra de Espino** *(tel 994-5527),* renowned nationwide for her polleras, which she has been sewing since 1946. Though now confined to a wheelchair, Sra. Saavedra exudes *joie de vivre* and will happily pose for photos with the medal presented by President Martin Torrijos for her years of service to Panama's folkloric tradition.

Continue to **Las Tablas** ⑥ (see pp. 180–181), stopping to view the church and museum. For the final 26 miles (42 km) to the sleepy town of **Pedasí** ⑦, you pass through an increasingly impoverished and somnolent landscape where the opposing vehicle is likely to be a creaky ox-drawn cart.

End your day with an overnight at **Villa Marina** (see p. 250) or **Villa Camilla** *(tel 6678-8555, www.azueros.com)* with a second day given to visiting the Isla Iguana and Isla Cañas wildlife reserves.

To turn this drive into a loop, continue west from Pedasí and follow the southern shore to **El Cacao,** then turn north to return to Las Tablas. This latter section via **Flores** and **El Muñoz** winds upward through exquisite mountain scenery, giving you magnificent views east over the coastal plains and Pacific Ocean. ∎

✚ See area map p. 169
▶ Interamerican Highway
⟷ 70 miles (112 km)
🕒 8 hours including sightseeing
▶ Pedasí

NOT TO BE MISSED
- Parque Nacional Sarigua
- Mask-making studio of Dario López, Parita
- Museo de Herrera, Chitré

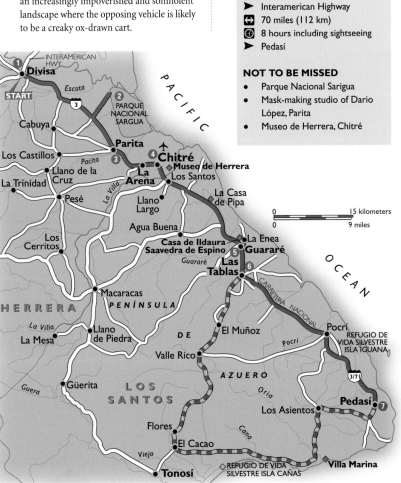

Refugio de Vida Silvestre Isla Cañas

Parque Nacional Cerro Hoya
⚠ 169 A1, B1
$ $
Visitor information
www.anam.gob.pa
☎ Anam, Los Santos, 994-7313

AROUND ISLA CAÑAS THERE ARE ALMOST ALWAYS TURTLES in the water, never more so than in the fall nesting season, when olive Ridley turtles storm ashore in battalions like helmeted troops during the D-Day invasion. The birdlife is also astounding.

Cañas Island Wildlife Refuge was created in 1947 to protect Panama's most important marine turtle nesting site. Hawksbills, leatherbacks, loggerheads, olive Ridleys, and Pacific greens struggle ashore to lay their eggs on the gray-brown sands of this 9-mile-long (14 km) island, with August through November the peak nesting season.

The 98-square-mile (254 sq km) refuge—four-fifths of which extends out to sea—also includes mangroves that stretch 10 miles (16 km) between the mouths of the Cañas and Tonosí Rivers and along the landward shore of the isle. They provide roosts for nesting colonies of cattle egrets, scissor-tail frigate birds, and white ibises.

At night, the lagoon waters literally glow, thanks to billions of microscopic dinoflagellates that emit a spectral bioluminescence when disturbed. Swimming is discouraged due to crocodiles… with luck you might see one moving stealthily, enveloped

by a greenish glow.

To get to the refuge, turn off the Pedasí-Tonosí road at the hamlet of Agua Buena; the junction is poorly marked, and four-wheel-drive is required in wet season for the 3-mile (5 km) dirt road. Boatmen will run you across the channel: a metal clanger is provided to summon a boat. The cooperative also offers compulsory guide service plus basic accommodation and a snack bar. Overnighting is virtually essential for seeing nesting turtles. Bring a mosquito net, plus insect repellent. A tiny restaurant serves seafood. ■

A water taxi makes its way through mangroves to Isla Cañas (top). A male frigate bird inflates its chest in a show of proving itself a viable mate (above right).

Parque Nacional Cerro Hoya

SECLUDED IN THE EXTREME SOUTHWEST OF THE AZUERO
Peninsula, Cerro Hoya—an island of dense primary vegetation amid
a sea of deforested land—receives only a handful of visitors. Yet ranging from offshore coral reefs to cool mountain heights, the park
teems with precious wildlife.

**Reserva Forestal
La Tronosa**
www.anam.gob.pa
✉ 1.2 miles (2 km) W
of Jobero

Occupying 512 acres (207 ha),
and with elevations ranging
from sea level to 5,115 feet
(1,559 m) atop **Cerro Hoya,**
the park's climate varies considerably. So, too, does its vegetation. Giant cedar, mahogany,
and ceiba trees tower over the
tropical forests (moist, premontane, and montane) that rise in
shades of green. At lower elevations, much of the park is being
regenerated after decades of
deforestation for cattle.

The forests resound with
the calls of scarlet macaws and
painted parakeets, two among
95 bird species recorded here.
Sightings of tamanduas, sloths,
agoutis, white-tailed deer, and
squirrel, white-faced, and howler
monkeys are regular rewards for
adventure seekers, although big
cats such as ocelots and jaguars
are ever elusive.

Extending south into the
Pacific Ocean, the park protects
pristine coral reefs and mangrove swamps as well as a
string of tiny offshore islands.
By night, marine turtles arrive
to nest on virginal beaches.

The park has two ranger
stations, plus administrative
centers at **Restingue** (in
Veraguas Province) and outside
the park at **Tonosí** (in Los Santos
Province). The easiest access is
from the west via the road from
Santiago to El Varadero, beyond
which with four-wheel-drive you
can reach Restingue, a short hike
from the park. From the east, you
can enter the park on horseback
or foot from **Jobero,** 16 miles
(22 km) west of Tonosi, at the
gateway to **Reserva Forestal
La Tronosa,** a forest reserve
adjoining the park. Alternately,
you can hire a boat at **Playa
Cambutal** (see p. 186) to the
park boundary at the isolated
hamlet of **Tembladera;** you can
even hike the shore at low tide—
an overnight journey involving
river crossings (a tide chart is
essential), or drive partway with a
four-wheel-drive vehicle
depending on seasonal conditions.
Basic accommodations and a
merendero (snack shack) exist
midway. Otherwise, you will need
a tent and supplies. ■

Arribadas

The olive Ridley turtle has
hit on a clever idea to
ensure its survival...an occurrence known locally as an *arribada.* When the moon is full,
thousands of turtles congregate offshore, then surge
ashore in an astonishing example of synchronized reproduction. Each arribada can occupy
an entire week as wave after
wave of turtles come ashore.
So many eggs are laid (and
destroyed by turtles digging up
existing nests) that residents
are granted rights to collect a
limited number in a designated
harvest zone. ■

More places to visit in the Azuero Peninsula

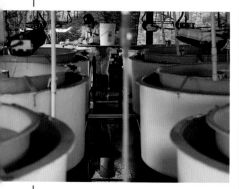

Tuna-breeding tanks at Laboratorio Achotines

LABORATORIO ACHOTINES
This hatchery and laboratory where scientists study tuna ecology borders beautiful Bahía de Achotines, whose narrow continental shelf and welling marine currents provide a year-round spawning ground for tuna. Ten species of tuna and billfish run in the offshore waters. Operated by the Inter-American Tropical Tuna Commission (IATTC, *tel 858-546-7100, www.iattc.org)*, the facility is part of IATTC's Tuna-Billfish Program, which researches the egg, larval, and early juvenile stages of tuna

life. It has incubation pools and tanks where juvenile tuna fatten. The site also includes 173 acres (70 ha) of tropical dry forest inhabited by howler monkeys, iguanas, and toucans. Guided tours are offered by appointment, Monday through Thursday, and can be arranged through Buzos de Azuero *(tel 995-2405, www.dive-n-fishpanama.com)* in Pedasí.

🗺 169 C2 ✉ Bahía de Achotines, 19 miles (31 km) SW of Pedasí ☎ 995-8166, e-mail: achotine@cwp.net.pa, www.iattc.org

PLAYAS CAMBUTAL & GUÁNICO
Playa Cambutal is a dark gray beach in three parts, hemmed in to the ocean by rugged mountains. Punta Morro de Puercos separates it from neighboring Playa Guánico, farther east. Until recently drawing only surfers, these lonesome lovelies are being primed for development. Cambutal is a launch site via rented fishing boat for visits to nearby Parque Nacional Cerro Hoya (see pp. 184–185), which can also be accessed by a rugged coastal hike. ANAM has an office in the sleepy cowboy and fishing village of **Cambutal,** about 0.6 mile (1 km) inland.

🗺 169 B1 ✉ 15.5 miles (25 km) SW of Tonosí ☎ 333-0700 (ANAM) ∎

Sombreros montunos

Panama hats—the sartorial splendors worn by FDR, Winston Churchill, and stars of the silver screen—don't come from the country of Panama. The overwhelming majority are made next door, in Ecuador. Nonetheless, the men of Panama do wear hand-woven *sombreros de paja toquilla,* locally made hats of native straw. Known as *sombreros montunos,* they hail principally from the villages of Ocú and La Pintada. The *ocueño* features a turned-up brim decorated with a single black or brown line, with a braided cord unique to the village; the *pintado* has a straight brim decorated with black patterns, often in multiple rings. The hats, which take between two weeks and

a month to produce, are made from the white fibers of a plant called *bellota.* The fibers are stripped from the leaves, boiled, and then sun-dried until they are bleached a creamy white. The same fibers are used for the pattern rings and derive their coloration (anywhere from rust-red to black) from being boiled. Ecuadorian hats lack the black trim characteristic of the Panamanian version and are woven crown to brim as a single unit. Panama's hats, however, are woven in half-inch strips that are wound around a wooden form and sewn together. The highest quality montunos are so finely woven that not even water can pass between the threads. ∎

Spanning remote surf-washed beaches and mist-shrouded volcanic heights, this diverse region abounds in dramatic landscapes, from sultry coastal plains thick with sugarcane to cool coffee-clad mountain vales. Chiriquí's Ngöbe-Buglé culture infuses the region.

Chiriquí & the cordillera

Ginger plant, Sitio Barriles, near Volcán

Chiriquí & the cordillera

THE MOST VARIED OF PANAMA'S PROVINCES, RANGING FROM BEACHES LIKE fresh-fallen snow to misty cloud forest, this region requires at least a full week. Plunging gorges and razorback ridges, marine wetlands and offshore isles teeming with game fish, and cool highland valleys sheltering flower gardens and coffee farms comprise a vastly diverse array of appealing options.

A busy commercial node and Panama's third largest city, David is the gateway to this region, divided between a long coastal plain narrowing eastward and a parallel mountain chain that is rugged in the extreme. Banana plantations and sugarcane smother much of the *llanura* (plain) west of town, where the Carta Vieja rum factory offers a chance to tipple the wares. Closer to shore, rivers meander through some of Central America's largest swamp systems: important nesting sites for wading and shore birds. The coastline is strung with gray-sand beaches popular equally with marine turtles and surfers. A necklace of isles redolent with forest and wildlife is protected within Parque Nacional Marino Golfo de Chiriquí. The surrounding waters are world-famous for sportfishing, offered out of the hamlet of Boca Chica.

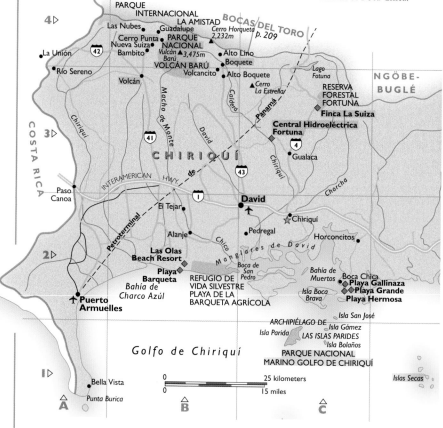

A real estate ad at Boquete's bus station points to things to come.

The lowlands can be suffocatingly hot and dry around David and oppressively humid by the shore. In contrast, the crisp highlands are marked by dozens of mild microclimates. The rivers cascade downhill in leaps and bounds, perfect for challenging Class III and IV whitewater runs.

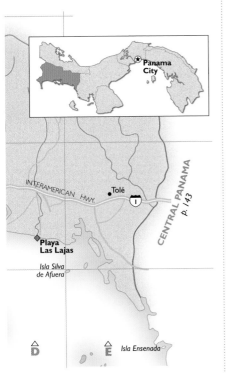

The country's highest peak offers exhilarating hikes through the cloud forests of Parque Nacional Volcán Barú and Parque Internacional La Amistad, a million-acre (400,000 ha) reserve shared with Costa Rica. The parks are literally steps from the mountain resort towns of Boquete—Panama's "Little Switzerland"—and Cerro Punta. Panama's well-heeled and, in recent years, its wave of expatriates have built houses here. Tourists are also flocking to the delightful hotels, gourmet restaurants, and cafés serving fresh-roasted coffees. The Cerro Punta region is the nation's breadbasket, thanks to rich volcanic soils from which the town of Volcán gets its name. Sitio Barriles preserves mementos of a pre-Columbian culture wiped out by a volcanic explosion.

Chiriquí is an ancient Guaymi word meaning "Valley of the Moon." The Guaymi, known today as Ngöbe-Buglé, live in remote mountain villages, many within a *comarca* (autonomous reserve) established in 1998. Most eke out a living on subsistence plots, selling crafts, or as laborers in the coffee fields.

Direct flights serve David from Panama City. Alternately, the drive takes about five hours along the Interamerican Highway. The eastern section linking Chiriquí Province with Veraguas Province is badly deteriorated; with one lane in each direction, it requires caution and should be avoided entirely at night. The Interamerican runs to the Costa Rican border at Paso Canoa, about 290 miles (470 km) west of Panama City. *Careful!* It is easy to drive straight through the border post. ■

David & around

PANAMA'S THIRD LARGEST CITY (POP. 120,000) SITS ON A coastal plain and, though short on sightseeing attractions, is centrally placed for hub-and-spoke exploration of Chiriquí Province. Congested David (Dav-EED) is known most for its weeklong mid-March fiesta honoring the city's patron saint, but despite its overriding modernity also boasts a handful of modest historic draws.

Religious icons in David's Museo de História y Arte

creak with age. It is filled with period furniture, best seen in a reproduction of a typical 19th-century bedroom. Downstairs rooms host exhibits on pre-Columbian culture, such as *metates* and ceramics. The Sala Colonial boasts swords, stirrups, and other pieces of the era, while cassocks and other forms of religious clothing are a highlight of the Sala de Arte Colonial. The exhibits are much deteriorated, being exposed to the heat and drenching humidity.

Next door, another charming colonial home hosts the **Fundación Gallegos y Culturama,** a research library with a miscellany of intriguing exhibits that include a 19th-century printing press plus pre-Columbian ceramics. Nearby stands **La Hermita San José de David** *(Ave. 10 Este at Calle A Norte),* with a recently restored (albeit weathered) stone bell tower now made complete by the addition of a church. Across the plaza, the school houses the **Museo Escolar del Colegio Félix Olivares** *(775-2854, closed Sat. & Sun., by appt. only Dec.–March),* displaying pre-Columbian artifacts.

Boats can be rented at the port of **Pedregal,** 3 miles (5 km) south of David, for trips through the **Manglares de David** (see p. 191) and to **Parque Nacional Marino Golfo de Chiriquí** (see p. 193). David is also linked by air to Panama City, Bocas del Toro, and San José, Costa Rica. ∎

David
⚐ 188 C2
Visitor information
www.ipat.gob.pa
✉ IPAT, Edificio Don José, Ave. Domingo Díaz
☎ 775-2839
🕑 Closed Sat. & Sun.

Museo de História y Arte José de Obaldía
✉ Ave. 8A Este, between Calle A Norte & Calle Central
☎ 775-1217
🕑 Closed Sat. & Sun.
💲 $

David—a major agricultural center—is surrounded by cattle country (rodeos are frequently held on Sundays). Although founded in 1602, there is comparatively little sense of the past (in 1732 the town was attacked and razed by indigenous peoples). The crowded town center bustles with business. Markets and street stalls spill their wares onto streets chockfull of tooting traffic. The whirligig of commercialism revolves around **Parque Cervantes,** overlooked by a ho-hum church, the 19th-century **Iglesia de la Sagrada Familia.**

Barrio Bolívar, the historic core, lies south of the main square and clings to a slower pace. David's few sites of interest are here. The **Museo de História y Arte José de Obaldía** occupies the former two-story home of the namesake founder (1806–1889) of Chiriquí Province. Built in 1880, its timbers

Golfo de Chiriquí shoreline

Bananas are sorted at a packing plant in Puerto Armuelles.

MANGROVES. BEACHES WASHED BY HIGH SURF. STUPENDOUS diving and fishing. Myriad emerald isles strewn like jewels in a sapphire sea. These are the appeals of the humid Chiriquí coast. Bring insect repellent to ward off the *chitras* (no-see-ums) that are particularly active by the shore around dawn and dusk.

South of David, the **Manglares de David**—the largest mangrove system in Panama—spans 28 miles (45 km) of estuaries in the delta of the Chiriquí, Chico, and David Rivers, which merge into Boca de San Pedro. The waterways form a convoluted lacework through dense mangroves and mudflats teeming with migratory shorebirds. Part of the system comprises **Refugio de Vida Silvestre Playa de la Barqueta Agrícola,** extending west from Boca San Pedro. Egrets lift up like silken kites and white ibises and black-crowned night herons breed in this 14,665-acre (5,935 ha) reserve, three-quarters of which protects offshore waters where marine turtles mate before nesting on **Playa Barqueta.** Driftwood adds to the dramatic beauty of this lonesome beach unspooling for 10 miles (16 km) like a ribbon of silver lamé. Poaching by locals

remains a problem despite the presence of a hatchery. Savage waves may tempt you to body surf, but caution is required due to fierce riptides. Other than the bargain-priced all-inclusive **Las Olas Beach Resort** (which sells passes for day or night visits; see p. 254), the only facilities are two simple restaurants.

The eastern shoreline of Chiriquí is heaven for surfers seeking a less crowded wave. A top draw is **Playa Las Lajas,** a 7-mile (11 km) slingshot of dun sands where tourism is beginning to stir. Offshore **Isla Silva de Afuera** is a small island with Big Kahuna rides.

BOCA CHICA & ISLA BOCA BRAVA
The mainland fishing village of Boca Chica lies 18 miles (25 km) south of the Interamerican Highway via the community of

Golfo de Chiriquí shoreline

🗺 188–189 B2, C2, D2, E2, & E1

Visitor information

www.ipat.gob.pa

✉ IPAT, Edificio Don José, Ave. Domingo Díaz

☎ 775-2839

🕓 Closed Sat. & Sun.

Horconcitos (a roadside hamlet known for its saddlemakers); the road resembles a tank-training course and is a serious challenge in the wet season. That may soon change, as a six-hotel complex broke ground in 2006 at nearby **Playa Hermosa** and **Playa Gallinaza;** and the Marina Playa Grande and Resort, with slips for 100 boats, is to be built at nearby **Playa Grande.** The ocean vistas could not have been bettered by Hollywood.

ISLA BOCA BRAVA

Isla Boca Brava floats in the Bahía de Muertos, about one-half mile (0.8 km) from Boca Chica; water taxis link the two. Howler monkeys holler as you hike trails through thick forest teeming with wildlife.

Activities include seasonal whale-watching. Gone Fishing Panama (*tel 6573-0151, www .gonefishingpanama.com*) and Panama Big Game Fishing Club (*tel 866-281-1225, www .panamabiggamefishingclub.com*) offer sportfishing in the Hannibal Bank. Buzos Boca Brava (*tel 6600-6191*) and Chiriquí Diving (*tel 6571-7512, www .chiriquidiving.com*) provide scuba-diving trips.

PUNTA BURICA

A needle-thin peninsula pierces the Pacific, marking Panama's extreme western tip. The gateway to this lonesome promontory is **Puerto Armuelles,** a rambling, relatively prosperous town surrounded by banana groves. The fruit is the town's entire raison d'être and has been since the United Fruit Co. (now Chiquita Brands) arrived in 1927. Chiquita shuttered locally in 2001, causing widespread unemployment at the time; a worker's cooperative now farms the fields. The company legacy still stands south of town in a *barrio* (district) of colorful, albeit tumbledown, clapboard houses. Beyond, a gray-sand beach, surf-washed and palm-lined, curls gently south toward the **Petroterminal de Panamá** oil terminal.

The road ends at Petroterminal, beyond which—at outgoing tide only!—you take to the beach as a roadway (after signing in at the terminal guardhouse). Mountains wrapped in dark folds of forest rise up behind, and long, lonesome beaches pounded by tubular surf stretch off into the green-blue infinity. Panama Surf Tours (*tel 6671-7777, www.panamasurftours .com*) offers eight-day surfing tours. Truck-buses run inland of the beach along a tortuous mud track as far as the hamlet of **Bella Vista,** from which it's an hour-long hike to the tip of **Punta Burica.** Here, the **Mono Feliz** hotel (see p. 254) is surrounded by monkey-filled forests and guarantees an end-of-the-world nature experience. ■

Crude oil

Charco Azul (Blue Ditch), 6 miles (10 km) west of Puerto Armuelles, is the Pacific terminus of an oil pipeline that crosses the continental divide, linking Charco Azul to Chiriquí Grande in Bocas del Toro Province. The 81-mile-long (131 km) pipeline, operated by Petroterminal de Panamá, was completed in 1982. Supertankers carrying oil from Alaska and Ecuador are too big for the canal. Hence, they discharge their cargo here for shipment to refineries in Houston and the Gulf states. ■

Parque Nacional Marino Golfo de Chiriquí

ANCHORED IN THE MIDDLE OF THE GOLFO DE CHIRIQUÍ, this stellar marine park known for its glorious beaches and pristine coral reefs embodies many of the physical attributes that visitors to Panama might hope to see. Overflowing with terrestrial wildlife, the hard-to-access park offers stupendous birding, plus palm trees and white-sand beaches.

The Gulf of Chiriquí Marine Park was established in 1994 to protect 57 square miles (148 sq km) of marine ecosystems and the two dozen or so islands of the **Archipiélago de las Islas Paridas** that speckle these Pacific waters.

The Goliath among these isles is **Isla Parida.** Its rolling hills are swathed in moist tropical forest and fringed by dense mangroves—perfect roosts for magnificent frigate birds, which wheel and slide overhead like kites on invisible strings. The forests vibrate with the squawks of parakeets and the stentorian roar of howler monkeys. ANAM has a ranger station.

Jade-colored and bathtub warm, the waters around **Isla San José** are a snorkeler's dream. So, too, are those surrounding **Isla Bolaños,** where at night hawksbill and leatherback turtles come ashore to lay their eggs. By day, turtles can be seen grazing among coral reefs nibbled upon by parrotfish in their Joseph's coats of many colors. Anglers rave about the explosive strike of cubera snapper, roosterfish, and other game fish.

Boaters are drawn to **Isla Gámez,** half a mile (1 km) northeast of Parida. Unfortunately, its beaches are often strewn with trash, courtesy of uncaring visitors.

Access to the park is by boat from Boca Chica (see pp. 191–192). Exploration Panama (tel 720-2470, www.explorationpanama .net) offers tours. ■

Sugar-fine sands dissolve into azure waters on Isla San José.

Parque Nacional Marino Golfo de Chiriquí
Visitor information
www.anam.gob.pa

188 C1
ANAM, Vía Aeropuerto, David
775-3163
Closed Sat. & Sun.

Parrots & macaws

abilities. Most birds waterproof their feathers using a special gland in the middle of their lower back with secretions that act as both an antibacterial and antifungal agent. The Amazons lack this gland and instead employ a powder from their down feathers.

The gaily colored macaws—the giants of the parrot kingdom—are as haughty and elaborately plumed as emperors, with authoritative voices to match. Five of the six species of Panama's macaws are endangered due to deforestation and to poaching both for the pet market and for their long trailing tail feathers, plucked for use in folkloric ceremonies.

Although not yet considered endangered, the rust-red green-winged macaw (*Ara chloroptera*) has nonetheless disappeared from part of its former range in Panama. The scarlet macaw (*Ara macao*), called *guacamayo* locally, is today found only in Cerro Hoya and Isla Coiba National Parks; named for its blood-red plumage, the scarlet macaw has wings of bold royal blue and yellow. The Caribbean-dwelling great green, or Buffon's macaw, has all but vanished in the wild and like most of Panama's macaw species is found only in Darién Province; uniquely, these bright-green birds blush when excited, their white featherless cheeks turning rose-petal pink. The amiable blue-and-gold macaw (*Ara ararauna*) is instantly recognizable by its dazzling coat of teal blue and chest of yellow. It, too, occupies the lowlands of eastern Panama, albeit in diminishing numbers. Measuring more than three feet (1 m) to the tip of its tail feathers, it's also the largest of the six macaws.

Panama boasts 18 of the world's 330-plus species of parrots, including 6 of the 16 macaws. The quintessential avians of the neotropics, these gregarious birds (flocks of several hundred are common) are character-ized by their uncanny intelligence and gift of the gab. Uniquely, parrots possess four toes on each foot, with two facing forward and two rearward, providing the dexterity to grasp fruits and nuts just as if the birds had oppos-able thumbs. Their hooked and immensely strong beaks have evolved to slice through nuts and seeds like metal cutters, while rasp-like ridges inside the upper bill can grind even the hardest pits to dust.

Most parrots are lime green, with varying colored markings that separate the species and subspecies. The most common genus includes the more than 50 species of so-called Amazon parrots—medium-size, stocky birds with heavy bills and slightly rounded, truncated tails. Savvy beyond their size, they have the intelligence and temperament of a two-year-old child. The country's very own Panama Amazon or yellow-fronted Amazon (*Amazona ochrocepala panamenis*) is the smallest and least colorful of the Amazons, its sole distinguishing marks being gray eye-rings, orange epaulettes, and a small patch of yellow on the forehead. Found only along the Pacific coast, the Panama Amazon prefers savannas and woodlands. An inquisitive and talkative fellow, the Panama adapts well to captivity and is an expert mimic renowned for its linguistic

Parrots and macaws make their nests in hollowed-out tree trunks. Males feed their partners by regurgitating food while females incubate the eggs and feed the young. Monogamous for life, parrots are often seen flying in pairs, the male and female squawking love notes as they sail overhead like double rainbows with their wings almost touching. ∎

The blue-and-gold (top left) and scarlet (right) macaws are among the most beautifully plumed of parrots.

Boquete

Boquete

📍 188 B3 & B4

Visitor information

✉ CEFATI, Alto Boquete

☎ 720-4060

KNOWN AS THE CITY OF ETERNAL SPRING, THIS POPULAR highland destination enjoys an enviably scenic location on the eastern flank of Volcán Barú. Roads lined with angel trumpetvine herald a world of exquisite beauty. Coffee estates, white-water rafting, and trails that offer superb hiking and birding are among the key draws.

A climber seeks a route up a rock-face of hexagonal basalt near Boquete.

The road from David ascends as smoothly as a line in a logarithmic equation—a 25-mile (40 km) straight shot that delivers you to the **Centro de Información Turística** (CEFATI) atop a bluff known as **Mirador de la Virgen de la Gruta** in Alto Boquete (Upper Boquete). CEFATI offers fabulous views over the town center, known as Bajo Boquete

(Lower Boquete), laid out below in the tight valley of the Río Caldera at an elevation of 3,950 feet (1,300 m). Boquete is cupped by lush mountains, with the brooding mass of Volcán Barú to the west and Cerro Azul and Cerro La Estrella to the east.

Founded in 1911, Boquete was settled early last century by immigrants from central Europe.

The Swiss, Germans, and even Slavs left their mark in building styles.

The past few years have witnessed an explosion in tourism along with an influx of foreign residents and an associated real estate boom. The area is also home to one of the largest concentrations of Ngöbe-Buglé Indians in the country, their simple dresses in primary colors adding to the charm of Boquete.

Gently sloping Bajo Boquete makes for delightful ambling. The heart of affairs is **Parque Domingo Médica,** where locals gather to gossip beneath redolent pines. On weekends, Ngöbe-Buglé set up stalls to sell their exquisitely colorful and creative crafts.

White-water rafting

Rafting the Chiriquí and Chiriquí Viejo Rivers provides the ultimate combination of natural beauty and thrill. These two rivers pour off the slopes of Volcán Barú and cascade down to the Pacific plains. The rivers are at their best May through December, but can be rafted year-round. Safety-conscious Chiriquí River Rafting (tel 720-1505, www.panama-rafting.com) offers trips aboard self-bailing rafts under the care and control of professional guides. The company supplies mandatory life vests and helmets. The intoxicating ride takes you through tricky cascades with names like The Fear and Three Humps. ■

An **antique railroad car** marooned on a slice of track on the plaza's east side is a reminder of the railway, built in 1912, that once linked Boquete to the coast. Diagonally across the plaza, **Parque de las Madres** features a statue of mother and child. A five-minute uphill walk to the lovely **Panamonte Inn & Spa** (see p. 251), dating from 1914, is well rewarded for its charming gardens and yesteryear ambience.

Orientation tours in an open-air jeep are offered by Boquete Mountain Cruisers *(tel 720-4697 or 6627-8829, e-mail: boquetecruisers @hotmail.com).*

BLOOMIN' LOVELY

Plants and shrubs love Boquete's climate. Flower cultivation is a local industry. Many *viveros* grow lilies, carnations, and even roses, while locals coddle their plants with an almost English obsession.

Jardín de Villa Marta,

El Explorador
✉ Calle Jarmillo Alto
☎ 720-1989
💲 $

Finca Lérida
www.fincalerida.com
✉ Alto Quiel, 6.5 miles
(10.5 km) NW of
Boquete
☎ 720-2285
💲 $

**Beneficio
Cafetalero Café
Ruíz**
www.caferuiz.com
✉ Hwy. 43, Alto
Boquete
☎ 720-1000 or 800-
2233
🕐 One- and three-hour
tours by appt., 9
a.m. Mon.–Sat.
💲 $$$

commonly known as **Mi Jardín es Su Jardín** (*Ave. Central, 0.5 mile/0.8 km NW of Boquete*), is a riot of color and scents. Spread over 12 acres (5 ha), the private garden of the González family draws visitors to admire ferns, azaleas, impatiens, hibiscus, and roses laid out in semi-formal fashion. Psychedelic cows and cut-out human figurines are among the eclectic oddities.

Each January, the Fería Internacional de las Flores y el Café (*Ave. Buenos Aires, tel 720-1466*),

COFFEE TOURS
The country's finest coffee is grown in Boquete, whose slopes are patterned in rows of green corduroy. Several producers and roasters welcome visitors to their *beneficios* (coffee mills). During harvest season, Ngöbe-Buglé Indians comprise the workforce and flock to pick ripe beans from the dark-green bushes.

The loveliest *cafetal* is **Finca Lérida,** combining a 110-acre (44.5 ha) coffee estate with 640 acres (259 ha) of primary forest and

Boquete coffee

The arabica coffee plant grows best in well-drained soils at elevations of 2,500 to 3,500 feet (760 to 1,070 m), with nearly constant temperatures between 59°F and 82°F (15°–28°C) and a distinct wet and dry season. The climate, slope aspect, and rich volcanic soils of the Chiriquí highlands are perfect for coffee cultivation and combine to produce a distinctly flavored coffee—mellow and aromatic, with a hint of acidity—that connoisseurs say is among the best in the world.

The glossy green bushes begin fruiting by their fourth year,

announced at the onset of rainy season by the appearance of tiny white blossoms that scent the air with a jasminelike fragrance. The beans are surrounded by lush green berries that turn blood-red by October, the time of the seasonal harvest. The hand-picked berries are shipped to beneficios, where the fleshy outer layers are removed to expose the beans, which are blow-dried or spread out in the sun in the traditional manner. The leathery skins are then stripped away, the beans are roasted and…java! ∎

the Flower and Coffee Fair, displays the finest examples of local gardeners' arts and crafts. The showground on the east bank of the Río Caldera boasts 10,000 varieties of flowers. It is open year-round, but is best seen during the Feria de las Orquídeas each April.

El Explorador, a roadside café with a garden full of wacky bric-a-brac, is an offbeat mountainside delight where flora and fun combine. Owner Deyanira Miranda and her gardeners have wielded their pruning shears like an artist's paintbrush.

another 140 acres (57 ha) given to crops such as lettuce and carrots. Visitors can savor a fresh-roasted brew in the coffeehouse overlooking the original beneficio, now a museum with exhibits relating to coffee production. Five miles (8 km) of manicured trails lead into the adjacent cloud-forest reserve where the two-tone whistles of quetzals promise potential sightings. Guided and self-guided tours are offered. Finca Lérida operates a lovely bed-and-breakfast (see p. 252).

Beneficio Cafetalero Café Ruíz also offers tours that include

the coffee fields in Palmira and beneficio in Boquete, ending with a delicious tasting in the coffee shop. You can sign up for a tour at Café Ruiz café at CEFATI in Boquete.

Estate Palo Alto, northeast of Boquete, offers daily group tours that include the **Kotowa Coffee Tour,** where visitors are shown the processing plant and a coffee mill—the oldest in Panama—that doubles as a cupping room for tastings. There are no signs to Estate Palo Alto, as drop-ins without reservations are discouraged. Kotowa hosts the **Boquete Tree Trek** *(tel 720-1635 or 6615-3300, www.aventurist.com),* a three-hour zipline ride along steel cables strung between treetop platforms. **Wild Orchid Coffee** *(Volcancito, tel 6672-7754, www.wildorchidcoffee .com)* also offers tours. The estate features gardens and an orchid trail.

MOUNTAIN HIGHS

To visit Boquete and not hike is akin to visiting France without tasting the wine. There are trails for every ability. Local hotels can recommend reputable guides.

Three short loops lead from Bajo Boquete to the trailheads. The most southerly loop departs the center of town and ascends through lush coffee fields to **Volcancito,** from which the hale and hearty can hike to the summit of **Volcán Barú** (see pp. 200–201). A second loop leads northeast to **Alto Lino,** where a less challenging trail leads up 7,323-foot (2,232 m) **Cerro Horqueta.** Another trail from Alto Lino transcends the continental divide and descends through La Amistad International Park to the Caribbean lowlands—an arduous four-day adventure!

The most dramatic drive is the 13-mile (20 km) **Bajo Mono** loop, switchbacking sharply upward through a canyon framed by a wall of hexagonal basalt columns formed by magma from an eons-old volcanic eruption. You can drive to the end of the road at **Alto Chiquero,** step from your car, and start walking the aptly named **Sendero Los Quetzales** (see p. 201), which wends around the northern slopes of Volcán Barú. If you've ever wanted to see a quetzal, then this is as good as it gets. ∎

Ngöbe-Buglé Indians provide the labor to bring in the crops, including coffee, around Boquete.

Kotowa Coffee Tour
www.myroaster.com
✉ Estate Palo Alto, 3 miles (5 km) NE of Boquete
☎ 720-1430
🕐 Tours 9:00 a.m. daily; Sun. & private tours by appt. through Coffee Adventures, tel 720-3852, www .coffeeadventures.net
 $$$$

The Sendero Los Quetzales offers fine views over Cerro Punta.

Parque Nacional Volcán Barú

PROTECTING THE BRAWNY, THICKLY FORESTED FLANKS OF Panama's sole volcano, this park is easily accessed, providing fantastic, albeit challenging hikes and prime quetzal viewing. On clear days you can see both the Caribbean Sea and Pacific Ocean from the mountain's summit—the highest point in the country.

Parque Nacional Volcán Barú

⚑ 188 B4

Visitor information

✉ ANAM, Vía Aeropuerto

☎ 775-3163

The 55-square-mile (142 sq km) park abutting Parque Internacional La Amistad (see p. 224) is centered on the eponymous 11,398-foot (3,474 m) volcano, which has slumbered peacefully for the last 500 years. Seven craters pock the summit (topped by communication towers). They are attainable from the east by the 8.5-mile-long (13.5 km) trail that begins at the ANAM ranger station above **Volcancito,** 5 miles (8 km) west of Boquete. Driving the steep rocky track to the station requires a high-ground-clearance four-wheel-drive vehicle with off-road tires; otherwise, it's a 45-minute hike from the end of the paved road at Volcancito. The **summit trail** is a challenging five-hour hike from the ranger station (the boulder-strewn track can also be driven—a brutal ordeal guaranteed to shake your teeth loose).

From the west side, a track that begins roadside about 2.5 miles (4 km) north of **Volcán** leads 4 miles (7 km) east to the summit trailhead. This is a steeper route than the Boquete trail;

Quetzals

The resplendent trogon, better known as the quetzal, is an exotic and elusive species that draws many birders to Panama. Its iridescent emerald plumage is so luxuriant that the Maya worshiped it as a sacred bird. The endangered pigeon-size bird is common at elevations of 3,500 feet (1.070 m), where cloud forests are found. The male boasts a chest of brilliant crimson and trailing tail feathers sinuous as feather boas, which it puts to good use in its mating displays. The quetzal prefers the avocadolike fruit of the aguacatillo, which it plucks from below in mid-flight. ■

allow a good 10 hours minimum to summit and return.

Hiking with a seasoned guide enhances the possibilities of spotting quetzals, whose melodious two-note whistles lure you on like the mysterious calls of Rima the bird girl from *Green Mansions*. Black-bellied and brown violet ear hummingbirds flit past, the metallic clang of the endangered three-wattled bellbird rings through the forest, and hikers thrill to sightings of such endemics as yellow-thighed finches and black-chested warblers. Set out before dawn to beat the clouds that often blanket the upper heights by mid-morning, and bring warm clothing and raingear.

The **Sendero Los Quetzales** trail threads the lush green blankets of the north slope and links the ANAM ranger stations at **Alto Chiquero,** which has a dorm with cold shower, and **El Respingo** at

Bajo Grande, near Cerro Punta (see p. 204). Six hours should be sufficient for this 12-mile (19 km) mostly uphill trail, which is well named. More than 300 breeding pairs of quetzals inhabit the park, and they are frequently seen tending their nests or in sweeping dip-and-rise flight. A government attempt to turn Sendero Los Quetzales into a paved highway has been postponed—but not canceled—due to outraged public reaction; for information, contact **Fundación para el Desarrollo Integral de Cerro Punta** (FUNDICCEP, *tel 771-2171, e-mail: fundiccep@cwpanama.net).*

The park's thriving mammal population includes all five species of cats. Pumas are particularly common, although infrequently seen. Wildlife viewing is enhanced by participating in guided hikes, offered from Boquete by Coffee Adventures *(tel 720-3852, www.coffeeadventures.net)* and Los Quetzales *(tel 771-2291, www.losquetzales.com). ■*

Around Volcán

One of many pre-Columbian ceramic urns at Sitio Barriles

THE TOWN OF VOLCÁN ENJOYS A GLORIOUSLY SCENIC setting on the western flank of Volcán Barú. Though its own appeal is limited, it draws adventure-minded visitors keen on kayaking, hiking, or birding, while coffee estates line a spectacular ridge-top drive that extends west to the Costa Rica border.

Volcán
🅰 188 B2

Sitio Barriles
✉ 4 miles (6.4 km) W of Volcán
☎ 6575-2121, e-mail: luislandau@mixmail.com
💲 By donation

All services locally are centered on the town of **Hato de Volcán** (more commonly known as Volcán), on a bare, high plateau on the southwestern slopes of Volcán Barú. The area was first settled by Swiss immigrants a century ago, and their architectural legacy is evident. The nondescript town serves as a gateway to sites farther afield. Plans to build a new road to link Cuesta de Piedra, 7 miles (10 km) south of town, with Boquete promise to increase tourist traffic.

Worth a quick visit, **Janson's**

Coffee House *(tel 771-4087 or 261-1488, www.jansoncoffee.net, closed Sun.)* is a hilltop coffee roaster and café above the company *beneficio*—roasting plant—on the south side of town. Free tours of the company's **La Torcaza Estate** coffee farm and beneficio are given by request. After sampling the coffees, birders should head to nearby **Lagunas de Volcán.** These three small lagoons enveloped by wetlands covering 352 acres (143 ha) are an important stop for purple gallinules, masked ducks, and other migratory waterfowl. The muddy access road begins on the north side of the airstrip and is suitable for four-wheel-drive vehicles only. Don't swim here, as it's easy to get caught in the weeds.

The Río Macho de Monte rises on the west flank of Volcán Barú and drops through the sheer-walled **Cañón Macho de Monte,** with waterfalls tumbling dramatically into cool pools. Access off the highway is via the track to a hydroelectricity plant that begins 7 miles (12 km) south of Volcán. Thrilling Class IV kayak runs are offered by Natahala Outdoor Center *(U.S. tel 888/905-7238, www.noc.com)* and inner tubes can be rented from El Manantial Spa & Resort (see p. 253) for more placid floats upriver. Finca Guardia *(0.5 mile/0.75 km S of Volcán, tel 6616-2521)* also offers horseback trips.

WEST OF VOLCÁN
The proverbially long and winding road that leads to Río Sereno west

of Volcán is to be enjoyed for its own sake as it snakes through mountains draped in cloud forest and coffee fields that ripple down the hillsides like folds of green silk.

The small roadside coffee farm of José Luis and Edna Landau doubles as an archaeological site—(from exquisite butterflies to rhinoceros beetles), and pre-Columbian artifacts, as well as accommodations in a lovely wooden lodge. At **Palo Verde** (the main coffee farm), 3 miles (5 km) of self-guided trails lead into 12 acres (5 ha) of primary forest.

Sitio Barriles—where the remains of a culture dating from 300 to 600 B.C. include a tomb, a large rock carved with an ancient map, plus remnants of what may have been an ancient temple. Pottery fragments and other pre-Columbian figurines are displayed higgledy-piggledy. In 1947, 18 life-size human figures hewn from basalt were discovered here (they are now in the Museo Reina Torres de Araúz in Panama City). The culture was probably destroyed by a volcanic eruption. Edna gives tours in Spanish and English.

Owned and operated by a keen conservationist, the **Finca Hartmann** coffee farm has its own forest reserve. The farm has two units. **Ojo de Agua** has a small museum with displays on coffee production, a large insect collection

Toucans, tinimus, and motmots are among the almost 300 bird species commonly seen, and deer, ocelots, armadillos, and monkeys abound.

Tucked in the forest nearby are **Los Pozos Termales Tisingal,** hot-water pools reached by four-wheel-drive via a convoluted dirt road. The road begins at a turnoff 6 miles (10 km) west of Volcán; signs to the springs are found along the way.

Río Sereno, 22 miles (35 km) west of Volcán, is a pleasant border town centered on a grassy plaza with a marble obelisk. The Costa Rica border runs by the hilltop radio tower, on the southwest side of town. A dirt road leads northwest from town through coffee fields to **La Unión,** where the (easily missed) border is marked by an obelisk. ∎

Ancient urns stud the mossy walls of a re-created pre-Columbian tomb at Sitio Barriles.

Finca Hartmann
www.fincahartmann.com
✉ Hwy. 42, 17 miles (27 km) W of Volcán
☎ 6477-1259
🕐 24 hours' notice required
💲 $$$

Around Cerro Punta

QUINTESSENTIALLY ALPINE CERRO PUNTA IS A MOST
unlikely tropical setting, conjuring images of *The Sound of Music*
without the snow. You'll be glad for blankets at night in this flower-
filled high-mountain valley at the gateway to Parque Internacional La
Amistad. Orchid, strawberry, and horse-breeding farms and a large
Ngöbe-Buglé population keep visitors enthralled when not hiking
and birding in the cloud forests.

North of Volcán, the road ascends
through **El Llano**—The Plain—
created by an ancient lava flow; it is
studded with massive boulders and
striated with old riverbeds. Set
amid pines between Volcán and
Cerro Punta, the twin communities
of **Bambito** and **Nueva Suiza**
(New Switzerland) cause you to do
a double-take with their Tyrolean-
style houses and lodges (many with
sod roofs) graced by gingerbread
trim and hanging baskets full of
pink, red, and white impatiens
(locally called *novia*). **Truchas de
Bambito** *(on the main road in
Bambito, tel 771-4373)* breeds

trout and rents rods—it's like
catching fish in a barrel.

About 2,200 feet (670 m) higher
than Boquete, **Cerro Punta,** at
6,463 feet (1,970 m) elevation,
occupies the crater of an extinct
volcano, with mountains all
around. The mild yet sunny alpine
climate and fertile soils are perfect
for cultivation of arable crops,
flowers, and strawberries. Cerro
Punta is also a center for the raising
of thoroughbred horses, a tradition
of animal husbandry dating back a
century to when European farmers
settled the region. **Haras Cerro
Punta** *(on the main road, 0.3*

**The thorough-
bred horses at
Haras Cerro
Punta are world-
renowned.**

mile/0.5 km N of Cerro Punta, tel 771-2057, www.harascerropunta .com) stud farm offers tours of its impressive facilities, where championship racehorses and French Percheron drays munch contentedly in lime-green pastures. Foaling season (January through May) is especially rewarding.

Above Cerro Punta, exquisite **Guadalupe,** the highest village in Panama, is the flower-festooned setting for **Los Quetzales Lodge & Spa** (see p. 253), an excellent base for riverside spa treatments and for hiking and birding in the hotel's 865-acre (350 ha) private reserve. Nearby, the **Jardín Botánico Finca Dracula** orchid sanctuary displays more than 2,200 orchid species—supposedly the largest collection in the Americas—including several from the genus *Dracula vampira* for which the *orquideario* is named. Guided tours of the greenhouses and laboratories (which produce 250,000 plants a year) provide orchid lovers with plenty to sink their teeth into.

At Guadalupe, the road loops and returns to Cerro Punta, a beautiful 4-mile-long (6.5 km) circular drive past flower and strawberry farms: **Finca Fresas Manolo** *(tel 6671-4871)* and **Panaflores** *(tel 771-2080)* welcome visits.

CLOUD FOREST HIKES

Only 158 acres (62 ha) of the 799-square-mile (2,069 sq km) **Parque Internacional La Amistad** (see p. 224) park is located in Chiriquí Province, yet the principal entrance and most accessible trails are here. Hiking La Amistad's lush cloud forests is reason enough to visit this region. The main entry and ANAM ranger station is 4 miles (7 km) northwest of Cerro Punta at Las Nubes. Three trails begin at the

A *Dracula vampira* orchid displays its spectacular petals at Finca Dracula orchid farm.

ranger station. The mile-long (1.6 km) **Sendero La Cascada** offers lookout points en route to a spectacular waterfall; slightly longer **Sendero El Retoño** ascends into the cloud forest, as does the more challenging **Sendero La Montaña.** The **Asociación Agroecoturística La Amistad** (ASAELA; *tel 771-2620),* a local cooperative, runs a delightful open-air restaurant at the entrance. The ranger station, a five-minute hike uphill, has a tiny exhibition center, plus a simple dorm and kitchen (bring your own food).

You can also set out along **Sendero Los Quetzales** (see p. 201), which begins at Bajo Grande *(3 miles/5 km east of the Cerro Punta–Guadalupe road)* and crosses the northern shoulder of **Parque Internacional Volcán Barú** before depositing you in Boquete (see pp. 196–199). The shorter and easier **Sendero Las Tres Rocas** leads to a rock formation and lookout with spectacular views. Los Quetzales Lodge & Spa's private reserve (see above) lies within the park and has trails that extend into Parque Internacional La Amistad. ■

Storm clouds gather over Lago Fortuna on the Caribbean side of the continental divide.

Driving across the continental divide

Surmounting Panama's serrated spine, this mountain drive begins almost at sea level and reaches cloud-draped heights before spiraling dizzily down to the Caribbean coastal plain. Stupendously scenic, the journey features numerous waystations of interest. While unpaved in part, the route described here is suitable for most sedans, although occasional landslides, ephemeral fogs, and steep switchbacks require more than the usual degree of caution.

Highway 4 begins at **Chiriquí ❶**, a nondescript town at the junction with the Interamerican Highway. From here the well-paved road sweeps north through cattle country lushly clad with green meadows. Drawing you forward are the rounded peaks of the Cordillera de Tabasará floating on the horizon in shades of bottle green. Turn left at the Y-fork at the entrance to **Gualaca ❷**, then left at the gas station half a mile (0.8 km) farther along. Soon the road begins to climb foothills strewn with volcanic boulders.

After 18 miles (29 km), a sheer-walled canyon parallels the road, which appears to slope downhill. You'll be shocked to note the water running in the opposite direction, albeit level with the road——the apparent slope is an **optical illusion.** A short distance farther you cross **Presa Chiriquí,** a dam tapping the Río Chiriquí for electricity.

Four miles (6.4 km) farther, turn right at the T-junction. Beyond the tiny community of **Caldera ❸** you'll pass a short trail to **Piedra**

Pintada, a giant riverside boulder carved with pre-Columbian petroglyphs, and a 1.5-mile-long (2.5 km) trail to the **Pozos de Aguas Termales** thermal springs (102°–108°F/39°–42°C), known locally as Las Calderas. Soaking in these tepid pools, ringed by stone walls and shaded by fruit trees, provides a pleasant break. Continuing, dramatic mountains open up as the road begins a roller-coaster ascent into the mountains. Some 36 miles (58 km) after starting out, turn right onto the dirt road at the junction marked "Casa de Control" (the left fork ends at the control center for the Central Hidroeléctrica Fortuna; see p. 208).

After 6.5 miles (10.5 km) you meet Highway 4; turn left. Immediately you enter **Reserva Forestal Fortuna ❹**, where trails lead up through 75 square miles (194 sq km) of protected forests swaddled in clouds. Beyond the **Centro Para la Investigación y Conservación de la Biodiversidad Tropical,** where the Smithsonian Tropical

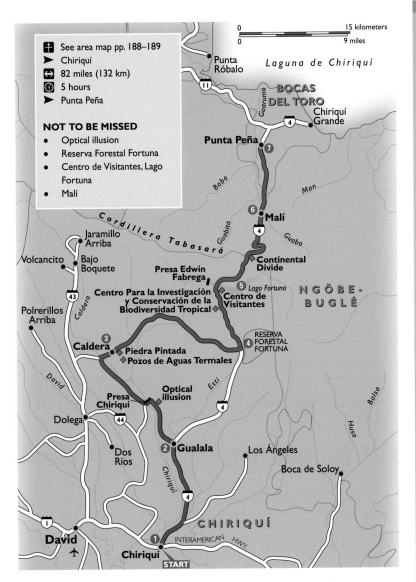

See area map pp. 188–189
► Chiriquí
↔ 82 miles (132 km)
⏱ 5 hours
► Punta Peña

NOT TO BE MISSED
- Optical illusion
- Reserva Forestal Fortuna
- Centro de Visitantes, Lago Fortuna
- Malí

Research Institute has a research facility *(tel 212-8016, www.stri.org)*, the road coils sharply downhill into the Valle de Las Sierpes and **Presa Edwin Fabrega,** a 100-foot-high (30 m) dam containing the waters of **Lago Fortuna** ⑤. Stop to peruse the nature exhibitions (in Spanish only) in the **Centro de Visitantes** *(www.fortuna.com.pa).*

Hereon, the mountain vistas inspire awe as you approach and cross the continental divide.

Drive with care as you descend the forest-clad eastern slopes with the road falling sharply, sinuous as a snake, to the Ngöbe-Buglé Indian village of **Malí** ⑥—a drop of some 5,000 feet (1,524 m). The road then follows the Río Guarumo through a lush valley framed by dramatic mountain scenes westward. The drive ends in **Punta Peña** ⑦, whose inhabitants are employed in the pineapple plantations north of town. ∎

More places to visit in Chiriquí & the cordillera

CARTA VIEJA RUM FACTORY

The plains west of David are covered in cane fields as level and as green as a billiard table. The yeasty smell of molasses hovers over them, luring you toward one of the oldest *centrales* (sugarcane processing factories) in Panama. The Central Industrial Chiricana rum factory, in the village of El Tejar, about 12 miles (20 km) west of David, was founded in 1915. It is known for making Panama's esteemed Carta Vieja—a dark, full-flavored rum aged for four years in white birch casks, which lend their own coloration and flavor. The distillery offers weekday tours. Two of the original stills are displayed outside. Every Holy Week, the nearby rural village of Alanje draws 10,000 devotees to the "miraculous" Cristo de Alanje, a statue laid out in the church.

🅰 206 B2 ✉ El Tejar, 2 miles (3.2 km) NW of Alanje (10 miles/16 km W of David) ☎ 772-7073, www.cartaviejapanama.com 🕐 Closed Sat. & Sun.

CENTRAL HIDROELÉCTRICA FORTUNA

The Fortuna Hydroelectricity Station, opened in 1984, generates 39 percent of Panama's electricity needs. Its three 100 MW turbines are fed by the waters of Lago Fortuna (see p. 207) 20 miles (32 km) away. The waters speed 4 miles (6 km) downhill through a pressure tunnel, dropping 2,392 feet (765 m) to the turbine station. The Casa de Máquinas—the turbine facility—occupies a vast subterranean cavern 1,419 feet deep (430 m) and is accessed via a mile-long tunnel. Guided tours are offered with one week's advance notice. Long pants and covered shoes must be worn.

🅰 188 C3 ✉ 3 miles (5 km) NW of Gualacá (19 miles/31 km NE of David) ☎ 206-1800 (in Panama City), www.fortuna.com.pa 🕐 Closed Sat. & Sun.

FINCA LA SUIZA

Set on 500 acres (200 ha) of premontane forest on the southeastern slopes of Volcán Barú, this Swiss-run lodge offers hiking along four well-marked and manicured forest trails—some steep, all-day adventures—that ascend into cloud forest full of chattering birdsong. Cascades cast misty rainbows, and it is congenial to sit and listen to the falling water change into music. Day access is offered to nonguests for a fee. The postprandial strawberry sundae is reason enough to dine and overnight at the lodge.

🅰 188 B4 ✉ 2.5 miles (4 km) N of Los Planes & 11 miles (18 km) N of Gualacá ☎ 6615-3774, www.panama.net.tc 🕐 Closed June, Sept., & Oct. 🅂 $$

ISLAS SECAS

The Islas Secas archipelago, southeast of Parque Nacional Marino Golfo de Chiriquí, is a privately owned archipelago of 16 small islands with one hotel served by its own charter plane. Limned by talcum-soft beaches, these isles answer the longing for a luxury take on the Robinson Crusoe experience. Each isle is distinct as a thumbprint, though most are craggy, densely forested, and ringed by coral reefs. Some have trails good for birding. White-tipped sharks are common, patrolling reefs that guarantee fantastic snorkeling and diving. Hawksbill, leatherback, and olive Ridley turtles flap leisurely by, and by night haul out to nest in hidden coves.

🅰 189 D1 ✉ 22 miles (35 km) SE of Boca Chica by charter boat or private charter flight

TOLÉ

Tolé is the most accessible of the Ngöbe-Buglé communities and sprawls across the foothills separating Veraguas and Chiriquí Provinces. During the coffee harvest, entire families commute to work in the highlands around Boquete. You can watch *chácaras* (woven handbags), exquisitely woven baskets, and dresses being made. If you're in a hiking mood, a trail that begins at **El Nancito,** 5 miles (8 km) west of Tolé, leads to boulders etched with pre-Columbian petroglyphs.

🅰 189 E2 ✉ 51 miles (82 km) E of David via the Interamerian Highway, then 1.5 miles (2 km) N ∎

Extreme in contrasts of
mountain and isle, this area
invites visitors to experience the
charm of Caribbean island culture, the thrill of premier snorkeling and surfing, and the insights of
engaging with indigenous peoples.

Bocas del Toro

**Waterfront living,
Bocas Town**

Bocas del Toro

THE MOST POPULAR TOURIST DESTINATION BEYOND PANAMA CITY, BOCAS del Toro Province is known for its funky, laid-back island lifestyle. There are really two Bocas del Toro, however: island and mainland. Banana plantations cover much of the hot and humid coastal lowlands, centered on Changuinola (the fruits are shipped from the port town of Almirante), while pineapples poke up around Chiriquí Grande. A huge chunk of the mainland province lies within Parque Internacional La Amistad and the Bosque Protector Palo Seco buffer zone. This wild and rugged region—a realm of peccaries, jaguars, and pumas—is virtually unexplored. Sluggish rivers spill from the mountains to long brown-sand beaches, drawing marine turtles to nest. Manatees forage the inshore waters, where black-as-night swamps such as San San Pond Sak are also inhabited by caiman, river otters, and waterbirds.

The offshore isles synonymous with the name Bocas del Toro—referred to simply as "Bocas" by locals—are another world altogether. This archipelago of about six major islands and several score atolls and cays is a watery world where water taxis (anything from powerful motor-launches to quieter, slower *cayucos*) are the only means of travel. Chilling in a hammock, catching a wave, or sipping cold beers in raffish tumbledown bars—such are the ways of the laid-back Bocas lifestyle (exemplified by the local use of *tranquilo* as a retort when asked how things are). Foreign investors have recently discovered Bocas's appeal, however. Big resorts and residential projects are bursting forth like mushrooms on a wet log, threatening to change the casual mood.

The vast majority of visitors to the region limit their visit to these islands, which

The sunlit waterfront of Bocas del Toro Town, an increasingly popular tourist destination.

rise up from year-round warm water where coral reefs support 74 of the Caribbean's 79 coral species. Snorkeling and diving are superb, although visibility is often an issue (especially after heavy rains) due to silt from the banana plantations. Patches of rain forest tower over the waters. Several species of poison dart frogs are endemic to the islands, as is a small sloth that resides among the mangrove leaves. Bring insect repellent against mosquitoes and *chitras,* tiny annoying sand flies that will eat you alive.

A key attraction in the area are the Ngöbe-Buglé

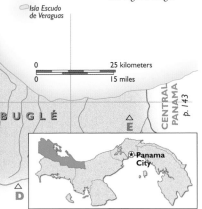

communities (and Naso-Teribe in the extreme north), many still clinging to their Ngabere language and culture in the face of hardship. Located throughout the archipelago and mainland (where many communities line the coast highway between Punta Peña and Almirante), they are accessible to every traveler. Increasingly, indigenous peoples throughout the region are turning to ecotourism. Though facilities—including ecolodges such as those at Wekso—are simple, visits provide an opportunity to experience the diversity of Panama while contributing to the well-being and eco-consciousness of indigenous people (from necessity, many still hunt wildlife, including turtles, illegally; visitors should refrain from eating turtle meat and even lobster, which is being overfished).

While the mainland population is mostly mestizo and Ngöbe Indian, a majority of islanders are black—descendants of slaves and of 19th-century Jamaican laborers. Most speak both Spanish and English, though the region's lingua franca is a lilting English patois laced with indigenous and Spanish terms called Guari-Guari.

Come prepared for rain. September through October and March through April offer you a better-than-average chance of sunny weather. ■

Isla Colón

Isla Colón

🗺 210 B3

Visitor information

www.ipat.gob.pa

✉ IPAT, Calle 1, Bocas Town

☎ 757-9642

🕐 Closed Sat. & Sun.

THIS 24-SQUARE-MILE (61 SQ KM) ISLAND IS THE LARGEST and by far the most populated of Bocas's isles, with the majority of hotels, restaurants, and services. Though its prime appeal is the mellow charm of the Bocas Town lifestyle, the island has patches of primary forest to explore, plus spectacular beaches seemingly tailored for surfing and for turtle-viewing by night. The entire place is easy to explore by bicycle, albeit along rough dirt roads.

GETTING TO BOCAS TOWN

By air

Bocas Town is served by air from Panama City, David, & Costa Rica.

By water taxi

🚤 Boteros Bocatorenos Unidos, 757-9760, e-mail: boterosbocas@yahoo.com

🚤 Expreso Taxi 25 (to & from Almirante & neighboring isles), tel 757-9028

By car ferry

🚤 A car ferry operates between Chiriquí Grande, Almirante, and Bocas Town.

Bocas Town, the archipelago's commercial hub, was founded in 1826 and was a base for British loggers and for harvesting sea turtles. In 1889, the United Fruit Co. established its local headquarters here; the building, erected in 1905, is now the **Hotel Bahía** *(tel 757-9626, fax 757-9692).* Jamaican laborers followed. The early 20th-century boom died along with banana plants when "Panama disease" struck and the company moved to the mainland. Meanwhile, a series of fires destroyed much of the town—a charming ensemble of clapboard houses in quintessential Caribbean vernacular, with gingerbread trim and facades painted in tropical ice cream flavors. After "Big Fruit" pulled out, the isle slumbered in limbo until a decade or so ago, when backpackers from Costa Rica put Bocas on the map.

Though the past few years have witnessed an explosion in tourism and foreign investment, this cozy and close-knit community still appeals mostly to offbeat tropical tramps and independent-minded travelers whose idea of a good time is lazing in a hammock until sundown, then chilling over reggae riffs and a cool beer in funky waterfront bars. Most hotels nestle over the waters, and many have their own wharves and restaurants resting on stilts, good for watching fiery vermilion sunsets.

The town is laid out in a simple grid with every place of import strung along the two main waterfront streets: Calle 1 and Calle 3. Between the two, and the heart of affairs, is **Parque Simón Bolívar,** shaded by rambling fig trees full of birdsong. A bronze **bust of Simón Bolívar** is the town's sole

monument. The *bomberos (Calle 1 at Ave. G),* or fire station, displays a 1920s fire engine; the **Biblioteca Pública de Bocas** *(Calle 3, closed Sat. & Sun.),* or library, has an exhibition on marine turtle ecology; and the **IPAT office** has exhibits on the history and ecology of the archipelago.

Cayo Carenero floats atop the waters just a three-minute boat-ride to the north. A crumbling cement path winds through its village—a smaller, sleepier version of Bocas Town—and leads to a killer reef break that surfers know simply as Carenero.

Bocas Town's beach, **Playa el Istmito,** a ten-minute walk north from the park along Avenida G, is the setting for the annual four-day Fería del Mar in September, when the entire community grooves to reggae. The beach has a volleyball court and a party atmosphere, although there are more scenic beaches farther out.

WINDWARD SHORE

Two dirt roads lead north from Bocas Town. One follows the eastern shore past the community of **Big Creek** to **Playa Paunch,** which tempts surfers with its reef break, and **Playa Bluff,** where nonsurfers can kick back and watch experienced surf dudes practicing on Hawaiian-size killer tubes.

At offbeat, vibrant restaurants and pubs throughout Isla Colón— such as here at Bocas Town's El Pecador del Sabor restaurant— locals and visitors mingle in laid-back ease.

Riptides and high surf preclude swimming. Stretching for 2 miles (3.5 km), this brown-sand beach is an important nesting site for marine turtles, June to September. The **Observatorio de Tortugas** (*0.5 mile/0.75 km N of Playa Paunch*) offers guided tours at night. By day, you can follow a trail beyond Playa Bluff to **La Piscina,** a lagoon with safe swimming. Inland, the forests teem with parakeets, monkeys, and sloths.

Birders will be enthralled by rare sightings at **Cayo del Cisne** (Swan Cay), sometimes called Isla de los Pájaros (Bird Island). Rising 131 feet (40 m), this small rugged islet 1 mile (1.6 km) off the north coast of Isla Colón is the only known nesting site in the southwest Caribbean for red-billed tropicbirds and one of only three nesting sites for brown boobies along Panama's Caribbean coast. The island is a popular destination for tourist boats, but stepping ashore is forbidden. If your guide offers to lead you ashore, refuse.

LEEWARD SHORE

A second, unpaved road cuts north through the heart of the island to **La Colonia Santeña,** a small community surrounded by cattle pastures. (You'll be glad for four-wheel-drive in the wet season.) Half a mile (1 km) east of town, a cavern known as the **Santuario Natural Nuestra Señora de la Gruta,** or more commonly as La Gruta (the grotto), contains a statuette of the Virgin Mary. Push aside the ferns and vines that curtain the entrance to discover a surreal world full of dripstone formations. Fruit bats roost in ceiling crevices and the pungent smell of ammonia seeps up from their excrement, soft underfoot (wear a bandanna mask to guard against inhaling toxic spores). The site draws pilgrims, especially each July 16 for the Festival de la Virgen del Carmen.

The dirt road, a fun cycling experience in the dry season, ends at **Bocas del Drago,** a sheltered bay with a gorgeous white-sand beach at the isle's far southwest tip. It's a great place to relax in a hammock, and the beachfront restaurant rents pedal boats and snorkeling gear. Boat taxis will run you here; it's wise to arrange a return pickup. The **Smithsonian Tropical Research Institute** operates a scientific research station (*tel 757-9794 or 212-8082 for visitors, www.stri.org*) close by. The early morning public bus to Bocas del Drago serves workers and returns only in the evening. ∎

Marine turtles

Five of the world's seven species of marine turtle—from the diminutive olive Ridley to Cadillac-size leatherbacks—lay their eggs on Panama's beaches. Their populations are endangered throughout their range thanks to human depredations, though all the major nesting sites in Panama are now protected. Male turtles spend their lives at sea; only the female returns to land, normally to the beach where she was born, and usually at night during a full-moon high tide. Finding a spot above the high tide mark, she digs a pit in which she lays 100 or so spherical, golf ball–size eggs. After covering them up, she heads back to sea. The eggs hatch after incubating in the warm sand for about seven weeks. Hatchlings are usually the same gender in each nest according to the temperature of the sand (cooler for males). ∎

Opposite:
The waterfront hotels of Bocas del Toro invite relaxation on decks with a view.

Islas Bastimentos & Solarte

Islas Bastimentos & Solarte

🗺 210 C3 & 219

Visitor information

www.anam.gob.pa

✉ ANAM, Calle 1, Bocas Town

☎ 758-6802

🕐 Closed Sat. & Sun.

THESE TWIN CAYS PARALLELING EACH OTHER EAST OF ISLA Colón boast rain forest with rewarding hikes, world-class snorkeling spots, and interesting Ngöbe-Buglé villages. Surfers rave about Hawaiian-size waves on Bastimentos, which is also known for its strawberry poison dart frogs; one-third of the isle is protected as a national park that extends into the marine environment.

ISLA BASTIMENTOS

Appealing mainly to nature lovers, this lush, 20-square-mile (52 sq km) island also pulses to the heartbeat of Afro-Antillean culture, centered on the small, down-at-heels settlement of **Old Bank** (also called Bastimentos Town). A ten-minute boat ride from Bocas Town, this funky, colorful community snuggles in a sheltered cove on the isle's southwest side. Dogs snoozing in the dust and old-timers playing dominoes in pools of shade sum up the pace of life. The predominantly Afro-Antillean population (most of whom speak the local Guari-Guari dialect) lives by fishing, by guiding tourists, or by selling Afro-Antillean cuisine, such as johnnycakes and *rondon* (rundown), a spicy Caribbean seafood stew. Reggae riffs mingle with the surf, and locals pick up the beat on Monday night calypso sessions by the world-famous Bastimentos Beach Boys.

A rough track begins near the football field and cuts east across the island, providing a lovely rain forest experience and stringing together a necklace of spectacular beaches. First up is **Playa Primera** (also called Wizard's Beach). Like most north-shore beaches, it is pummeled by high surf and therefore unsafe for swimming. Farther east, frosty-white **Playa Rana Roja** (Red Frog Beach) is slated for major residential development. Surf crashes ashore onto **Playa Larga,** whose miles-long sugary sands draw nesting sea

turtles. The beach lies within the Marino Isla Bastimentos national park (see p. 220), whose inland forests can be accessed from here by trails. Nearby, **The Silverback**—as in gorilla—is so-named because its waves can snap your board like a twig; this is the Big Kahuna of Bocas surfing with waves that on occasion reach 25 feet (7.5 m).

Connecting Playa Rana Roja to the southern, inward shore, the jungle-shaded **Sendero de la Rana Roja**—named for the many enameled strawberry-red frogs hopping among the leaf litter—leads via pools full of caimans to the tiny and teetering Ngöbe-Buglé community of **Bahía Honda,** tucked tight into the head of a cove of the same name. Here, guides will take you out in cayucos to spot crocodiles and caimans and the region's endemic species of

isle that locals call Cayo Nancy is slated for a large residential community project. For now there are few houses and no roads. Bicycles and golf carts follow narrow trails. And there's walking, of course. A short trail ascends through the forest from the humble community of

A water taxi sets out from Bastimentos for Isla Colón. These simple craft form the sole links between isles.

mangrove-munching sloth.

The **Cueva Nivida,** a cavern tucked up a small creek off Bahía Honda, can be reached by sea kayak. Exploring involves wading chest-deep through grottoes; Oscar Powell, at Roots Restaurant in the center of Old Bank, guides tours and provides helmets with lanterns.

ISLA SOLARTE

Slung beneath the underbelly of Isla Bastimentos and 1.5 miles (2 km) east of Bocas Town, the 3-mile-long (5 km) by half-mile-wide (1 km)

Solarte, where the mostly Ngöbe-Buglé inhabitants live by fishing and lobstering.

There's great snorkeling and diving in the little bay off the western tip of **Punta Hospital,** although it can get crowded with tour boats bringing snorkelers. The point is named for a hospital—now in ruins—established by the United Fruit Co. to treat workers suffering malaria. Starfleet Scuba *(Calle 1A 2374, Bocas Town, tel 757-9630, www.starfleetscuba.com)* offers dive trips. ■

A boat tour around the archipelago

Sprinkled across almost 60 miles (100 km) of teal waters, the Bocas del Toro archipelago offers isles within isles. All the islands have things in common, but each has its own character and even distinct culture and natural wonders. This full-day boat tour combines cultural highlights, wildlife encounters, and opportunities for snorkeling in bathtub-warm waters the color of melted peridots.

Ngöbe-Buglé Indians paddle a hand-hewn log canoe past Cayo Agua.

Several boat operators in **Bocas Town** ❶ offer tours or hire out a boat and guide for a personal tour. They can be found at the waterfront docks on Calle 1; Gallardo Livingstone *(tel 757-9388)* is recommended. The price can top $100 for a day's boat ride and is best shared with a group. Be sure that the boat is seaworthy and has life-jackets—which you should wear—and a 75-hp motor. You'll be at sea all day, so a sun hat and sunscreen are de rigueur even if your boat has a canopy. Take snorkel gear, which can be rented in Bocas Town.

Begin by heading south for **Isla San Cristóbal** ❷—note the lighthouse on the northwestern point marking the channel through which large cargo ships pass en route to load bananas at Almirante. Cruising along the mangrove-lined shoreline, your destination is **Laguna Bocatorito,** a calm lagoon teeming with fish. Bottlenose dolphins are almost always around and seem to delight in leaping alongside speeding boats. The Ngöbe-Buglé community of **Bocatorito** overlooks the lagoon. Step ashore briefly to learn about the Comité Local de Conservación y Pesca, a local fish conservation group that has established tanks of tilapia to feed the impoverished village.

Next head to **Isla Popa** ❸, passing **Popa II,** a Ngöbe-Buglé community that lives on fishing and diving for lobster. An ecotourism project sponsored by ANAM has laid trails; the **Sendero de Sandubidi** provides a magnificent rain forest experience should you choose to stop and hike (be aware of your surroundings at all times, as fearsome fer-de-lance snakes abound here). If hungry, you can eat at the restaurant here, or continue east along the shore of Isla Popa to **Punta Cayo Tigre** and the rocky isle that rises from the channel to its east; here, **Restaurante El Morro** offers lunch from a perch with a view,

A BOAT TOUR AROUND THE ARCHIPELAGO

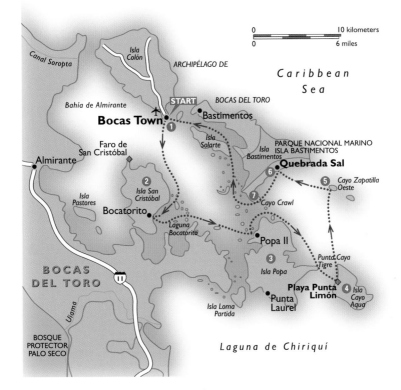

and you can snorkel close to shore.

It's a five-minute ride to the next island, **Cayo Agua** ❹, drawing few visitors but fascinating for its rickety homesteads in vibrant colors overhanging the waters. Passing **Playa Punta Limón** at the isle's northwest point, note the exposed coral embedded in cliffs more than three million years old. Next, turn north across open water toward the enchanting **Cayo Zapatilla Oeste** ❺, whose white sands beckon you for an hour or more of snorkeling in the glassy shallows, with coral only 9 feet (3 m) down. Stay close in to shore due to strong currents farther out.

Satisfied? Head back west toward Isla Bastimentos and the land-locked community of **Quebrada Sal** ❻ (Salt Creek), where a mix of Ngöbe-Buglé and *afrocaribeños* live surrounded by mangroves; look for sloths as you motor up the channel. The community still practices traditional healing, and guides will lead you along a mile-long (1.5 km) forest

trail to a mirador with lovely views back to Cayo Zapatilla. Then, continue south around the tip of Isla Bastimentos, passing **Cayo Crawl** ❼, a tiny cay off the southeast tip of Bastimentos. Stop to snorkel the reefs in crystal-clear shallows.

Return to Bocas Town via the channel running between Isla Bastimentos and Isla Solarte. ■

✚ See area map pp. 210–211
► Bocas Town
🔁 60 miles (100 km)
🕐 8 hours
► Bocas Town

NOT TO BE MISSED
- Laguna Bocatorito
- Cayo Zapatilla Oeste
- Cayo Crawl

Cayo Zapatilla Uno—the perfect spot for a relaxed stroll on the beach

Parque Nacional Marino Isla Bastimentos

COVERING 51 SQUARE MILES (132 SQ KM) OF LUSH ISLA Bastimentos and surrounding tropical waters and cays, this marine park was established in 1988 to protect the most extensive coral reefs and Caribbean mangrove swamps in the country. Superlative snorkeling and spectacular wildlife viewing are key appeals.

Parque Nacional Marino Isla Bastimentos
🗺 210 C2 & C3
Visitor information
www.anam.gob.pa
✉ ANAM, Calle 1ra, Bocas Town
☎ 758-6802
🕐 Closed Sat. & Sun.
💲 $$. Permit can be purchased in Bocas Town

Girding the wide waist of Isla Bastimentos, the park covers one-third of the island. Along the shores, channels braid through vast expanses of mangroves whose stilt roots rise from translucent waters. Inland, dense moist tropical forest makes a fecund habitat for capuchin and night monkeys, sloths, agoutis, and 28 other species of mammal, including bulldog bats that swoop over **Lagunas de Bastimentos** after dusk to seize fish on the fly. The freshwater lagoon is a hangout for turtles, caimans, and crocodiles: Swimming is not recommended! You may spy the strawberry poison dart frog, one of 28 reptile and amphibian species in the park. Trails into the forest are basic. Hire a local guide.

You can follow a trail from Old Bank to access the park at **Playa Larga.** Four marine turtle species nest along this 8-mile-long (13 km) beach. Frigate birds soar overhead and parrots add their squawks and screeches to the calliope of birdsong.

Two-thirds of the park spans the waters to both west and east of the island. Stealing the show are the **Cayos Zapatilla,** named for the *zapatilla* fruit that grows here. Sitting atop a coral plateau, these twin isles are ringed by palm-shaded talcum-fine beaches. Nurse sharks cruise among the coral heads and point their noses into caves that begin about 30 feet (9 m) down. Ashore, the **Bosque Detrás del Arrecife** interpretive trail begins at the ANAM ranger station on Cayo Zapatilla Este, where camping is permitted for a small fee. ∎

Bosque Protector Palo Seco

FORMING A BUFFER BETWEEN PARQUE INTERNACIONAL LA Amistad and the coast, this 603,000-acre (244,000 ha) protected zone acts as a biological corridor for wildlife connecting the park with Reserva Forestal Fortuna.

Bosque Protector Palo Seco

🏔 210 B2

Visitor information

www.anam.gob.pa

✉ ANAM, Changuinola

☎ 758-6822

The fragile ecological region incorporates six different forest types extending from about 600 feet (182 m) to more than 6,500 feet (1,981 m) above sea level. Most of the terrain is rugged, mountainous, and jungle clad. The vistas looking up from the lowlands are dramatic. Nonetheless, the lowland terrain bordering the zone is under pressure. Slash-and-burn agriculture and illicit logging have followed the recent opening of the Punta Peña–Almirante highway, gnawing away at the rain forest with frightening speed. Lone ceiba and balsa trees tower above vast swathes cleared for cattle.

Two projects—Corredor Biológico Mesoamericano del Atlántico Panameño and the Modelo de Comunidad Ecológica los Valles—work with dozens of small Ngöbe-Buglé communities scattered throughout the lowlands to establish sustainable ecological models. Several are focusing their efforts on ecotourism, including the community of **Bajo Cedro,** which has a women's crafts cooperative using natural fibers and dyes, 3 miles (5 km) west of the highway, about 22 miles (35 km) south of Almirante. The community of **Nance de Riscó,** about 3 miles (5 km) inland of Almirante, lies within the Bosque Protector and is a center for the production of the woven handbags and other indigenous crafts sold in Bocas. And nearby **Miraflores,** on the highway 4 miles (6.5 km) north of Almirante, has a *zoocriadero* (breeding farm) for iguanas. All these communities are active in reforestation and offer guide services into the nearby forest along community trails.

ANAM has a ranger station at Km 68.5 on the Fortuna highway, near Altos de Valle, 18 miles (29 km) south of Chiriquí Grande. Here, the **Sendero Los Tucanes** leads through thick montane forest. Nearby **Willie Mazu Rancho Ecológico** (*tel 442-1340, www.natturpanama.com),* at Km 68.7, also has trails and tent accommodations. It makes a fine base for spectacular birding. ∎

Iguanas

The iguana is found in forested lowlands from Mexico to Brazil. Primarily herbivorous, it spends most of its time in the treetops or basking in the sun in forest clearings. It can grow up to 6 feet (1.8 m), half of which comprises a flickable tail ribbed with spines. This hardy, solitary creature is capable of withstanding a 50-foot (15 m) fall from a tree; it's a good swimmer, and its rough, scaly skin is water resistant. Nonetheless, the iguana faces threats from hunting, loss of habitat, and capture for the pet trade. Impoverished *campesinos* consider its meat and eggs to be delicacies, and indigenous communities also kill iguanas for medicinal purposes. The Smithsonian Tropical Research Institute (see p. 104) heads a successful breeding program in Panama. ∎

Wild cats

Of the ten species of neotropical wild cats, six are present in Panama and are found from the shoreline to the highest mountain slopes. Supremely camouflaged and armed with keen vision, these elusive hunters stealthily prowl their habitats, silent as a cloud.

Four species——the jaguar, margay, ocelot, and oncilla—have spotted coats; all are listed as facing extinction due to poaching and deforestation. The puma and jaguarundi, with their single-colored coats, fare slightly better.

Worshiped by pre-Columbian Indians, the muscular jaguar *(Panthera onca)* can weigh up to 330 pounds (150 kg) and measure almost 9 feet (2.7 m) in length, nose to tail. It has short, stocky legs and a large head with powerful jaws built for piercing its prey's skull with one bite (*yaguara* is a South American Indian word meaning "a beast that kills its prey with one bound"). An adept swimmer, this forest-dweller lives close to water and is skilled at scooping up fish. Despite its size, it can even scale trees to hunt monkeys. Melanistic or black jaguars are frequently born into litters alongside normally colored siblings; their rosette markings can faintly be seen, slate against jet-black sheen. The jaguar is one of the first animals to disappear in habitat suffering deforestation.

Found throughout Panama in a wide range of environments, the sleek and furtive ocelot *(Leopardus pardalis),* known locally as the *manigordo,* is the phantom of the night. About twice as long as a house cat, this agile climber spends most of its time slinking along branches like a catwalk diva. Ocelots often pair up to stalk prey. The cat's exquisite fur can vary from a rich yellow cream in arid areas to a deeper rust brown in darker forests. Its white-tipped ears are well rounded and dotted with a single white spot on the back; white markings surround the eyes and mouth and twin black lines run up over its shoulders. Rows of beige blotches ringed in black run along its body, while its short tail is ringed in black bands like a raccoon.

The ocelot's smaller cousin, the margay *(Leopardus wiedii),* known to Panamanians as

the *tigrillo,* also prefers a life in the trees and has evolved specially adapted claws and a unique ankle joint—which it can rotate 180 degrees for pirouetting like a ballerina—for an arboreal lifestyle. It can even run headfirst down trees! The margay has a longer tail and legs than the ocelot, and its rosettes are less distinct, sometimes appearing as solid blotches. The population has dwindled dramatically, and the margay is now found only in isolated pockets of Panama. The similarly colored, house cat–size oncilla *(Leopardus tigrinus),* or tiger cat, is found in higher-elevation forests in Panama's cordilleras. Far less adept at arboreal living than its larger cousins, it hunts on the ground,

feeding primarily on rodents, reptiles, and insects. It has a shorter tail than the margay and a narrower body.

Known to North Americans as the mountain lion, the puma *(Puma concolor)* is common throughout the isthmus and South America. Colored from tawny to taupe or chocolate, the 6-foot-long (1.8 m) cat has a small, broad head with small rounded ears, a long slender body, and an equally long black-tipped tail. A full-grown adult can tackle domestic cattle with trademark running jumps ending with a huge lunge of its powerful hind legs.

The long-tailed jaguarundi *(Herpailurus yagouarundi)* has an elongated slender body,

Like most big cats, the ocelot has been hunted to near extinction for its exquisite fur.

short front legs, slightly longer hind legs, and a small head with tiny weasel-like ears and narrow yellowish eyes. This lowland dweller is expert at scooping up fish with its probing front paws. A full-grown male can measure up to some 30 inches (76 cm) and, though spotted at birth, its lustrous adult coat is solid, ranging from coffee-colored to chocolate or even charcoal. Known to Panamanians as the *león breñero* (scrub lion), it is the most adaptable of the neotropical cat species to environmental changes wrought by humans. ∎

Parque Internacional La Amistad

**Parque
Internacional
La Amistad**
🗺 210 A1 & B2
Visitor information
www.anam.gob.pa
✉ ANAM, Changuinola;
Vía Aeropuerto,
David
☎ 758-6822
(Changuinola), 775-
3163 (David)

BEYOND THE EDGE OF HUMAN INCURSION, THE VAST Talamanca massif is a last frontier for tourism. Panama's wildest mountain terrain has been enshrined for posterity in a mammoth park that the country shares with its northern neighbor, Costa Rica. Panama's portion lies almost wholly within Boca del Toro Province, though the tiny fraction that spills westward into Chiriquí offers by far the easiest access.

Spanning 1,550 square miles (4,000 sq km) of Panama and Costa Rica, the International Friendship Park girdles the rugged Cordillera Talamanca mountains, a great tectonic massif thrust from the ocean over several million years and twisted into a number of ranges. Rising with a heart-aching loveliness from 150 feet (46 m) above sea level on the Caribbean lowlands to a cool 10,945 feet (3,336 m) atop the dizzying heights of **Cerro Fábrega,** these mountains span a width of 50 miles (80 km). The steep knife-edged peaks are rain-sodden year-round.

Panama's 799-square-mile (2,069 sq km) portion spans 7 of the country's 12 life zones. Vegetation varies from rain-drenched lowland tropical rain forest to a prodigious expanse of cloud forest—home to the largest concentration of quetzals in Central America. Named a UNESCO World Heritage site in 1990, this pristine wilderness is a last refuge for many endangered species. The wildlife viewing is superlative, offering creatures from tapirs to tayras. Poison dart frogs are abundant underfoot, and well-camouflaged fer-de-lances lie coiled in deathly anticipation of passing prey. Birders are no less rewarded: More than 225 species have been recorded within the park. Harpy eagles, locally extinct in much of

Central America, still soar over the southern Talamancas. In all, the park holds at least 60 percent of the nation's species of flora and fauna.

Three indigenous tribes—the Bribrí, the Ngöbe-Buglé, and the Naso-Teribe—also cling to vestiges of their traditional lifestyles in the remote lowland valleys. The vast majority of this choking terrain, however, is uncharted, uninhabited, and immensely difficult to explore.

Hiking is a true adventure and should be undertaken only with adequate preparation and never alone. Access on the Caribbean side requires a 40-minute boat trip up the Río Teribe from **El Silencio,** 6 miles (10 km) south of Changuinola. Kingfishers, parrots, and river otters are frequently seen. The ANAM ranger station is at the hamlet of **Wekso** (see p. 227), where a short trail leads into the park. Other barely discernible trails penetrate the mountainous heart of La Amistad along remote, often overgrown, muddy tracks. A guide and hiking shoes are essential, as are food and camping gear for overnights. It's best to hike in the dry season (May to December).

Even more appealing are the subalpine highlands. The best base for exploring these areas is **Cerro Punta** (see p. 204) in the Chiriquí highlands, where you do not have to be Indiana Jones to make your way to the park. ∎

**Opposite:
Festooned with
epiphytes and
mosses, the rain
forests of Parque
La Amistad are a
mecca for birders.**

Around Changuinola

The inky black waters of San San Pond Sak open out to the sea.

THIS ZONE, IN THE FAR NORTHEAST CORNER OF THE country, is engulfed in a sea of bananas. The unlovely regional center of Changuinola offers no inherent attractions and is a place to pass through en route to precious wetlands and to indigenous communities that are evolving an ecotouristic aesthetic.

Changuinola
🗺 210 B3

San San Pond Sak Wetlands
www.eco-index.org/ong /aamvecona-pa-eng.html
✉ AAMVECONA (Association of Friends and Neighbors of the Coast and Nature), 3 miles (5 km) N of Changuinola
☎ 758-6794
💲 $

Bananas were first planted in the Bocas del Toro lowlands in 1890, and the business expanded rapidly when the United Fruit Co. arrived in 1899. Today the vast plantations (now owned by Chiquita Brands) stretch north to the Costa Rica border and far inland up the valley of the Río Sixaola. The company established Changuinola and built most of the town infrastructure, including a canal (see p. 228) stretching 9 miles (15 km) to the Bahía de Almirante. Bocas Marine & Tours (*tel 758-9858, www.bocamarinetours.com*) operates a scheduled water taxi

service from Changuinola to Bocas Town.

SAN SAN POND SAK WETLANDS

These coastal wetlands cover 39,845 acres (16,125 ha) extending from Río Sixaola—the Costa Rica border—to Bahía de Almirante. They include seasonally flooded forest dominated by oreys (a swamp-loving tree), mangroves, palms, and peat marshes. San San Pond Sak was designated an Internationally Important Wetland under the Ramsar Convention in 1994 and is a precious habitat for endangered species, including manatees, river otters, and the tucuxi dolphin. The ecosystem, a spawning ground for tarpon, is threatened by agricultural chemicals washing out from the banana plantations and by hunting from the hard-pressed community of **San San Pond Sak**.

A poorly maintained and, at times, partially inundated boardwalk leads from the ANAM station at the entrance to the refuge to a nesting beach for green, hawksbill, and leatherback turtles. Rain forest rises up from ink-black waters, in places forming dark glades that explode with the roar of howler monkeys. Iguanas, sloths, and dozens of waterbird species can also be seen. The **Asociación de Amigos y Vecinos de la Costa y la Naturaleza,** Association of Friends and Neighbors of the Coast and Nature *(e-mail: keruiz@cwpana ma.net),* sponsors ecotourism, including views of nesting turtles.

WEKSO CENTRO ECOTURÍSTICO NASO

This project, also known as Proyecto ODESEN—Organization for the Sustainable Development of Naso Ecotourism *(tel 758-9137 or 6522-5591, e-mail: turismonaso_o desen@hotmail.com or efraincc@cw panama.net)*—was established in 1995 to orient the indigenous Naso-Teribe people toward sustainable practices, including ecotourism, reforestation, and production of quality native crafts. The Naso retain their own language and are attempting to revitalize centuries-old practices of shamanism and medicinal plant use. They live in 27 communities in the Río Teribe valley, on the border with Parque Internacional La Amistad (see pp. 224–225). The largest communities are **Sieykin** and **Sieyik.**

Wekso Ecolodge (see p. 255), on the banks of the Teribe, occupies the site of a former military jungle survival school called Pana-Jungla, set up in 1983 under Gen. Manuel Noriega. Camouflaged ruins of concrete army barracks can be still be seen. A visit to Wekso proves an incredible cultural experience. Trails include the relatively easy 2-mile (3.5 km) **Sendero Los Heliconias** loop trail; red-eyed tree frogs, monkeys, and sloths are easily seen. Guided hikes are also offered to Sieyik, returning via an exciting rafting trip. Ecocircuitos *(tel 314-1586, www.ecocircuitos .com)* offers guided three-day trips to Wekso, and day trips can be booked in Bocas Town. Wekso is best visited December to May.

A hydroelectric project planned for the Teribe valley has split the Naso community, which awaits the government's legalization of a Naso-Teribe autonomous district.

VALLE DE TALAMANCA

This lush valley extends west from the border town of **Guabito** and follows the Río Sixaola. A railway track serving the banana farms runs to **Las Tablas,** 11 miles (18 km) west of Guabito. Jeep taxis in Las Tablas negotiate the rugged track to the Bribrí Indian community of **Las Delicias.** Once reliant on hunting in the nearby forests, the locals now focus on ecotourism and the establishment of a nascent nature reserve. Two short eco-trails that begin at the ecolodge lead to a mirador with fine views over the valley and through old-growth forest abounding with wildlife, including a host of butterflies. You can ride on horseback or hike to the **Catarata Colorado** waterfall, plus take river trips up the Río Yorkín to the Bribrí community of Yorkín. Las Delicias has basic thatched accommodations with a lovely view over the Sixaola. ■

Wekso Centro Ecotúristico Naso
www.odesen.org
✉ About 10 miles (16 km) SW of Changuinola via dirt road to El Silencio, then one-hour, 5-mile (8 km) boat journey
☎ 758-9137 or 6522-5591

Las Delicias
✉ 20 miles (32 km) W of Guabito
☎ 600-4042

More places to visit in Bocas del Toro

ALMIRANTE

Fascinating for its Caribbean vernacular wooden houses (many in ramshackle condition) built over estuaries, this sprawling, hardscrabble banana-loading port and fishing village is the gateway to Bocas del Toro via water taxis that leave from unmarked *muelles* (wharves). Anyone arriving by car will be hit upon by touts on bicycles eager to guide you to the wharves, which are otherwise a devil to find; it's best to resign yourself to hiring a guide, who will also be happy to carry your luggage to the boat. The smell of sewage at wharf-side does not inspire confidence: Don't fall in! The few hotels are dour.

△ 210 B3 ✉ 18 miles (29 km) SE of Changuinola

CANAL SOROPTA

Initially known as the Snyder Canal and more commonly called the Changuinola Canal, this artificial waterway runs parallel to the Caribbean shore and extends from the Río Changuinola to the western edge of Bahía de Almirante. Initiated in 1897 by the Snyder Banana Co., the canal was completed in 1903 and permitted shipment of bananas by barge in calm waters protected from the sea. It was

abandoned following construction of a railroad. The canal is still a liquid highway of commerce used by public water taxis—usually fast-paced launches—and slower dugout cayucos ferrying bananas and other agricultural produce. Cut through tropical rain forest and wetland, the 100-foot-wide (30 m) channel has been severely deforested in recent years, and cattle graze in clearings cut from the grasslands and sedge. Still, it's a thrilling journey as your boatman runs your craft with the throttle wide open; ask him to slow down to maximize wildlife viewing. Freshwater turtles and small caimans sunning themselves on logs will plop into the waters as you putter past. Egrets and other stilt-legged waders stalk the grassy banks in search of tasty tidbits. Kingfishers skim like low-level jet fighters. Jacanas strut across water hyacinths munched on by manatees. Early morning and late afternoon are best for viewing wildlife.

△ 210 B3 ✉ 7 miles (11 km) E of Changuinola ⛴ Water taxi from Finca 63 or Bocas Town

LAGUNA DE CHIRIQUÍ & PENÍNSULA VALIENTE

The Bocas del Toro archipelago shelters Chiriquí Lagoon, held in the grip of the claw-like Península Valiente hooking around the bay to north and east. Much of the shore is lined with mangroves and freshwater swamps. Most of the land lies within the Ño Kribo region of the Comarca Ngöbe-Buglé. The indigenous village of **Boca Guariviara,** at the mouth of the Río Guariviara, can be reached by four-wheel-drive vehicle from Chiriquí Grande and has a women's artisan cooperative; the community of **Punta Siraín,** at the tip of Península Valiente, can be accessed only by boat. Game fish put up a fight to remember in the sheltered waters of **Punta Valiente.** Offshore, the **Cayo Tigre** (Tiger Cay) is one of only two known nesting sites for Audubon's shearwater in the southwest Caribbean. Brown boobies nest on **Isla Escudo de Veraguas,** 11 miles (18 km) off the coast.

△ 210 C2 & D2 ∎

Manatees

The West Indian manatee inhabits warm coastal tropical and subtropical waters from Florida through Panama to northern Brazil. This gray marine mammal resembles a tuskless walrus and propels itself using its spatulate tail. Males grow to about 10 feet (3 m) in length and can weigh 1,200 (540 kg) pounds. Manatees live in shallow, slow-moving river estuaries and calm saltwater bays, eating up to 20 percent of their body weight in aquatic plants daily. They can live for 60 years, but reproductive rates are low: Females reach sexual maturity at five years of age, after which they calve on average every two years. Although protected as an endangered species, they are still threatened by loss of habitat, pesticides, and accidents with boats. ∎

Travelwise

Bocas del Toro nightlife

TRAVELWISE INFORMATION.

PLANNING YOUR TRIP

WHEN TO GO

Time your visit to Panama according to the area you wish to visit, as the country's climate varies by region. In general, December through April is "dry season," which in most parts of the country means less rainy; "wet season" is May through November. The *arco seco*, a dry belt centered on the Azuero Peninsula, sizzles during the dry season when temperatures soar. Elsewhere, be prepared for stifling humidity in the lowlands. The Caribbean coast can be cooler in summer, when the trade winds pick up. In Darién Province, torrential rains can occur at any time of year. Panama lies outside the hurricane belt, although tropical storms are frequent in late summer.

Temperatures vary with elevation, rather than with latitude. The highlands of central Panama and Chiriquí enjoy a year-round springlike climate. Caribbean-facing slopes receive significantly more rain than Pacific-facing slopes.

Most tourists visit in the dry season, when Panamanians also vacation en masse—mostly at beach resorts, which can be sold out at this time. November is also busy, especially in Azuero, as towns nationwide host their patron saint festivals. Lenten week is the biggest holiday in Panama, and much of the country shuts down; hotels in cities hosting *carnavales* are usually fully booked. The end of the wet season is a perfect time to visit, when everything is lush.

WHAT TO TAKE

Panama has a hot, tropical climate, so dress accordingly. Lightweight, loose-fitting cotton and synthetic clothes are best. You'll want some elegant wear for nighttime. A sweater and/or lightweight jacket are useful for the heavily air-conditioned restaurants and stores and essential for visits to highland areas. A poncho works well against downpours.

Hiking shoes will prove useful on mountain trails or in wilderness areas, where you should expect to get muddy. Avoid bright colors (which can frighten away wildlife) if you plan on birding or nature hikes.

You'll need insect repellent, particularly for coastal areas and during wet season, even in cities.

Sunglasses are a necessity, as the tropical light is intense, and a hat is mandatory, even for brief periods outdoors.

Medicines are widely available. However, you should bring a basic first-aid kit that includes aspirin, Lomotil, antiseptic lotions, band-aids, and essential medications. Make a note of the generic name of any prescription medications you take before you leave home; they may be sold by a different trade name in Panama.

Similarly, bring all the photographic film and equipment you'll need, as these are in short supply and expensive.

INSURANCE

Travel insurance is a wise investment. Companies that provide coverage for Panama include:

American Express, tel 800/234-0375, www.americanexpress.com

Travelers, tel 800/243-3174, www.travelers.com

TravelGuard International, tel 800/826-4919, www.travelguard.com

Assistcard, tel 305/381-9959, www.assist-card.com. Based in Florida, it has a regional assistance center in Panama.

ENTRY FORMALITIES

Citizens of the United States, Canada, and most European nations require a valid passport and a return ticket to enter Panama. No visas are necessary for these citizens. Tourists are permitted stays of 30 days; tourist cards ($5) are issued upon arrival and can be extended an additional 90 days by applying to the Dirección Nacional de Migración, Ave. Cuba & Calle 28, Panama City, tel 507-1800. There are also immigration offices in David, Chitré, Changuinola, and Santiago.

FURTHER READING

Getting to Know the General (1984) by Graham Greene. Britain's beloved novelist writes of his real-life friendship with Panamanian strongman president Omar Torrijos.

A Guide to the Birds of Panama (1992) by Robert S. Ridgely & John A. Gwynne, Jr. A beautifully illustrated field guide to local birds and key birding sites.

Our Man in Panama: How General Noriega Used the United States—and Made Millions in Drugs and Arms (1990) by John Dinges. A critical exposé of U.S. involvement in Panamanian affairs.

The Path between the Seas: The Creation of the Panama Canal (1977) by David McCullough. Mesmerizing text tells the history of construction of the Panama Canal.

The Tailor of Panama (1996) by John Le Carré. A tale of espionage, blackmail, and deceit.

HOW TO GET TO PANAMA

BY AIR

The majority of flights arrive at Tocumen International Airport, tel 238-2700, 15 miles (25 km) east of Panama City. A small number of international flights land at David's Aeropuerto Enrique Malek, tel 721-1072 or 721-1071, in the northwest of the country. Bocas Town, in Bocas del Toro, is served in Panama by daily flights on Aeroperlas and Mapiex.

The national carrier, **Copa**

Airlines, tel 800/359-2672, or 217-2672 in Panama, www.copaair.com, serves more than 30 destinations throughout the Americas, including several in North America.

The following U.S. airlines offer regular flights to Panama:

American Airlines, tel 800/433-7300, www.aa.com

Continental Airlines, tel 800/231-0856, www.conti nental.com

Delta Airlines, tel 800/221-1212, www.delta.com

BY SEA

More than a dozen major cruise lines include Panama on their itineraries. Many feature a transit of the Panama Canal. For information, contact the Cruise Lines International Association, tel 212/921-0066, www.cruising.org.

Cruise West, tel 888/851-8133, www.cruisewest.com, offers in-depth eight- and ten-day educational cruises of Panama and Costa Rica focusing on cultural and nature encounters.

GROUP TOURS

Most packaged tours cater to anglers, scuba divers, and surfers. A few others focus on nature (especially birding) and cultural encounters, such as those offered by **The World Outdoors,** tel 800/488-8483, www.thewor ldoutdoors.com. Contact the Panamanian Tourism Institute (IPAT; see p. 234) for a list of recommended tour companies.

GETTING AROUND

IN PANAMA CITY

By bus

Diablos rojos—red devils—operate throughout Panama City and the Canal Zone. Public buses can be confusing in the city and should be used only on main routes; fares are fixed at $0.25, payable when you step off the bus. No public buses serve the airport.

By taxi

Taxis are the staple form of transport in town. They are safe, cheap, and numerous. Point-to-point fares in Panama City are based on a zone system. For touring and multiple points, rates are negotiable. Tourists are usually charged more than locals. Stick with local taxis; taxis with "SET" on their license plates are *Servicio Especial Turista,* which charge considerably more. The official rate for a tourist taxi between Tocumen International Airport and downtown is $25 for one person, $14 per person for two people, and $10 per person for up to four people. Local taxis are not allowed there, but penny-pinchers can catch local taxis outside the airport.

AROUND PANAMA

By air

Flights departing Aeropuerto Marcos A. Gelabert, tel 501-9272, in Albrook, connect Panama City with key tourist destinations throughout the country. Smaller charter planes serve the country's 150 or so airstrips. Be prepared for white-knuckle rides.

Two domestic carriers offer scheduled flights; both use 20- to 46-passenger aircraft:

Air Panama, tel 316-9000, www.flyairpanama.com. Flies to 22 destinations throughout Panama.

Aeroperlas, tel 315-7555, www.aeroperlas.com, serving 24 destinations.

By boat

Travel between islands within the San Blas and Bocas del Toro archipelagos, and along the coast and rivers of Darién, is primarily by motorized water taxis *(lanchas),* motorized dugout canoes *(piraguas),* or paddled dugouts *(cayucos).* Except for Bocas del Toro, where regular services operate, prices are often negotiable; be sure that any agreed-upon price includes fuel. Usually only *lanchas*

operate with lifejackets.

Calypso Queen Ferries, tel 314-1730, depart every day except Thursday from Amador Causeway to Isla Taboga. The round-trip ticket is $10 for adults and $7 for children up to 12 years.

By bus

Buses to destinations throughout Panama depart Gran Terminal de Transporte, tel 303-3030, in the Albrook district of Panama City. There is no national network. Several private companies compete and offer fast *(directo)* and slower *(regular)* service. Long-distance service is typically by large, modern, air-conditioned bus. However, regional buses can mean anything from a former school bus to minivans *(chivas).*

Buses are usually crowded; avoid travel on weekends if possible, and guard against pickpockets and luggage theft. Most companies sell advance tickets; on others you pay when boarding. Fares are reasonable; the most expensive route—Panama City to Changuinola—costs about $25 one-way.

By car

To rent a car you should be over 25 (some agencies permit younger drivers with credit cards) and hold a passport and a valid driver's license (a U.S. license is fine). You will also need a credit card and will have to leave a hefty deposit (about $500). Beware additional charges that might appear on your bill when you return the car or get your credit card statement. Loss damage waiver *(renuncia a daños o pérdida)* and liability insurance are mandatory; some companies refuse to honor insurance issued abroad. For off-road driving, a rugged four-wheel-drive vehicle *(carro con doble)* is essential. Rental cars cannot be taken into Costa Rica.

The local **Hertz** franchise, tel 263-6511, www.hertz.com .pa, has a reputation for reliability. In addition, most other major international car rental companies are represented:

Alamo, tel 236-5777, www.alamopanama.com

Avis, tel 278-9444, www.avisworld.com

Budget, tel 263-8777, www.budgetpanama.com

Dollar, tel 214-4725, www.dollarpanama.com

National, tel 265-2222, www.nationalpanama.com

Main roads throughout the country are in excellent condition. However, portions of the Interamerican Highway (notably in Chiriquí Province) are in a poor state of repair and should be avoided at night. A four-wheel-drive vehicle is recommended for more remote areas, including Darién east of Metetí, and for access to many national parks. Many Panamanian drivers are reckless—there is a high auto fatality rate, especially during Carnival season, when drunk drivers are a menace. Drive slowly, and be on your guard. Stray cattle and pedestrians in the road are additional hazards outside cities. Talking on a cell phone while driving is illegal, and wearing a seatbelt is mandatory.

See p. 235 for what to do in a car accident.

By train
The country's sole railroad connects Panama City with Colón and runs alongside the Panama Canal. Trains leave Panama City's Corozal train station daily at 7:15 a.m. and return at 5:15 p.m. Contact the **Panama Canal Railway Company,** tel 317-6070, www.kcsi.com/corporate/pcrc .html, e-mail: info@panarail.com.

Group tours
Panama has several dozen reputable tour agencies, including:

Ancón Expeditions, tel 269-9415, www.ancon expeditions.com. Renowned for its eco-tours and top-ranked

bilingual nature guides. Operates nature lodges in Darién.

Panama Travel Experts, tel 304-0251, www.panamat ravelexperts.com. Specializes in half-day and day-long excursions.

PRACTICAL ADVICE

COMMUNICATIONS

Post offices
It costs $0.35 to mail a letter or postcard to North America, and $0.45 to Europe. Never mail anything of value; theft is common. Most towns have a post office, usually open 7 a.m.–5:45 p.m. Allow a week for mail to the U.S. or Canada, and at least 10 days for mail to Europe.

There is no home delivery in Panama. Mail is delivered to postal boxes (*apartados postales,* abbreviated *Apdo.*). However, service is unreliable and many people use private mail and courier services.

Telephones
Public pay phones are yellow or blue and usually accept both coins and prepaid phonecards (some accept only phonecards), which can be bought at supermarkets and Cable & Wireless outlets nationwide. Insert the card into the phone and the cost of your call is deducted. "Telechip Total" cards can be used in any phone booth; "Telechip International" cards work only in specific phones. In remote areas, the public phone may serve the entire community.

Making calls
Local calls cost $0.10 for the first three minutes, then $0.05 per minute. Hotels often charge a high fee for calls from in-room phones. Some Internet cafés double as call centers and have cheaper rates than most hotels.

For direct-dial international calls from Panama, dial 00, the country code (U.S.: 1; U.K.: 44) and area code, then the number. For operator-assisted calls

inside Panama, dial 101. For operator-assisted calls to countries outside, dial 106. For directory inquiries, call 102.

Calling to Panama from the U.S., dial 011 plus Panama's country code 507 and the number. From the U.K., dial 00 plus Panama's country code 507 and the number.

Cellular numbers within Panama usually have eight digits starting with 6.

E-mail & Internet
Most towns and villages have Internet cafés (usually charging $1–$2 per hour), and most upscale tourist hotels are wired for Internet use or have business centers, though fees can be high.

CONVERSIONS
Panama uses the metric system. However, gasoline (petrol) is sold in U.S. gallons. Useful conversions are:

1 mile = 1.61 kilometers
1 kilometer = 0.62 mile
1 meter = 39.37 inches
1 liter = 0.26 U.S. gallon
1 kilogram = 2.2 pounds
1 pound = 0.45 kilogram

Weather reports use Celsius:
0°C = 32°F
10°C = 50°F
20°C = 68°F
30°C = 86°F

ELECTRICITY
Panama operates on 110-volt AC (60 cycles) nationwide, although a few more-remote places use 220 volts. Most outlets use U.S. flat, two-, or three-pin plugs. Many more-remote parts of the country do not have electricity; here restaurants and hotels rely on generators or solar power, and often service is limited to certain hours of the day.

ETIQUETTE & LOCAL CUSTOMS
Panamanian society is diverse. Life in Panama City is cosmopolitan and relatively liberal, while smaller towns and

rural villages are far more conservative. Society remains extremely class conscious. Panamanians respect professional titles and use them when addressing title-holders, such as engineers (e.g. Ingeniero Arosemena) and architects (Arquitecto García).

Adults are addressed as Señor (Mr.), Señora (Mrs.), or Señorita (Miss). The terms Don (for men) and Doña (for women) are used for high-ranking or respected individuals and senior citizens.

Panamanians are courteous and normally use the formal *usted* form of "you," while the informal *tu* form is reserved for intimates. Hugs and kisses are generally used only among close friends and family. The normal greeting is *buenos días* (good morning), *buenas tardes* (good afternoon), or *buenas noches* (good evening). A more informal greeting is *hola* (hi!).

Panamanians are proud of their country and sensitive to criticism by foreigners, particularly U.S. citizens. The Kuna Indians of the San Blas are extremely sensitive to intrusions or insults to their culture: Dress modestly away from the beach, and photograph individuals only if you are prepared to pay the expected $1 per photo.

Outside the main tourist areas and business centers, you may not be understood in English, so it is advisable to learn a few Spanish phrases. Most restaurants in cities have menus in English, although you may have to ask for them.

HOLIDAYS

In addition to Christmas, New Year's, and Easter, Panama observes the following national holidays:

January 9, Martyrs' Day
May 1, Labor Day
August 15, Foundation of Old Panama
November 3, Independence from Colombia Day
November 4, Flag Day
November 10, First Call for

Independence (*Primer Grito de Independencia*)
November 28, Independence from Spain Day
December 8, Mother's Day

The biggest holiday of the year is *Carnaval*, the four days leading up to Ash Wednesday. Most tourist sites and services stay open for these holidays, but banks and government offices close.

LIQUOR LAWS

Drinking alcoholic beverages is legal at 18 in Panama, though the law is rarely enforced. Driving while under the influence is illegal; a conviction of drunk driving will nullify any insurance coverage for rented cars.

MEDIA

Newspapers & magazines

Panama has three major national newspapers. The excellent daily *La Prensa* is the most conservative and complete, and covers everything from politics to fashion; *El Panama América* and *La Estrella de Panama* are also good.

Such publications are usually sold at small streetside stands or supermarkets. Major U.S. magazines and dailies are usually available at hotel gift stores.

There are no English-language newspapers. However, *The Bulletin*, www.bulletinpa.com, and the weekly *Panama News*, www.thepanamanews.com, publish news online in English.

Television & radio

Television reaches everywhere in Panama, which has five TV stations. Panama also has dozens of radio stations. All but a few broadcast local news and Latin music. The BBC World Service and Voice of America offer English-language news.

MONEY MATTERS

Currency

Panama's official currency is the balboa, which is pegged to the U.S. dollar (1 balboa = 1 dollar).

There are 100 *centesimos* to a balboa. Circulating paper money is usually dollars, and U.S. coins are accepted as well as Panamanian ones.

Some international banks in larger towns have foreign-exchange counters to serve travelers arriving without U.S. dollars, but you shouldn't count on this; most banks have no such service. The state-owned Banco Nacional tends to be less efficient than other, private, banks. There are few private exchange bureaus.

Take all the cash you think you'll need for a stay in the San Blas Islands; there are only two banks in the entire comarca, and banks in Darién are also few and far between. In these out-of-the-way spots, it is best to carry plenty of small-denomination bills, as $50 and $100 bills often cannot be changed.

Visitors may experience trouble cashing traveler's checks anywhere but banks, due to widespread fraud and holds imposed by banks. Many shops will refuse to accept them.

Automated teller machines

Most banks have 24-hour automated teller machines (ATMs). There is usually a small charge. Using ATMs during regular banking hours is advisable in case of problems (e.g., machines not returning cards, etc.). Avoid using ATMs in poor neighborhoods and in dark locations, where crime may be a problem.

Credit cards

Credits cards (*tarjetas de crédito*) are widely accepted. Visa is the most commonly accepted, followed by MasterCard and American Express. In the San Blas Islands and Darién, you will need to operate on a cash-only basis.

OPENING TIMES

Most stores are open Monday to Saturday 9 a.m. to 6 p.m., but malls, supermarkets, and many souvenir stores have longer hours and also open on Sundays.

Banks are typically open Monday through Friday 8 a.m. to 3 p.m. (some until 6) and Saturdays 9 a.m. to noon. Businesses are typically open Monday through Friday 9:30 a.m. to 7 p.m.; travel agencies and tourist-related businesses are also open on Saturdays 8 a.m. to noon and do not close for lunch. Most government offices are open weekdays 7:30 a.m. to 3:30 p.m.

PLACES OF WORSHIP/RELIGION

Most communities have at least one Roman Catholic church and often a Protestant church. Panama City also has mosques. Local tourist information offices and leading hotels can usually supply a list of places of worship.

REST ROOMS

There are very few public rest room facilities (baños). Most restaurants and bus stations have rest rooms, although standards of cleanliness vary.

In the San Blas Islands, most accommodations have only shared bathrooms (many are over-the-water affairs that dump waste directly into the sea), as do some budget hotels in Bocas del Toro and Darién. Toilet paper is rarely available in these places; bring your own.

SMOKING

Smoking is officially forbidden in public areas. However, a large percentage of Panamanians smoke. Only the more upscale restaurants have nonsmoking sections. Elsewhere, "No Smoking" signs are regularly disobeyed.

TIME DIFFERENCES

Panama time is the same as U.S. Eastern Standard Time (EST), five hours behind Greenwich Mean Time (GMT). Panama does not observe daylight savings time.

TIPPING

Tipping is not a fact of life in Panama except in tourist areas. However, a tip is an acknowledgement of good

service: If the service is not satisfactory, do not tip.

A 10 percent service charge is often added onto restaurant bills, where a tip should be given for good service. Many cafés and budget eateries do not expect to receive tips. Hotel porters should be given 50 cents per bag (airport porters expect $1), and room service staff $1 per day. Taxi drivers do not expect a tip.

In the countryside, park rangers, boat guides, etc., often provide services for which a tip is in order, albeit not expected.

TRAVELERS WITH DISABILITIES

Although paying lip service to the theme, Panama does not display great sensitivity to the needs of visitors with disabilities. Few buildings have wheelchair access or provide special toilets. Buses are not adapted for wheelchairs, and few curbs are dropped at corners. Some modern, upscale hotels and a few restaurants in Panama City have wheelchair access, and a few hotels provide special suites.

The following agencies provide information for visitors with disabilities:

Gimp on the Go, www.gimponthego.com, an Internet-based newsletter and forum for disabled travelers.

Instituto Panameño de Habilitación Especial (Panamanian Institute for Special Rehabilitation), tel 501-0508, www.iphe.gob.pa. A government organization to assist disabled people.

Society for Accessible Travel & Hospitality, 347 5th Ave. Ste. 610, New York, NY 10016, tel 212/447-7284, www.sath.org.

VISITOR INFORMATION

Panama's environmental agency, **Autoridad Nacional del Ambiente** (ANAM), administers national parks and other protected areas throughout Panama. Though the main office in Panama City

provides little help to visitors, the regional offices are generally more helpful; they're also essential stops before visiting parks where permits are needed or if you want to spend the night in a refuge. The website is: www.anam.gob.pa.

Panama's government also runs the **Instituto Panameño de Turismo** (IPAT, tel 800/231-0568 in the U.S.), which maintains a website: www.visitpanama.com. IPAT is headquartered in the ATLAPA Convention Center, Panama City, tel 526-7000, and has regional bureaus through the country.

Focus Panama is a tourist-oriented publication published twice-yearly in English and Spanish and widely available in hotels. The Panama Visitor newspaper is published twice-monthly in Spanish and English.

EMERGENCIES

CRIME & POLICE

Panama is a relatively safe destination and crime is no more prevalent than in most North American towns and cities; overall, violent crime against tourists is extremely rare. However, caution should be exercised at all times, particularly in impoverished parts of Panama City (including the El Chorrillo area bordering Casco Viejo and Curundú, northeast of Ancón) and in Colón, where the threat of muggings is severe. In towns, there is a danger of pickpockets and snatch-and-grab theft, so be especially wary in crowded areas, such as buses and markets. Scams are common, especially in private street transactions; never take your eyes off any items you purchase. And keep your possessions in a locked suitcase in hotels, as theft by cleaning staff is common.

Never hike alone, particularly in national parks close to Panama City and the Canal Zone, where robberies have been known. And never leave items unguarded on beaches. Avoid leaving luggage or valuables in cars; do not carry large quantities of cash or wear expensive-looking jewelry, and keep passports and credit cards out of sight. If anything is stolen, report it immediately to the police and/or your hotel.

The eastern half of Darién Province close to the Colombia border is considered unsafe for travel due to infiltration by guerrillas, armed insurgents, drug traffickers, and lawless bandits. A heavily armed branch of the police maintains fortified bases throughout the region, but cannot guarantee travelers' safety.

Tourism police patrol Casco Viejo and a few other heavily touristed areas, including Colón. Traffic police (tránsitos) patrol the highways. A new professionalism to Panama's police force belies their reputation for corruption. However, dishonest officials still exist. The Policía Técnica Judicial (PTJ), tel 512-2222, www.ptj.gob.pa, handles criminal investigations, including reports of police corruption.

EMBASSIES & CONSULATES

United States Embassy, Ave. Balboa at Calle 38, Bella Vista, Panama City, tel 207-7000, http://panama.usembassy.gov/, e-mail: Panamaweb@state.gov
British Embassy, Calle 53, Marbella, Panama City, tel 269-0866, www.britishembassy. gov.uk/panama, e-mail: britemb@ cwpanama.net.pa
Canadian Embassy, Calle 53E, Marbella, World Trade Center, Panama City, tel 264-9731, www.dfait-maeci.gc.ca

EMERGENCY TELEPHONE NUMBERS

Most, but not all, communities are served by the following emergency numbers:

Fire (bomberos), tel 103
Police (policia), tel 104
Tourism police, tel 512-2269

Ambulance service is provided by the Red Cross, tel 228-2187,

and private companies such as SEMM, tel 264-4122, and Alerta, tel 269-1111.

Emergency care is free in public hospitals, in Panama City's **Hospital Santo Tomás,** in the Central Provinces, **Hospital Cecilio Castillero** (Los Santos) and **Aquilino Tejeira** (Penonomé), but all other medical services cost.

WHAT TO DO IN A CAR ACCIDENT

In the event of an accident, do not move the vehicle or permit the other vehicle to be moved. Take down the license plate numbers and cédula (legal identification) of any witnesses. Call the transit police and await their arrival; they will fill out a report that you will need for insurance purposes.

If someone is seriously injured or killed, contact your embassy.

HEALTH

Most towns have private physicians and clinics. In Panama City and David, medical service is up to North American standards. In Panama City, three of the best facilities are the **Hospital Nacional,** Ave. Cuba & Calles 38 and 39, tel 207-8100, **Centro Médico Paitilla,** Ave. Balboa & Calle 53, tel 265-8800, and **Clinica Hospital San Fernando,** Vía España, Las Sabanas, tel 278-6300. Government-run centros de salud (health centers) serve virtually every town in the country and offer treatment for nominal fees. However, the service is of low standard and visitors are advised to seek treatment at private facilities.

Full travel insurance should cover all medical costs. A medical evacuation clause is also important in case you need to return home.

Most hotels keep a list of doctors and medical centers. Keep any receipts or paperwork for insurance claims.

Panama's main health

hazards—other than traffic accidents—relate to its tropical climate, where bacteria and germs breed profusely. Wash all cuts and scrapes with warm water and rubbing alcohol. The tap water is safe in most of the country. However, avoid drinking water from faucets in Bocas del Toro and other destinations along the Caribbean shore, and in all other impoverished communities, where you should drink (and brush your teeth with) bottled water. Boil water when camping to eliminate giardia, a parasite that thrives in warm water. Avoid uncooked seafood (except ceviche, which is normally safe) and vegetables, unwashed salads, and unpeeled fruits.

Be liberal with sunscreen and build up your tan slowly, as the tropical sun is intense. Drink plenty of water to guard against dehydration.

Biting insects abound, particularly in the humid lowlands. Malaria is present in lowland areas and is a problem mainly on the Caribbean coast and Darién. Consult your doctor for a suitable malaria prophylaxis. Dengue fever is also spread by mosquitos and occasional outbreaks are reported in the Caribbean and Pacific lowlands. There is no preventative medication, so it is wise to try to avoid being bitten. Use insect repellents liberally, and wear earth-colored clothing with long sleeves and full-length pants when hiking.

Venomous snakes are common in wilderness areas. Wear closed-toed shoes that cover the ankle to reduce the chance of snake bites, and don't put your hand in places you can't see. Give snakes a wide berth. If you are bitten, get immediate medical help. Avoid wading in the shallows along the central Pacific shore, where stingrays abound.

Riptides are an extreme danger along much of the coast, particularly where high surf comes ashore.

HOTELS & RESTAURANTS

Accommodations in Panama are varied and reasonably priced, although standards vary widely. There are great differences between the facilities available, and it will help you to understand these differences when deciding where to stay. Remember that large areas of the country are remote, and the availability of accommodations is limited; more desirable accommodations can fill quickly during busy months and especially during festivals such as Carnaval. In much of Darién and the San Blas Islands, the only available accommodation may be extremely basic. Eating out can be a great pleasure in Panama City, which offers a wide variety of possibilities, including many world-class options. Elsewhere, menus are typically restricted to traditional fare and seafood, with more cosmopolitan options in tourist destinations and upscale hotels. In the San Blas Islands, meals are often bland and your options are extremely limited.

ACCOMMODATIONS

There are several types of accommodations. Panama City is blessed with top-of-the-class hotels to international standards. These range from small, family-run boutique hotels that combine intimacy and charm to high-rise international chain hotels, usually with business and or convention facilities. Several have casinos. Some of these hotel chains have toll-free numbers:

Country Inn & Suites, tel 800/201-1746, www.countryinns.com
Intercontinental Hotels Group, tel 800/424-3685, www.intercontinental.com
Marriott Hotels & Resorts, tel 888/236-2427, www.marriott.com
Radisson, tel 888/201-1718, www.radisson.com

The El Valle and Boquete regions have some of the best accommodations in the country, including intimate bed-and-breakfast country inns, and Bocas del Toro also offers wide options (note that the party-hearty bars and discos of Bocas Town can wake the dead). Large-scale beach resorts are relatively few in number; the few that exist are generally all-inclusive and cater mainly to a local clientele. Mid-range hotels are widely available, offering a modicum of services; standards vary. However, certain areas of the country, such as Azuero,

have relatively few hotels; the options that exist sell out fast during Carnaval, when accommodations can be impossible to find.

Panama has relatively few wilderness lodges. Exceptions are in Darién as well as the Chiriquí highlands, where facilities range from tent camps to cozy, no-frills wooden lodges and a couple of more sophisticated options with spas and saunas. Specialized lodges also serve anglers and surfers, although most of the latter are fairly simple. Camping is available along beaches and in most national parks.

In the San Blas archipelago, hotels are few and invariably basic, even spartan: Expect homespun *cabañas* made of palm trunks and bamboo reeds, with thatch or tin for a roof. Few have electricity (lighting is usually kerosene lanterns) and fewer still have flushing toilets—over-the-water outhouses are the norm.

Vacation rental and long-term properties—everything from beachfront bungalows to Spanish colonial haciendas—can be rented through **Haciendas Panama,** tel 265-2801, www.haciendaspanama.com.

In budget hotels, sink plugs may be missing, showers are often cold, and mattresses are thin and usually past their prime. Warm (tepid) water may be provided by an electric element above the shower. Ensure windows and doors are secure.

Avoid "motels," which are

usually rented by the hour for sexual trysts.

Unless otherwise stated, all hotels listed here have dining rooms and private bathrooms and are open year-round.

Hotel rates generally are about 15 percent higher in high season, December through April. In mid-range and budget hotels, ask to see several rooms, as the same price often applies to rooms of vastly different size and standard.

A 10 percent sales tax is added to most hotel bills.

RESTAURANTS

Seafood is the staple along the coasts, while chicken and pork form the heart of typical Panamanian fare. Restaurants usually open 11 a.m. to 2 p.m. and 6 p.m. to 11 p.m. Many close on Mondays. Make reservations for the more expensive restaurants, particularly on weekends. In Panama City, service is usually fast, but elsewhere it is often slow.

Local fare can be enjoyed for less than $5. Look for *comida corriente,* set lunch plates (usually a choice of meat, rice, beans, and vegetables, or salad) at bargain prices.

In the San Blas Islands, restaurants can be counted on one hand; most are extremely basic. Here, expect to eat rather blandly in your hotel; avoid lobster (if possible) due to overexploitation, and squid, which are often fished by dumping bleach in the water.

A selection of the best quality restaurants for each area is given below.

CREDIT CARDS

Giving a card number is often the only way to reserve rooms in upscale hotels. Some hotels add a fee of up to 3 percent for credit card payments. Most quality restaurants accept payment by credit cards.

MAKING RESERVATIONS

Although we have tried to give comprehensive information,

please check details before booking. This applies particularly to facilities for disabled guests or nonsmoking rooms, acceptance of credit cards, and rates. Do not rely on booking by mail; fax or e-mail your hotel reservation, and take your written confirmation with you.

If a Panamanian tour operator informs you that the hotel of your choice is full, check directly with the hotel; even the most reputable tour operators have been known to intentionally steer clients toward hotels that pay preferential commissions.

For disabled access, it is recommended that you check with the establishment to verify the extent of their facilities.

ORGANIZATION
The hotels and restaurants listed here have been grouped first according to their region (by chapter), then listed alphabetically by price category. L = lunch   D = dinner

CREDIT & DEBIT CARDS
Abbreviations used are: AE (American Express), DC (Diners Club), MC (Mastercard), V (Visa).

◼ PANAMA CITY
HOTELS
SOMETHING SPECIAL

🏨 HOTEL BRISTOL
🍽
Unequivocally the city's finest hotel, this splendid boutique option—a member of the Leading Hotels of the World—sparkles with mahogany and marble while exuding a London-style Old World class and charm. Tastefully deluxe furnishings include locally themed highlights, such as colorful mola pillows. The restaurant is among the city's finest.
$$$$$

HOTELS
An indication of the cost of a double room without breakfast is given by $ signs:
$$$$$ Over $200
$$$$ $100–$200
$$$ $50–$100
$$ $25–$50
$ Under $25

RESTAURANTS
An indication of the cost of a three-course dinner without drinks is given by $ signs:
$$$$$ Over $35
$$$$ $20–$35
$$$ $10–$20
$$ $5–$10
$ Under $5

CALLE AQUILINO DE LA GUARDIA, CALLES 51 & 52
TEL 265-7844
FAX 265-7829
www.thebristol.com
ⓘ 56 🅿 🔄 🆂 🎽 🚠
AE, MC, V

🏨 MARRIOTT HOTEL
🍽 **$$$$$**
CALLE 52 & CALLE RICARDO ARIAS
TEL 210-9100
FAX 210-9110
www.marriott.com
This 20-story hotel is centrally located, with easy access to key restaurants, shops, and nightclubs. Focusing on a business clientele, rooms are elegant and functional. It has casino and convention facilities, plus a gorgeous outdoor pool.
ⓘ 296 🅿 🆂 🔄 🆂 🚠
🎽 🅰 AE, MC, V

🏨 CROWNE PLAZA
$$$$
AVE. MANUEL ESPINOSA. BAUTISTA
TEL 206-5555
FAX 206-5557
www.cppanama.com
This full-service upscale hotel in the heart of the commercial zone has tastefully appointed rooms with all

---

modern conveniences. Rooftop pool and sports bar are highlights. Breakfast is included.
ⓘ 150 🅿 🆂 🔄 🆂 🚠
🎽 🅰 All major cards

SOMETHING SPECIAL

🏨 HOTEL DEVILLE
🍽
Furnished with an eclectic assemblage of globe-spanning pieces, this all-suite luxury boutique hotel combines the best of both worlds: tasteful (albeit sometimes mismatched) decor and comprehensive, modern accoutrements. Themed rooms and cavernous bathrooms sparkle with marble floors topped with oriental throw rugs. Guaranteeing angelic slumber are orthopedic mattresses, Egyptian cotton linens, and pillows as soft as a sigh. Its leafy location in the heart of the dining and entertainment district is a bonus. Chef Fabien Migny's trendy Ten Bistro restaurant adjoins (see p. 240).
$$$$
AVE. BEATRIZ CABAL N OF CALLE 50
TEL 206-3100
FAX 206-3111
www.devillehotel.com.pa
ⓘ 33 🅿 🔄 🆂
🅰 AE, MC, V

🏨 INTERCONTINENTAL
🍽 MIRAMAR PANAMA
$$$$
MIRAMAR PLAZA, AVE. BALBOA
TEL 206-8888
FAX 223-4891
www.miramarpanama.com
Soaring 25 stories over Panama Bay, this handsome, contemporary high-rise combines luxe and convenience, including a full-service business center and banqueting facilities, plus Turkish baths. Spacious rooms are beautifully appointed and are wired for Internet. Spectacular views through wall-of-glass windows are a high point. The ground-floor

---

🆂 Nonsmoking 🔄 Elevator 🆂 Air-conditioning 🕳 Indoor/🚠 Outdoor pool 🎽 Gym 🅰 Credit cards   **KEY**

Bay View Restaurant offers a splendid buffet and Sunday brunch; the fifth-floor Miramar Restaurant is noted for its gourmet seafood.

🛏 183 🅿 ⬛ ➡ ⬛ ☰
☷ ⬓ AE, MC, V

🏨 RADISSON DECAPOLIS
🍴 $$$$
AVE. BALBOA, BEHIND
MULTICENTRO PLAZA
TEL 215-5000
FAX 215-5715
www.radisson.com
This slick avant-garde high-rise thrusting 29 stories over Marbella boasts minimalist contemporary furnishings, fabulous views, hip dining options, plus a fashionable martini bar. Business travelers are well served—it even has executive floors reserved for businesswomen—and all rooms have broadband Internet. A casino and shopping mall adjoin. Breakfast included.

🛏 300 🅿 ⬛ ➡ ⬛ ➤
⬓ ⬓ AE, MC, V

🏨 VENETO HOTEL &
🍴 CASINO
$$$$
BETWEEN VIA VENETO &
EUSEBIO A. MORALES, EL
CANGREJO
TEL 340-8888
FAX 340-8899
www.venetocasino.com
In the heart of the financial and shopping district, this stylish hotel has luxurious rooms with flat-screen TVs, plus marble-clad bathrooms with robes. Choice of quality restaurants, plus full-service spa and enormous in-house casino. Breakfast included.

🛏 301 🅿 ⬛ ➡ ⬛ ➤
⬓ ⬓ AE, MC, V

🏨 ALBROOK INN
$$$
CALLE LAS MAGNOLIAS #14,
ANCÓN
TEL 315-1789
FAX 315-1975
www.albrookinn.com
On the far west of the city

and close to the airport, perfect for exploring Ancón and Balboa. Graciously furnished with rich red fabrics, dark contemporary hardwoods, and cream walls. Suites have large kitchenettes. Small free-form pool in pleasant garden. Continental breakfast included.

🛏 30 🅿 ⬛ ⬛ ➤ ☰
⬓ AE, MC, V

🏨 B&B LA ESTANCIA
$$$
CASA 35, QUARRY HEIGHTS
TEL 314 1417
www.bedandbreakfastpanama.com
Cozy bed-and-breakfast surrounded by woodland on the northwest slopes of Cerro Ancón. Rooms are sparsely furnished with rattan and hardwood pieces and have piping-hot water in spacious showers; most have views. Monkeys and plentiful birds at fingertip distance. Full breakfast and free Internet.

🛏 9 🅿 ⬛ ⬛ ⬓ MC, V

🏨 BEST WESTERN LAS
HUACAS HOTEL &
SUITES
$$$
CALLE 49, EL CANGREJO
TEL 213-2222
FAX 213-3057
www.bestwestern.com
Pleasant, well-placed mid-range property. Furnishings are a mishmash of styles. Simple restaurant supplied by many neighborhood restaurants. Breakfast included.

🛏 33 🅿 ⬛ ➡ ⬛ ⬓
⬓ AE, MC, V

🏨 COUNTRY INN &
SUITES PANAMA
CANAL
$$$
AVE. AMADOR & AVE.
PELICANO, 2 MILES (3.2 KM) W
OF CASCO VIEJO
TEL 211-4500
FAX 211-4501
www.countryinns.com
/panamacanalpan
With dramatic views toward

the Bridge of the Americas and canal entrance, this Amador Causeway hotel has balconies for every room; also high-speed Internet connections. Ho-hum decor. TGI Friday's for dining, plus convention facilities. Breakfast included.

🛏 150 🅿 ⬛ ➡ ⬛ ➤
⬓ ⬓ All major cards

🏨 EXECUTIVE HOTEL
$$$
TEL 265-8011
www.executivehotel-panama.com
Impeccable high-rise hotel in the banking zone focusing on business clientele. Quality furnishings and modern conveniences. The jazz bar is a favorite. Café dining only, but local restaurants are close at hand. Breakfast included.

🛏 96 🅿 ⬛ ⬛ ➤ ⬓
⬓ All major cards

🏨 EL LITORAL
$$$
CALLE 49, EDIFICIO ISABELITA
16, BELLA VISTA
TEL 265-8662
www.litoralpanama.com
Colorful, French-run bed-and-breakfast in a colonial-era wooden home with tasteful decor and simple appointments. Ultra-clean rooms; two share a bathroom. Close to major restaurants and shops.

🛏 5 🅿 ⬛ ⬛ (4 rooms)
⬓ MC, V

🏨 PLAZA PAITILLA INN
$$$
VÍA ITALIA, PUNTA PAITILLA
TEL 208-0600
FAX 208-0619
www.plazapaitillainn.com
Modern, circular high-rise with fabulous city views through walls of glass. Pleasant decor and understated elegance in guest rooms. Special rates offer bargains.

🛏 255 🅿 ⬛ ➡ ⬛ ➤
⬓ AE, MC, V

RESTAURANTS

SOMETHING SPECIAL

EURASIA

Housed in an aged mansion tastefully furnished classical Bella Vista style with a contemporary feel. World music plays as patrons enjoy such French-Asian fusion dishes as grilled tuna filet with caramelized onions in Dijon mustard sauce. Start with the shrimp rolls and save room for the fondant—the decadent house chocolate soufflé. Eclectic art adds further interest. Impeccable service, including from the charming host, Kim Young.

$$$$
CALLE 48, BETWEEN PARQUE URRUCÁ & AVE. FEDERICO BOYD, BELLA VISTA
TEL 264-7859
100 Closed Sun.
  MC, V

BARANDA'S

$$$$
CALLE AQUILINO DE LA GUARDIA, CALLES 51 & 52
TEL 265 7844
www.thebristol.com
Mahogany panels and classical European elegance at an upscale restaurant in the Hotel Bristol (see p. 237). Exemplary service. The nouvelle-inspired menu features an exceptionally smooth and delicious *crema de maíz* appetizer, while entrée standouts include corvina in tamarind sauce and chicken in coconut and curry sauce served with gnocchi, plantains, rice, and black beans.
80   AE, MC, V

LIMONCILLO

$$$$
CALLE 47, BETWEEN AQUILINO DE LA GUARDIA & URUGUAY, MARBELLA
TEL 263-5350
www.limoncillo.com
One of the city's most

fashionable eateries, this hip option exudes tasteful contemporary sophistication. The inspired nouvelle menu is superbly executed by Chef Clara Icaza, one of Latin America's top chefs. Recommended are the fried jumbo coconut shrimp with mango salsa, and herb-crusted salmon with balsamic glaze and spinach. Walls are hung with contemporary art. Try the house Hemingway daiquiri at the hip bar. Exemplary service. Reservations recommended.
24 Closed Sun. & L Sat.   MC, V

SOMETHING SPECIAL

PALMS

With the chic-est, most minimalist decor in town (charcoal gray tile floors, brushed steel rails, walls of glass, halogen lighting), this recent addition to the dining scene delivers creative and superbly executed cuisine. The eclectic, globe-trotting fusion menu offers such temptations as prawn tempura and potato samosa appetizers; grilled octopus *escabeche* with capers, and sweet red peppers; sole ourlade with black butter, capers, and lemon; and pumpkin ravioli in sage butter sauce. Impeccable service.

$$$$
CALLE 48, BELLA VISTA
TEL 265-7256
E-MAIL palmsrestaurant @cableonda.net
50 Closed Mon.   AE, MC, V

AL TAMBOR DE LA ALEGRÍA

$$$
CALZADA DE AMADOR, AMADOR
TEL 314-3380
Típico (traditional) Panamanian fare at this touristy restaurant with a hour-long folkloric dinner show ($10 cover) Tues., Thurs., Fri., and Sat. beginning at 9 p.m. Waitresses wear polleras. Reservations

required for dinner shows.
100 Closed Sun.   AE, MC, V

CAFÉ BARKO

$$$
ISLA FLAMENCO, AMADOR CAUSEWAY
TEL 314-0000
Open-air dining under thatch at this seafood restaurant. Live music at night, when patio trees are lit by fairy lights.
120   AE, MC, V

HABIBI'S

$$$
CALLE RICARDO ARIAS
TEL 264-3647
Popular Levantine-themed restaurant in a converted colonial mansion with a contemporary motif and mellow vibe. The menu features staples such as hummus, shish kebab, and shaslik, but also Western favorites. Belly dancers perform on weekends. Hookahs are passed around upstairs in the tented lounge!
60   MC, V

MACARENA

$$$
CALLE 1, 50 YARDS (46 M) N OF PLAZA DE FRANCIA, CASCO VIEJO
TEL 228-0572
Colonial-themed Spanish-style tapa bar with a hip contemporary mood and eclectic decor. Revolving menu includes seafood and nouvelle themes. Large Spanish wine list; the adjoining bar serves cocktails.
40   AE, MC, V

MADAME CHANG

$$$
CALLE 48, BELLA VISTA
TEL 269-1313
World-renowned restaurant with warm, inviting, and sophisticated decor, and some of the best Chinese cuisine this side of Shanghai, from eggplant and tofu to Madame Chang's roast chicken special.

HOTELS & RESTAURANTS

Thai dishes also served. Madame Siu Mee Chang and her daughter Yolanda preside.
🛏 90 🅿 📶 📶 📶 MC, V

SOMETHING SPECIAL

🍴 MANOLO CARACOL

This fashionable conversion of a colonial structure has lively, eclectic decor and an open kitchen. It features superbly executed fusion dishes and tapas using fresh ingredients. The Spanish-inspired menu includes such delights as gazpacho Andaluz with cucumber and sorbet, but runs to sashimi tuna. Prix-fixe daily menu. Doubles as an art gallery, with changing exhibitions.
$$$
CALLE 3RA & AVE. CENTRAL, CASCO VIEJO
TEL 228-4640
www.manolocaracol.net
🛏 100 🕐 Closed Sun. & L Sat. 📶 📶 📶 MC, V

🍴 S'CENA

$$$
CALLE IRA, CASCO VIEJO
TEL 228-4011
Bare stone walls adorned with brass instruments, black-and-white prints of jazz musicians, and live jazz (in the bar below) provide a lively ambience for enjoying the creative Mediterranean dishes of Spanish chef José Luis Rodríguez. Fresh filet of fish in Roquefort sauce, and roast lamb are among the tasty treats. A wine cave features a top-class selection from around the world.
🛏 34 🕐 Closed Mon. & D Sun. 📶 📶 📶 MC, V

🍴 SUSHI ITTO

$$$
REAR OF EDIFICIO PLAZA OBARRIO, BETWEEN CALLE SAMUEL LEWIS & CALLE 55
TEL 265-1222
Milan meets Tokyo in the contemporary Japanese restaurant. Sophisticated without being pretentious, it

has walls of glass and bright lighting. The menu includes such non-Japanese oddities as pastas, alongside sushi, tempura, and other Japanese staples of average quality. Patio dining is an option.
🛏 80 🅿 📶 📶 📶 MC, V

🍴 TEN BISTRO

$$$
CALLE 50 & BEATRIZ CABAL, INSIDE HOTEL DEVILLE, EL CANGREJO
TEL 213-8250
www.devillehotel.com.pa
The hip new restaurant of French chef Fabien Migny in Hotel Deville (see p. 237) is a sophisticated eye-pleaser. Trendy contemporary decor, plus progressive music in the lounge bar. All entrées (ten meat dishes, ten seafood dishes) cost $10.
🛏 36 🅿 📶 📶 📶 AE, MC, V

🍴 LAS TINAJAS

$$$
CALLE 51, BELLA VISTA
TEL 263-7890
FAX 264-4858
Touristy restaurant renowned for its traditional folkloric shows (Tues. & Thurs.–Sat. at 9 p.m., $5 cover) featuring women dressed in polleras. The menu plays on a local theme, with dishes such as *sopa borracha*, tamales, and *frituras*. Rustic colonial-themed decor. Reservations essential for dinner shows.
🛏 80 🅿 📶 📶 📶 MC, V

🍴 CAFÉ CAPPUCCINO

$$
AVE. BALBOA & ANASTACIO RUIZ, MARBELLA
TEL 264-0106
Clean and pleasant, well-lit café with air-conditioning, plus an option for shaded patio dining under fans. Excellently prepared and filling dishes with a Mexican twist (ceviche, chicken flautas) plus sandwiches and fresh fruit *batidos* (shakes). Baked

desserts and cappuccinos.
🛏 50 🅿 📶 📶 📶 AE, MC, V

🍴 EL PAVO REAL

$$
CALLE 51, CAMPO ALEGRE, BEHIND MARRIOTT HOTEL
TEL 269-0504
Styled as a traditional English pub. Go for the fish and chips cooked in beer batter and served in newspaper with salt and vinegar. Menu also includes burgers, sandwiches, French onion soup, and salmon mousse. Wash your meal down with some hearty beer and follow with a game of darts.
🛏 80 🅿 📶 📶 MC, V

🍴 EL TRAPICHE

$$
VÍA ARGENTINA, EL CANGREJO
TEL 269-4353
Hearty traditional Panamanian fare from the central provinces. Start with chicken-stuffed fritters or ceviche followed by the "Panamanian Fiesta" combo. Decor includes a *trapiche*: a traditional sugar press. Slow service.
🛏 44 🅿 🕐 Closed Mon. 📶 📶 📶 MC, V

HOTELS
An indication of the cost of a double room without breakfast is given by $ signs:
$$$$$	Over $200
$$$$	$100–$200
$$$	$50–$100
$$	$25–$50
$	Under $25

RESTAURANTS
An indication of the cost of a three-course dinner without drinks is given by $ signs:
$$$$$	Over $35
$$$$	$20–$35
$$$	$10–$20
$$	$5–$10
$	Under $5

SOL AZTECA

$$

CALLE 51 #28, BELLA VISTA

TEL 214-3910

A fine choice for Veracruzan Mexican fare. Pleasant ocher-and-purple color scheme. The fare is tasty and filling rather than distinguished. Recommended is the *pulpo a la José Alfredo*—octopus in a perfect chili sauce.

48 ☐ ☐ Closed Mon., L Sat. ☑ ☑ ☒ AE, MC, V

GRANCLEMENT

$

AVE. CENTRAL & CALLE 3RA, CASCO VIEJO

TEL 228-0737

www.granclement.com

Gourmet ice creams and sorbets made from all-natural ingredients. Flavors range from pineapple and mango to honey, cinnamon, and Earl Grey tea. Cool colonial surroundings.

6 ☑ ☑ ☒ No credit cards

NIKO'S CAFÉ

$

ANTIGUA BOLERA, BALBOA

TEL 228-8888

Excellent value at this large, popular, café-style restaurant serving buffet style. An excellent range of tasty local fare, including desserts. Panoramic black-and-white historic photos of the Canal Zone.

120 ☐ ☑ ☑ ☒ No credit cards

CENTRAL CARIBBEAN & THE CANAL

ARCHIPIÉLAGO DE LAS PERLAS

SOMETHING SPECIAL

HACIENDA DEL MAR

Billed as an "eco-resort by the sea," this gorgeous hotel is an escape in all senses of the word.

No TVs. No phones. A 20-minute flight from the mainland. Poised on a promontory with balconies suspended over azure waters, the bungalows here are cozy and include junior suites and two-room "VIP cabañas." Slate-lined swimming pool. Superb (albeit expensive) seafoods in the dramatic open-air bamboo restaurant. Sportfishing, all-terrain-vehicle tours, etc., available at extra charge.

$$$$$

ISLA SAN JOSÉ

TEL 269-6634

FAX 264-1787

www.haciendadelmar.net

14 ☑ ☑ ☒ ☒ AE, MC, V

HOTEL CONTADORA

$$$$

PLAYA LARGA, ISLA CONTADORA

TEL 214-3719

FAX 264-1178

www.hotelcontadora.com

Hawaiian-style resort overlooking stunning white sands. Rooms are graciously furnished and exude comfort and romance; fabrics are striped in bold colors while white ceramic tiles glisten underfoot. ATV tours and watersports. Rates include meals and drinks.

300 ☑ ☑ ☒ ☒ ☒ AE, MC, V

SOMETHING SPECIAL

PERLA REAL INN

Spanish-colonial-themed inn with courtyard fountain, minutes from gorgeous white beaches. Classically elegant rooms boast wrought-iron pieces, tilework, and gaily colored walls with stencil designs, pure white linens, and hand-painted blue-and-white tilework and sinks in spacious bathrooms. Offers tours and activities. Breakfast included. A solid bargain.

$$$$

ISLA CONTADORA

TEL 250-4095

www.perlareal.com

6 ☑ ☑ ☒ ☒ MC, V

HOTEL PUNTA GALEON RESORT

$$$

ISLA CONTADORA

TEL 250-4134

FAX 250-4135

E-MAIL reservas@pun tagaleon.com

Set amid landscaped, palm-shaded grounds with a raised beachfront boardwalk. Simply appointed rooms. Exquisite free-form pool and thatched open-air beachfront restaurant offering sandwiches and seafoods.

48 ☐ ☑ ☑ ☒ ☒ MC, V

CERRO AZÚL

SOMETHING SPECIAL

HOSTAL CASA DE CAMPO COUNTRY INN & SPA

Delightful modern family-run hilltop inn decorated in Old World style. Rooms in cabins set on lush grounds boast rich color schemes and fabrics. Home-cooked meals are served, and the spa has wide-ranging treatments. Minutes from Parque Nacional Chagres. Birding tours are offered. Rates include tax.

$$$

28 MILES (45 KM) E OF PANAMA CITY

TEL 226-0274

www.panamacasadecampo.com

11 ☐ ☑ ☒

SIERRA LLORONA

$$$

SABANITAS, SANTA RITA ARRIBA, 12 MILES (19 KM) SE OF COLÓN

TEL 442-8104 OR 6614-8191

www.sierrallorona.com

A handsome contemporary-style two-story nature lodge set amid rain forest and popular for birding. Airy,

HOTELS & RESTAURANTS

spacious bedrooms featuring tile floors, a mix of wicker and Spanish colonial furniture, and ceiling fans open to verandas with hammocks. Dining is family style, and there's a cozy lounge with bar. Guided birding, hiking, and mountain biking are offered.

ⓘ 8 🅿 � 🔲 🅂DC, MC, V

🏨 LA POSADA DE FERHISSE
$$
CALLE DOMINGO DÍAZ, 9 MILES (14.5 KM) E OF TOCUMEN INTERNATIONAL AIRPORT
TEL 297-0197
With both lake and mountain views, this family-run inn sits at the edge of Parque Nacional Chagres. Dowdy furnishings. Hammocks on verandas. Restaurant serves Panamanian and Cuban cuisine.

ⓘ 6 🅿 🔲 🔳 🅂V

COLÓN

🏨 HOTEL NEW 🍴 WASHINGTON
$$$
CALLE 1, AVE. BOLÍVAR, COLÓN
TEL 441-7133
FAX 441-7397
E-MAIL nwh@sinfo.net
This venerable grande dame of a hotel recently received a much-needed facelift. Chandeliers and marble staircases gleam, although rooms remain dull. A casino adjoins and the restaurant offers a broad seafood menu.

ⓘ 124 🅿 🔲 🔳
🅂AE, MC, V

🏨 HOTEL ANDROS
🍴 **$$**
AVE. HERRERA, BETWEEN CALLES 9 & 10
TEL 441-0477
FAX 441-7921
www.hotelandros.com
This modern high-rise is tastefully furnished and has state-of-the-art conveniences,

including wi-fi Internet. Suites have whirlpool tubs. Rooftop restaurant and bar with views. A splendid bargain.

ⓘ 60 🅿 🔲 🅂AE, MC, V

🏨 MERYLAND HOTEL
$$
CALLE 7 & SANTA ISABEL
TEL/FAX 441-7055
Modern hotel in Spanish neo-colonial style close to Colón 2000 in an upscale part of town.

ⓘ 79 🅿 🔲 🅂MC, V

GAMBOA

🏨 GAMBOA RAINFOREST 🍴 RESORT
$$$$
AVE. GAILLARD, 15.5 MILES (25 KM) NW OF PANAMA CITY
TEL 314-9000
FAX 314-9020
www.gamboaresort.com
Large, modern facility enjoying a supremely beautiful position overlooking the Río Chagres. Forest trails and a wide range of nature-oriented activities. Spacious rooms are tastefully furnished and have balconies overlooking the grounds, Chagres River, and rain forest. Also 48 apartments in renovated 1930s Panama Canal Administration homes decorated with charming tropical furniture. Choice of eateries includes the elegant Chagres River View restaurant and the lakeside Los Lagartos for Sunday brunch.

ⓘ 107 🅿 🔲 �️ 🔲 🔳
🔲 🅂DC, MC, V

ISLA GRANDE

🏨 BANANAS VILLAGE 🍴 RESORT
$$$
13 MILES (21 KM) E OF PORTOBELO
TEL 263-9510 OR 448-2252
www.bananasresort.com
Quintessentially tropical resort amid a coconut grove overlooking a palm-shaded beach, with hammocks under thatch umbrellas. Beach

volleyball plus kayaks and other watersports. Twin-story cottages of Caribbean pastels overhanging azure waters have king-size beds and uninspired yesteryear decor in pinks and mauves. Restaurant serves traditional American breakfasts, plus seafood, pork, and chicken staples.

ⓘ 28 🅿 🔲 🔳 🔲 🔳
🅂DC, MC, V

🏨 SISTER MOON HOTEL
$$$
14 MILES (22.5 KM) E OF PORTOBELO
TEL 226-9861
www.hotelsistermoon.com
Shaded by palms on the slopes of a rocky cove. Thatched stilt-legged cabins, including bunks for budget travelers. Billiard table and darts in the sundeck bar. Watersports and fishing. Breakfast included.

ⓘ 14 🅿 🔲 🔳 🅂MC, V

ISLA TABOGA

🏨 VEREDA TROPICAL HOTEL
$$$
ISLA TABOGA
TEL 250-2154
www.veredatropicalhotel.com
This colorful hotel has a cliff-top perch with beach views. Tastefully furnished rooms around a central courtyard are themed to span the globe; colorful tilework is a highlight. Oceanview restaurant.

ⓘ 14 🔲 🔳 (some rooms)
🅂MC, V

LAGO GATÚN

🏨 MELIÁ PANAMA 🍴 CANAL
$$$$
LAGO GATÚN, 4 MILES (6.4 KM) W OF COLÓN
TEL 470-1100
FAX 470-1200
www.solmelia.com
Stylish conversion of former U.S. military headquarters on the shores of Lake Gatún. Spacious rooms offer elegant

Edwardian-style furnishings; "Royal Service" suites have butler service. Convention center, choice of restaurants, plentiful sports options, plus a treetop zipline.

🛈 286 🅿 ⬛ 🅢 🅢 🈂 🎾 🅢 All major cards

LAS CUMBRES

🏨 AVALON GRAND PANAMA RESORT
$$$$
5 MILES (8 KM) N OF PANAMA CITY
TEL 800/261-5014 OR 268-4499
FAX: 268-8654
www.avalonvacations.com
Hilltop rain forest setting adjoining Parque Nacional Camino de Cruces, accessed by trails. Elegantly appointed guest rooms and villas. Children's water park.

🛈 171 🅿 🅢 🅢 🈂 🅢 AE, MC, V

MIRAFLORES

🍴 TOP DECK
$$$
MIRAFLORES LOCKS VISITOR CENTER, 5 MILES (8 KM) W OF BALBOA
TEL 276-8325
All-you-can-eat (albeit expensive) buffet restaurant with shaded terrace for a bird's-eye view over the Miraflores Locks. Ground-floor snack bar with sandwiches, salads, coffees, etc. You will need to pay an entrance to the visitor center for the upper-level restaurant.

🍴 60 🅿 🅢 🅢 MC, V

PARQUE NACIONAL SOBERANÍA

SOMETHING SPECIAL

🏨 CANOPY TOWER ECOLODGE & NATURE OBSERVATORY

An ascetic conversion of a former radar facility, this unusual entity appeals mostly to birders. First impressions upon

entering are of being inside a grain silo, with its bare metal walls and "industrial" beams. Expensive first-story rooms are small, basic, and share bathroom facilities. Upper-story rooms, shaped like pie slices, are more spacious and romantically furnished. Avoid rooms with views into the parking lot. A cozy library doubles as a dining room. A rooftop observatory looks down over the forest. Meals and birding tour included.

$$$$
PARQUE NACIONAL SOBERANÍA
TEL 264-5720
FAX 263-2784
www.canopytower.com

🛈 12 🅿 🅢 🅢 DC, MC, V

PORTOBELO

🏨 COCO PLUM
🍴 $$$
3 MILES (5 KM) W OF PORTOBELO
TEL 448-2102
www.cocoplum-panama.com
Lovely beachfront hotel with watersports and beach games. Colorful decor in spacious rooms with cool tiles underfoot. The airy Restaurante Las Anclas specializes in seafood and Colombian-style *patacones*.

🛈 12 🅿 🅢 🅢 AE, MC, V

🍴 RESTAURANTE LOS CAÑONES
$$
0.5 MILE (0.8 KM) W OF PORTOBELO
TEL 448-2980
This thatched restaurant overlooking a cove specializes in seafood. The house specialty is *pulpo en leche de coco*: octopus in tomato sauce on coconut rice. Chitras strike at dusk—bring insect repellent.

🍴 34 🅿

⬛ KUNA YALA

ACHUTUPU

🏨 DOLPHIN ISLAND
🍴 LODGE
$$$
ISLA UAGUITUPO, 400 YARDS (366 M) E OF ACHUTUPU
TEL 263-7780
FAX 263-2559
www.uaginega.com
On its own private island. Two types of thatched, beachfront cabins, served with satellite Internet. Delightful, albeit rustic, bamboo-sided junior suites with hardwood floors are preferred to the simpler concrete-and-wood standards. Private bathrooms have flush toilets and cold showers. Facilities include hammocks and volleyball court, plus waterfront bar and seafood Bohío Restaurant with ocean views (rates include meals). Solar electricity during set hours. Nighttime beach bonfires are a highlight.

🛈 14 🅢 MC, V

AILIGANDI

🏨 DAD IBE ISLAND
🍴 LODGE
$$$$
10-MINUTE BOAT RIDE FROM DOMESTIC AIRPORT
TEL 6487-6239
www.dadibelodge.com
Simple thatch-and-bamboo huts overhang waters surrounding this tiny island, with safe waters for swimming thanks to flush toilets and septic tank. Simple seafood restaurant. Rates include meals. Bilingual guides available.

🛈 3 🅢 No credit cards

ÁREA SILVESTRE PROTEGIDA NARGANÁ

SOMETHING SPECIAL

🏨 BURBAYAR LODGE
🍴

Sitting astride the summit of the Serranía San Blas, this rustic family-run ecolodge immerses guests in unspoiled nature. Run to strict ecological principles, the simple wood-and-thatch lodge has rustic bamboo-and-hardwood cabañas with basic furnishings, shared bathrooms, and solar-powered lamps. Some rooms have bunks. Delicious meals served family-style at candlelit rough-hewn tables with lovely views over landscaped grounds and forest (meals are included in rates). Guided hikes. Gates are locked in the evening; advance reservations are essential.

$$$

NUSUGANDI, 9 MILES (14.5 KM) N OF EL LLANO (ON THE INTERAMERICAN HIGHWAY)
TEL 390-6674 OR 6654-0952
www.burbayar.com
ⓘ 6 🅿

BAHÍA EL ESCRIBANO

SOMETHING SPECIAL

🏨 CORAL LODGE
🍴 RESORT

This intimate, Polynesian-inspired, U.S.-owned and -operated resort, on the western boundary of the Kuna Yala comarca, features thatched, octagonal "water villas" on piers overhanging the turquoise waters. Sitting rooms feature glass floors for close-up viewing of reef life, while king-size beds with wraparound net drapes, hammocks slung on sundecks, rattan furnishings, and whirlpool tubs with ocean views add to the romantic ambience. Casual elegance is the watchword. Scuba diving and kayaking are specialties. Two restaurants.

$$$$$

COSTA ARRIBA, COLÓN, SAN BLAS
TEL/FAX 317-6754
www.corallodge.com
ⓘ 6 🚫 ⚡

ISKARDUP

🏨 SAPIBENEGA KUNA
🍴 LODGE

$$$$$

3 MILES (4.8 KM) W OF PLAYÓN CHICO
TEL 215-1406
FAX 215-3724
www.sapibenega.com

Squeezed onto a tiny islet, this pleasant lodge operates under the motto "nature is our life." Bamboo-walled duplex cabins on stilts over the water have private flush toilets and tiled showers. Fresh seafood is served in an open-air waterfront restaurant lit by tiki lights at night. Guided nature hikes and cultural tours. Meals included in rates. Solar power and generator supply electricity 24 hours.

ⓘ 13 🚫 MC, V

ISLA YANDUP

🏨 CABAÑAS YANDUP

$$$

0.75 MILE (1.2 KM) NE OF PLAYÓN CHICO
TEL 261-7229 OR 261-6347
www.yandupisland.com

Pleasant, albeit simple, thatched bamboo-walled cabins with oceanfront patios and shared toilets. Forest hikes, snorkeling, and meals (served in an open-air dining room) included in rates. Bring insect repellent.

ⓘ 14 🚫 No credit cards

KUANIDUP

🏨 CABAÑAS KUANIDUP
🍴 **$$$**

KUANIDUP, 4.5 MILES (7.2 KM) N OF RÍO SIDRA
TEL 6635-6737
FAX 227-1396
www.kuanidup.8k.com

Simple thatched, woven-

HOTELS

An indication of the cost of a double room without breakfast is given by **$** signs:

$$$$$	Over $200
$$$$	$100–$200
$$$	$50–$100
$$	$25–$50
$	Under $25

RESTAURANTS

An indication of the cost of a three-course dinner without drinks is given by **$** signs:

$$$$$	Over $35
$$$$	$20–$35
$$$	$10–$20
$$	$5–$10
$	Under $5

bamboo cabins enjoy a splendid, unpolluted beachside location. Rough-hewn beds with foam mattresses, sandy floors, and outside shared toilets. Rates include all meals, snorkeling, plus transfers from Río Sidra airstrip.

ⓘ 7 🚫 No credit cards

NARGANÁ

🏨 HOTEL NORIS
$

NARGANÁ
TEL 299-9009 (PUBLIC PHONE)

The only option on Narganá, this concrete building offers air-conditioning—a rarity in these islands. Rooms are basic, however; some share bathrooms and lack a/c. Room #1 outranks the rest. Boat transfers are offered.

ⓘ 7 ⚡ (some rooms)
🚫 No credit cards

🍴 RESTAURANTE NALI'S CAFÉ

$

NARGANÁ
TEL 299-9009 (PUBLIC PHONE)

One of the few restaurants in the archipelago. Seafood is tasty and usually trustworthy. Lobster, fresh crab, rice, and beans are the staples. Traditional American breakfasts are served.

🪑 20 🚫 No credit cards

EL PORVENIR

🏨 UKUPTUPU HOTEL
$$$
UKUPTUPU, 0.2 MILE (0.3 KM)
W OF EL PORVENIR
TEL/FAX 293-8709
E-MAIL ukuptupu@ukuptupu.com
This former Smithsonian Institution research facility takes up most of the tiny isle and offers delightful vistas. Spacious yet basic accommodations have tin roofs, bamboo walls, foam mattresses, and linoleum floors. Shared bathrooms have flush toilets. Hammocks are slung on shaded balconies. Rates include meals.
🛈 15 🚫 No credit cards

🏨 KUNA NISKUA LODGE
$$
ISLA WAILIDUP, 0.5 MILE (0.8 KM) SW OF EL PORVENIR
TEL 259-3471
www.kunaniskua.com
No frills at this simple, clean, thatch-and-bamboo lodge where corner rooms are preferable. Three rooms have shared bathrooms and solar electricity. Seafood served at a simple thatched restaurant. Meals and snorkeling trip included.
🛈 12

◼ DARIÉN

BAHÍA PIÑA

SOMETHING SPECIAL

🏨 TROPIC STAR LODGE
Originated in 1961 as a home away from home for a Texas oil tycoon and drawing an A-list clientele, this upscale U.S.-owned sportfishing lodge enjoys a tranquil setting on the mountain-rimmed east shore of Pineapple Bay. Accommodations are a mix of cabins and rooms, some with king beds, furnished in Old World colonial style. El Palacio, the original owner's three-bedroom ridgetop home, can be rented and is reached by funicular or a flight of 122 steps. Dining is family style and features top-notch meals, predominantly seafood, enjoyed while fishing videos are screened. Fishing is aboard a fleet of 31-foot (9.5 m) Bertrams. One-week minimum stay during high season.
$$$$$
BAHIA PIÑA
TEL U.S. 800/682-3424 OR 407/423-9931
FAX 407/839-3637
www.tropicstar.com
🛈 18 🛗 🏊 🚫 AE, MC, V

LA PALMA

🏨 HOTEL BIAQUIRÚ 🍴 BAGARÁ
$$
LA PALMA
TEL 299-6224
The nicest among a motley collection of hotels in La Palma, this one is well maintained, though rooms vary. Six rooms have inside bathrooms; the rest share. There's a TV lounge and pay phone. Meals are prepared by request.
🛈 13 🅿 🔆 (two rooms only) 🚫 No credit cards

PARQUE NACIONAL DARIÉN

🏨 CANA FIELD STATION
$$$$
CANA, PARQUE NACIONAL DARIÉN
TEL 269-9415
FAX 264-3715
www.anconexpeditions.com
At 1,600 feet (488 m) of elevation in the heart of Parque Nacional Darién, this simple nature lodge is administered by Ancón Expeditions, which has sole use of the facility. Surrounded by rain forest offering spectacular birding. Communal bathrooms. The dining room looks out to the forest. Accommodation is usually provided only as a multiday package. Ancillary accommodation is offered at a cloud-forest tent camp at 4,200 feet (1,280 m), a 6-mile (9.6 km) hike.
🛈 8 🚫 MC, V

PLAYA DE MUERTO

🏨 MAMA GRAJALES'
$
18 MILES (29 KM) SW OF GARACHINÉ
TEL 299-6428 (ASK FOR GISELA DE OLMEDO)
A one-of-a-kind cultural experience in one of the most remote and welcoming Emberá villages in Panama. Simple thatched huts of bamboo reed attended by matriarch Mama Grajales are raised on stilts on the black-sand beach, plus platforms for pitching tents. Running water and clean outdoor bathrooms. Simple but tasty and filling meals included.
🛈 2 🚫 No credit cards

PUNTA PATIÑO

🏨 PUNTA PATIÑO LODGE
$$$$
RESERVA NATURAL PUNTA PATIÑO
TEL 269-9415
FAX 264-3713
www.anconexpeditions.com
Blufftop nature lodge within Punta Patiño Nature Reserve, with magnificent views. Individual cabins in tropical pastels set amid lawns have loft bedrooms and private bathrooms with cold showers; six are air-conditioned. A balcony wrapping around the dining room has hammocks. Nature hikes are a specialty. Bugs abound. Bring insect repellent.
🛈 10 🅿 🔆 🚫 MC, V

RÍO SAMBÚ

🏨 SAMBÚ HAUSE BED & BREAKFAST
$$$
SAMBÚ

TEL 217-8224 (DAY)
FAX 260-4030
http://sambuhausedarienpana
ma.com
This spacious wooden lodge
with BBQ deck and mosquito
screens offers a true jungle
experience with comforts in
the heart of a small Emberá
indigenous community. Two
rooms share a bathroom; a
third is air-conditioned and
has its own bathroom. A
jungle treehouse is to be
added. The American/Afro-
Antillean owners offer birding
and cultural trips. Meals
included.
🛏 3 🅢 🚫 No credit cards

CENTRAL PANAMA

CAPIRA

🍴 PAPPASSITOS
$
INTERAMERICAN HWY.
NO TEL
FAX 348-6227
Large restaurant on the
Interamerican Highway.
Specializes in Tex-Mex, but has
accomplished fresh seafood
dishes. The conical thatched
roof soars overhead.
🅿 🅢 🚫 MC, V

EL VALLE DE ANTÓN

🛏 CANOPY LODGE
$$$$
CALLE CERRO MACHO
TEL 264-5720
FAX 263-2784
www.canopylodge.com
Lovely contemporary
riverside hotel in a private
nature reserve next to the
protected area of Cerro
Gaital Natural Monument.
Birding is a specialty. Light
and spacious guest rooms
with Japanese-inspired
aesthetic open to terraces
overlooking the forest, as do
airy public spaces.
🛏 12 🅿 🅢 🚫 AE, MC, V

SOMETHING SPECIAL

🛏 LA CASA DE LOURDES
🍴
Recalling a Tuscan villa, this
gem tucked into a quiet
corner of El Valle could
justifiably claim to be Panama's
finest boutique hotel. Exquisite
gardens. Tile floors and elegant
furnishings, including four-
poster beds in spacious rooms
and villas. Doubles as the
weekend home of Chef Lourdes
Fábega de Ward, owner of
Panama City's acclaimed
Golosina restaurant. The dining
here is the finest outside the
capital city, with nouvelle
Pananamian fare enjoyed on a
terrace with pool. The changing
menu features such hits as
blackened fish in tamarind sauce
and *guavina* (a light whitefish) in
champagne sauce with capers. A
spa offers complete treatments.
$$$$
200 YARDS (185 M) W OF
ESCUELA DE PRIMER CICLO,
OFF CALLE EL CICLO
TEL 983-6450 (EL VALLE) OR
264-3210 (PANAMA CITY)
FAX 212-0114
www.losmandarinos.com
🛏 14 🅿 🅢 🏊 🍸
🚫 AE, MC, V

🛏 CRATER VALLEY
RESORT &
ADVENTURE SPA
$$$$
CALLE CATIRITA & RANITA DE
ORO
TEL 215-2328
FAX 215-2329
www.crater-valley.com
Gorgeous landscaped grounds
provide a perfect setting in
this large estate hotel and
spa. Spacious but modestly
furnished rooms have beamed
wooden ceilings and ceramic
floors, warm earth tones, and
heaps of light. The spa offers a
panoply of treatments.
Continental breakfast
included.
🛏 8 🅿 🅢 🅢 🏊 🍸
🚫 MC, V

SOMETHING SPECIAL

🛏 PARK EDEN BED &
BREAKFAST
An exquisite garden sets off
this European-style timber-
and-stone lodge. Intimate decor
in individually styled rooms,
which vary in size; all have ceiling
fans. The live-in Panamanian-
Ecuadorian owners lavish pride
on their fine home-hotel, which
also includes a two-bedroom
house for rent. Full-course
breakfasts are a treat, and English
tea is served mid-afternoon.
$$$$
CALLE ESPAVE #7
TEL 983-6167
FAX 226-8858
www.parkeden.com
🛏 6 🅿 🅢 🅢 (some
rooms) 🚫 AE, MC, V

🛏 HOTEL CAMPESTRE
$$$
CALLE EL HATO
TEL 983-6146
FAX 983-6469
www.hotelcampestre.com
This charmingly rustic alpine
lodge at the base of
mountains has heaps of
ambience, although furnishings
are aged. Go for the
ambience, which extends to
the beamed restaurant.
🛏 14 🅿 🅢 🅢 🚫 MC, V

🛏 RINCÓN VALLERO
🍴 HOTEL
$$$
100 YARDS (90 M) S OF CALLE
DE LOS MILIONARIOS
TEL 983-6175
FAX 983-6791
www.rinconvallero.com
Hacienda-style hotel with
flagstone floors set on lovely
grounds with artificial lake and
waterfall. Offers tastefully
appointed, individually themed
rooms and bungalows, including
a honeymoon suite with
sunken stone whirlpool. Lovely
El Pez de Oro restaurant and
bar is romantically inviting. Try
the fried ceviche.
🛏 14 🅿 🅢 🅢
🚫 MC, V

LOS CAPITANES ECO RESORT
$$
CALLE EL CICLO
TEL 983-6080
FAX 983-6505
www.los-capitanes.com
A modest hotel with tin roof enfolded by lush gardens. Charmingly old-fashioned furnishings; some rooms have loft bedrooms. Cozy TV lounge. The owner, a retired German sea captain, is a delightful host. A solid bargain. The octagonal restaurant is heavy on Teutonic fare.
10 P 🚭 🖫
🖎 MC, V

ISLA TABORCILLO

TABORCILLO—THE JOHN WAYNE ISLAND
$$$$
ISLA TABORCILLO
TEL 214-7407 OR 214-7408
FAX 214-7407
www.isla-taborcillo.com
Hokey but endearing family-focused resort themed around a Hollywood-style cowboy town. Nature attractions include birding and marine turtles. Accommodations range from John Wayne's personal bedroom to modest cabins, all with terra-cotta floors and slightly aged furnishings. Full complement of activities, including—need we say—riflery. Meals and tours included.
24 🖫 🗟 🎯
🖎 MC, V

MARIATO

RÍO NEGRO SPORT-FISHING LODGE
$$$$$
MARIATO, 40 MILES (64 KM) S OF SANTIAGO
TEL 646-0529 OR 912/786-5926
www.panamasportsman.com
Run by a team of dedicated U.S. anglers, this comfortable, no-frills lodge has a shaded deck for sipping cocktails and sharing fishy tales. Simply appointed cabins. Rooms are

part of pricey all-inclusive fishing package.
4 P 🚭 🖎 No credit cards

PARQUE NACIONAL ALTOS DE CAMPANA

HOSTAL HACIENDA DOÑA VICTORIA
$$
CAMPANA, 2 MILES (3.2 KM) W OF CAPIRA
TEL 236-4152 OR 248-5075
Set in a beautiful garden, this intimate old Spanish hacienda is fronted by a stone courtyard with fountain, wrought-iron grills, and hammocks on terra-cotta patios. It has a lovely swimming pool with waterfall. Horseback riding and a carriage tour are offered. Meals included.
7 P 🗟 🖎 MC, V

RICHARD'S PLACE
$$
PARQUE NACIONAL ALTOS DE CAMPANA, ENTRADA DE CHICA
TEL 601-2882
Within the national park, this private home of a long-time U.S. expat takes in guests. Eccentric in the extreme, the old house is full of dusty yesteryear miscellany. Each room is unique and has a hot-water bathroom. Camping is permitted (tents are available).
5 P 🖎 No credit cards

PARQUE NACIONAL COIBA

PESCA PANAMA
$$$$$
ISLA COIBA
TEL 6614-5850, 6524-3851, OR 800/946-3474
FAX 623/362-2732 (U.S.)
www.pescapanama.com
A floating lodge catering primarily to sportfishers. Cozy wood-paneled bar/lounge with bamboo furnishings, plus outdoor dining. Sleeps 12, including bunks. Scuba diving and kayaking are offered.

Fishing on 27-foot (8 m) center-console boats. Week-long packages only.
3 🚭 🖫 🖎 MC, V

PENONOMÉ

SOMETHING SPECIAL

TRINIDAD SPA & LODGE
Boasting a hard-to-beat ridgetop setting with spectacular vistas, this hacienda-style spa hotel is among Panama's finest provincial options. Spacious fourplex cottages boast terra-cotta floors, Spanish colonial–style furniture, comfortable king-size beds, and vast windows for enjoying the views; each also has a small veranda with hammock. Ceiling fans are a thoughtful feature. Rawhide chairs and flame-colored wall lanterns are charming features of the dining room, which offers wraparound views and accomplished fare based on local ingredients. A full-service spa offers treatments with views, and guided forest hikes and other activities satisfy nature-loving visitors.
$$$
CHIGUIRÍ ARRIBA, 17 MILES (27 KM) NE OF PENONOMÉ
TEL/FAX 983-8900
www.posadaecologica.com
19 P 🚭 🖫
🖎 MC, V

ALBERGUE ECOLÓGICO LA IGUANA
$$
CHURUQUITA GRANDE, 9 MILES (14 KM) NE OF PENONOMÉ
TEL 983-8056 OR 6623-7480
FAX 983 8056
www.laiguanaresort.com
Approached by a long glade, this thatched nature lodge in the foothills is perfect for birders, although it is slightly run-down. Simply appointed rooms decorated with pre-Columbian motifs; some have loft bedrooms. Cold showers

only. Meals served indoors and on a lovely patio. Trails lead to a waterfall and into a forest teeming with wildlife.

🛈 8 🅿 🔲 🏊 🚫 No credit cards

🏨 HOTEL & SUITES 🍴 GUACAMAYA
$$
INTERAMERICAN HWY., 100 YARDS (90 M) E OF AVE. JUAN DEMOSTENES AROSEMENA
TEL 991-0117
FAX 991-1010
E-MAIL hotelguacamayahow@ hotmail.com
A comfortable, well-run hotel. Standards offer better value than the "suites," which merely provide more space. Choose mountain-view rooms to the rear. The Chinese restaurant is recommended.

🛈 40 🅿 🔲 🚫 MC, V

PLAYA BLANCA

🏨 PLAYA BLANCA HOTEL & RESORT
$$$$
6 MILES (9.6 KM) SW OF RÍO HATO
TEL 264-6444
FAX 300-7797
www.playablancaresort.com
An all-inclusive beach resort catering to Panama's middle-class and international package groups. Guest rooms occupy a series of three-story units arranged haphazardly around two large free-form pools. Lively contemporary decor. Complete dining, entertainment, and activities such as watersports included in the fee. Boisterous on weekends and holidays.

🛈 219 🅿 🔲 🔄 🔲 🏊 🚫 MC, V

🍴 PIPA'S BEACH BAR
$$
FARALLÓN, 1 MILE (1.6 KM) W OF DECAMERON
NO TEL
Ramshackle and colorful beach bar and restaurant serving delicious seafood.

Listen to reggae tunes, play beach volleyball, and dine with the sand between your toes. Usually open until the last guest leaves.

🍴 20 🅿 🚫 No credit cards

PLAYA CORONADO

🏨 CORONADO GOLF & 🍴 BEACH RESORT
$$$$
PLAYA CORONADO
TEL 264-3164 (PANAMA CITY), 240-4444 (CORONADO)
FAX 223-8513 (PANAMA CITY), 240-4899 (CORONADO)
www.coronadoresort.com
Based around a championship 18-hole golf course, this low-rise upscale resort can be boisterous on weekends when the Panama City crowd flocks in. Its wide-ranging facilities include eight restaurants, a spa, plus tennis, a stable, watersports, and convention facilities.

🛈 78 🅿 🔲 🔄 🔲 🏊 🚫 All major cards

PLAYA GORGONA

🏨 CABAÑAS DE PLAYA GORGONA
$$$
PLAYA GORGONA
TEL 269-243 OR 240-6160
http://propanama.com/gorgona
Somewhat soulless yet popular beach hotel with thatched umbrellas and acres of concrete around the pool (plus kiddies' pool). Efficiency cabins have kitchenettes, plus hammocks on balconies. Beach volleyball and other activities make this a noisy option on weekends.

🛈 40 🅿 🔲 🏊 🚫 MC, V

PLAYA KOBBE

🏨 INTERCONTINENTAL 🍴 PLAYA BONITA RESORT & SPA
$$$$
4 MILES (6.4 KM) W OF PANAMA CITY
TEL 211-8500 OR 206-8880

FAX 316-1463
www.playabonitapanama.com
A sprawling Mediterranean-inspired hotel set amid 20 acres (8 ha) of lush rain forest along a mile-long (1.6 km) stretch of brown sand. Guest rooms are a classy indulgence, with rich hardwood furnishings, divinely comfortable king beds, and wireless Internet access. Four swimming pools, three restaurants, and a huge spa. Open-air oceanfront dining under thatch.

🛈 300 🅿 🔲 🔄 🔲 🏊 🚫 All major cards

PLAYA EL PALMAR

🏨 BAY VIEW RESORT
$$$
58 MILES (93 KM) W OF PANAMA CITY, PLAYA EL PALMAR, SAN CARLOS
TEL 240-9621
FAX 240-9875
www.bayviewelpalmar.com
Popular family-oriented beach resort. Modestly furnished rooms in two-story units. Breeze-swept seafood restaurant and bar with fabulous views. Rents surfboards and boogie boards.

🛈 14 🅿 🔲 🏊 🚫 MC, V

🏨 PALMAR POINT SURF HOTEL
$$

9 MILES (14 KM) W OF CHAME, PLAYA EL PALMAR, SAN CARLOS

TEL 240-8004 OR 236-1940

Simply appointed two-story beachfront lodge catering to surfers. Minimal furnishings in standard rooms; the suite with kitchenette is recommended. Broad veranda with plastic chairs. A rustic bar, but no meals. Camping permitted.

🛈 10 🅿 🍴 🌊 🗺 MC, V

PLAYA SANTA CATALINA

🏨 PUNTA BRAVA LODGE
$$$

PUNTA BRAVA, 2 MILES (3.2 KM) E OF PLAYA SANTA CATALINA

TEL 6614-3868 OR 202-5505

www.puntabrava.com

Pleasant surf lodge enjoying spectacular views from its hilltop perch. Large, clean rooms with TV. Simple outdoor restaurant has large-screen TV. Surf packages, plus fishing trips, diving, and tours.

🛈 11 🅿 🍴 🗺 V

🍴 PIZZERÍA JAMMIN'
$

BETWEEN PLAYA SANTA CATALINA & PUNTA BRAVA

NO TEL

A favorite of surfers, who flock for the thin-crust pizzas served beneath thatch. Has hammocks and bench tables.

🔲 24 🅿 ⊕ Closed Mon. 🗺 No credit cards

PLAYA SANTA CLARA

🏨 HOTEL LAS
🍴 VERANERAS
$$$

PLAYA SANTA CLARA, 1.5 MILES (2.4 KM) SE OF INTERAMERICAN HWY.

TEL 993-3313

FAX 993-2528

E-MAIL lasveraneras@

cwpanama.net

Splendid setting overlooking a silvery beach. Accommodations range from simple thatched rooms with bunks to bungalows and two-story thatched cottages, all with TV and balcony. A ten-person house is also available. The thatched beachfront restaurant and bar doubles as a disco on weekends.

🛈 16 🅿 🍴 🌊 🗺 MC, V

🏨 LAS SIRENAS
$$$

PLAYA SANTA CLARA, 1.5 MILES (2.4 KM) SE OF INTERAMERICAN HWY.

TEL 993-3235 OR 264-1964

www.panamainfo.com/lassirenas

Crickets chirp you to sleep at this charming beachfront option. A choice of modestly appointed clifftop villas or smaller beachfront units, all with verandas with hammocks. Larger units have wireless Internet, kitchens, and outside dining terrace.

🛈 11 🅿 🍴 🗺 MC, V

PUNTA CHAME

🍴 RINCÓN CATRACHO
$$

CALLE 2DA SUR, GORGONA, PUNTA CHAME

TEL 240-5807

Sidewalk café with an eclectic menu running from Central American to German fare, including seafood.

🔲 20 🅿 🗺 No credit cards

SANTA FÉ

🏨 HOTEL SANTA FÉ
$

CARRETERA SANTIAGO–SANTA FÉ, 600 YARDS (550 M) S OF SANTA FÉ

TEL 954-0941

E-MAIL santafeexplorer @hotmail.com

A favorite of birders, this hotel on the edge of the village has lovely valley views. Simply yet cozily furnished

rooms with cold showers; some are air-conditioned. Guided hiking and birding tours, plus horse rental.

🛈 21 🅿 🍴 🗺 No credit cards

SANTIAGO

🏨 HOTEL LA HACIENDA
🍴 **$$**

INTERAMERICAN HWY., 1.5 MILES (2.4 KM) W OF TOWN CENTER

TEL 958-8580

FAX 958-8579

www.hotel-lahacienda.com

A hotel with a sunny disposition, this colorful Mexican-themed stopover beside the Interamerican Highway is a popular way station for business travelers and is the nicest hotel in town. Ceramic sun and moon faces smile at every turn. Rooms are furnished in simple hacienda style. Firm mattresses are a bonus. Undistinguished Mexican fare in the colorful restaurant, where the upright chairs are back-killers.

🛈 42 🍴 🍴 🌊 🗺 MC, V

🍴 RESTAURANTE MAR DEL SUR
$$$

INTERAMERICAN HWY., OPPOSITE CENTRO PYRAMIDAL

TEL 998-6455

Peruvian seafood, including delicious shrimp chowder, and ceviche with habanero pepper, red onions, and cilantro. The small lobster tails are also good.

🔲 40 🅿 🍴 🍴 🗺 MC, V

🍴 RESTAURANTE LOS TUCANES
$$$

CENTRO COMERCIAL VERAGUENSE, INTERAMERICAN HWY.

TEL 958-6490

A favorite rest stop for buses, this popular roadside restaurant is a good place for

---

🍴 Nonsmoking 🔼 Elevator 🍴 Air-conditioning 🌊 Indoor/🌊 Outdoor pool 🏋 Gym 🗺 Credit cards **KEY**

sandwiches, salads, and Panamanian staples, from fried chicken to spicy shrimp *criolla* (in tomato sauce).
🍴60 🅿 🔲 MC, V

SORÁ

🏨 TANGLEWOOD WELLNESS CENTER
$$$$
9 MILES (14.5 KM) NW OF BEJUCO
TEL 6671-9965 OR 301/637-4657 (U.S.)
www.tanglewoodwellnesscenter.com
A health and fasting retreat enjoying a superb mountain setting at a 1,500-foot (460 m) elevation. Guest lounge with wicker furnishings and library. Cozy cottages have been added, and organic meals are served. Best suited to travelers seeking a wellness package. One-week minimum.
🛏10 🅿 🔲 🔳 All major cards

AZUERO PENINSULA

CHITRÉ

🏨🍴 HOTEL LOS GUAYACANES
$$$
VÍA CIRCUNVALACIÓN
TEL 996-9758
FAX 996-9759
www.losguayacanes.com
A quality albeit soulless hotel in quasi-Teutonic style around an artificial lake with waterfall. Hard-carved hardwood furnishings in guest rooms. Facilities include tennis courts, disco, and convention space. The open-air Restaurante Las Brisas—graced by glistening hardwoods—has an eclectic menu. We like the grilled chicken breast in lemon mushroom sauce.
🍴88 🅿 🔲 🔲 🔳 AE, MC, V

🏨 HOTEL VERSALLES
$$
PASEO ENRIQUE GEENZIER,

CHITRÉ
TEL 996-4422
FAX 996-2090
www.hotelversalles.com
This clean, no-frills modern hotel on the main road on the outskirts of town offers simple comforts. Spacious family rooms are a better value than smaller standards. High-speed Internet is a bonus, but the swimming pool is tiny.
🛏60 🅿 🔲 🔲 🔳 MC, V

🍴 RESTAURANTE EL MESÓN
$$
HOTEL REX, CALLE MELITÓN MARTÍN
TEL 996-4310
You get value for money at this pleasant restaurant with patio overlooking the main square. Everything from sandwiches to lasagna, seafood, and excellent Mexican fare. Paella is served on Sundays. The roast pork *(loma al horno)* is recommended any day.
🍴66 🔲 🔳 AE, MC, V

LA VILLA DE LOS SANTOS

🏨 HOTEL LA VILLA
$$
BARRIADA DON MARCEL
TEL/FAX 966-8201
Tucked into a quiet cul-de-sac, this sprawling hotel is adorned throughout with *tinajas* (earthenware jars) and other folkloric pieces. Rooms vary in size and appeal; newer rooms are preferred. The restaurant, albeit gloomy, appeals.
🍴38 🅿 🔲 🔳 MC, V

🍴 KIOSCO EL CIRUELO
$
3 MILES (4.8 KM) SE OF LA VILLA DE LOS SANTOS
NO TEL
Charming Old World ambience at this roadside shack where you dine under a corrugated tin roof. Chickens run around underfoot. The delicious

tamales are cooked in a traditional wood-fired oven.
🍴20 🔳 No credit cards

PEDASÍ

🏨 DIM'S HOSTAL
$
AVE. CENTRAL, PEDASÍ
TEL/FAX 995-2303
E-MAIL mirely@iname.com
A simple bed-and-breakfast in an aged two-story wooden home. Sparsely appointed rooms with cold showers only. Breakfasts are served under the shade of a mango tree. Friendly English-speaking hostess.
🛏5 🅿 🔲 🔳 No credit cards

PLAYA DESTILADEROS

🏨 POSADA LOS DESTILADEROS
$$$$
7 MILES (11.3 KM) SW OF PEDASÍ
TEL 675-9715 OR 995-2771
www.panamabambu.net
French-run ecolodge made entirely of hardwoods and thatch. Cross-ventilated Amazonian-themed rooms exude a one-with-nature feel. Exquisite touches include hand-carved wooden washbasins. Ocean views from wooden deck with Adirondack chairs. Gourmet cuisine by the French professional chef.
🛏9 🅿 🔳 🔳 MC, V

PLAYA VENADO

SOMETHING SPECIAL

🏨 VILLA MARINA
Set on 220 acres (90 ha) of grounds, this gorgeous historic Spanish hacienda–style beach property revolves around a terra-cotta courtyard with fountain. Red-tile roofs and traditional blue-and-white painted walls and posts add to the gracious yesteryear ambience, as do antiques in guest rooms, which have tasteful

fabrics plus French doors opening onto oceanview balconies with hammocks beneath shady eaves. Some rooms share bathrooms. The main house has graceful lounges. Lush lawns sweep down to the 1.2-mile-wide (2 km) beach. Quality meals are served in the atmospheric dining room. Horseback rides are a specialty and a 23-foot (7 m) Boston Whaler is available for sportfishing.

$$$$
PLAYA VENADO
TEL 211-2277 OR 6673-9445
www.playavenado.com
🅘 10 🅿 🅢 🅢 AE, MC, V

🏨 LA PLAYITA RESORT
$$$
PLAYA ACHOTINES, 1 MILE (1.6 KM) W OF PLAYA VENADO
TEL 6639-2968 OR 996-6727
Set above its own cove, this ascetic resort on lovely grounds is a work in progress, with an abundance of colorful tilework. Spacious yet basic stone-and-timber cabins with few accoutrements barely suffice. Despite this, the hotel has plenty of quirky charm. You can camp. Wildlife abounds, including ostriches, a rhea, and other exotics.
🅘 4 🅿 🅢 MC, V

LAS TABLAS

🏨 HOTEL LA MEJORANA
🍴 **$**
VÍA NACIONAL
TEL 994-5794
FAX 994-5796
Effusive bougainvillea makes a delightful first impression. Decorated with devil masks and folkloric-themed photos. Choice of small or larger rooms; both are merely functional. The high point is the restaurant serving tasty, filling, bargain-priced seafood.
🅘 2 🅿 🅢 MC, V

🍴 RESTAURANTE LOS PORTALES
$

AVE. BELISARIO PORTRAS & CALLE LOS SANTOS
NO TEL
In a colorful colonial home with courtyard dining. Meat dishes, spaghetti, and seafood ranging from calamari to garlic bass (corvina con ajo). Also recommended for its Panamanian breakfast of steak with corn patties.
🅘 40 🕙 Closed D Sun.
🅢 MC, V

▇ CHIRIQUÍ & THE CORDILLERA

BOCA CHICA

🏨 GONE FISHING PANAMA RESORT
$$$
2 MILES (3.2 KM) S OF BOCA CHICA
TEL 6573-0151
www.gonefishingpanama.com
Owned by Floridian mariners, this modern posada in neo-colonial style has a hillside setting with splendid ocean views from the open bar or horizon pool. Hardwood furnishings and tropical fabrics and murals, plus ceiling fan. Additional rooms are being added. Boaters can berth at the hotel's marina; whale-watching and sportfishing are offered.
🅘 3 🅿 🅢 🅢 🅢
🅢 MC, V

BOQUETE

🏨 CIELO PARAÍSO
$$$$$
CIELO PARAÍSO, 6 MILES (9.6 KM) SE OF BOQUETE
TEL 720-2431 OR 720-2661
FAX 720-2432
www.cieloparaiso.com
A boutique hotel in the midst of a forest reserve and 18-hole championship golf course, slated to open in late 2008. Deluxe rooms, suites, and villas all offer oversize bathrooms and terraces boasting golf-course views. Highlights include an infinity pool and spectacular

mountain vistas.
🅘 72 🅿 🅢 🅢 🅢 🍴
🅢 All major cards

SOMETHING SPECIAL

🏨 COFFEE ESTATE INN
Chiriquí's preeminent family-run inn exudes a home-away-from-home appeal. Surrounded by lush forest at 4,200 feet (1,280 m) of elevation, this coffee and citrus estate proves that a fine jewel is made complete by its setting. The inn offers stupendous volcano views from the cozy, delightfully furnished bungalows, each with bedroom, bathroom, kitchen, TV lounge, and terrace; comfy beds feature down-filled duvets and pillows. Run lovingly by an erudite Canadian couple who pay meticulous attention to guests' well-being and comfort. Candlelit gourmet dinners are served alfresco on your balcony, and the owners will prepare boxed lunches. Free Internet is a bonus, and the charming and conscientious owners are a trove of useful tour information. Trails offer fabulous birding.
$$$$
JARAMILLO ARRIBA, 1 MILE (1.6 KM) NE OF BOQUETE
TEL/FAX 720-2211
www.coffeeestateinn.com
🅘 3 🅿 🅢 🅢 MC, V

🏨 LOS ESTABLOS
$$$$
JARAMILLO ARRIBA, 1.5 MILES (2.4 KM) NE OF BOQUETE
TEL 720-2685
www.losestablos.net
A boutique inn with fantastic views. Converted from horse stables, this luxury hotel is surrounded by lawns and coffee fields. Lovely furnishings include antiques; guest quarters have patios and marble bathrooms. Internet access. Breakfast included.
🅘 7 🅿 🅢 🅢 MC, V

HOTELS & RESTAURANTS

SOMETHING SPECIAL

🏨🍴 PANAMONTE INN & SPA

This family-run gem dates back to 1914. Furnished with period pieces, it exudes warmth and individuality, multiplied by the presence of gracious hostess Inga Collins. A log fire burns in the cocktail lounge that opens onto lush gardens. Individually styled nonsmoking guest rooms are welcoming and cozy in the manner of a classic English country inn; all have ceiling fans, Internet service, and telephones. The elegant restaurant offers top-notch traditional staples, including fresh trout and succulent Black Angus beef dishes, served with fresh local vegetables and conjured into a sublime treat by Chef Charlie Collins. Who can resist his grilled pork chop served with onion ragout and potatoes, with a veal stock reduction wine sauce? The signature dessert is the inn's famous lemon pie. A spa offers all manner of treatments.

$$$$
BOQUETE
TEL 720-1324 OR 720-1327
FAX 720-2055
www.panamonteinnandspa.com
🛏 19 🅿 🚇 🚭 🚱 AE, MC, V

🏨 BOQUETE GARDEN INN

$$$
PALO ALTO, 1.75 MILES (2.8 KM) N OF BOQUETE
TEL 720-2376
www.boquetegardeninn.com
On the banks of the Río Palo Alto, amid effusive gardens, this charming hotel is steeped in nature. Guest rooms are modestly yet exquisitely furnished, with rich earth tones, crisp linens, and warm duvets. The Canadian/American owners run their inn with caring concern for detail.
🛏 10 🅿 🚇 🚱 MC, V

🏨 FINCA LÉRIDA BED & BREAKFAST

$$$
ALTO QUIEL, 6 MILES (9.6 KM) NW OF BOQUETE
TEL/FAX 720-2285
www.fincalerida.com
In the heart of a coffee estate, this delightful romantic inn appeals to nature lovers and oozes ambience and good taste. Choose one of the rooms in the vintage family home (or adjoining cottages) built in 1922 and wood-paneled throughout in cedar. The cozy lounge-library has a stone fireplace. Furnishings are original period pieces; bathrooms are Swiss-clean. Some rooms have private porches with Adirondack chairs. Newer rooms in a modern block overlook the manicured lawns and coffee fields; one room is equipped for handicapped visitors. Trails lead into the forest and tours are offered on the estate.
🛏 16 🅿 🚇 🚱 MC, V

🏨 HOSTAL PETIT MOZART

$$
BAJO VOLCANCITO, 1.5 MILES (2.4 KM) W OF BOQUETE
TEL/FAX 720-3764
www.centrodereservas.net
Delightful though simply furnished alpine bed-and-breakfast with soft earth tones (a contrast to the harsh primary colors of the exterior). Two rooms boast views. A perfect budget option. Live-in German-Peruvian owners are artists. Cloud-forest hikes are offered.
🛏 4 🅿 🚱 MC, V

🍴 DELICIAS DEL PERÚ

$$$
AVE. LOS FUNDADORES & CALLE 2DA
TEL 720-1966
Terrific seafood restaurant with a cozy ambience and superlative ceviche and other regional dishes. Outdoor dining patio with view.
🪑 80 🚱 AE, MC, V

HOTELS

An indication of the cost of a double room without breakfast is given by $ signs:

$$$$$	Over $200
$$$$	$100–$200
$$$	$50–$100
$$	$25–$50
$	Under $25

RESTAURANTS

An indication of the cost of a three-course dinner without drinks is given by $ signs:

$$$$$	Over $35
$$$$	$20–$35
$$$	$10–$20
$$	$5–$10
$	Under $5

🍴 MACHU PICCHU

$$$
AVE. BELISARIO PORRAS
TEL 720-1502
Attentive Peruvian chef Jaime Breña Aristoteles conjures outstanding Peruvian seafood and meat dishes. Rich decor of royal blue and white, with blond wood furniture.
🪑 65 🚱 AE, MC, V

🍴 BISTRO BOQUETE

$$
AVE. CENTRAL & CALLE 1RA SUR
TEL 720-1017
A delightful main-street bistro with eclectic menu: salads, sandwiches, quesadillas, trout dishes, filet mignon, even curried chicken. Cheesecakes to die for!
🪑 40 🚱 MC, V

🍴 PALO ALTO RESTAURANTE

$$
AVE. 11 DE ABRIL, PALO ALTO
TEL 720-1076
Specializing in fresh-caught trout dishes, this charming riverside restaurant with outdoor patio is set in a delightful garden full of trees. Also chops and steaks, plus a few Asian options. Reservations advised.
🪑 65 🅿 🕓 Closed Mon. 🚱 MC, V

KEY
🏨 Hotel 🍴 Restaurant 🛏 No. of guest rooms 🪑 No. of seats 🅿 Parking 🕓 Closed

🍴 CAFÉ KOTOWA
$

CEFATI, ALTO BOQUETE
TEL 720-1430

Adjoining IPAT's information office, this coffee shop boasts fabulous views over Boquete—perfect for enjoying cappuccino and a chocolate brownie or other scrumptious desserts.

ⓘ 20 🅢 🅢 MC, V

CERRO PUNTA

🏨 EL MANANTIAL SPA & 🍴 RESORT
$$$$

BAMBITO, 3 MILES (4.8 KM) S OF CERRO PUNTA
TEL 771-5126
FAX 771-5127
www.manantialspa.com

Charming wooden cabins facing manicured grounds on one side and lush forest on the other. Massage and other treatments in a spa with stone-walled hot tubs. La Carreta restaurant has walls of glass with forest views and a patio for dining on sunny days. River tubing and other activities.

ⓘ 20 🅿 🅢 🅥
🅢 AE, MC, V

🏨 HOTEL Y CABAÑAS 🍴 LOS QUETZALES
$$$$

GUADALUPE, 2 MILES (3.2 KM) NE OF CERRO PUNTA
TEL 771-2182 OR 774-5555 (DAVID)
FAX 771-2226
www.losquetzales.com

Nature-themed Swiss-style alpine lodge with meagerly furnished budget dorms, chalets, and suites. Cozy library-lounge and charming restaurant serving excellent and filling fare make amends. Five spacious, rustic cabins within Parque Nacional La Amistad (quetzals are often seen from the balconies) have butane-powered lamps and stoves; meals can be delivered from the lodge. Guided birding and hikes.

ⓘ 24 🅿 🅢 AE, MC, V

🏨 CIELITO SUR BED & BREAKFAST
$$$

NUEVA SUIZA, 2 MILES (3.2 KM) S OF CERRO PUNTA
TEL/FAX 771-2038
www.cielitosur.com

This peaceful bed-and-breakfast enjoys a magnificent setting overlooking the trout-filled Río Caldera. Spacious, quaintly furnished alpine cottages, plus open-air dining on a shaded porch with fireplace good for birding. A thatched *bohio* has hammocks, and a bath house has a hot tub.

ⓘ 4 🅿 🕑 Closed Oct. 🅢
🅢 MC, V

🏨 HOTEL BAMBITO 🍴 RESORT
$$$

BAMBITO, 3 MILES (4.8 KM) S OF CERRO PUNTA
TEL 771-4373, 771-4374, OR 215-9000 EXT. 9443 (PANAMA CITY)
FAX 771-4207
www.hotelbambito.com

This contemporary-themed hotel with strong alpine hints has a lovely garden setting with duck pond and cascade, plus modestly furnished accommodations. Glass-enclosed heated indoor pool, plus activities such as guided horseback rides and hiking. Weekend all-inclusive package rates are a bargain. The Restaurante Las Truchas specializes in trout; a prix-fixe Sunday brunch offers an all-you-can-eat treat.

ⓘ 47 🅿 🅢 🅢 🅢 🅥
🅢 AE, MC, V

DAVID

🏨 GRAN HOTEL NACIONAL
$$$

CALLE CENTRAL & AVE. I ESTE
TEL 775-2222
FAX 775-7729
www.hotelnacional.com.pa

Favored by the local business crowd, this modern option is the best of an uninspiring choice of hotels. Modest-size rooms have comfortable

mattresses but cramped bathrooms. An adult TV channel airing at night cannot be screened out. A casino adjoins.

ⓘ 75 🅿 🅢 🅢 🅢
🅢 All major cards

🍴 PANAMA BILL'S AMERICAN BAR & GRILL
$$$

AVE. DOMINGO DÍAZ & CALLE C NORTE
TEL 774-4686
www.panamabills.com

American-run restaurant in a converted colonial home serving *yanqui* favorites, including burgers, prime rib, and Texas chili; paella on Tuesdays. Indoor and outdoor dining. Music is oldies but goodies, plus live bands—usually far too loud.

🍽 40 🅢 🅢 🅢 AE, MC, V

🍴 RESTAURANTE EL FOGÓN
$$$

AVE. I RA & C SUR
TEL 775-7091

A pleasant open-air ambience to this modern restaurant serving a large menu of meat and seafood dishes. Latin music is usually playing.

🍽 90 🅿 🕑 Closed L Sun.
🅢 🅢 🅢 MC, V

🍴 HELADERÍA JACKELITA
$

CALLE E NORTE BETWEEN AVE. I OESTE & AVE. CENTRAL
TEL 774-6574

Open-air snack bar serving delicious homemade ice creams, yogurts, and *batidos* (shakes) using fresh fruits—everything from coconut to strawberries and *guanabana* (soursop). Also serves burgers and fried chicken, etc., at ludicrously low prices.

🍽 12 🅿 🅢 No credit cards

🅢 Nonsmoking 🛗 Elevator 🅢 Air-conditioning 🅢 Indoor/🅢 Outdoor pool 🅥 Gym 🅢 Credit cards   **KEY**

HOTELS & RESTAURANTS

ISLAS SECAS

SOMETHING SPECIAL

🏨 ISLAS SECAS RESORT

Unpretentious luxury at this eco-conscious resort spread over 10 acres (4 ha) of palm-studded coastline. Spacious cabins—actually wood-framed canvas yurts—overlooking an oceanfront cove come with queen bed, wraparound screened open windows, and sensuous decor. Absent are TV, phone, or radio—you come here for a Robinson Crusoe escape. Gourmet fare on the deck beneath spreading mango trees might start with plantain-crusted crab cakes, followed by Manchego cheese and roasted garlic aioli as an entrée. Rates include meals, alcoholic beverages, and watersports such as scuba diving. Arrival is by charter plane. Four-night minimum.

$$$$$
ISLA CAVADA
TEL 805/729-2737 (U.S.)
www.islassecas.com
🛈 6 🅢 🅢 AE, MC, V

LOS PLANES

🏨 FINCA LA SUIZA JUNGLE LODGE
$$
HWY. 4, 26 MILES (42 KM) N OF CHIRIQUÍ
TEL 6615-3774
www.panama.net.tc
Panoramic mountain views and cloud-forest trails are high points at this Swiss-run mountain lodge with its own reserve where forest hikes are offered. Gourmet dinners are a surprising treat. Two-night minimum.
🛈 3 🅿 🕓 Closed June, Sept., & Oct. 🅢 🅢 No credit cards

PLAYA BARQUETA

🏨 LAS OLAS BEACH RESORT
$$$$
PLAYA BARQUETA, 16 MILES (26 KM) SW OF DAVID
TEL 772-3000 OR 800/535-2513
FAX 772-3619
www.lasolasresort.com
Modern, all-inclusive hotel adjoining the wildlife refuge. Pink rooms all have oceanfront terraces; standards are small, and junior suites offer a better bargain. Activities from beach volleyball to horseback rides, plus spa.
🛈 39 🅿 🅢 🅢 🅢 🖵 🅢 AE, MC, V

PLAYA LAS LAJAS

🏨 LAJAS CLUB
$
100 YARDS (90 M) INLAND OF PLAYA LAS LAJAS
TEL 6647-9566 OR 6661-9556
http://lajasclub.tripod.com
Italian-owned option offers a choice of simply appointed rooms in two-story units, pie-slice-shaped rooms, and free-standing cabins. A thatched open-air restaurant is matched by an open-air disco-bar that could cause early-to-bedders problems on weekends.
🛈 10 🅿 🕓 (some rooms) 🅢 🅢 No credit cards

PUNTA BURICA

🏨 MONO FELIZ
$$
BELLA VISTA, 28 MILES (45 KM) S OF BOQUETE
TEL 6595-0388
E-MAIL mono_feliz@hotmail.com
End-of-the-road, North American–run nature lodge at the tip of Punta Burica. Fabulous wildlife viewing. Simple cabins have mosquito nets and cold showers, and camping is permitted; guests have use of a kitchen, but meals are also served for an extra fee. Getting here requires hiking.
🛈 3 🅢 🅢 No credit cards

VOLCÁN

🏨 HOTEL DOS RÍOS
$$$
1.5 MILES (2.4 KM) W OF VOLCÁN
TEL 771-5555
FAX 771-5794
E-MAIL hoteldosrios @cwpanama.net
Colorful, modestly equipped rooms at this friendly, service-oriented, all-wood riverside hotel. Outdoor-indoor restaurant with a quaint country feel (offering quality meals), plus the kitschy bar-disco Barriles. Alas, boardwalk passageways amplify footsteps. Breakfast included.
🛈 19 🅿 🅢 🅢 MC, V

🍴 RESTAURANTE ACROPOLIS
$$
AVE. CENTRAL NUEVA CALIFORNIA, NEXT TO ACCELL GAS STATION
TEL 6624-9687 OR 6651-4777
Run by retired Greek sea captain George Babos and his Panamanian wife, Elizabeth, this Greek restaurant offers the menu you'd expect—from moussaka to a superb baklava—using fresh herbs from their garden. Also burgers, pastas, etc.
🍴 20 🅿 🅢 🅢 MC, V

BOCAS DEL TORO

BOSQUE PROTECTOR PALO SECO

🏨 RANCHO ECOLÓGICO WILLIE MAZU
$$
KM 68, HWY. 4, 18 MILES (29 KM) S OF CHURUQUÍ GRANDE
TEL 442-1340
FAX 442-8485
http://natturpanama.com
Camping retreat for nature lovers just below the continental divide. Tents beneath thatch, with hot showers in shared bathroom. Trails lead into pristine montane forest; guided birding

is offered. Rates include meals. Reservations essential.

🛈 8 🅿 🚫 No credit cards

CHANGUINOLA

🏨 WEKSO ECOLODGE
$$

APPROX. 12 MILES (19 KM) W OF CHANGUINOLA

TEL 758-9137 OR 6522-5591

www.odesen.org

Isolated, rustic riverside ecolodge run by the Naso Indian community on the edge of Parque Internacional La Amistad. Simple thatched accommodations in stilt-legged cabins surrounded by jungle; cold showers. Hearty meals, but bring bottled water. Transportation is by boat from El Silencio.

🛈 6 🚫 No credit cards

ISLA BASTIMENTOS

SOMETHING SPECIAL

🏨 LA LOMA JUNGLE LODGE

Accessible solely by boat, this ecolodge borders the national park. Incredible snorkeling and wildlife viewing combine with romantic decor. Open-walled bamboo-and-thatch ranchos with glistening hardwood floors and simple, locally crafted furniture; beds have hardwood planks spanning tree trunks. Private bathrooms have hot water. Two cabins require a steep climb. Health-conscious meals are included. Wooden *cayucos* available.

$$$$

BAHÍA HONDA, 6.5 MILES (10.5 KM) E OF OLD BANK

TEL 6592-5162

www.thejunglelodge.com

🛈 3 🚫 🚫 No credit cards

🏨 AL NATURAL
$$$

PUNTA VIEJA

TEL 757-9004

www.bocas.com/alnatura.htm

Overlooking a white-sand beach near the northeast tip

of Isla Bastimentos, this lonesome lodge is accessed by boat. Delightfully rustic, open-walled, log-and-thatch bungalows with mosquito nets and hammocks enhance the jungle experience; tile bathrooms have hot showers. Simple family-style meals, plus kayaks and snorkeling.

🛈 5 🚫 🚫 No credit cards

🏨 HOTEL TRANQUILO BAY
$$$

CAYO CRAWL

TEL 713/589-6952 OR 507/380-0721

FAX 713/344-1125

www.tranquilobay.com

Amid mangroves, modest tin-roofed cabins on stilts have simple handmade furniture, granite countertops, and raised oceanfront porches with hammocks and Adirondack chairs. Main lodge has a bar and TV lounge. Meals included in all-inclusive package rate.

🛈 6 🚫 🚫 🚫 AE, MC, V

🏨 TREEHOUSE HOTEL
🍴 **$$**

PLAYA PRIMERA

TEL 6494-3163

E-MAIL shantydan@earthlink.net

This laidback, colorful beachfront property has log-and-thatch cabins with hammocks and rockers on patios. Live music will suit night owls.

🛈 7 🚫 No credit cards

ISLA CARENERO

🏨 BUCCANEER RESORT
$$$

SE SHORE

TEL/FAX 757-9042

www.buccaneer-resort.com

Upscale jungle-themed lodge with thatched, wood-paneled bungalows (including two-story suites) and cabins shaded by palms. A cheerful, thatched open-air bar-restaurant hangs over the waters. Catches the thumping beat from nearby disco bars.

🛈 12 🚫 🚫 🚫 MC, V

🏨 HOTEL AND
🍴 **RESTAURANTE DOÑA MARA**
$$$

1 MILE (1.6 KM) N OF BOCAS TOWN

TEL 757-9551

E-MAIL donamara@cwpanama.net

Tucked behind a picket fence on the beach, this tiny charmer offers spotless, simply appointed (and overpriced) rooms—ask for end units with ocean views. Hammocks under thatch, lounge chairs on the sands, plus Caribbean-style seafood.

🛈 6 🚫 🚫 MC, V

ISLA COLÓN

SOMETHING SPECIAL

🏨 PUNTA CARACOL
🍴 **ACQUA-LODGE**

Romantic, eco-sensitive, Polynesian-style lodge. A boardwalk leads to thatched wooden cabinas on stilts above jade waters. Quality hand-crafted hardwood furnishings include king-size four-poster beds with netting. Soothing Caribbean pastel schemes grace the choice of one- or two-story suites. Solar-powered electricity, bio-digesters for waste water, and state-of-the-art aerobic sewage treatment earn thumbs-up. The open-air restaurant focuses on seafood with local flavors, such as snapper in virgin olive oil and rock salt with rice, and guandu in coconut milk.

$$$$$

PUNTA CARACOL

TEL 6612-1088

www.puntacaracol.com

🛈 9 🚫 🚫 🚫 AE, MC, V

🏨 TROPICAL SUITES
🍴 **$$$$**

CALLE 1RA NEXT TO POLICÍA NACIONAL AND IPAT, BOCAS TOWN

TEL 757-9880

FAX 757-9081

www.tropical-suites.com

For travelers preferring a self-catering option. Functional but uninspired suites with maid service have orthopedic mattresses and tile floors. Watercraft are available and the property has its own dock.

[i] 16 [P] [S] [⇄] [S] [cc] MC, V

🏨 BOCAS INN
$$$
CALLE 3 & AVE. G, BOCAS TOWN
TEL 757-9600 OR 269-9415
FAX 757-9600 OR 264-3713
www.anconexpeditions.com
This well-respected establishment run by Ancón Expeditions hangs over the waters on the northeast side of town. Spacious, modestly furnished, wood-paneled rooms open onto broad verandas with hammocks. Filling breakfasts are served, and there's a tiny bar.

[i] 6 [S] [cc] AE, MC, V

🏨 HOTEL EL LIMBO BY 🍴 THE SEA
$$$
CALLE 2DA, BOCAS TOWN
TEL 757-9062
www.ellimbo.com
Lovely little three-story hotel on the water with large windows opening to balconies. Waterfront bar, plus sea kayaks and snorkeling gear for rent.

[i] 18 [P] [S] [cc] AE, MC, V

🏨 HOTEL SWANS' CAY 🍴 $$$
CALLE 3, BETWEEN AVES. E & F, BOCAS TOWN
TEL 757-9090
www.swanscayhotel.com
Striking exterior with lush hardwoods bespeaks a natty rehab for this aged building. Rooms around an atrium courtyard have colorful furnishings. Italian-themed restaurant, plus oceanfront pool in a nearby annex.

[i] 46 [P] [S] [≋] [cc] MC, V

🏨 HOTEL DEL PARQUE 🍴 $$
CALLE 2DA & PARQUE BOLÍVAR, BOCAS TOWN

TEL 757-9008
E-MAIL delparque35@hotmail.com
Lovely older hotel in its own garden overlooking the park. Simple furnishings include wicker and hammocks.

[i] 18 [P] [S] [S] [cc] V

🍴 MR. ROBERTS STEAK HOUSE
$$$
CALLE IRA & AVE. E, BOCAS TOWN
NO TEL
Modern, open-air, waterfront bar and restaurant popular with North American expats. The eclectic menu ranges from burgers to fish and chips to New York steak. Leave room for the brownie with vanilla ice cream.

[≡] 40 [P] [cc] No credit cards

🍴 EL PARGO ROJO
$$
CALLE 3 & AVE. H, BOCAS TOWN
TEL 6597-0296
Overhead fans stir a whirlwind at this atmospheric open-air restaurant with world music, a hip motif, and an international menu. Pastel decor and contemporary wall lamps add just the right romantic touch. Thai soup and shrimp in coconut and curry sauce are recommended.

[≡] 60 [⊘] Closed Mon. [S] [cc] MC, V

🍴 OM CAFÉ
$$
AVE. H, BETWEEN CALLES 3 & 4, BOCAS TOWN
NO TEL
Iconoclastic restaurant in a creaky old home serving superb East Indian fare on an upstairs balcony to a hip world-music beat. Bargain rates, including for vegetarian dishes and tropical fruit lassis. Also filling breakfasts (such as spicy eggs vindaloo).

[i] 20 [P] [⊘] Closed Wed. [cc] No credit cards

HOTELS
An indication of the cost of a double room without breakfast is given by **$** signs:

$$$$$	Over $200
$$$$	$100–$200
$$$	$50–$100
$$	$25–$50
$	Under $25

RESTAURANTS
An indication of the cost of a three-course dinner without drinks is given by **$** signs:

$$$$$	Over $35
$$$$	$20–$35
$$$	$10–$20
$$	$5–$10
$	Under $5

🍴 YARISNORI
$$
BOCAS DEL DRAGO, 9 MILES (14.5 KM) NW OF BOCAS TOWN
TEL 6615-5580
E-MAIL yarisnori@hotmail.com
Pleasant beachfront bar and restaurant with sand underfoot and shady open-air dining, including medieval-style tents. Lobster, shrimp, and other seafood such as red snapper with coconut rice. Hammocks, snorkeling, and kiddie playground.

[i] 60 [P] [⊘] Closed Tues. [cc] No credit cards

ISLA SOLARTE

🏨 SOLARTE DEL CARIBE INN
$$$
3 MILES (4.8 KM) E OF BOCAS TOWN
TEL 757-9032 OR 6488-4775
www.solarteinn.com
Classic Caribbean-style inn of cedar with gingerbread trim. The lounge with simple cane furniture has satellite TV. Five minutes by water taxi from Bocas.

[i] 7 [S] [S] [cc] MC, V

SHOPPING IN PANAMA

As a major crossroads of the world, Panama is a shopping mecca, not least for such high-end goods as jewelry and designer clothing. The Colón Free Zone (one of the world's largest free-trade zones) supplies many retailers in Panama City, which pass on the benefits from low freight costs. Large malls in Marbella and the Tumba Muerto district of Panama City offer a complete selection of world-renowned names from Bulgari to Yves Saint-Laurent.

Panama's other strong suit is indigenous crafts. Most upscale hotels have gift stores selling high-quality crafts. However, artisans' markets have by far the widest choice, and you might have more fun bargaining with the artisans themselves. Almost every town has an artisans' market selling intricate woven baskets, colorful bead necklaces (*chaquiras*), intricately knitted Ngöbe-Buglé bags called *chácaras*, small animal figurines carved from the *tagua* palm nut, and colorful stitched-appliqué *molas*. Many crafts use hardwoods, such as lignum vitae, purpleheart, and rosewood, often carved into the form of jungle animals and birds or *cayucos*. Other mementos include devil masks from the Azuero region, *sombrero montuno* straw hats, and dolls dressed in polleras.

Bargaining is expected for crafts and, unlike most Central American nations, even for items such as electronics and jewelry.

The country's renowned coffee is available nationwide. And Panamanian cigars make a popular souvenir. (Cuban cigars are also sold; it is illegal for U.S. citizens to purchase them here.)

OPENING TIMES
See pp. 233–234.

PANAMA CITY

Panama City's main shopping street is Vía España. The shopping district centered in Marbella and El Cangrejo districts is chock-full of designer stores and malls, including Multiplaza Pacific Mall and Multicentro, with 177 stores. The new Albrook Mall (near Aeropuerto Marcos A. Gelabert) sprawls over almost 5 million square feet (460,000 sq m). Kuna Indian women sell their crafts streetside in Casco Viejo and in dedicated artisans' markets where crafts from every indigenous group in the country are represented. Pedestrian-only Avenida Central is lined with street vendors and shops—beware of pickpockets.

ARTS & ANTIQUES
Art America Calle Aquilino de la Guardia, tel 214-9612. Original art with more than 3,600 works for sale.
Arts & Antiques Balboa Bay Plaza, Ave. Balboa & Calle Anastasio Ruíz, tel 264-8121. Crystals, furniture, porcelains, rugs, etc., representing styles from Louis XV to art deco.
Habitante Calle Uruguay #16, Bella Vista, tel 264-6470, e-mail: jvillala@ns.sinfo.net. Small art gallery focusing on contemporary works by leading Panamanian and Latin American artists.
Imagen Galería de Arte Calle Uruguay & Calle 47, tel 226-2649. This gallery, in a colonial mansion, displays and sells works by the nation's top artists.

BOOKS & MAPS
Exedra Books Vía España & Vía Brasil, tel 264-4252, www.exedrabooks.com. Modest range of texts in both Spanish and English, plus magazines.
Instituto Geográfico Nacional Tommy Guardia Calle 57 Oeste & Ave. 6A Norte (off Vía Simón Bolívar), tel 507-9684. Detailed maps of all kinds, especially useful for hikers; it does not sell tourist maps.

Librería Argosy Vía Argentina & Vía España, tel 223-5344. Small, cluttered bookstore is a treasure trove of antiquarian and new books, with a strong emphasis on Panama.

CLOTHES & ACCESSORIES
La Fortuna Vía España, 50 yards (45 m) E of Vía Argentina, tel 302-7890, e-mail: venta@lafortunapanama.com. Suits and shirts from the *real* tailor of Panama. Anyone who is anyone dresses here.
Outdoors Multiplaza, Vía Israel, tel 302-4828, Multicentro, Ave. Balboa, Paitilla, tel 208-2647, Albrook Mall, Corredor Norte, tel 303-6120. Casual outdoor wear and Indiana Jones–style gear.
Polleras Artesanias Ave. A & Calle 8, Casco Viejo, tel 228-8671. This tiny shop makes hand-stitched polleras and men's montuno shirts.

CRAFTS & JEWELRY
Emerald Plaza Multicentro #362, Ave. Balboa, tel 208-2784. Jewelry made with Colombian emeralds and 18-carat gold.
Galería Bernheim Edificio Madison 50, Calle 50, El Cangrejo, tel 6672-3052. Large selection of indigenous crafts, plus other souvenirs including fine art.
La Ronda Calle Primera, Casco Viejo, tel 211-1001. *The* place for quality indigenous crafts, such as Emberá-Wounaan baskets, Ngöbe jewelry, and sombreros montunos.
Reprosa Ave. Samuel Lewis & Santuario Nacional St., Obarrio, tel 269-0457. Pre-Columbian gold replicas (*huacas*) plus contemporary jewelry. Shopping here includes a factory tour.

GIFTS & MISCELLANEOUS
Panafoto Calle 50 & Calle 49A Este, tel 263-0102. Electronics store with a modest selection of cameras and photographic equipment, plus binoculars.

MALLS
Albrook Mall Corredor Norte, tel 303-6333, www.albrookmall.com. A huge mall with more than one hundred stores.
Multicentro Mall Ave. Balboa, Marbella, tel 208-2500. Multistory complex incorporating a casino and hotel.
Multiplaza Pacific Vía Israel, Punta Pacífica, tel 302-5380, www.mallmultiplazapacific.com. Multistory complex with seven department stores and 52 shops.

MARKETS
Centro de Artesanías Internacional Old YMCA Building, Ave. Arnulfo Arias Madrid, tel 6529-0678. Indigenous-run market selling hammocks, masks, carvings, baskets, molas, and other tribal arts and crafts.
Mercado de Buhonerías y Artesanias Ave. 4 Sur & Calle 23 Este, Calidonia. Outdoor market where artisans from around the country sell molas and other indigenous crafts, plus sombreros montunos, hammocks, etc.
Mercado Nacional de Artesanías Vía Cincuentenario, Panama Viejo. Dozens of stalls attended by Kuna Indians and other indigenous people selling everything from straw hats to hammocks.
Mi Pueblito Ave. de los Mártires, Ancón. This re-creation of typical Spanish colonial, Caribbean, and Emberá villages has stores selling crafts representative of each region.

CENTRAL CARIBBEAN & THE CANAL

Colón is the main entrepôt for goods entering and leaving Panama via the Zona Libre de Colón (Colón Free Zone). This vast complex serves wholesalers and retailers. Strict customs regulations apply to retail sale to tourists, who cannot leave the zone with any items. Purchased items must be sent to the airport or cruise port, where they are delivered to departing passengers. Colón's cruise ports have arts-and-crafts markets, and you can journey to Emberá Indian villages to buy exquisite baskets, necklaces, and other items at the source.

CRAFTS & JEWELRY
Emberá Parará Púru, Emberá Drua, and **Emberá Púru** Parque Nacional Chagres. Indigenous villages selling native bead jewelry, wood and tagua-nut carvings, carved gourds, beautiful woven baskets and plates, plus traditional masks. Bring small-denomination bills.

GIFTS & MISCELLANEOUS
Colón 2000 Paseo Gorgas, www.colon2000.com. This small but modern cruise-ship port has half a dozen duty-free and souvenir stores, plus folkloric performances when ships are in port.
Miraflores Visitors Center Miraflores Locks, tel 276-8325. Splendid gift shop with everything you could wish to buy relating to the canal, from trinkets such as mugs and key-chain rings to books and fine art prints.
MUCEC Calle 2 & Ave. Amador Guerrero, Colón, tel 447-0828, http://musec.org. This nonprofit charity supports distressed women in Colón and has a development workshop producing pillowcases, children's clothing, pottery, etc., sold in the on-site store.

MALLS
Zona Libre de Colón Ave. Roosevelt & Calle 13, tel 475-9500, www.colonfreezone.com. This city-size entity sprawls over 1,000 acres (400 ha) and has scores of warehouses and showrooms stocked with every imaginable item sold duty free. Permits, obtainable at the main gate, are required to enter. Most items sold here that are of interest to tourists can be bought as cheaply at airport duty-free stores.

MARKETS
Mercado de Artesanía 50 yards (45 m) SW of Iglesia de San Felipe de Portobelo, Portobelo. This tiny market on the west side of the plaza hosts Kuna Indians selling molas, hammocks, and jewelry.

KUNA YALA

Ground zero for the production of gorgeous, brightly colored molas, the San Blas Islands are a magical mystery tour of indigenous Kuna crafts, which include beaded bracelets, coral and shell jewelry, Pan-style wooden flutes, and embroidered blouses and shirts with appliqué panels. Certain islands excel. There are no fixed-roof stores: Vendors display their wares along village pathways, while others paddle out in their watercraft to pitch to cruise ships and yachts. Vendors can be quite aggressive in their sales pitch. Although a limited degree of bargaining is acceptable, the Kuna are tough negotiators and most prices are fair to begin with. Expect to pay at least $15 for molas, with the largest and highest-quality examples costing several hundred dollars. When buying molas, look for the following: a well-balanced design with harmonic contrasts of color; evenly spaced lines with smooth edges; small, almost invisible stitches. Also look for *nuchanaga* wooden figures representing spirit gods.

Avoid the islands of Wichub-Huala and Carti Suituipo when the cruise ships are in. Credit cards are not accepted. You will need lots of small-denomination bills. Narganá has a bank if you run out of cash.

DARIÉN

The Emberá-Wounaan people are gifted at crafts. While their exquisite products can be bought in Panama City, bargaining with the artist directly in an Emberá or Wounaan village is far more fun. The local communities are trying to adjust to environmental threats, such as deforestation, by turning to ecotourism and a more productive use of their natural habitat than slash-and-burn. Sales of crafts to tourists now form a significant source of income. Look for highly colored chaquiras of colorful shells and/or beads; bowls, animal figurines, and miniature canoes carved from iron-hard cocobolo hardwood; and smaller figurines—anteaters, marine turtles, macaws, and sloths— hewn from the ivorylike, hen-egg-size nut of the tagua palm. Most impressive are the decorative baskets made of *naguala* and *chunga* palm fibers. The cream-colored baskets and platters are woven by Emberá women using a coil technique, and inlaid with black and red geometric shapes or representations of animals and birds. The finest examples can take two months or longer to make. Expect to pay at least $10 for a platter, and no less than $50 for a basket.

Most communities set up stalls selling their crafts upon arrival of visitors. Afro-Antillean people also inhabit the region; some sell drums and other musical instruments.

CRAFTS & JEWELRY

The following villages are good sources:

Boca Lara 4 miles (6.4 km) S of Santa Fé and 5 miles (8 km) SW of the Interamerican Hwy. Wounaan community prized for the quality of its crafts.
Emberá Arimae Interamerican Hwy., 18 miles (29 km) W of Metetí. Emberá community known for its crafts.
Ipetí Emberá 1 mile (1.6 km) S of Interamerican Hwy., 54 miles (87 km) E of Chepo, tel 333-0803. Emberá community selling crafts.
Ipetí Kuna 1 mile (0.6 km) N of Interamerican Hwy., 53 miles (85 km) E of Chepo. Small Kuna community selling molas and other typical Kuna craft items.

Vista Alegre Río Tuira, 2.5 miles (4 km) E of El Real de Santa María. The entire community makes hand-woven plates and baskets.
Wererá Perú 2 miles (3.2 km) W of Sambú. Emberá and Afro-Antillean community with an artisan's workshop selling crafts.

GIFTS & MISCELLANEOUS

ECODIC Santa Fé, 2 miles (3.2 km) W of the Interamerican Hwy. and 92 miles (148 km) E of Chepo. Indigenous community workshop producing and selling medicinal plants, paintings (including murals by local youths), and scented soaps.
Pajaro Jai Furniture Factory Mogue, 3 miles (4.8 km) up the Río Mogue, 15 miles (24 km) SW of La Palma, www.pajarojai.org/furniture.htm. A small-scale furniture factory run by the Emberá community that makes world-class hardwood benches and other furniture for export.
Talabartería Echao Palante, Tortí, Interamerican Hwy. Pedro Guerra owns this saddlery where you can have a hand-crafted saddle custom-made in a single day.

CENTRAL PANAMA

The road that winds up to El Valle de Antón is lined with stalls selling wicker crafts and ceramics, while *viveros* (nurseries) sell orchids. This is one of the best areas in the country to buy a *sombrero montuno* (cream-colored with narrow trims of black or brown), made locally around the community of La Pintada and sold here for about half the price of one in Panama City. Lesser-quality hats can be bought for as little as $15, although the best hats sell for $100 and up. Look for a barely discernible weave. Other good bargains include embroidered montuno men's shirts (similar to the Cuban *guayabera*) and dolls dressed in polleras.

CRAFTS & JEWELRY

David's Shop Ave. Central, El Valle de Antón, tel 983-6536. This crafts store and workshop represents a wide range of crafts, many made on-site in the workshop to the rear. Folk art from throughout the Americas is represented.

GIFTS & MISCELLANEOUS

Artesanías Típicas Panameñas Interamerican Hwy., Km 50 near Capira, tel 248-5313. This roadside store sells devil masks and ceramics from Azuero, as well as a wide choice of hammocks, plus rustic rocking chairs of leather and lathe-turned wood.
Café El Tute Santa Fé, tel 954-0914. This Ngöbe-Buglé worker's cooperative sells organic coffees fresh from the roaster.
Cigarros Joyas de Panama La Pintada, tel 991-0013. A small cigar factory where you can buy any of 12 types of surprisingly high-quality hand-rolled smokes for a pittance. A box of Churchills costs $45, and individual cigars cost $1–2.

MARKETS

Cooperativa Santa Fé Santa Fé. Good for Ngöbe-Buglé chacaras and jewelry.
Mercado Artesanal Veragua La Peña Interamerican Hwy., 3 miles (4.8 km) W of Santiago. This small artisans' market is worth the stop for its reproduction pre-Columbian figurines, plus contemporary indigenous crafts.
Mercado de Artesanías Ave. Central, El Valle de Antón. This small, pulsating market is one of Panama's best, especially on Sunday when a wide variety of Ngöbe-Buglé jewelry, soapstone carvings, and other crafts, plus sombreros pintados, hammocks, and Kuna molas, are sold. Specialties include orchids, hardwood serving trays *(bateas)*, and painted figurines.
Mercado de Artesanías Cocle Interamerican Hwy., Penonomé. Good selection of

traditional craft items, from hammocks to men's embroidered montuno shirts.

AZUERO PENINSULA

Azuero is renowned for the production of polleras and *diablitos* (brightly colored devil masks), while La Arena, on the outskirts of Chitré, is the nation's leading ceramics center. Feel free to enter *talleres* (workshops) to see ceramics being fired in clay wood-burning ovens. Guararé and Ocú are centers for polleras, which can take six months or longer to make and cost $1,000 or more.

CLOTHES & ACCESSORIES
Casa de Ildaura Saavedra de Espino La Enea, tel 994-5527. Sra. de Espino is renowned for the quality of her hand-sewn polleras.
Talabartería González Calle Pablo Arosemena, Las Tablas. Saddlery and leather shop, with fine belts.

CRAFTS & JEWELRY
Artesanía Ocueña San José, 3 miles (4.8 km) W of Ocútel, tel 974-1047. Makes sombreros montunos and montuno shirts for men and polleras for women. Also lace tablecloths.
Casa de Carlos Ivan de León Calle Tomás Herrera, Los Santos. A foremost mask-maker; his masks are collectibles.
Casa de Dario López Carretera Nacional, opposite the Shell gas station, La Parita, tel 974-2015, 6534-1958. Fearsome papier-mâché devil masks from one of the most acclaimed mask-makers in Panama.
Cerámica Calderón Carretera Nacional, La Arena, tel 974-4946. This *taller* produces some of the nicest ceramic pieces in town, including dinner sets and pre-Columbian reproductions made to order.

MARKETS
Mercado de Artesanías de Herrera Carretera Nacional, La Arena. This two-story building represents works by several ceramic talleres.
Mercado de Artesanías de Las Tablas Carretera Nacional, Las Tablas. Comparatively small market good for devil and other masks.

CHIRIQUÍ

Ngöbe-Buglé people produce exquisite bead jewelry and woven bags. The Interamerican Hwy. is lined with indigenous crafts stalls. Boquete has several quality gift stores, as well as superb coffee, which can be bought fresh-roasted on the estates. David has malls and the main street is a major commercial thoroughfare. Paso Canoas is lined with duty-free shops selling CDs, cheap clothes, and the like.

BOOKS & MAPS
Bookmark Dolega, 10 miles (16 km) N of Interamerican Hwy., tel 776-1688. U.S.-owned secondhand bookshop full to the rafters; many rare travel books.

CRAFTS & JEWELRY
Casa de Artesanal Ngöbe-Buglé Cruce San Felix, Interamerican Hwy., 2 miles (3.2 km) N of Las Lajas, tel 727-0783. Large Ngöbe-Buglé cooperative with the widest range of indigenous crafts in the region.
Tolé Interamerican Hwy. Ngöbe-Buglé center of crafts, sold roadside.

GIFTS & MISCELLANEOUS
Café de Eleta Coffee & Gift Shop Cerro Punta. Coffees plus Ngöbe-Buglé handicrafts.
Conservas de Antaño 400 yards (366 m) SE of Parque Domingo Médica, Boquete, tel 720-1539. Homemade tropical fruit jams.
Finca Dracula Orchid Sanctuary Guadalupe, tel 771-2070. Rare orchids sold in vials ready for export.
Hacienda Carta Vieja El Tejar, 2 miles (3.2 km) NW of Alanje,

tel 772-7073. Quality bottles of rum can be purchased after a factory tour.
Souvenir El Cacique SW corner of Parque Domingo Médica, Boquete, tel 720-2217. Quality Ngöbe-Buglé crafts, plus books, maps, and more.

MARKETS
Avenida 3 de Noviembre David. Stores and stalls selling CDs, hammocks, clothes, etc.
Mercado Municipal NE corner of Parque Domingo Médica, Boquete. Market crammed with fresh produce stalls.

BOCAS DEL TORO

Bocas Town has lots of shops selling hammocks, molas, and other indigenous crafts, which can also be bought at the source in Ngöbe-Buglé and Bribrí villages in the Bosque Protector Palo Seco and isles of the Bocas del Toro archipelago. Many places sell chocolate bars made from locally grown organic cocoa.

CLOTHES & ACCESSORIES
Tropix Surf Shop Calle 3, Isla Colón, Bocas Town, tel 757-9297. Custom surfboards and surf duds.

CRAFTS & JEWELRY
Artesanías Bribrí Emanuel Calle 3, Bocas Town, tel 757-9652. Large selection of native crafts and souvenirs.
Pachamama Calle 3, Bocas Town. Hammocks and indigenous crafts.

MARKETS
Gourmet Groceries Calle 3 & Ave. Central, next to Hotel Bahía, Bocas Town, tel 757-9357. Specialty food store.
Super Gourmet Avenida F & Calle 2, Bocas Town. Wide stock of imported foodstuffs.

ENTERTAINMENT

Panama City has something for everyone, from theater and movies to casinos, sports bars, and discos, many concentrated in the Bella Vista and El Cangrejo districts. Nightclubs and bars in Panama City begin to get in the groove on Wednesday, peak on Friday, and wind down on Saturday. Folkloric festivals are a staple of Azuero Province, which also hosts the nation's wildest Carnaval. Festivals and events are listed in *La Prensa*.

PANAMA CITY

THE ARTS
Asociación Nacional de Conciertos tel 214-7236, www.conciertospanama.org. Promotes the performing arts.
Atlapa Convention Center tel 236-7845 or 526-7112. The city's main venue for classical performances and shows.
Ballet Nacional de Panama tel 501-4112, www.inac.gob.pa /balletnacional. Acclaimed ballet company performs at the Teatro Nacional.
Orquestra Sinfónica Nacional tel 501-4111
Teatro Balboa tel 228-0327, e-mail: teatrobalboa@inac.g ob.pa. Art deco theater hosting classical performances and plays.
Teatro Nacional tel 262-3525. The city's leading theater.

CASINOS
Fiesta Hotel Panama, 111 Vía de España, tel 213-1274.
Veneto Hotel & Casino Vía Veneto between Vía España & El Cangrejo, tel 340-8888.

FESTIVALS
Panama City Jazz Festival (Jan.), www.panamajazzfestival .com. Four days of music with international performers.
Festival Nacional de Ballet (Oct.), tel 232-7627. International ballet festival.

NIGHTLIFE
Most dance clubs don't get going until well past midnight.
Oz Bar & Lounge Calle 53 Este, Marbella, tel 265-2805, www.ozpanama.com. Trendy upscale club. Occasional live bands.
Platea Calle 1ra, Casco Viejo, tel 228-4011. Live jazz and salsa in atmospheric surroundings;

piano bar on Saturdays.
Sahara Calle 48, Bella Vista, tel 214-8284. Hot party venue with live rock music.

CENTRAL CARIBBEAN & THE CANAL

CASINOS
Casino David Calle D Norte & Ave. 2, David, tel 775-6536
Fiesta Casino Hotel Washington, Ave. del Frente, Colón, tel 433-2174

FESTIVALS
Festival de Diablos y Congos (New Year's Eve & March 3), Portobelo. Satirical festival recalling slave days.
Los Congos (Jan.–Feb.), Escobal, 15 miles (24 km) SW of Colón. Celebration of Afro-Antillean heritage. Draws large crowds.
Carnaval (four days preceding Ash Wednesday), Isla Grande. Costumed revelry calypso style.
Patronales de la Virgen del Carmen (July 16), Isla Grande. Religious procession by sea and land.
Día de la Raza (Oct. 12), Viento Frío, Colón. Celebration of Columbus' landing.
Black Christ Festival (Oct. 21), Portobelo. Pilgrimage with religious parade, plus music, dance, and feasting.

NIGHTLIFE
Lum's Bar & Grill Corozal, tel 317-6303. Sports bar popular with Zonians; live music.

KUNA YALA

FESTIVALS
Carnaval (four days preceding Ash Wednesday), Río Azucar. Four days of music, dance, and drinking of *chicha* (fermented

corn alcohol).
Nogagope (Oct. 10–17), Isla Tigre. Celebration of traditional *nogagope* dance, plus canoe races and games.

DARIÉN

FESTIVALS
Emberá-Wounaan Cultural Festival (Oct.), Emberá Purú. Traditional music and dance.

CENTRAL PANAMA

CASINOS
Decameron Casino Royal Decameron Beach Resort, Playa Farallón, tel 993-2255
Money Casino David David, tel 774-8887

FESTIVALS
Carnaval Acuático (four days preceding Ash Wednesday), Penonomé. Mardi Gras–style carnival, begins with the carnival queen and attendees floating on a raft.
Feria de las Orquídeas de Santa Fé (Aug.), Santa Fé de Veraguas. Orchid festival.
Festival del Toro Guapo (Oct.), Antón. Three-day celebration with floats, beauty contests, and bullfighting.
Festival del Topon (Dec. 8 & 9), Penonomé. Christmas procession with participants bearing the figure of the patron saint.

NIGHTLIFE
Magic Place Calle Lastenia Campos, Aguadulce. Disco with occasional live bands.

AZUERO PENINSULA

CASINOS
Casino Chitré Chitré, tel 996-9758, fax 996-9759
Casino Colón Ave. Central, Colón, tel 433-2675
Fiesta de Los Reyes Magos (Jan. 6), Macaracas. Celebration of Epiphany with the three wise men on horseback.

FESTIVALS
Carnaval (four days preceding

Ash Wednesday), Las Tablas. Panama's most popular, crowded, and colorful Mardi Gras–style carnival.

Festival de Corpus Christi, (May/June), Villa de los Santos. Two weeks of elaborate devil dances, parades, fireworks, and merry-making.

Festival de la Pollera (July), Las Tablas. Young women model the national costume, vying to become the National Queen.

Fiestas Patronales de Santa Librada (July 20), Las Tablas. Part religious procession, part irreligious revelry.

Festival Nacional de la Mejorana (Sept.), Guararé. The nation's most important folkloric festival, with ox-cart parade and villages queens in polleras, plus folkloric music and dance.

El Grito de la Villa de los Santos (Nov. 10), La Villa de los Santos. Parade celebrates the first call for independence.

NIGHTLIFE
Centro Turístico Los Guayacanes, Chitré, tel 996-9759. Two bars plus nightclub adjoining the hotel.

CHIRIQUÍ

THE ARTS
Chiriquí Eventos Cultural
http://chiriquieventos.blogspot
.com. Excellent resource for events.

CASINOS
Fiesta Casino Calle Central & Ave 1 Este, David, tel 775-9667

FESTIVALS
Feria de las Flores y el Café (mid-Jan.), Boquete. Hugely popular flower festival.
Feria Internacional de San José de David (mid-March), David, tel 775-2128, www.feriadedavid.com. Agricultural fair, with livestock, rodeo, and folkloric performances.
Fiesta Patronal de San José (week of March 19), David. Celebrates the town's patron saint with music and dance.

Independencia de Panamá de España (Nov. 28), Boquete. Independence day celebration.
Festival del Tambor (Nov. 28), David. Folkloric presentations in celebration of Panama's independence.

NIGHTLIFE
Panama Bill's Ave. Domingo Díaz, David, tel 774-4686. Sports bar popular with expatriate males.
Zanzibar Boquete, tel 6515-2174. Hip, African-themed bar with live jazz and great cocktails.

BOCAS DEL TORO

FESTIVALS
Carnaval (last week in Feb.), Bocas Town. Party Brazilian-style, with floats, beauty contests, and nonstop music and dance.
Fiestas Patronales de la Virgen del Carmen (third Sun. in July), La Colonia Santeña, Isla Colón. Religious pilgrimage.
Feria del Mar (Sept.), Bocas Town. Four days of dancing, feasting, and merry-making on the beach.
Fundación de la Provincia de Bocas del Toro (Nov. 16), Bocas Town. Parades and street parties celebrating the founding of Bocas del Toro Province.

NIGHTLIFE
Cantina La Feria Old Bank, Isla Bastimentos. Popular reggae bar with "Blue Monday" parties.
Like Tiki Playa Istmito, Isla Colón. This laid-back beachfront bar is a favorite at happy hour.
Roots Old Bank, Isla Bastimentos. Colorful reggae bar.

ACTIVITIES

The nation supplements its entertainment scene with activities that make the most of the natural diversity. Below you'll find a general primer on activities and various outfitters throughout Panama, followed by a listing of region-specific ones. Note that the companies described may cover additional activities and areas than the ones featured here.

GENERAL

ADVENTURE TRIPS
Adventures in Panama tel 236-8146, www .panamapeteadventures.com. Offers birding, canyoning, canal transits, fishing, helicopter adventures, jungle survival training, kayaking, mountain biking, scuba diving, and more.
Ancón Expeditions tel 269-9415, www.anconexpeditio ns.com. A variety of adventures offered throughout Panama, including exploring Darién by dugout canoe, a trek along the Camino Real, and a family trip to Panama's best places.
Expediciones Tropicales tel & fax 317-1279, www.xtrop.com. Adventure travel experiences throughout Panama with a conservationist emphasis. Custom itineraries offered.
Panama Explorer Club tel 215-2330, fax 215-2329, www.pexclub.com. Adventure trips in Chiriquí, Cocle, and Panamá Provinces.
Panama Travel Experts tel 304-0251, www.panamatrav elexperts.com. Ecotourist trips throughout Panama, including boat safaris, birdwatching, and Panama Canal tours.

BIRDING
Observing birds and wildlife is best done with a guide.
Ancón Expeditions tel 269-9415, www.anconexpeditio ns.com. This outfitter has some of the best guides in the country.
Birdingpal www.birdingpal.org /panama.htm has a list of freelance birding guides.
Exotic Birding 877/247-3371, www.exoticbirding.com. Birding trips throughout Panama, including photography tours.

FISHING
Sportfishing focuses on the Hannibal Bank in the Pacific northwest. Fishing excursions are also offered from Panama City. Lake Gatún is considered world-class for peacock bass.
Panama Fishing & Catching tel 6622-0212 or 6505-9553, www.panamafishingandcatching .com. Fishing trips throughout Panama, including Lake Gatún, Bayano River, and Tuna Coast.

GOLF
Panama has about a dozen 9- and 18-hole courses. Premier golf courses are concentrated around Panama City and the Pacific beach resorts of central Panama.

HORSEBACK RIDING
Horseback riding is available nationwide, notably in Boquete and the Azuero Peninsula.

MOTORCYCLING
Adventures in Motorcycling tel 236-7232. One- to ten-day group motorcycle tours throughout Panama.

MOUNTAIN BIKING
Mountain bikes can be rented in popular tourist spots such as Bocas del Toro, Boquete, and El Valle de Antón.

NATURE CRUISING
Cruise boats travel mostly at night, with days spent at wilderness sites, at indigenous communities, and in passage through the Panama Canal. Wildlife guides lead hikes and excursions by boat. Snorkeling at prime coral reefs.
Cruise West 2401 4th Ave., Suite 700, Seattle, WA 98121, tel 888/851-8133, www.cruisewest.com. Nature-focused cruises on small ships, including along the canal.

NATURE TOURS
Panama abounds in opportunities for enjoying nature, which is best done with a licensed naturalist guide. The following companies specialize in nature trips.
Adventures in Panama tel 236-8146, www.adventuresinpanama.com
Ancón Expeditions tel 269-9415, fax 264-3713, www.anconexpeditions.com
Aventuras Panama tel 260-0044, fax 260-7535, www.aventuraspanama.com
Panama Travel Experts, tel tel 304-0251 or 866/637-8871, www.panamatravelexperts.com

SAILING & CRUISING
There are splendid anchorages on both Caribbean and Pacific shores, plus a wide range of marina facilities cater to private yachters. Several companies offer day-long to ten-day boating adventures, and sunset cruises are available at some locales.
Panamaniac tel 6718-2824, www.panamaniac.net
Panama Sailing & Diving Adventures tel 6668-6849, www.panamasailing.com
Panama Yacht Tours tel 263-5044, www.panamayachttours .com

SCUBA DIVING
Manta rays, sharks, and other large pelagics can be seen on the Pacific side, with the waters around Isla Coiba and Archipiélago de Perlas offering the best opportunities. On the Caribbean side, Bocas del Toro has fabulous reef diving, and Spanish galleons litter the ocean floor around Portobelo.
Scuba Panama tel 261-3841, www.scubapanama.com. Dive in some of the best places in Panama, including the canal. Offers scuba trips, a dive resort near the town of Portobelo, and courses.

SURFING
The Pacific coast has superb surfing spots good enough to host international competitions.

ACTIVITIES

Playa Venado and Santa Catalina are especially good. On the Caribbean side, Bocas del Toro and Isla Grande offer worthy challenges. You can rent boards at dedicated surf camps. **Panama Surf Tours**, tel 6671-7777, www.panamasurftours .com. Surfing trips to all major surf sites in Panama, including Catalina, Isla Grande, Punta Burica, and Bocas.

PANAMA CITY

WATERSPORTS
Balboa Yacht Club Fort Amador, tel 228-5794. In Balboa Harbor, with haul-out service for yachts.
Flamenco Yacht Club and Marina tel 314-0665, www.fuer teamador.com. Modern marina, but with only 12 slips, usually full.
Panama Yacht Tours tel 6614-1114, www.panamayachttours .com. Fishing and motorized sailing tours.

CENTRAL CARIBBEAN & THE CANAL

BIRDING
Canopy Tower Parque Nacional Soberanía, tel 264-5720, www.canopytower.com. Renowned birders' hotel with rooftop lookouts and telescopes.
Selvaventuras, Portobelo, www.geocities.com /selvaventuras. Personally customized trips led by residents of Portobelo.

BOAT TOURS
Canal & Bay Tours tel 227-2000, www.canalandbaytours .com. Guided transits of the Panama Canal.
Gatun Explorer tel 260-8205, www.gatunexplorer.com. Boat tours of Lake Gatún.
Pacific Queen tel 226-8917, www.pmatours.net. Partial and full transits of the Panama Canal.

FISHING
Kingfisher Bay Marina & Golf Resort tel 200-1122,

www.kingfisherbay.net. Located on Isla del Rey in the Archipelago de las Perlas, this resort offers sublime sportfishing plus snorkeling, diving, and gorgeous beaches.

GOLF
Summit Golf & Resort tel 232-4653, www.summitgolfpanama.com. 18-hole championship course.

RAFTING
Aventuras Panama tel 260-0044, fax 260-7535, www.avent uraspanama.com. White-water trips on the Chagres and Mamomi Rivers.

SCUBA DIVING
Centro de Buceo Isla Grande Isla Grande, tel 6501-5374, www.buceoenpanama .com. Diving trips at Isla Grande, plus Isla Coiba and San Blas.
Coco Plum Eco-Lodge 3 miles (4.8 km) W of Portobelo, tel 448-2102, www .cocoplum-panama.com. Dive shop with trips to the nearby reefs.
Coral Dreams Isla Contadora, tel 6536-1776, www.scubacontadora.com. Diving in the Islas de las Perlas.
Scuba Panama tel 261-3841, www.scubapanama.com. Dive trips at Portobelo.

KUNA YALA

BIRDING & HIKING
Burbayar Lodge, Nusugandi, tel 390-6674, www.burbayar .com. Guided hiking and birding.
Ecocircuitos tel 314-1586, www.ecocircuitos.com. Multiday San Blas excursions that include hiking.
Exotics Adventures tel 223-9283, www.panama exoticsadventures.com. Hiking and kayaking adventures.

SAILING
San Blas Sailing tel 314-1288 or 314-0195, www.sanblassailing .com. Four- to 21-day itineraries in the San Blas Islands.

SCUBA DIVING
Coral Lodge Costa Arriba, tel 317-6754, www.corallodge.com. Also arranges sea kayaking and horseback riding.

SEA KAYAKING
Expediciones Tropicales tel/fax 317-1279, www.xtrop .com. Sea kayaking in the San Blas.

DARIÉN

ADVENTURE TRIPS
Ancón Expeditions tel 269-9415, www .anconexpeditions.com. Specializes in birding, hiking, and other nature programs in Darién.
Ecocircuitos tel 314-1586, www.ecocircuitos.com. Three-day "Darien Ethnic Expedition."
Exotics Adventures tel 223-9283, www .panamaexoticsadventures .com. Three-day hiking, kayaking, and horseback adventure.

SPORTFISHING
Tropic Star Lodge tel 232-8375 or 800/682-3424, www.tropicstar.com. World-class sportfishing.

CENTRAL PANAMA

ADVENTURE TRIPS
Crater Valley Adventure Center El Valle de Antón, tel 983-6942, www.pexclub.com. Rock climbing, canyoneering, etc.
Panama Explorers Club tel 215-2330, www.pexclub.com. Full menu from hiking, kayaking, and mountain biking to corporate and kids' adventure retreats.

BOATING
Santa Catalina boat tours www.santacatalinaboattours .com. Boat and surfing tours to remote beaches and outer islands.

CANOPY TOURS
Canopy Adventure El Valle de Antón, tel 983-6547, http://panamabirding.com

/adventure. Zipline tours between treetops in a private tropical forest reserve.

GOLF
Coronado Golf Course
Coronado Beach & Golf Resort, tel 264-3164, www.coronadoresort.com. Tom Fazio-designed course; hotel guests only.
Costa Blanca Playa Farallon, tel 214-2016, www.costablanca.com.pa. 18-hole golf course at the Royal Decameron Beach Resort.
Vista Mar Resort Playa San Carlos, tel 215-1111, www.vistamarresort.com. The first 9 holes of this new 18-hole championship course opened in late 2006.

HORSEBACK RIDING
Alquiler de Caballos El Valle de Antón, tel 6646-5813. Horseback trips from one hour to half day.

KITEBOARDING
Machete Kiteboarding, Punta Chame, tel 674-7772 or 6674-7772, www.machetekites.com. Kitesurfing school Nov.–April.

SCUBA DIVING
Scuba Coiba Playa Santa Catalina, e-mail: info@scubac oiba.com, http://scubacoiba.com. Dive trips twice daily, plus multiday trips with overnights in the park.

SPORTFISHING
Coiba Adventure tel 999-8108, www.coibadventures.com. Fishing trips in the waters around Isla Coiba.
M/V Coral Star tel 985/845-0113 or 866/924-2837, www.coralstar.com. Six-day fishing packages with accommodations aboard this live-aboard vessel.
Pesca Panama tel 800/946-3474 (U.S.), www.pescap anama.com. Fabulous fishing adventures around Isla Coiba.

AZUERO PENINSULA

SCUBA DIVING & SPORTFISHING
Buzos de Azuero Pedasí, tel 995-2405, www.dive-n-fishpanama.com. Diving at Isla Iguana and Islas Frailes, plus sportfishing along the Tuna Coast.

CHIRIQUÍ

CANOPY TOURS
Boquete Tree Trek Boquete, tel 720-1635 or 6615-3300, www.aventurist.com. Glide between treetops on this steel cable system.

FISHING
Gone Fishing Panama Resort tel 6573-0151, www.gonefishingpanama.com. A secluded vacation eco-resort focusing on families in Gulf of Chiriqui National Marine Park.

GOLF
Cielo Paraíso tel 720-2431, www.cieloparaiso.com. 18-hole championship golf course with spectacular ocean and mountain views.

KAYAKING
Nantahala Outdoor Center tel 888/905-7238, www.noc.com. Eight-day trips for intermediate and advanced kayakers.

RAFTING
Chiriquí River Rafting tel/fax 720-1505, www.panama-rafting.com. Half-day rafting trips on seven rivers.

SCUBA DIVING
Centro de Buceo Isla Grande tel 6501-5374, www.buceoenpanama.com. Dive trips to Isla Coiba.

SPORTFISHING
Panama Big Game Fishing Club tel 866/281-1225, www.panama-sportfishing .com. All-inclusive three-, four-, five- and six-day fishing packages.
Pesca Panama tel 6614-5850,

www.pescapanama.com. Live-aboard floating fishing lodge.

BOCAS DEL TORO

BOAT TOURS
Panama Jet Boat Explorer tel 6604-7736, www.panamajetboatexplorer .com. Boat tours combining travel by jet boat and cayuco.

CULTURAL TOURS
ODESEN 758-9137 or 6522-5591, www.odesen.org. Immersions in Teribe Indian culture.

FISHING
Caribbean Blue Fishing Charters tel 6628-8033, www.bocascharters.com. Half- and full-day fishing trips.

SCUBA DIVING
Starfleet Scuba Bocas Town, tel 757-9630, www.starfleetscuba.com. Reputable dive resort and operator with a full complement of PADI programs and trips.

SURFING
Del Toro Surfing Bocas Town, tel 6570-8277, e-mail: deltorosurf@yahoo.com.ar. Offers surfing lessons and trips.
Panama Surf Tours tel 6671-7777, www .panamasurftours.com. Surfing trips to all major surf sites in Panama, including Bocas.

ILLUSTRATIONS CREDITS

Cover photographs by Gilles Mingasson/Getty Images

All interior photographs by Gilles Mingasson/Getty Images, unless otherwise noted:

26, Hulton Archive/Getty Images; 28-29, Hulton Archive/Getty Images; 30, Time Life Pictures/Mansell/Time Life Pictures/Getty Images; 32, Hulton Archive/Getty Images; 33, Hulton Archive/Getty Images; 35 (UP), Stephen Ferry/Liaison/Getty; 35 (LO), MANOOCHER DEGHATI/AFP/Getty Images; 36-37, TERESITA CHAVARRIA/AFP/Getty Images; 56, Paul Hawthorne/Getty Images; 98, Mattias Klum/National Geographic/Getty Images; 104, George F. Mobley; 108-109, Hulton Archive/Getty Images; 113, Danny Lehman/CORBIS; 121, Diana Walker/Time & Life Pictures/Getty Images; 137, George Grall/National Geographic/Getty Images; 164-165, Wolcott Henry/National Geographic/Getty Images; 184 (LO), Tim Graham/Getty Images; 191, ALBERTO LOWE/Reuters/Corbis; 193, Dave G. Houser/Corbis; 194, Scott Sroka/National Geographic/Getty Images.

Founded in 1888, the National Geographic Society is one of the largest nonprofit scientific and educational organizations in the world. It reaches more than 285 million people worldwide each month through its official journal, NATIONAL GEOGRAPHIC, and its four other magazines; the National Geographic Channel; television documentaries; radio programs; films; books; videos and DVDs; maps; and interactive media. National Geographic has funded more than 8,000 scientific research projects and supports an education program combating geographic illiteracy.

For more information, please call 1-800-NGS LINE (647-5463) or write to the following address: National Geographic Society,1145 17th Street N.W.,Washington, D.C. 20036-4688 U.S.A.

Visit us online at: www.national geographic.com/books

For information about special discounts for bulk purchases, please contact National Geographic Books Special Sales: ngspecsales@ngs.org

Printed in Toledo, Spain.

Order *Traveler* today, the magazine that travelers trust. In the U.S. and Canada call 1-800-NGS-LINE; 813-979-6845 for international. Or visit us online at www.national geographic.com/traveler and click on SUBSCRIBE.

National Geographic Traveler: Panama
by Christopher P. Baker.

Published by the National Geographic Society
John M. Fahey, Jr., *President and Chief Executive Officer*
Gilbert M. Grosvenor, *Chairman of the Board*
Nina D. Hoffman, *Executive Vice President;*
    President, Book Publishing Group

Prepared by the Book Division
Kevin Mulroy, *Senior Vice President and Publisher*
Leah Bendavid-Val, *Director of Photography Publishing*
    and Illustrations
Marianne R. Koszorus, *Director of Design*
Elizabeth Newhouse, *Director of Travel Publishing*
Carl Mehler, *Director of Maps*
Cinda Rose, *Art Director*

Staff for this book:
Barbara A. Noe, *Series Editor and Project Editor*
Kay Kobor Hankins, *Designer*
Dana Chivvis, *Illustrations Editor*
Patricia Daniels, *Text Editor*
Margarita Chiurliza, *Researcher*
Michael McNey, Nicholas P. Rosenbach, and Mapping Specialists,
    Map Research and Production
Mike Horenstein, *Production Manager*
Robert Waymouth, *Illustrations Specialist*
Margie Towery, *Indexer*
Jack Brostrom, Michele T. Callaghan, Sonia Harmon, Lynsey Jacob,
    Contributors

Jennifer A. Thornton, *Managing Editor*
R. Gary Colbert, *Production Director*

Artwork by Maltings Partnership, Derby, England (pp. 64–65 & 96–97)

National Geographic Traveler: Panama (2007)

ISBN-13: 978-1-4262-0146-2

Printed and bound by Mondadori Printing, Toledo, Spain.
Color separations by Quad Graphics, Alexandria, VA.

The information in this book has been carefully checked and to the best of our knowledge is accurate. However, details are subject to change, and the National Geographic Society cannot be responsible for such changes, or for errors or omissions. Assessments of sites, hotels, and restaurants are based on the author's subjective opinions, which do not necessarily reflect the publisher's opinion. The publisher cannot be responsible for any consequences arising from the use of this book.

NATIONAL GEOGRAPHIC
TRAVELER
A Century of Travel Expertise in Every Guide

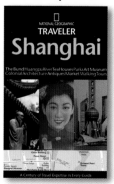

- **Alaska** ISBN: 978-0-7922-5371-6
- **Amsterdam** ISBN: 978-0-7922-7900-6
- **Arizona** (2nd Edition) ISBN: 978-0-7922-3888-1
- **Australia** (2nd Edition) ISBN: 978-0-7922-3893-5
- **Barcelona** (2nd Edition) ISBN: 978-0-7922-5365-5
- **Berlin** ISBN: 978-0-7922-6212-1
- **Boston & environs** ISBN: 978-0-7922-7926-6
- **California** (2nd Edition) ISBN: 978-0-7922-3885-0
- **Canada** (2nd Edition) ISBN: 978-0-7922-6201-5
- **The Caribbean** (2nd Edition) ISBN: 978-1-4262-0141-7
- **China** (2nd Edition) ISBN: 978-1-4262-0035-9
- **Costa Rica** (2nd Edition) ISBN: 978-0-7922-5368-6
- **Cuba** (2nd Edition) ISBN: 978-1-4262-0142-4
- **Egypt** (2nd Edition) ISBN: 978-1-4262-0143-1
- **Florence & Tuscany** (2nd Edition) ISBN: 978-0-7922-5318-1
- **Florida** ISBN: 978-0-7922-7432-2
- **France** (2nd Edition) ISBN: 978-1-4262-0027-4
- **Germany** (2nd Edition) ISBN: 978-1-4262-0028-1
- **Great Britain** (2nd Edition) ISBN: 978-1-4262-0029-8
- **Greece** (2nd Edition) ISBN: 978-1-4262-0030-4
- **Hawaii** (2nd Edition) ISBN: 978-0-7922-5568-0
- **Hong Kong** (2nd Edition) ISBN: 978-0-7922-5369-3
- **India** (2nd Edition) ISBN: 978-1-4262-0144-8
- **Ireland** (2nd Edition) ISBN: 978-1-4262-0022-9
- **Italy** (2nd Edition) ISBN: 978-0-7922-3889-8
- **Japan** (2nd Edition) ISBN: 978-0-7922-3894-2
- **London** (2nd Edition) ISBN: 978-1-4262-0023-6
- **Los Angeles** ISBN: 978-0-7922-7947-1

- **Madrid** ISBN: 978-0-7922-5372-3
- **Mexico** (2nd Edition) ISBN: 978-0-7922-5319-8
- **Miami & the Keys** (2nd Edition) ISBN: 978-0-7922-3886-7
- **New York** (2nd Edition) ISBN: 978-0-7922-5370-9
- **Naples & southern Italy** ISBN 978-1-4262-0040-3
- **Panama** ISBN: 978-1-4262-0146-2
- **Paris** (2nd Edition) ISBN: 978-1-4262-0024-3
- **Piedmont & Northwest Italy** ISBN: 978-0-7922-4198-0
- **Portugal** ISBN: 978-0-7922-4199-7
- **Prague & the Czech Republic** ISBN: 978-0-7922-4147-8
- **Provence & the Côte d'Azur** ISBN: 978-0-7922-9542-6
- **Romania** ISBN: 978-1-4262-0147-9
- **Rome** (2nd Edition) ISBN: 978-0-7922-5572-7
- **St. Petersburg** ISBN 978-1-4262-0050-2
- **San Diego** (2nd Edition) ISBN: 978-0-7922-6202-2
- **San Francisco** (2nd Edition) ISBN: 978-0-7922-3883-6
- **Shanghai** ISBN: 978-1-4262-0148-6
- **Sicily** ISBN: 978-0-7922-9541-9
- **Spain** ISBN: 978-0-7922-3884-3
- **Sydney** ISBN: 978-0-7922-7435-3
- **Taiwan** (2nd Edition) ISBN: 978-1-4262-0145-5
- **Thailand** (2nd Edition) ISBN: 978-0-7922-5321-1
- **Venice** ISBN: 978-0-7922-7917-4
- **Vietnam** ISBN: 978-0-7922-6203-9
- **Washington, D.C.** (2nd Edition) ISBN: 978-0-7922-3887-4

AVAILABLE WHEREVER BOOKS ARE SOLD